ALL HELL WILL
BREAK LOOSE

All Hell
Will Break Loose

AUSTIN CURRIE

THE O'BRIEN PRESS
DUBLIN

First published 2004 by The O'Brien Press Ltd,
20 Victoria Road, Dublin 6, Ireland.
Tel: +353 1 4923333; Fax: +353 1 4922777
E-mail: books@obrien.ie
Website: www.obrien.ie

ISBN: 0-86278-815-3

British Library Cataloguing-in-Publication Data
Currie, Austin
All hell will break loose
1.Currie, Austin
2.Politicians - Northern Ireland - Biography
3.Northern Ireland - Politics and government - 1969-1994
I.Title
941.6'0824'092

1 2 3 4 5 6 7 8
04 05 06 07

Typesetting, editing, layout, design: The O'Brien Press Ltd
Printing: Creative Print and Design

PICTURE CREDITS
The author and publisher wish to thank the following for permission to reproduce images:
courtesy of PA Photos, picture section 1, p.7, bottom; courtesy of the *Irish News*, picture
section 2, p.2, bottom; courtesy of the *Belfast Telegraph*, picture section 2, p.5, top and
bottom. Back cover photograph: Tony Higgins.
While every effort has been made to locate the holders of copyright, we would ask any
copyright holder(s) who have been omitted to inform the publisher.

DEDICATION

To Annita

Without whom this book could not have been written
And to Estelle, Caitríona, Dualta, Austin and Emer.

ACKNOWLEDGEMENTS

This is not a history book. It is the autobiography of a politician. Yet I hope the account I give here, from the perspective of one who has been close to historic events and helped to initiate and shape some of them, will be of interest to historians.

I had, from the beginning of the civil rights campaign, been conscious of being involved in politics at a time of change, indeed, in the context of Northern Ireland, of dramatic change. And my time in the History Department of Queen's University had made me aware of the importance of documents and contemporary records. I once overheard John Hume telling a group of SDLP Executive members, 'Don't leave bits of paper lying around. Currie will squirrel them.'

I wish to thank those who, in 1977, made it possible for me to utilise a Research Fellowship at Trinity College, Dublin, to put together a record which has been invaluable in the writing of this book.

In a political autobiography it is impossible to avoid being a victim of hindsight and self-justification. I have done my best to minimise these abuses, but I am conscious of my limitations and deficiencies. I have, on occasion, been angered by the attempted rewriting of history, particularly since the end of the Provisional IRA campaign and specifically the efforts made to portray that unnecessary 'war' in the context of civil rights and to suggest that until Hume–Adams there was no alternative to violence. I have attempted to put the record straight.

Despite my record-keeping and my surprisingly good recollection of most events, I have, on occasion, needed the assistance of a number of people to jog my memory and to fill in some factual gaps. I am particularly grateful to Michael McLoughlin, John C Duffy, Sean Donlon, Edmund Haughey, Pat Hughes and Gerry Cosgrave. They, of course, have no responsibility for the opinions expressed or any factual errors, for which I accept full and sole responsibility.

The order in which public events occurred could have caused me problems except for the assistance of Paul Bew and Gordon Gillespie in their *Northern Ireland A Chronology of the Troubles 1968–1999*. I thank them.

A good personal friend and brave journalist, as a staffman with the *Tyrone Democrat* and as a stringer with the national media, was Sean Hughes, until his tragic drowning in Lough Erne in 1978. Sean got all my press releases and covered all developments in the Coalisland/Dungannon area, 'the cradle of civil rights'. Sean's reports have been essential to my narrative. May he rest in peace.

My thanks are also due to the Western Education and Library Board, and to Elizabeth McAleer and Patrick Brogan, in particular; to Mary McVeigh of the Southern Education and Library Board in Armagh; to Gerry Kavanagh and the staff in the National Library of Ireland; and to Dr Patrick Melvin and Seamus Haughey of the Oireachtas Library.

To my brothers and sisters, Raymond, Sean, Brian, Mairead, Collette, Aidan, Vincent, Brendan and Annette, thanks for the memories, and the reminiscences of shared family life, and additionally to Brendan for his work in helping to compile the family history. I remember too, with love and gratitude, the contribution to family folk memory of our deceased brother, Seamus, who for banter and slagging had no equal.

Thanks also to Michael O'Brien and Íde ní Laoghaire of The O'Brien Press for their confidence in me, and to my editor, Rachel Pierce, for her friendship and for keeping me on the straight and narrow.

To Estelle, Caitríona, Dualta, Austin and Emer, with love and gratitude, and my apologies for causing so much stress in their young lives.

And finally to my companion of almost forty years. Every single word in this book and the drafts which preceded the final version were typed by Annita. This mammoth task was the least of her contribution. The book, after all, is only a book. I will never be able to repay her for her contribution to my life.

CONTENTS

PROLOGUE

O n Wednesday, 19 June 1968, near the end of an acrimonious debate in the Stormont Parliament, I was ordered by the Speaker to leave the House. As I left, I angrily threw my speaking notes at the jeering Unionist benches and shouted, 'All hell will break loose, and by God I will lead it.'

It was no accident, or act of injustice by the Speaker, that I was thrown out. I had deliberately precipitated it. I knew the lexicon of unparliamentary expressions, and when I described the remarks of John Taylor, MP for South Tyrone, as 'a damned lie', repeated the accusation twice and then refused to withdraw it, I knew the Speaker had no alternative but to expel me from the House. I was escorted from the precincts, given barely enough time to collect my coat and briefcase from the Nationalist room and, under the watchful eye of the RUC, directed to my car. I didn't wish to hang around anyway. I knew what I had to do.

When I arrived home in Donaghmore, County Tyrone, my wife, Annita, was a little surprised as I was a number of hours earlier than usual; my little rumpus at Stormont had not yet made the news. Surprise turned to shock when I asked her to sit down and told her of my intentions. Later that night, in response to my phone calls, the small front room of our home was overcrowded as I told those present that a Member of Parliament, whose job it was to make the law, was now intending to break it. We went on to discuss in detail what I intended to do and how they could assist me in doing it. We examined the practicalities and the likely legal and political consequences. I confided in my visitors, without elaboration, that I had further plans in mind, that what I intended to do would not be an isolated incident. They departed sometime after midnight.

Annita and I knew that my proposed action was serious, that a certain amount of physical risk to me was possible, and that the stress involved might not be good for her and the baby she was carrying. However, we agreed that I had reached a point in my political career where I really had no alternative.

Had I known the consequences of what I intended to do later that day, at Caledon, would I have proceeded with it? I have asked myself that question many, many times over the years. Would I have gone ahead had I known, or even suspected, that the action I was about to take would initiate a process that would lead to the loss of nearly four thousand lives? Would I have gone ahead had I known that my intended action and other actions stemming from it would transform the political scene in Northern Ireland and destroy a political regime which, at that time, appeared permanent and unchallengeable; would I have proceeded? These are some of the questions I have wrestled with for more than thirty years, particularly in the aftermath of barbarous events, such as have occurred at Enniskillen and Omagh, McGurk's bar, Greysteel and Bloody Sunday, or when people personally known to me, such as Jim and Gertie Devlin, were murdered in cold blood.

The answer is 'No', I would not have proceeded if I had had knowledge of these things. The injustices being suffered by the Catholic population of Northern Ireland were great and caused much suffering to individuals. And the initial injustice of a nation divided by a foreign country against the wishes of the great majority of its inhabitants was also great. But none of these injustices justified the loss of a single life, never mind close to four thousand.

What occurred over the following three decades was not inevitable. The deaths resulted from the decisions and actions of individuals, organisations and governments. The men, women and children who lost their lives in the Troubles did so because of hundreds of decisions, some intentional, others unintentional, which resulted in their deaths. Amongst those many decisions were my own – taken in good faith, with all the available information at the time and always, I can honestly say, from a desire to put right the wrongs that proliferated in Northern Ireland, and yet, not all correct, not all productive, not all to be proud of. It was not inevitable, I have repeated to myself so many times over the years.

1 : ORIGINS

S ave for the imminence of war – which Britain had declared the previous month, on 3 September, after German troops invaded Poland – I would have been born an Englishman at South Empsill, near Pontefract in Yorkshire. My parents had been living in Yorkshire, with my father's eldest brother, Joe, and his wife, Marion, since their marriage in December 1938. But now they were expecting their first child and the threat of war had concentrated their minds on the need to return home for the birth. It was not so much the fear of war that was the deciding factor, rather my parents' determination that I would not be liable for conscription in some future conflicts. The actual outbreak of war and the obvious danger of living in an industrial area so accessible to German bombers merely confirmed their decision to return home, to County Tyrone.

I was born on 11 October 1939 at Derry, Coalisland, County Tyrone, the eldest of the eight sons and three daughters of John and Mary Currie. I was christened Joseph Austin: Joseph after my father's eldest brother, who had been his best man, and Austin after a Passionist priest, Fr Austin Tierney, whose eloquence had greatly impressed my mother at a parish Mission. The house I was born in was an end-of-terrace house owned by a local farmer called McAvoy, and rented from him by my mother's Aunt Charlotte and her husband, Arthur O'Neill. My parents, known as Johnny and Minnie, were both locals, born within two miles of my birthplace.

The townland of Derry adjoined Coalisland and effectively consisted of two rows of terraced homes. 'Derry Corner' was well-known locally, long before 'Free Derry Corner' became part of history. It was here that the males of the locality, young and old, congregated to converse, to gossip and to play pitch-and-toss. 'The Corner' adjoined Kettle Lane, named after Tom Kettle, a Dubliner who had represented the area as MP for East Tyrone between 1910 and his death in the First World War.

Back in 1939, Derry was a peaceful hamlet less than ten minutes' walk from the centre of Coalisland, itself a village which no stranger dared describe as such. Coalisland, which was known locally as 'the Islan', received its name for obvious reasons: coal had been mined in the locality for hundreds of years, while the 'Island' was the peninsular piece of land at the head of the canal. The nearest town to 'the Islan' was Dungannon, less than five miles away.

The Curries were long associated with the Dungannon–Coalisland area, but they also boasted a close association with Scotland. My mother, an O'Donnell with a fierce pride in her Irish ancestry, would on occasion refer to 'the Scotch Curries'. My father would retort that Scotland had been created by the Irish, and that he and his family had merely returned to their homeland. His sister, Anna Bella, told me on more than one occasion that the Curries originally came from Ireland and had been renowned for poetry, singing, book learning and piety. This information I took with a very large dollop of salt. Unlike the O'Donnells, my father's generation of Curries and mine didn't have a musical note in their heads nor had I noticed any inclination among them to be Gospel greedy. But Anna Bella may have been more accurate than she realised. The Scottish Clan Currie can trace their ancestry back to Muiredach O'Dallaidh (1180–1222), a hereditary bard to Cathal Crodhearg of Connacht, who was forced to flee Ireland in 1213. It would have been a cause of much bantering between my father and mother had they known that the reason for Muiredach's forced emigration was a row with an O'Donnell, who had sent his steward to demand rent from the Royal bard. Muiredach split the poor messenger's head with a battleaxe.

Muiredach was a founder and name father of the clan Mac Mhuirrick who, as well as being hereditary bards, had responsibility, from the time of Muiredach's son, Niall, for inaugurating the MacDonalds, Lord of the Isles. The Lordship of the Isles merged with the Scottish Crown in 1545 and then, of course, with the English Crown in 1603. The current holder of the title is Charles, Prince of Wales. Enough to make a Currie mind boggle!

The Curries, who apparently arrived in the Coalisland–Dungannon area in the early nineteenth century, were, at least on the face of it, somewhat removed from this noble lineage: their interest was in coal rather than ermine. I say 'apparently' because I have found no direct evidence of this and I am relying on my father's eldest sister, Anna Bella, for this information. Marriage, birth and death records are complicated by a variation of the spelling between Currie and Curry, indicating a Scottish influence, or someone's inability to spell correctly. It is likely that there was regular movement between Tyrone and Scotland. The first record I have found is: 'Edward, born 11th December 1825 to James Curry and Mary McGowan of Glebe, Parish of Dungannon.' My grandfather, Thomas, was born on 8 December 1869 and married Margaret McGurk of the same townland, Atkinsallagh, on 8 January 1898. My father, John, was the second youngest of ten, born on 29 April 1910.

The economy of Coalisland at that time was largely based on its mineral resources and their extraction and exploitation. Coal had been mined in the area from the seventeenth century; the first instance recorded in the townland of Derry dates to 1654. The other major industries and areas of employment were the fire clay industry, which manufactured bricks, tiles, pipes, earthenware and fine china, and the Coalisland sand deposits, which were valuable for the building industry and were used as far away as Belfast.

In the late nineteenth and early twentieth century, Coalisland was, in many respects, more like a small English town developed by the Industrial Revolution than an Irish town evolving as a market centre for its hinterland. The topography, until fairly recent times, contributed to the comparison: chimney stacks, abandoned coal workings and scars on the landscape left by the extraction of clay and sand did not leave the impression of a typical small Irish town. Another distinguishing feature of Coalisland was its canal. The original purpose was to transport coal via the canal, the River Blackwater, Lough Neagh and the Newry canal and then by sea to Dublin. Later, in an effort to further reduce the cost of transportation, the canal system was extended to serve mines west of Coalisland. After 1789, when the main canal was completed, mines were opened in nearly every townland around Coalisland and between Coalisland and Dungannon.

There were, and still are, abundant supplies of coal. The problem for miners was that geological movements millions of years ago created earth faults, which meant coal seams would suddenly end, only to reappear above or below the previous level. Miners working a good thick seam of coal would find they had to sink another expensive shaft in order to continue. Such a development meant the end of many promising undertakings.

Working conditions for the miners and others employed in the coal industry were harsh, badly paid and often dangerous, with the ever-present threat of flooding or asphyxiation. In 1895, at the Congo pit, six miners (four English and two Irish) were drowned when they unwittingly released the full force of a huge volume of water contained in an old, abandoned shaft. My grandfather, Tom Currie, was working the other shift that day!

Despite the expenditure of much money and effort, the introduction of modern machinery and methods (as at Annagher, 1924–1926) and the employment of English and Scottish miners, coal-mining never became a viable proposition for the area. Indeed, the canal, built largely for the purpose of exporting coal from East Tyrone mines, became the conveyor of Scottish and English coal imported to Coalisland for use in local industries.

Coalisland people were proud of their canal, but Coalisland wasn't exactly 'the Venice of the North'. It was, however, where my mother's people came from. There was no problem over the ancestry of the O'Donnells, as my mother frequently reminded my father. The family was as old as Irish history itself. Although, there was one matter to which she did not refer. Her mother was a Hughes and 'Irish World' family history researchers in Coalisland unearthed the following record: 'James Hughes, collier and Rebecca Atkinson, both of Derry, Parish of Tullynisken, were married in Dungannon Registrar's office on 4th February 1873; both over 21 and bachelor and spinster respectively; fathers, James Hughes, collier and Francis Atkinson, labourer, Witnesses Alexander Patterson and N. Irwin.' So, my mother's grandfather not only married a Protestant but in a Registry Office! Those unionists who alleged I had bad blood in me somewhere may have been right after all. But to be serious, could the introduction of Presbyterian blood have contributed to the radicalism of my grandfather and, down the line, to the politicisation of his sons and grandsons?

My maternal grandparents were Neal and Bridget O'Donnell. My mother, Mary, or Minnie, was born on 30 March 1918, the only girl in a family of five, one of whom, Mark, died in infancy. From the perspective of history, Neal O'Donnell was involved with two organisations which appear to be incompatible. He was a member of the Ancient Order of Hibernians (AOH) and an official of the Transport and General Workers Union (TGWU). The former was and is a political and religious body with characteristics which led critics to describe it as the other side of the political and religious coin from the Orange Order. Its objective was the promotion of 'friendship, unity and true Christian charity', but only practising Catholics could be members and its origins lay in older secret societies, such as The Defenders and The Whiteboys of the eighteenth century and earlier. Politically, the AOH had supported the Irish party and post-Partition provided the electoral muscle for Nationalist MPs. Joe Devlin, the MP for West Belfast, was National President, while on the local level Joe Stewart MP was a leading light in Tyrone. The Order took extremely seriously its motto of 'Faith and Fatherland', never deviated from official Catholic Church teaching, was a force for moderation in opposition to men of violence and, of course, was conservative, if not reactionary, in social views. Membership of such an organisation did not naturally chime with being an official of a trade union.

There was, however, one very strong point of contact. The AOH was a registered Friendly Society and in the period after 1912, when the Irish

Parliamentary party got credit for the extension to Ireland of the National Health Insurance Act, the Order was enthusiastic to join it. The introduction of even minimal payments in the event of sickness or death was a great humanitarian advance and the AOH seized upon the opportunity offered to help provide the benefits for its members and their families. Of the sixty-five societies operating the Health Insurance Act in Ireland, the AOH secured one in five of insurable persons.

Neal O'Donnell found it entirely compatible with his trade union duties to collect the pennies to insure the less well-off in the East Tyrone area against illness and death. Later, in 1927, he took on the duties of councillor for the Coalisland division of Meenagh on Dungannon Rural Council. As the following report from the *Irish News* of 28 August 1923 indicates, he was acquiring a reputation for militancy:

TRADE UNIONIST CHARGED IN TYRONE

'At a special court in Dungannon before Mr Robert Newton, JP, District Inspector Walshe charged Neal O'Donnell, Coalisland, local organiser of the Workers' Union, with intimidation.

Constable Woods, Coalisland, stated that the accused went up to workmen employed by Messrs Teggart, Belfast, and told them that if they had the spirit of a dog they wouldn't work for Teggart. Witness ordered defendant to leave the works and he refused and witness arrested him to prevent a breach of the peace.

A number of houses were being erected for Sir Samuel Kelly's employees and the defendant used the statement directly towards the men employed at the work.

Teggart stated that he was paying the men and defendant arrived at the buildings.

Witness asked defendant to clear off the field and defendant refused to leave. Witness called the police who removed defendant to the road.

O'Donnell, when he got to the road, said to the men: "If you had the spirit of a dog you wouldn't work for Teggart. You are yellow dogs, anyway, and I'll get you yet."

Witness said a number of workers were members of the B-force and witness believed the remark about yellow dogs referred to their loyalty. Defendant called the workers blacklegs but witness looked on the defendant himself, under the circumstances, as a blackleg.

Defendant said he was local labour organiser in Coalisland and was sometimes engaged in settling labour disputes.

Mr Teggart was paying two shillings and sixpence per week less to the labourers than the district rate of wages.

O'Donnell told the police he had committed no crime, only looking for the money the men had earned.

Mr Bennett, JP, said it was a scandal in view of the unemployment in the district to see so much opposition to a gentleman who was prepared to spend thousands and perhaps millions of pounds in promoting employment.

It was playboys such as they had heard giving evidence that day that were destroying any industry promoted for the good of the district.

Mr Skeffington strongly protested against Mr Bennett giving his decision until the other magistrates were consulted and this in turn led to a sharp altercation between the chairman and Mr Skeffington ...

If the defendant would give an undertaking not to go to the premises again, they would deal leniently with him. Defendant gave the undertaking and the magistrates imposed a fine of 5 pounds and bound the defendant over to keep the peace for two years, himself in 20 pounds and two sureties of 10 pounds each.'

The fine of £5 was a severe one in 1923, being well in excess of what even the best-paid working man earned in a week. Compare it, in terms of real value, with the same £5 fine imposed on his grandson forty-five years later, in 1968, at Caledon!

Nonetheless, the plight of ordinary working people in a predominantly nationalist and Catholic area, in the immediate aftermath of Partition and amid the social, economic and political conditions then prevailing, demanded militancy. I am proud my grandfather had fire in his belly.

Neal O'Donnell went into hospital in 1928 for what was considered a minor operation, but died on the operating table. He left behind him a wife and eight children, for he had married again after the death of his first wife. His widow returned to her native Glasgow, bringing her four children with her. His eldest child, Jimmy, was only fourteen years of age, my mother, nine. My grandfather's death was a devastating blow not only in terms of personal sorrow but also to the advancement of a family which, despite the loss of a mother, seemed destined for significant economic, educational and social betterment. At the time of his untimely death, at the age of forty-two, two of his sons, Jimmy and Nealie, were already at secondary school (St Patrick's Academy, Dungannon) and in due course my mother, third in the family, would have expected to follow them into further education. Such hopes and expectations were now closed off. Aunt Charlotte, who took over the rearing of the family, did her best, but the wages were needed at the earliest opportunity, and so my mother graduated not to St Patrick's Academy or Donaghmore Convent but to the Coalisland Weaving Company.

2: CHILDHOOD

When my parents married, in 1938, my father was twenty-eight years old and my mother twenty. Like my mother, my father had left school at the end of compulsory education, aged fourteen, and had apprenticed as a motor mechanic in Lyttle's Garage in Coalisland. At the time of my birth his occupation was given as lorry driver, first for a private haulier in Dungannon, TW Reynolds, and then for the nationalised transport company, the Northern Ireland Road Transport Board (later the Ulster Transport Authority).

My earliest memories are related to my mother's Aunt Charlotte, even though I was only about four when she died. I have already related that I was born in her house when my parents returned from England, shortly before the outbreak of war. My mother's mother died in childbirth, when Mammy was three, and seven years later her father died too, leaving her and her three brothers orphans. It was Aunt Charlotte who took responsibility for them and brought them up. 'It was that or the workhouse,' my mother used to say. Charlotte had married late in life to Arthur O'Neill, who worked sporadically in the Derry coalmines, and they had no children of their own.

Shortly after my birth we moved out of Aunt Charlotte's house in Derry to rented accommodation elsewhere in Coalisland. However, my parents were determined to have their own house and renting made saving difficult. And so we moved again, to the old Engine Bridge, between Coalisland and Dungannon, to a terraced house at a low rent owned by local businessman and publican Willie Campbell.

Even by the standards of the time it was poor accommodation. Comprising two rooms, one for cooking, eating and living and the other for sleeping, it had earth floors, no electricity or running water or, of course, internal WC. The house was originally an outhouse to a shop and pub and, years later, part of the extended pub. I have derived some amusement from having lived the early years of my life in Ye Olde Stagger Inn.

These were, of course, the war years, but although American soldiers were billeted in Coalisland, we did not see much of them. This was unfortunate, as on the few occasions when US jeeps called at Campbell's pub and shop the GIs had been generous with their chocolates. I remember Lord Haw Haw on the wireless with his famous introduction, 'Germany Calling', and my father's description of Churchill as 'only an oul' warmonger'. My mother's half-brother, Brian, was captured at Arnhem and spent the rest of the war as a prisoner in Dresden, a city that was the target of some of the worst Allied bombing in the last days of the war. The bombings were particularly barbaric as Dresden was a centre to which thousands of refugees had fled to avoid the Soviet Army advancing from the east. In later years, Brian would describe how the Germans ordered the prisoners of war to carry out fire fighting and rescue missions in the aftermath of the bombings.

When he was eventually released, Brian visited us at the old Engine Bridge in uniform. My mother felt it necessary to explain to the neighbours that though he was her half-brother, he had been reared in Glasgow and could not avoid conscription. We were not a terribly pro-British family.

To revert to my earliest memories, my mother appeared to visit Aunt Charlotte almost every day. At least, that's what my memory suggests. The distance between the old Engine Bridge and Derry is less than three miles, but for a child of about three years of age it was a marathon. I remember the high pram, my two younger brothers in it and there not being enough room for all three of us, I had to walk part of the way to give my mother a rest from carrying one child and pushing the pram. My clearest memory is of the day Aunt Charlotte died. My father brought me to the wake house. The occasion is clear in my memory for two reasons. First, we travelled by bus and it was my first experience of a bus journey. Secondly, when I was brought to see the corpse I was forced, despite my protests, to kiss her cold cheek. The person responsible for this was my Uncle Jimmy's wife, and for the rest of her life I never forgave her.

An event occurred at the end of the war which was not only significant for the Currie family but which contributed, twenty-three years later, to developments that would help to change the political future of Northern Ireland.

There were now four children in the family, all boys, and another was on the way. In our case, four children in a two-room house, without any amenities, was making life virtually intolerable. My parents had been able to save some money in the hope of buying their own house. My father had been able to do a lot of overtime during the war years, neither of them smoked or drank and they were living where they were because the rent was low: yet they still did not have enough savings and my mother was at her wits' end.

It was at this stage that a council house became available locally and, under pressure from my mother, my father decided to do his best to get the tenancy.

The chairman of the unionist-dominated Rural Council was a Mr Moses Busby, farmer and Justice of the Peace, who lived about ten miles away, near the village of Dyan, on the road to Caledon (of all places!). When my father arrived on his bicycle he was received hospitably by Mosie, as he was called, because he was a decent enough man, doing his job according to his lights. He listened to my father put forward his case – the condition of the house, dampness, earthen floors, no basic amenities, the overcrowding because of four children and another on the way, the danger to the health of the children and the stress caused to his wife by the intolerable conditions. Mosie listened sympathetically, nodding his head on occasion in agreement. Then my father did something which went against the grain, but which he had been advised was customary on such occasions and without which he would have no chance of getting the house. He handed over a £5 note, one of the large English ones of the time, which represented a considerable amount for a working man – almost a week's wages. Mosie accepted the fiver, rolled it up and put it in his waistcoat pocket. He then said to my father, 'Mr Currie, you have made a good case. There is no doubt you badly need a house. I promise you, you will get the first suitable one vacated by one of your own kind.'

It was a very angry, but determined, Johnny Currie who returned to his wife and children. He said to my mother, 'We'll find a better use for the next fiver than giving it to Mosie Busby.'

As luck would have it, or, as my mother believed, in answer to prayer, a short time after this event a female relative of my father's rather surprisingly announced her intention to marry and her house and small farm came on the market. My father had first choice, and so in 1946 we moved approximately two miles from our home at the old Engine Bridge to the townland of Mullaghmarget, near to the village of Edendork, two miles from Coalisland, three miles from Dungannon and forty-two miles from Belfast. As might be expected, a house on eight acres of land purchased for £450, even from a relative, was no mansion, but it was infinitely better than the shack we had left. I will always remember my first visit to my new home shortly before Maggie McGurk left. It was a Sunday afternoon and Maggie had gone to some trouble to provide a ham tea. As we sat at the table facing a small window high up on the front wall, I was shocked to see a bearded face looking in at us. It was Maggie's goat standing on a mossy bank!

An early recollection of life in the new house is being wakened early in the morning, at first light, by the sound of hammering as my parents knocked down a portion of wall in preparation for the builder later that day. Building was to become an almost constant feature. Mammy was always improving, always changing. You could leave home in the morning only to return at night to find some change had taken place, even if it was only the furniture that had been rearranged. We did not have electricity at this stage and sometimes 'the wee red lamp', which was the Sacred Heart lamp, was used to guide one to bed. I remember at least one occasion when I was unable to find the bed – and this long before I discovered the 'Devil's buttermilk'.

By the time we moved to Mullaghmarget there were five boys in the family – Austin, Raymond, Seamus, Sean and Brian. The day Mairead was born was a major occasion. Three of us were waiting when the new Daddy got off the bus from his work that evening, yelling excitedly, 'there is a girl in our house'.

Life was tough for a woman in those days, particularly for a woman who was pregnant as often as my mother. At this stage, in 1948, she had six children under the age of nine, and five more would follow. We did not have electricity or running water, and therefore no washing machine, or hot water, or internal toilet, or any of the amenities of modern living.

At age thirteen, on a trip to the Gaeltacht on a scholarship from Edendork GAA, I was amazed to find that in a remote area of Donegal, in the poverty-stricken Free State the unionists had told us about, there was electricity in houses halfway up the mountain. We did not live in a remote area – though rural, it was well-populated – yet we did not have electricity until 1961, while the piped water supply arrived just two years earlier, in 1959. The Black North may have been ahead of the South in some respects, but certainly not in terms of rural electrification.

Many years later I brought my children to the Ulster American Folk Park outside Omagh, which reproduces the lifestyles of those who left for the New World in the eighteenth and nineteenth centuries. I was able to point to items like churns and pots and crooks on the fire and tell them that I remembered them in use. My eldest daughter, Estelle, wasn't too impressed. 'Daddy,' she said, 'I know you are old, but I didn't think you were ancient.' I then had to explain how much a revolution was the installation of electricity. Prior to electrification, in terms of domestic living and lifestyle, things had changed little in generations.

So things were done in the old-fashioned way at Mullaghmarget prior to 1961: reading by the oil, then the tilley lamp, churning by hand, washing clothes manually, or using a scrubbing board, laying out sheets on the grass to bleach, storing butter and milk in a cool corner on the tiled floor and milking the cows by hand. We children were given jobs to do as soon as we were able, starting with helping in the house, then graduating to work on the farm. The most hated job was picking potatoes from the pit in winter. Daddy would open the pit, usually with some difficulty because of the frost, then all the potatoes had to be removed for storage inside. Some of them were rotten, their putridness adding to the pain of cold hands. For a boy aged eight or nine, it was not a pleasant task.

There wasn't much in the way of social life. Until I was old enough to babysit, my parents rarely went out. When they did, it was to *céilídh* at a neighbour's house and the compliment would be returned a week or so later. They rarely went anywhere separately on social occasions. Even at Sunday Mass in Edendork church, where there was a 'men's side' and a 'women's side', my mother insisted on sitting on the men's side along with her husband and children. The pub was the obvious meeting place for men, but my father didn't drink until well into his forties, when he endured the first and only illness that forced him to stay in bed. The family doctor prescribed a bottle of Guinness per day. This became a nightly pantomime for the younger children as they fought over who would bring the bottle to him, watch as he uncorked it and then laugh at the contortions of his face as he drank, complaining all the while about how awful it was. After a while we older ones noticed the contortions and the protestations seemed less real, and so it wasn't entirely a shock to hear that, upon his recovery, when he and my mother shopped together in Dungannon on a Saturday night, Mammy continued to visit her friend, Mrs Donnelly, the butcher's wife, while Daddy slipped into Charlie McKenna's pub next-door.

There was, of course, no television, but there was a lot of reading – even by the meagre light of the oil lamp. Comics for the children and magazines for my mother came with the breadman on Wednesdays and Saturdays, and books came from the local library in Dungannon. Reading was my mother's great release from the hard work and drudgery of ordinary life, and this love of reading she passed on to me. In the early years, particularly before I was old enough to babysit (at an age modern childcare regulations would not allow), she was rarely able to leave the house without an entourage of children. Even later, when going out was feasible, her visiting was confined to Saturday night shopping in Dungannon, Mass on Sunday and occasional *ceilidhing* with local neighbours. It was a hard life, particularly for an intelligent woman whose potential for advancement had been thwarted by being orphaned at such a young age.

My first 'holiday' came about when I was around twelve years of age. My father borrowed a car for the day and we visited Warrenpoint, enjoying a picnic lunch along the way, with tea prepared on a Primus stove. The big thrill, long remembered, was to travel by boat to Omeath in 'the Free State'. The phrase 'Free State' did not then, and does not now, hold the same political implications and considerations among Northerners as it does for those living in the Republic. It is commonly used, irrespective of the political allegiance of the user, be they nationalist or unionist. Indeed, in areas adjacent to the border the South is often referred to as 'the State'. This can be a source of some bewilderment to people from the Republic who are used to the phrase 'Free State', or 'Freestaters', being used in a narrower political and historical context. Once, at a football match in South Derry, one of my future Fianna Fáil colleagues, a TD from the deep South, was mortally affronted to be described as a 'Free State bastard'. I didn't enquire which epithet offended him most!

Anyway, on the occasion of this holiday, which was my first visit to the South, the excitement of travelling by boat was followed by a jaunting-car ride to a seminary where, very briefly, two of my uncles had attended, and then the delights of a southern Sunday on the dodgems and roundabouts. Even though we were nationalist to the core, we experienced some of the pleasures of visiting a 'foreign' country.

Our small farm was the last Catholic holding on the road between the Dungannon–Coalisland road and 'The Bush', an entirely Protestant village. Our immediate neighbours, except for the Girvans, were Protestants: the McMinns, Whites, Burrowes, Bradleys, Abernethys and Bleaks. They were good neighbours and we got on well with them. Religion and politics were never discussed. We went our way and they went theirs. We attended each other's funerals, but they did not enter our church and we did not enter theirs. There was, of course, the occasional jibe. Funeral 'offerings' survived in the Archdiocese of Armagh until the early 1970s. At each funeral, two male relatives of the deceased would stand at the altar rails, along with the priest, as the mourners, led by the chief male mourners, queued up to make a financial contribution, or 'offering', which went to the church. The men paid first, and when they were finished the women formed their line. Each contribution was entered in a book and called out, name and amount. There was always intense interest in the final amount as an indicator of the standing of the deceased in the community. Part of my father's job as a lorry driver was to collect pigs from farms and deliver them to the bacon factory. His objection to the system of offerings increased substantially when a Protestant workmate once enquired after a funeral, 'How much did they get for him, dead weight?'

My brothers and I worked for neighbours at such jobs as gathering potatoes or making the hay because the money was badly needed. We particularly liked working for the Abernethys because they had a tractor which we were allowed to drive on occasion. My brother Raymond became particularly proficient in the driving seat at a young age.

We were poor, but then we were no different from nearly everyone else we knew. We very rarely had meat, but we reared our own chickens and grew our own potatoes and vegetables and milked our own cows. We didn't have many eggs to eat, except at Easter, because the eggs were for sale and were collected weekly. In his job travelling around the country, my father was able to keep abreast of farming developments. He was the first in our area to introduce the deep litter for hens. I remember a neighbour, Frank Marlow, who came to *céilídh* one night saying, 'Johnny, I was thinking about what you were saying about mushrooms. I don't think they will catch on here.' We were poor and in many ways disadvantaged, but we did have an advantage over poor town children in that basic food was always available.

When I started at Edendork Primary School, aged four (almost five), the principal was Tom Kelly and there were two assistants, Miss Steele and Miss Brannigan. My first visit to the school had been at the end of the previous year when a party had been held for the retiring principal, Master Molloy. I remember the party for two reasons. First, seated on the bar of my father's bike, I had dropped my tin mug, which had bounced on the road and into thick undergrowth. We had to return home for another mug, otherwise, said Daddy, I wouldn't have had any tea. Secondly, meat sandwiches were served: my first, and long remembered.

Master Molloy had been a teacher of the old school. My father would recount stories of the pretty brutal corporal punishment inflicted on him and his schoolmates, which, he averred, never did any of them any harm. Indeed, my father, with only a primary education, was able to recite long passages from Shakespeare, a feat credited to Master Molloy and his cane. Master Kelly, who used the cane only as a last resort, was, in my father's opinion, 'too soft'. Despite this criticism of Master Kelly, my father, in his dealings with his own sons, was also 'too soft'. He was fond of telling people that a man walking along the road should always carry a stick ready for use, for 'if you meet a young fellow you should give him a slap because if he isn't coming from trouble he will be going into it'. Nevertheless, in a family with five boys, close to each other in age, where discipline was continually required, he always looked for an alternative to the stick, unlike many, if not most, parents at the time. When I hear reports of the brutality administered in Church institutions and in Christian Brothers' schools, I judge them in the context of the standards of the time. Wrong, yes, but in line with the Victorian maxim, 'spare the rod and spoil the child'.

Our father had devised one particularly successful alternative to the cane. Whenever there was an unresolved dispute, he would threaten, 'I will bring you to the Dean. He will take one look at you and know which of you did it and who is telling lies.' The Dean was not only the parish priest of Dungannon but Dean of the Archdiocese of Armagh and a Monsignor to boot. If that threat didn't produce immediate results, Daddy would proceed to the next stage, which was to start on the journey to Dungannon, three miles away. By this time, and usually early in the journey, the guilty one, fearful of the wrath of God through his servant the Dean, would confess. Being the eldest, I caught on to this ploy earlier than my brothers. I noted we walked by the railway rather than the road, which was nearer, and that as we neared our Aunt Maggie Jane's house, close to the railway line, the pressure to confess intensified. A confession having been obtained, we would then stop off at her house for tea. On one occasion, the last in which I was involved, I was the guilty party, but was determined to brazen it out. Imagine my relief to hear my brother, Raymond, confess to the crime. Either he had committed the offence on a previous occasion, or the baleful power of the Dean was particularly impressive to him.

There were a small number of Protestants at the school, five or six children who lived close and for whom it would have been inconvenient to travel to Protestant schools in The Bush, Newmills, Coalisland, or Dungannon. There wasn't anything different about them, except when it came to prayers, at which point they would leave the classroom to wait in a cloakroom until we were finished. When Catholic prayers were being taught, I would watch them with envy as they played in the yard outside. I had a particular problem with the Catechism. No Confirmations had taken place during the war, so there was a serious backlog. Additionally, it was decided that since Confirmation would not take place again for three years, those under the normal age would be administered the Sacrament, if they were capable of taking the instruction. The job of teaching me the Catechism, most of which I couldn't read never mind understand, fell to my poor father. So I was confirmed before I received my first Holy Communion.

Edendork was a good school with three dedicated teachers. I rarely missed a day, never mitched (that was saved for secondary school), but was late often enough to remember the rhyme Miss Brannigan used on such occasions:

Timothy took his time to school,
plenty of time he took,
some he spent by the Tadpole pool
and some by the sticky back brook.

The Butler Education Act 1944 was introduced in Northern Ireland in 1947, and so the new Qualifying Examination, or the Eleven-Plus as it later became known, was only in its fourth year when I sat it in 1951. There was little recognition then of the revolutionary potential of the exam – it was certainly not foreseen among the pupils and parents at Edendork St Malachy's – but Principal Tom Kelly recognised the opportunity it offered to children from poorer backgrounds. 'Cramming' would be much too strong a word, but a small number of us were selected, of whom I think I was the youngest, for extra tuition, mostly comprised of attempting intelligence tests from previous years. After the exam, which was held in the alien atmosphere of Union Place and Drumglass Protestant schools in Dungannon, Master Kelly held a *post-mortem*. He was disappointed with my answer to the question, 'The man was hung/hang/hanged this morning', but very pleased with my originality in the English paper, where we had been asked to complete a story about a boy and girl who find a chest in a cave. Instead of the predictable smuggling story, my chest contained a genie's lamp from which the genie emerged with a flaming sword. Faced with a certain and swift ending to their young lives, the boy shouted to his sister to dive into the sea. The genie followed and disappeared when he touched the water. The boy then explained that he had read that the best way to get rid of a genie was to put salt on its tail! In my lifetime I have let many genies out of the bottle; not all of them have been as easily dealt with.

Five of us, three boys and two girls, passed the Qualifying Exam that year, helping to establish for Edendork a reputation that has transformed it from an ordinary country school into one attracting pupils from a much wider area. The reputation has continued to the present day, and perhaps explains why Edendork is sometimes pronounced 'Eton'dork.

Also at this time I experienced my first political event, in 1948, at the age of eight, when Margaret Pearse, sister of the executed 1916 brothers Pádraig and Willie, spoke at an anti-Partition meeting in the Square in Coalisland. The following year Coalisland Fianna Gaelic Football Club opened its new pitch,

McRory Park. The identification between Gaelic football and nationalist politics was underlined by the presence on the platform of Major Vivian de Valera, son of the former and later Taoiseach, and Cork GAA star and future Taoiseach, Jack Lynch TD. An event took place the following day which illustrated that I had caught the political bug: a small procession took place in a field at Mullaghmarget, Dungannon, home of the Curries. The procession was led by a small boy carrying what appeared to be a flag, but on closer inspection turned out to be a Green's meal bag, which was coloured green, white and yellow. Behind him were four other boys, banging on a variety of tins and buckets. The procession proceeded to the vicinity of a tar barrel, where the flagpole was erected, and the oldest of the boys made a stirring speech, the central and oft-repeated theme of which was 'the border must go'. Thus was the political career of Austin Currie launched.

3: POLITICAL STIRRINGS

And so it came to pass that I arrived, in September 1951, at St Patrick's Academy Grammar School in Dungannon. Known as 'The Academy', it had been established in 1891 and catered for, as the Reverend Manager Dean MacDonald noted, 'boys and girls, mostly those whose parents couldn't afford to send their children to a boarding school'. There was one Board of Management, but effectively two schools: The Boys' and The Girls'. The President of the school from 1919 to 1942, Fr Alfie McKernan, was a character and an eccentric about whom stories, real and apocryphal, are still told at school gatherings. The school history records say of him: 'students who attended the Boys' Academy in the McKernan years went on to become teachers, doctors, civil servants, soldiers, policeman, priests – they joined all the professions. The school was not noted, however, for its academic achievements. Most of the students looked forward to attending school, if only for the "Crack" which was a feature of school life during those years. Some mothers in fact were apprehensive about allowing their sons to attend the Academy, fearing that they would "turn wild" under Fr McKernan's regime.'

I'm glad to say that things had changed for the better when I arrived through the impressive, decorative, wrought-iron railings and gates. The school was still sadly lacking in resources and amenities, inside and outside the building. It was still catering for many pupils whose parents could not afford to send them to boarding school. Parents who considered themselves a bit above the ordinary ('Tuppence halfpenny looking down on tuppence,' as my father would have said) sent their children to St Patrick's, Armagh. To be fair, the Academy was not a seminary school and those parents who wished to see their boys become priests had no alternative but to send them to Armagh. Indeed, some transferred to Armagh from the Academy for that purpose.

The presidency of Dr McLarnon, known as 'the Wee Doc', had eventually been successful in eliminating the reputation of the McKernan era. The 1947 Education Act had provided new challenges and opportunities. The number of boys had increased to 133, from ninety-eight, before the introduction of the Qualifying. In my class, A1, we were all qualifiers and the presumption was that we were the best of the local talent.

It was some time before I realised that I was not at the new school to play football. It took me even longer to come to the conclusion that, despite my great enthusiasm, I was never going to be an Eddie Devlin, or Iggy Jones, the great Tyrone football stars of the time, never mind a Jody O'Neill, who, in my second year, captained the most successful Academy team yet seen. From the beginning I was a model for those students whose school reports read, 'He works well at the subjects he likes'. I was reading history even at primary school, and not just Irish history, when most children of my age were still reading comics. I did, of course, read Irish history with avid interest, willing the pages to tell me different from what I had heard: that in Ireland's long struggle with England, the Saxons had always beaten us.

Being at school in Dungannon increased my interest in Irish history. Dungannon was, of course, the ancient capital of the O'Neills. The first article I ever wrote, for a local magazine and reproduced in the local newspaper, *Dungannon Observer*, was about a row between the O'Neills and the Pope in the twelfth century. Dungannon was also where the Volunteer Convention had met in 1782. Bulmer Hobson had founded the Dungannon Clubs there, and it had been the birthplace of Thomas Clarke, the first signator of the 1916 Easter Proclamation. Dan Breen's *My Fight for Irish Freedom* was my favourite book at about nine years of age. When the *Sunday Press* appeared, the only paper to be sold after Mass in Edendork, articles about the 'Four Glorious Years' encouraged my nationalism. Incidentally, it was the *Sunday Press,* and specifically its strip cartoon, The Looneys, which led to my first flutter on the horses. The Sunday before the Grand National, Mr Looney made a jocular reference to *ESB* and I invested six pence each way on the runner of that name. Standing on a chair, with my ear close to the old wireless, I listened in tense delight as *ESB* romped home at the expense of the Queen's horse, which was safely in the lead – until it jumped an imaginary fence and fell on the run-in.

Strangely, my interest in Irish history was not reflected in a similar interest in the language. It wasn't unusual for me to get a mark as low as 10% in class tests, or indeed lower. However, the necessity of having to pass a language subject for the Junior Certificate exam focussed my interest. I was always very good at 'spotting' questions and the streaming of subject choice until only three were necessary at A-level suited my inclinations.

When I first came to the Academy some food rationing, a hangover from the war years, was still in place, and sweets were one of the affected items. Because of the size of our family and the lack of money for such luxuries, the 'sweetie coupons' were rarely used in our house. Unknown to my parents, I developed quite a lucrative wee business selling the coupons to my more well-off classmates.

I learned other self-improving subjects at the Academy. Belatedly, at about thirteen, I took up smoking and a little later I was introduced to poker. I was never much of a singer and my lack of interest in that department was increased by the fact that non-singers had a free period that coincided with the PE class at the girls' High School, just two fields away. And they were Protestants! Not only did they not wear the thick stockings of the Academy girls but they had a reputation for being 'easy'. It was years later I found out that the Protestant boys at the Royal School had the same mistaken impression of the Academy girls.

I have already described my first brush with political activism at the tender age of eight. The year 1949, in particular, was an important year for Northern nationalism. The Anti-Partition League (APL) was established, supported by all the political parties in the South, and intensive efforts were made to put pressure on the Labour government at Westminster through the manipulation of the Irish vote in British constituencies. The campaign was a failure, indeed it was self-defeating. Basil Brooke, the unionist Prime Minister, had seized the opportunity of the challenge to unionism to call an election (the Chapel Gate election, so-called because of the manner in which funds were collected for Nationalist candidates), and the Unionists had triumphed. Additionally, the decision of the Southern government to declare a Republic created a situation that led the British government to introduce the Ireland Act, which actually strengthened Partition.

These setbacks to constitutional nationalism, and the frustration that they engendered, had the usual effect of boosting support for nationalism of the more violent variety, as soon became apparent with the increased support for abstentionism from Parliament on the political level, alongside increased IRA activity on the military level.

Events occurred while I was at the Academy certain to stir the political blood in most young fellows from a nationalist background, and I was no exception. Liam Kelly, expelled from the IRA in 1951, formed Clann Uladh and in 1953 was elected MP for Mid-Tyrone, defeating a Nationalist. He was charged with making a seditious speech at his victory rally and sentenced to six months' imprisonment. On his release, 10,000 gathered in the village of Pomeroy to welcome him home. An attempt by the RUC to seize the tricolour, under the terms of the recently passed Flags and Emblems Act, had predictable consequences and scores were injured. Clann Uladh (and its military wing, Saor Uladh) were further boosted, at the expense of the Nationalist party, by Kelly's nomination to the Irish Senate at the instigation of Seán MacBride, leader of the Clann na Poblacht element of the coalition government. Fianna Uladh and Saor Uladh (Free Ulster) were in competition with Sinn Féin and the IRA. In the early 1950s both military organisations sought arms and ammunition and the funding to purchase them. One dull afternoon at the Academy was enlivened by reports of a raid on the Labour Exchange in Dungannon, with shots being fired as the perpetrators were pursued by the RUC. The headline in that week's *Dungannon Observer* colourfully put it: 'Wild West Scenes in streets of Dungannon'.

There were other happenings to stir the juvenile imagination – and, indeed, the imagination of others supposedly more mature. The IRA raided Gough Military Barracks in Armagh and escaped with a considerable number of weapons. The Territorial Army camp in Dungannon was blown up in 1954 and a botched IRA raid at Omagh army camp would prove to have considerable political influence in the future, when the IRA men captured stood as candidates in later elections. There were other raids, mostly unsuccessful, in England, at Felstead in Essex and Arborfield in Berkshire, as well as a raid at Eglinton in Derry, but being farther away these were of less interest.

Dramatic political events accompanied these paramilitary developments, one sustaining the other. In 1955 the Anti-Partition League, or Nationalists as they were generally described, decided not to contest the Westminster general election, thereby leaving the field open to Sinn Féin. Fighting on an abstentionist policy of not taking their seats if elected, and emphasising that a vote for them would not be considered a mandate for the IRA campaign, Sinn Féin achieved considerable success and won seats in Fermanagh–South Tyrone and Mid-Ulster. However, as their candidates, Phil Clarke and Tom Mitchell, had been convicted of the Omagh raid and were still guests of Her Majesty at Crumlin Road jail, steps were taken by the Unionists to have them unseated as 'convicted felons'. In Fermanagh–South Tyrone the seat was given to the defeated Unionist candidate, but in Mid-Ulster a second election was declared. Mitchell was once again nominated and duly won, with an increased majority. By order of the Court, the seat was given to the defeated Unionist, Charles Beattie.

The saga was not yet over, however. Beattie was discovered to hold 'an office of profit under the Crown' and was consequently disqualified, and the seat was declared vacant once again. This time the Unionist party decided they had had enough and that the proceedings so far were only helping the Republicans. Their selection convention decided not to nominate a candidate against Mitchell, and in the circumstances the Nationalists decided to contest. At almost the last minute, indeed with only ten minutes to go before nominations closed, an independent Unionist, George Forrest, was nominated. The result was a foregone conclusion, with the Republican–Nationalist majority split. The Nationalist candidate, Michael O'Neill, lost his deposit after a bitter campaign, which is still remembered to this day in certain quarters. The Nationalists never recovered from the blow at Westminster election level, although the different circumstances at Stormont level, plus a law requiring candidates to give prior commitment to taking their seats if elected at Stormont, minimised the effect in subsequent Stormont elections.

Despite the assurances given by the Republican movement in its election manifesto, including a commitment that 'We are not asking Irish men and women to go out bearing arms for freedom', the election results were used as a mandate for an IRA campaign. Saor Uladh struck first, however, attacking Roslea RUC station in November 1955. The IRA campaign began in the early hours of 12 December 1956, when targets were hit in each of the Six Counties. They were not exactly crucial military targets, including among their number, for example, an Orange hall that doubled as a training centre for the B Specials, but the number of attacks, the spread of locations and the Proclamation addressed to the Irish people modelled on the 1916 proclamation certainly made an impact. The attack on Brookeborough RUC station was a farce, but the two IRA men killed, Seán South and Fergal O'Hanlon, became heroes, whereas the real courage was shown by the RUC defenders. The funerals of the two IRA men were massively attended, and the body of South was paraded through the Republic on the way to his military funeral in Limerick. The effect of all this on opinion in the Republic was evident three months later when four Sinn Féin TDs were elected to Dáil Éireann.

While these events were occurring, I was of course still a schoolboy at the Academy in Dungannon, but a schoolboy intensely interested in public events and responding emotionally to them. It was, as I have said earlier, a time of deep disillusionment with politicians, North and South, who had been involved in the abortive anti-Partition campaign. The general feeling was that we had been let down once again by southern politicians of all political hues – de Valera, Costello, MacBride, Brown, the lot. The Anti-Partition League, the 150th anniversary of 1798, the rise of Clann na Poblachta, the establishment of the Republic, the campaign of opposition to the Ireland Act, de Valera's anti-Partition tours in the USA and Britain, Australia, New Zealand, Canada and even in India, had all created expectations which had been summarily dashed. Now there was only disillusionment with these politicians and their ineffective political process.

For a fifteen-year-old boy engrossed in Irish history and seduced by stirring nationalism, these developments were bound to have an effect. Popular ballads celebrating 'Seán South of Garryowen' were bound to resonate. It was, in truth, satisfying to see someone putting the boot into the arrogant and dominating unionists. I had little short of hatred for the B Specials, some of whom were known to me, who would frequently stop me on the road demanding to know my name and address, which they already knew. The unionists were not only politically wrong, they were morally wrong as well. They had, with the help of the British, partitioned our country. They had divided us up in such a way as to maintain a permanent majority for themselves. They didn't know the meaning of the word 'democracy', they discriminated against us in jobs and in housing, as my own family had experienced. People were being imprisoned without trial, the Protestants held all the good land, which had been confiscated from Catholics, even the church in Newmills had been converted to a Church of Ireland place of worship. They didn't even allow us to call ourselves by an Irish name. Two of my brothers, Seamus and Sean, and my sister, Mairead, were registered as James, John and Margaret Mary because the registrar told my parents, 'no such names exist in Northern Ireland'. The political failures of the thirty-five years since Partition meant the alternative had to be tried and despite what the clergy said was morally justified. Such sentiments were shared by many of my fellow pupils. The day after the successful IRA raid on the Armagh military base, and for the first time in my experience, a group of us walked through a group of boys from the Royal School and elbowed them off the footpath.

And yet, to my knowledge, only two of my fellow students were active in the Republican movement. One was caught with documentation detailing the movements of police and Army personnel and was interned. The other was also interned, and in a later phase of 'the struggle', in 1972, was shot dead by the British Army.

I knew there would be strong parental disapproval if I became involved with the Republican movement. My mother was a strong nationalist, but her family background was Hibernian and trade union. My father had a more down-to-earth approach despite, or maybe because of, a cousin's involvement with the IRA. Seamus Donnelly had fled across the border after the shooting of Constable Forbes in Dungannon in 1942 and had not been able to return, not even for the funerals of his parents. 'A wee bit of education is easy carried,' my father would say, and I and others would serve ourselves and our country better by getting a good education and proving ourselves as good as, or better than 'the other kind'. So I soon came to terms with the emotional pull of violent republicanism and instead I threw my energies, if not entirely into my studies, into playing for and supporting the Academy and St Malachy's Gaelic football club, Edendork.

It soon became clear that the IRA was on a hiding to nothing. Internment was introduced immediately in the North, and in mid-1957 de Valera did likewise in the 'Free State'. Politically, the high tide of Sinn Féin soon receded after the high-water marks of 1955 and 1956. In 1958 the Nationalists made an almost miraculous recovery. The Catholic electorate had always distinguished between Stormont and Westminster elections. It was widely felt that a maximum of three seats at Westminster, in a House of over six hundred, was not as important as representation at Stormont. Voting for abstentionist candidates was a luxury which could be afforded at Westminster elections, but Stormont elections were viewed differently. Here, matters of importance to survival, such as housing, education, social welfare and agricultural grants, were decided and even though the Nationalist opposition was invariably ignored, it was still important to have a presence there. The letters 'MP' after one's name were essential for representations on the bread-and-butter issues affecting ordinary people. So, in the 1958 Stormont elections the Nationalist MPs survived, even in East and West Tyrone, losing only in Mid-Tyrone and that because of a split vote: a very considerable achievement considering the lost deposit of Michael O'Neill just two years earlier.

I had my first, small involvement in electoral politics in that 1958 election in my home constituency of East Tyrone. Joe Stewart, the sitting Nationalist MP, made a request to the Academy for helpers to assist in addressing election communications. A friend of 'wee Joe' on the staff asked if anyone would like to volunteer. Ed Haughey and I, albeit not great supporters of 'wee Joe', preferred this new experience to a double period of Latin. We amused ourselves by addressing the election communications to some of our Protestant neighbours on the electoral register, contrary to instructions. An even greater source of amusement were the stories of our supervisor, who claimed to have experience of some of the seedier night clubs in Nairobi. There was one anecdote concerning a donkey which was received with some incredulity!

In 1959 the Westminster election confirmed that the Republican tide had indeed gone out. In 1962 the inevitable happened when the IRA called off its campaign with the instruction to dump arms. I, for one, believed it was the end of them for all time as a force in politics!

There was one event during these years which sticks out in my memory. In 1957 Tyrone won the Ulster football championship and were due to play in Croke Park, Dublin, in the All-Ireland semi-final. It was a momentous occasion, only the second such achievement for Tyrone at senior level, the first having been the previous year, 1956. Everyone who could get to the match was going. My uncle, Eddie O'Donnell, who was working in England, returned for the historic match and stayed with his uncle by marriage, Arthur O'Neill, at his house in Derry, Coalisland – indeed, the same house in which I was born. It was arranged that Eddie, Arthur, my mother's uncle, James Hughes, and I would travel to Dublin by train, and as the train station was close to the O'Neill house and the train was leaving early on a Sunday morning, I would stay at O'Neills' on Saturday night. So, on Saturday, 17 August 1957, I left my family home at Edendork, two miles from Coalisland, and travelled there by bus. My mother had taken the precaution of giving me an alarm clock, as she knew Arthur O'Neill didn't have one and she suspected we might oversleep and miss the train.

As I disembarked from the bus in Coalisland there was a loud explosion. People stopped on the streets to listen and to question and soon there were signs of great activity at the RUC barracks. As I walked up the Derry Road, the half-mile to the house where I was to stay the night, a number of police vehicles passed by me, travelling at speed. We did not get any sleep that night because of the sound of sirens and the noise of engines. It was obvious that the explosion had occurred very close to us. The following morning the train was delayed, we believed unnecessarily and deliberately, as each intending passenger was questioned and searched by RUC and B men. The B men, in particular, were in angry mood and it was obvious something serious had happened. It was only when we got to Dundalk and saw the headline in the *Sunday Press* being sold on the platform that we knew, for certain, what had happened: 'RUC Sergeant killed in Coalisland'. Sergeant Ovens, the local Sergeant in Coalisland, had been lured to a derelict house at Kettle Lane and had been killed instantly when he opened the door, which triggered a booby-trap bomb. Another brave blow for Ireland in the name of the Irish nation!

After our defeat in Croke Park, we returned to Coalisland with some trepidation and, predictably, the following morning the RUC arrived to question us. The circumstances were sufficiently suspicious to ensure a lengthy grilling and a further visit by Special Branch a few days later. Uncle Eddie had just returned from England to a house only a half-a-mile from the explosion, while I had travelled to Coalisland from Edendork, from where the phone call that lured the Sergeant to his death had been made. I have often wondered what would have happened had I travelled on a later bus, when road blocks would have been set up, and had been found with a ticking parcel in my overnight bag. Two Coalisland men, Kevin Mallon and Francie Talbot, were charged with the murder of Sergeant Ovens. They were defended by the then Recorder of Bristol and later British Attorney-General, Elwyn Jones, and were acquitted of the murder, although later they both received custodial sentences for other offences: Mallon was sentenced to fourteen years' imprisonment, Talbot to eight years.

In later years I would get to know Kevin Mallon quite well. He was involved as a steward in the early days of the civil rights campaign, and later again was a founder member of the Provisional IRA, a member of the Army Council, one of the reputed kidnappers of *Shergar,* the unrivalled and extremely valuable racehorse, and one of those who made a daring escape from Portlaoise prison by helicopter. He was clearly a man totally committed to the Republican cause. He also had a dark sense of humour. On one occasion, during the civil rights campaign, he said to me, 'Austin, I admire you for what you have done and are doing. But if I thought a bullet through your head would help the cause, I would not hesitate.' I didn't laugh, or even smile.

Another major contribution to my education were my experiences as a bus conductor in Bournemouth, on the south coast of England. I first went there at seventeen years of age and continued to return to work during summer holidays from university. In many ways, I grew up on the buses in Bournemouth. It was my first time away from home, except for that month in the Donegal Gaeltacht. It was a testing experience to be in a strange town, where I was new to the job, in a situation were a large percentage of the passengers were holidaymakers who didn't know where they were going either, and where the conductor had to jump on and off at fixed points on the journey to adjust the trolleys. The money was good and I soon learned how to maximise 'shonk', the local word for overtime. I also joined the union in my first year, one of the few students to do so, and attended branch meetings. In my third year of bus conducting, this experience of the union and its procedures proved useful. During the winter the regular bus conductors had moved to protect their own interests by passing a motion that students should not get overtime until the regulars had got all they wanted. This was fair enough since most of the regulars had families to look after and it was their full-time occupation. From a student's point of view, however, we had not been informed of the change before signing up and we felt aggrieved by the potential loss of income. I had rejoined the union and now I persuaded a number of fellow students to do likewise. At the first branch meeting, we rescinded the motion, which could not then be changed for six months. My O'Donnell grandfather would have been proud of me for joining the union, particularly his union, the TGWU, although his loyalty would undoubtedly have been to the regular, full-time members.

I loved the job and became so good at it that some of the drivers did deals to have me as their conductor. I made friends among the students, some of whom went on to hold responsible positions in medicine, law, teaching and the civil service and are still, I'm glad to say, numbered among my friends. In 2002 I returned to Bournemouth as a TD and former minister to attend a meeting of the British–Irish Interparliamentary body. Also in attendance was Daithí Ó Ceallaigh, Irish Ambassador to Britain, who had soldiered alongside me as a bus conductor. We both agreed that had we remained in the job, we would, in all probability, have reached the rank of Inspector!

My second summer in Bournemouth ended in disappointment on my return home for the A-level results. Out of a total of 1,200 marks over three subjects, I had failed to win a university scholarship by just three marks. So it was back to the Academy for another year's study, with the result that I arrived at Queen's University, Belfast, in 1959, instead of 1958.

4: UNIVERSITY YEARS

My only knowledge of Belfast was to pass through it to the Heysham boat on my way to Bournemouth. The first time I saw Queen's University was when I went there to register as a student. My first thought was that it looked like a university. Well, it looked like my impression of a university, for it had cloisters and quadrangles and rustic brick and lawns. But it also seemed alien to someone from my background, with the Union Jack flying from the roof and buildings called Sir William this and Sir David that, portraits of the Queen and long-dead British worthies and the English accents of so many of the professors and lecturers. There were few recognisable Catholic names on the staff or administration that I could detect.

My best friend from the Academy, Ed Haughey, who had spent two years at St Patrick's, Armagh, joined me in lodgings on Malone Avenue. When we arrived there we found, already in residence, a brother and sister from Belleek, County Fermanagh. In the fullness of time Ed would marry Sive Egan. Her brother, Bowes Michael, would later make a name for himself as a brilliant, if eccentric, undergraduate and later again would give the House of Commons a whiff of its own medicine when he threw a CS gas canister from the gallery in protest against internment. Bowes had been resident in Belfast for some time and was able to give Ed and me an early introduction to university politics. In terms of my response to this new environment, it was similar to adding a detonator to a stick of gelignite.

Queen's was still quite a small university at that time. In 1962 there were only 3,895 students: to be there at all was an achievement and a privilege. When I think back to those days I am reminded of Neil Kinnock's famous speech during the British 1990 general election, 'Why am I the first Kinnock in one thousand generations to have gone to university?' My generation of Curries was also the first to achieve that distinction. My father and mother could have done it, and probably their parents, too, but I was of the lucky generation, the first to benefit from free second- and third-level education, and it was all due to politics. I never forgot that lesson.

My extra year at the Academy, the experience of dealing with the public as a bus conductor in Bournemouth and being comfortable with living away from home all made me more confident in myself, yet I found the environment and atmosphere at Queen's so alien that it took me quite a while to adjust. I found the company of those wearing Pioneer pins more congenial than those wearing poppies. Except for my neighbours at home, I had never had any dealings with Protestants (the English didn't count), and certainly never had any discussions with them about religion or politics. Initially, the other freshers and I gravitated towards the Catholic Chaplaincy, where we were among 'our own', but gradually we became more assimilated as our interests widened. Nonetheless, throughout my time at Queen's, although I made a number of friends from a unionist background, some of them still friends to this day, the segregation that was such a hallmark of Northern society was only slightly dented for the great majority of students. For the relatively small number of those who engaged in student politics and who were prepared to engage in debate in the Student Union, the Student Representative Council (SRC) and in the debating and political societies, a whole new world was opened up.

Why Queen's? Why not one of the British universities, or even UCD or TCD? The thought never really entered my head. As far as I was concerned, the choice lay between Queen's and Teachers' Training College. I enrolled in the Arts faculty and took Modern History, English and Geography, with the hope of being accepted for honours History at the end of my first year. However, a new joint honours course was established and I found myself, at the beginning of my second year, working for an honours degree in Modern History and Politics. There were two disadvantages, only one of which I recognised at the time. I did not have to sit exams between the end of my first year and the end of my fourth, and I happily behaved accordingly; and Professor JC Beckett's magnificent course in Irish history was not part of my syllabus. Rarely would I get out of bed for early lectures on subjects which were part of my course, but I was a regular at Professor Beckett's nine o'clock lectures, which were not on my course. No greater tribute could be paid to that wonderful teacher, JC Beckett!

No period of my life have I enjoyed more than my four years at Queen's. As the eldest of eleven children, I was entitled to a full scholarship plus a maintenance grant. I worked in Bournemouth every summer, except for the summer before my finals, and even though I gave my mother most of what I earned, this supplement to my scholarship meant I was rarely broke, particularly as I did not start drinking until my third year.

Belfast itself was a disappointment, however, especially at weekends when it was aptly described as 'a cemetery with traffic lights'. But there was enough 'diversion' around Queen's thanks to 'the hop' on Saturday nights and dances in Fruithill Park Tennis Club on Sundays. An occasional problem arose in attempting to ensure that the girl from the hop didn't meet the one from Fruithill: it didn't always work out!

Living in a flat had many advantages, and for three years Ed Haughey, Gerry Wills and I shared a succession of them. The most interesting was in Donegall Pass, situated only about a half-mile distance from the university, but off the beaten track for students looking for a party to gatecrash. Our flat was above Ellie's, a second-hand clothes shop, and above us was another flat, with whose inhabitants we shared cooking facilities. Among the occupants of the top-floor flat was a young Derry man, majoring in French but turning his attention more and more to a career in music; his name was Phil Coulter. I well remember one Saturday afternoon when the rather staid Lord Mayor's parade was processing along the Pass and proceedings were somewhat enlivened by the amplified music coming from the open window of Phil's flat. And then there was the party to which we invited girls from the next street, Virginia Street. I don't know about Phil, but I had no reason to question the veracity of the name.

Shortly after my arrival at Queen's I started to attend the weekly meetings of the university debating society, the Literific (the Literary and Scientific Society). There had not been a debating society at the Academy, and the only speech I had ever made was 'the border must go' oration for the benefit of my brothers. I found the atmosphere of the Literific intimidating, and the presiding chairman and the Secretary had what I considered to be la-de-dah accents. But the contributors from the floor were much more down-to-earth and I quickly caught the debating bug. However, I lacked the confidence to get to my feet and speak out, and my first year was spent in frustration as points were made that I felt ought to be challenged.

Ironically, it was Lord Brookeborough, Prime Minister of Northern Ireland, who rescued me from my self-imposed silence and launched me on my public-speaking career. He visited Queen's early in my second year, at the invitation of the Unionist Association. The meeting was open only to unionists and invited guests, but I managed to infiltrate, along with a few others. To me, Brookeborough epitomised all I hated about unionism, and when his speech ended and the few planted questions had been answered, I found myself on my feet, insisting on my right to ask a question. Despite the opposition of the Chair and barracking by most of the audience, I attacked the Prime Minister for discrimination against Catholics in houses and jobs. The following week I had no difficulty in contributing to the debate at the Literific. I told myself that anyone capable of taking on Brookeborough at a unionist meeting should have no difficulty in speaking anywhere else. It worked. And just four years later, in the Stormont House of Commons, I was able to thank Brookeborough in person for the boost he had given my political career.

In 1962 the student newspaper, *Gown*, estimated that of 3,895 students only 10% took an active interest in politics. Until 1961, there were student political organisations for Unionists, Labour and Liberals, but none for Nationalists. In April of that year a number of us who were active in the Literific and the SRC founded the New Ireland Society, with the stated aim of 'bringing together all those interested in the eventual reunification of Ireland and the political, social, economic and cultural advancement of the country'. Of the eleven who appended their names to a publicity handout, eight were from a traditional nationalist background and three were from a unionist background. The prime originator and first President was Michael Bradley, a lawyer who was flamboyant of speech and dress and more mature in years than the rest of us. He had studied at Queen's, then Trinity in Dublin and was now back at Queen's again. I succeeded him as President in 1962 and my successor, in turn, was Peter D Smith, later to become a distinguished lawyer and a leading member of the Unionist party Executive. Smith defeated Gerry Loughran for the position – later Sir Gerry, the first Catholic to lead the Northern Ireland Civil Service. John C Duffy, later a General Secretary of the SDLP, was also one of the founding members.

The formation of the New Ireland Society was an assertion of growing nationalist confidence, and within a short time its debates and symposia attracted the largest attendance of any student society. Among those who spoke to its members during my year as President were politicians who were current serving Ministers, former and future Ministers and indeed two future Taoisigh, Charles Haughey TD and Liam Cosgrave TD. The others included Brian Lenihan TD, Gerry Fitt MP, Cahir Healy MP, Paddy Gormley MP, Roderick H O'Connor MP, Walter Scott MP, Vivian Simpson MP, Robert Bailie, a Young Unionist, and Mr Brian McRoberts, a former Unionist candidate who described himself as 'but for the whims of a mountain electorate MP for South Armagh'. These and other politicians addressed such issues as, 'That minorities have nothing to fear in a united Ireland' and 'Ireland's future depends on a Socialist revival'. But New Ireland did not confine itself to purely political issues. Speakers like Micheál Mac Liammóir, Sir Tyrone Guthrie, John B Keane, Myles na Gopaleen (aka Brian O'Nolan) and Dónall Ó Moráin addressed us on cultural matters, while the headmasters of Methodist College, Belfast, St Andrew's College, Dublin, St Patrick's

Intermediate School, Belfast, and the Rector of Clongowes Wood, County Kildare, spoke on educational diversity in Ireland. At a time when there was little communication North and South, New Ireland provided an important platform for people who had not met before to speak together, to voice their opinions and to discuss topics which had not previously been discussed. It provided a forum where, unlike some other universities and colleges, a good hearing was guaranteed and also, of course, publicity for those invited – something which, on occasion, was not welcomed by the university authorities, or indeed the Northern Ireland government.

One such instance occurred in November 1962, during my term as President. A major row erupted when the then Minister for Justice in the Republic, Charles J Haughey, agreed to propose the motion, 'That minorities have nothing to fear in a united Ireland'. The Vice-Chancellor of Queen's, Michael Grant, wrote to inform me that the public and press should not be admitted to the debate. University authorities had the right to impose such a ban, but it had not been imposed in recent memory and the suspicion was that it was aimed at New Ireland, which had been receiving considerable publicity. I found it easy to get around the ban by inviting the Press to meet the speakers in a local hotel, and it was not so easy for the stewards to identify reporters among the large crowd that turned up. Indeed, as might have been expected, the meeting received greater publicity, including a first television interview for the President of New Ireland at a time when appearing on television was an event of some importance. I paid for it, of course, when forced to make an appearance before the university authorities to explain the photographs and reports, but wiser counsels prevailed with the recognition that disciplinary action against me on an issue of 'censorship' and 'political bias' would not have helped the university's image.

On my part, there was an awareness that a row with the powers-that-be might not be advisable in my final year with my degree exams looming. I exercised similar discretion in relation to the two letters I received from the Vice-Chancellor during the controversy. Both started, 'Dear Curry'. Misspelling my name was bad enough, but my lack of experience with British public school practice led me to question why I should not be addressed as, 'Mr Currie', or indeed, 'Austin'. The first draft of my reply began, 'Dear Grant'. I had second thoughts; the imminence of degree exams makes cowards of us all! And I was no exception.

There are other memories, less serious. One of the most amusing anecdotes came – aptly enough – from that wonderful actor and raconteur,

Micheál Mac Liammóir. The New Ireland Society invited him to speak and, following a magnificent performance, the officials of New Ireland accompanied their guest back to the Wellington Park Hotel for post-talk beverages. Mac Liammóir was seated at a table, very obviously wearing make-up, when a young student approached, whom I recognised as Nell McCafferty from Derry. 'Are you queer?' she demanded bluntly. He looked her up and down, in her sweater and 1962 equivalent of jeans, gently patted the chair beside him as an invitation to sit down and said drily, 'Don't worry, young man, you have nothing to fear.'

The New Ireland Society had an influence and importance outside that of an ordinary student debating society. It came into existence at a time when things were beginning to change, albeit slowly and with severe gestation pains, in Northern Ireland generally and within the nationalist community in particular: Brookeborough was about to be replaced by Terence O'Neill and new expectations accompanied the transfer of power from the old guard; Lemass had already indicated that he was prepared to pursue a more pragmatic line on the North; the IRA campaign had eventually fizzled out in 1962 and its arms had been dumped; the economic situation was improving with the hope that more jobs would mean less discrimination; there was persistent questioning of the role nationalists would play in the future of Northern Ireland, with a new organisation, National Unity, coming to prominence; and the general feeling of change, hope and challenge emanating from John F Kennedy and Pope John XXIII.

New Ireland promoted and reflected this sense of change. The growing confidence of young nationalists at the university was further boosted by their increasing numbers – the result of the Butler Education Act. By the early 1960s nearly every household had a television, exposing the minds of the young, in particular, to new experiences and enabling them to see that what was taken for granted in Northern Ireland was not always the best, or even the norm. Experience of New Ireland, the Literific, SRC and the Student Union indicated that those from Catholic and nationalist backgrounds were at least as able as, if not better than, those from traditional Protestant and unionist backgrounds. The debating stars were mostly non-unionist, young men such as Bowes Egan, John Murtagh, Vincent Hanna, Barney Cavanagh, Eamon McCann, John Duffy and others. At all levels within the university they were beginning to make their mark in scholarship, culture and in sport – everywhere the new self-confidence was making itself felt.

I was lucky and privileged to be there at that time, and I enjoyed every minute of it. I don't know if I could have achieved a first-class degree, but my extra-curricular activities in my final year, particularly as President of New Ireland, effectively put an end to that possibility, and I was very satisfied with my second. Thankfully, I very rarely have nightmares, but when I have they are never about the stressful and dangerous situations I have lived through, instead they are nearly always about failing my finals. Perhaps it had something to do with cramming three years' work into three months while continuing my involvement in university politics. My rather unique solution was to go to bed at 6.00pm, wake at midnight, study through the night and then spend the day in limited lectures and major politicking. My great consolation during the night was the night security man on duty on the road outside our flat, with whom I would break the monotony with a mug of tea and a cigarette at around 4.30am.

Queen's was good to me and I have always appreciated that. The practical experience I gained there, which proved greater than the influence of my degree in Politics and History, stood me in good stead and was an extremely valuable asset in the career I would follow shortly afterwards. At the same time, in some respects life at Queen's was artificial. It is true that it reflected the divisions in Northern Irish society: Prods were still Prods, Teagues still Teagues, and the great majority of students kept to their own tribe. But for the 10% or so who got involved in student affairs, most engaged in dialogue across the traditional divide, a dialogue that was challenging and liberating. I needed, and relished, the opportunity and the challenge of discussion and debate with the likes of Alf McCreary, Don Anderson, Geoff Martin, Peter D Smith and others from a unionist background, some of whom I am honoured to still have as personal friends. I was forced to recognise that there were other points of view which were worthy of consideration and which might actually be as credible as my own. I certainly left Queen's less of a bigot than when I arrived there. In particular, I learned to accept that unionism was an arguable proposition, a viable political philosophy that had to be respected if I were to expect them to respect my political beliefs in return. What I didn't fully appreciate at the time was that the 90% of students who did not participate in student politics, or the dialogue across the traditions, had better prepared themselves for the reality of earning a living and participating in the divided society of Northern Ireland. I would soon learn that the reality of living in Aughnacloy, or Aghohill had not changed.

5 : FIRST STEPS

When I graduated in June 1963 I still had no firm idea what I wished to do with my life, apart from the conviction that I did not want to do what so many of my contemporaries had done, ie, drift into teaching for lack of an alternative. So, I did what I knew best. The very evening of my graduation, instead of celebrating I took the Heysham boat and returned to bus conducting in Bournemouth, where I remained until the end of September. I then spent a week or so in London, staying with student friends and pondering the future. Conscious of the fact that my Bournemouth savings were draining away fast, and consoling myself that it was purely temporary, I applied to London Council for a position as a supply teacher. The same day I also applied for a job as a night security officer, and then returned home while my applications were being processed.

Back at home, the following week, I decided to get my hair cut. I have always found the traditional barber one of the most interesting, informative, not to say nosey, members of society. Jim Corrigan had all of those attributes, and more. As well as being a deft barber, he was also a part-time journalist (later editor of the *Tyrone Democrat*), performer in plays and musicals and a member of Dungannon Urban Council. Halfway through the haircut, out of the blue and without any lead-up, he told me that Joe Stewart, our local MP and leader of the Nationalist party, had a terminal illness and enquired whether I would be interested in succeeding him.

Joseph F Stewart had been MP for East Tyrone at Stormont for thirty-five years. He had also been at Westminster when, in 1934, he had succeeded Joe Devlin in the old joint constituency of Tyrone–Fermanagh. He became leader of the Nationalist party in 1958 and held that position until his death. Joe's political base was the Ancient Order of Hibernians, for which he served for many years as Tyrone County President and as a member of the National Executive. East Tyrone was a marginal seat, but that very fact, ironically, made it safer. A larger majority encouraged other Nationalists and Republicans to try their luck, but the infamy of handing the seat to the Unionists through a 'split vote' was a deterrent in a marginal. Joe was returned unopposed on many occasions, but won the five elections he fought. His closest call had been in 1958, in the aftermath of the disastrous Nationalist intervention in Mid-Ulster, when he scraped through by 236 votes in a poll of 20,000.

I had met him only once, when I had called at his constituency office, pub, auctioneering and undertaking business in Irish Street, Dungannon, to ask him to become a patron of the New Ireland Society. I had often seen him, sitting on a bench outside his pub, a small man wearing a bow-tie, lifting his hat to the ladies who passed by. He was also a Tyrone County Councillor and a member of Dungannon Urban Council. Like most of his Stormont colleagues, he was a member of the Knights of St Columbanus and had held office in that Catholic layman's organisation as Grand Knight, Provincial Knight and member of the Supreme Council.

I had known 'wee Joe' was not in good health, and he was elderly, but the severity of his illness came as a shock. I didn't answer Jim Corrigan's question at that time, but he later told me that the nature of my response betrayed my interest. The thought of attempting to succeed Joe Stewart at some stage had already occurred to me, but now a decision on such an action had become a matter of pressing urgency. In one respect, the timing could not have been better: I had not committed myself to any other career, the two jobs I had applied for were temporary and would provide me with the wherewithal to return home to seek the nomination when the time came. It did not take me long to reach a decision; I had nothing to lose.

On my return to London, I started work as a night security officer at an industrial estate at Brixton. My shift was from 5.00pm to 8.00am, starting on Sundays and concluding on Saturday morning. The work principally involved visiting about thirty locations every two hours, where the insertion of a key into a clock proved that that area had been visited. Additionally, a phone call had to be made twice during the night to indicate that everything was all right, and a mobile security officer visited during the night to ensure no disaster had befallen me. There remained the problem of accommodation. Since my non-working hours were between 8.00am and 5.00pm during the week and between 8.00am on Saturday and 5.00pm on Sunday, there didn't seem any point in paying for a place of my own if an alternative could be found. Luckily, for me at any rate, an old friend from Queen's, Eamon McLochlann, a Derry man who had been a founder member of the New Ireland Society, had a flat and he allowed me to use his place as a base. Effectively, this meant his bed was still warm when I crawled into it after my nightshift. Saturday night was a complication, but as we usually found a party to gatecrash the settee was adequate for my needs.

After about a month of these arrangements a further complication arose. I was appointed to a comprehensive school near Crystal Palace as a supply teacher. I decided that I would do both jobs, night security and teaching, for as long as I could. Only a young man with a burning ambition would have attempted such madness. For the next two months, until Christmas, I taught from 9.00am until 3.30pm and then got the bus to Brixton where I did the security job from 5.00pm until 8.00am. By the nature of supply teaching, little preparation or homework-marking was required. I could not be sure from day to day what classes I would be taking as it depended on which teacher I had to stand in for. Occasionally, I had to take a religion class. On the first occasion I did so, I asked a small group why they were leaving as I entered. 'Please sir, we are Catholics. We don't have to stay for religion,' one replied. It made me wonder about the value of RE in that school.

The security job, on the other hand, required much more ingenuity and creative thinking. The first thing I did was to draw a map of the location of the thirty sites which had to be visited at two-hour intervals. Some took longer to reach than others, so I devised a rota system whereby a few of the more distant locations were visited only every second round. An exercise that was supposed to last an hour was down to half the time. I then made an arrangement with my mobile supervisor that, in exchange for tea and a sandwich at 4.30am, he would make my check-in call at 3.00am and wake me at 4.15am. By doing my 2.00am round early, I was therefore assured of two-and-a-quarter hours' sleep in the middle of the night, as well as cat-napping at other times. I still continued to meet up with Eamon McLochlann on Saturday mornings, but invariably the day was spent between Fleet Street (where I kept up-to-date with events at home per the *Irish News*), the bookies, the pub and often a party. Then a few hours' sleep before clocking in at the security job again at 5.00pm on Sunday. Fortunately for my soul and my conscience, Mass was celebrated just up the road in Brixton at 6.00pm.

After Christmas, when I returned to teach again, I made an arrangement with one of my fellow teachers at the school to share a flat with him when I required it and I ceased to be a burden on Eamon, though we still met up on Saturdays. I will always be grateful to him for his help in relation to my accommodation problem, but also his generous, if sometimes cynical, contribution to my political development. Another person who assisted the development of my political ideas at this time was my old mentor and predecessor as President of New Ireland, Michael Bradley, then practising as a solicitor in Belfast.

The long evenings and nights with only radio for company gave me plenty of time to think about my political future and to put my thoughts in writing. I was convinced that the central weakness of nationalism in Northern Ireland was the lack of a democratically organised political party. The Nationalist MPs were effectively individuals who came together as a group at Stormont, but who did not have party membership, or annual conferences, or any of the characteristics or affiliations of a modern political organisation. A party structure similar to that of Fianna Fáil, Fine Gael or Labour in the South would, I felt sure, attract young and able people to the party who, through the organs of the party, would develop left-of-centre social and economic policies that would in turn win support beyond the ranks of traditional nationalism. If the party were radical enough in thought and action, it might, in the new TV age, win over republicans committed to abstention and might also cross the sectarian divide. The philosophy of Sinn Féin in terms of independent action, as suggested by its name, whereby it refused to rely on other bodies, be they government and political parties in the South, or the Catholic Church, or organisations like the AOH, were the attributes I sought to encourage. There were other possible avenues of advance, too. The new party should consider the possibility of becoming the official opposition at Stormont. Granted, this would mean having to overcome the highly emotional hurdle of becoming 'Her Majesty's loyal opposition', but this was one of the decisions which could be better taken by a mass membership, democratic organisation than by a small, isolated group of MPs. Once this structure was in place, the party I envisaged could then examine the further, even more emotive and far-reaching decision as to how the future of Northern Ireland should be determined – by the majority of votes within the State itself, or by the traditional, nationalist preference of a majority vote on the whole of the island? That would have to be decided by as democratic and representative a decision-making body as possible.

Some of these matters were for decision down the road, but there was one urgent priority demanding immediate action: a vigorous, no-holds-barred campaign, aimed at British public opinion, to highlight discrimination against Catholics in houses and jobs. Unionists were not concerned about such allegations as long as they were confined to Northern Ireland. What they feared, however, was that exposure of such practices in Britain would lead to pressure from the British government and public for redress.

My thinking on this issue was conditioned by the circumstances in my home area of Dungannon and the leadership which had been given by Conn and Patricia McCluskey. I did not know it then, of course, but events in

Dungannon the previous year, 1963, would play a crucial role in the development of the later civil rights campaign. To put developments in context it is necessary to provide the background to the formation of the Homeless Citizens League and the Campaign for Social Justice in Northern Ireland.

The word 'gerrymander' derived from Elbridge Gerry, a Governor of the State of Massachusetts, who gained a reputation for converting electoral minorities into majorities, and vice versa, by boundary manipulation. Northern Ireland unionists were among his best students.

The system in Dungannon operated on the same basis as elsewhere in the North where unionists were in a minority, or held only a narrow majority: the council area was divided into three wards, one of which had an overwhelming Catholic majority while the other two had much smaller Protestant majorities, but each ward returned sufficient councillors to ensure a unionist majority on the council. Had boundaries been fairly drawn and elections been held on the basis of one person, one vote, there would have been a nationalist majority. The most blatant examples of gerrymander were: Derry, where 20,102 voters elected eight Nationalist councillors and 10,274 voters elected twelve Unionist councillors; Fermanagh, where, according to the 1961 census, there were 27,291 Catholics and 24,322 Protestants, but the County Council had thirty-six unionists and seventeen anti-unionists in 1967; Omagh, with a population 61.2% Catholic and represented by a council composed of twelve unionists and nine non-unionists; and Armagh, 53.5% Catholic with twelve Unionist and eight non-unionist councillors. Dungannon Urban Council was the most marginal in terms of the religious headcount (50.3%), but was nonetheless represented by fourteen Unionist and seven non-unionist councillors.

Since voting entitlement was confined to a householder and their spouse, every house allocated or built became a subject of political attention. As the Urban and Rural Councils allocated council housing, the County Council was responsible for planning permission and the whole system was supervised by the Stormont government, the Unionist party was in a position to do what it liked to ensure its supremacy. The applicants for housing accommodation, or for planning permission to build a house, were effectively pawns in a one-sided political game.

The system did allow for some houses to be allocated to Catholics, as long as the house was located in the right ward and therefore not a threat to unionist control. Reallocations tended to be on the basis of allocation to 'your own kind'. Indeed, in Dungannon a so-called 'gentleman's agreement' had ensured that Nationalist councillors in the West Ward were allowed to allocate houses there. Not only were such allocations safe from a political point of view but they had the added advantage of dividing the nationalist councillors, who squabbled among themselves for the rare allocations since there were many applicants and only one could be satisfied.

In 1963, 142 houses were nearing completion in one of the unionist wards and the members of the recently formed Homeless Citizens League, set up to demand fair allocations, were hopeful that if they campaigned strongly, their entitlement on the basis of need would be recognised. Pickets, protest marches and publicity in the local Press followed, but their innocent optimism and hope was dashed by the predictable allocations to less needy Protestants. The League responded to this injustice by squatting in the prefabricated bungalows vacated by successful applicants. The council cut off electricity and water supplies to force them out, however this action was proven to be illegal, and the council had to accept the reality that it would be extremely difficult to eject more than 120 people from thirty-five dwellings, and that even if it was successful, a heavy price would be paid in bad publicity. Eventually the 'Fairmount Park squatters' were rehoused in the politically safe West Ward. The example was important for the future. The new militancy had been partially successful. The most disadvantaged in local society had shown that they were prepared to get up off their knees and fight for their rights. And, most importantly, a new leadership had emerged.

Mrs Patricia McCluskey first came to prominence as Chairman of the Homeless Citizens League. For the next ten years she and her husband, Conn, contributed substantially to the betterment of the quality of life and to the eradication of injustice and inequality for the Catholic minority in Northern Ireland. In so doing they inspired others, myself included, by their courage, leadership and sheer hard work.

Conn was a local GP in Dungannon and when he and Patricia became involved in the affairs of the Homeless Citizens League they were described as 'middle-aged and middle-class'. People of their background just did not become involved in pickets and marches on behalf of the homeless; it was not even a topic worthy of mention at the golf club or the rugby club. The example shown by the McCluskeys encouraged others from a similar background to become involved, particularly when they formed the Campaign for Social Justice in Northern Ireland (CSJ) in 1964.

The press release for the launch of the CSJ in January 1964 outlined its objective: 'to collect comprehensive and accurate data on all injustices done against all creeds and political opinions, including details of discrimination in jobs and houses, and to bring them to the attention of as many socially minded people as possible.'

One could be excused for thinking that, forty years after a system of government had been established based on injustice and inequality, the collection of accurate data would have already been done. Previous efforts had been made, especially in the late 1940s and early 1950s when the anti-Partition campaign was at its height. However, the data collected at that time was in the context of the injustice of Partition and was now out of date. The CSJ, on the other hand, rarely mentioned Partition. The facts and figures they collected and published stood alone as an indictment of unionist misrule. Their main focus was on British public opinion, in an attempt to force the British government to intervene by invoking Section 75 of the Government of Ireland Act 1920. The McCluskeys and the mostly professional people represented on the committee of the CSJ did not describe themselves as nationalists. Instead, their major concern was the humanitarian one of removing discrimination and inequality from public life in Northern Ireland.

The facts and figures were, of course, useful to Nationalist politicians and they were badly needed. Around this time there was a public confrontation that was to have a considerable influence on the nationalist population. The Unionist MP Brian Faulkner and the Nationalist MP for Mourne, James O'Reilly, participated in a televised debate on discrimination. It was a resounding triumph for Faulkner. Shortly after this debate I became a colleague of James O'Reilly at Stormont. I found him to be articulate, intelligent and extremely hard-working, but on the relatively new medium of TV he was simply no match for the slick Brian Faulkner. Even allowing for James' lack of television technique, had he had available to him the CSJ publication *The Plain Truth* and been able to quote the damning statistics contained therein, there was no way Faulkner would have won the debate. The debacle encouraged those like the McCluskeys to continue to gather the necessary statistics. For the nationalist community, it also hammered home the importance of television and the necessity for their public representatives to be able to handle the medium. It was a lesson well learned for the future.

In the course of their data collection, the McCluskeys brought into their circle, and into the CSJ, professional and middle-class people, some of whom would later contribute to public life. In particular, the person largely responsible for compiling the statistics of discrimination in Lurgan, County Armagh, was a local teacher and dentist's wife, Bríd Rogers, later to become Chairperson of the SDLP and Minister for Agriculture in the second power-sharing Executive. Members of the medical and legal profession were encouraged to lend their expertise and local knowledge. In 1964, Mrs McCluskey headed a reform team in the Dungannon local elections and thereby helped to bring into public life people who would distinguish themselves shortly thereafter in the leadership of the civil rights movement, people such as, Michael McLoughlin, John Donaghy, Patsy McCooey, Bids McAleer, Jim Corrigan and others.

Meanwhile *The Plain Truth* and other CSJ publications were being sent to opinion-formers in politics and the media all over the world, but particularly in Britain. Material was made available to international conferences and to the annual meetings of organisations such as the British National Council for Civil Liberties. Various contacts were used to courier the CSJ publications to these conferences and meetings, among them the young graduate Austin Currie, returning to his teaching post in London after the Easter holidays and cursing at the unexpected weight of hundreds of *The Plain Truth*, which were for distribution to Westminster MPs.

Before I left for London, however, and after my conversation with my knowledgeable barber, I became aware that members of National Unity were planning a conference to discuss the future of nationalism. This organisation, led by progressive thinkers like Michael McKeown and Professor James Scott and dedicated to a united Ireland brought about by the consent of the majority in the North, had been in existence since 1959 and had been energetically organising meetings North and South and publishing pamphlets and articles. I was collecting copies of *The Plain Truth* from McCluskeys' when Conn told me that an interesting and important meeting was being held shortly and suggested that I might like to be present. I don't know whether the word was out and my ambitious intentions known, but I suspect Conn McCluskey did not know at that time; he was much too blunt not to have asked me directly.

The conference was eventually held on Sunday, 19 April in Mackle's Hotel in Maghery, just across the River Blackwater from my intended constituency. The fact that the meeting was held at all was an indication of widespread disillusion with the lack of progress by nationalists generally, and the Nationalist party in particular, and about three hundred people turned up, including most of the Nationalist politicians. The proceedings were dominated by teachers – an early indication of the role this profession was to play in the later organisation of the SDLP. The tone was set by Gerry Quigley, Northern Secretary of the Irish National Teachers Organisation, in one of the best speeches I have ever heard. He opened his remarks with the words, 'I came here out of frustration'. The gale was so strongly in favour of an organised political party that even those MPs and Senators who were less than enthusiastic trimmed their sails and a resolution was passed setting up a National Political Front 'to stimulate the growth of Nationalist constituency organisations, to facilitate Nationalist candidates being selected and to secure adequate representation in all public bodies, to decide in conjunction with other Nationalist parliamentary representatives and other MPs who support the National ideal, to take immediate steps to create the democratic machinery of a normal political party.'

Maghery was an important development in the move towards the creation of an organised, card-bearing, left-of-centre political party. Had the Nationalist party embraced fully the proposals made there and harnessed the enthusiasm and commitment of the majority of those present, it would have had a future. Indeed, it would have been converted into what the SDLP later became. Instead, the vested interests had too firm a grip, and it was destined to disband in the 1970s. Too many of the MPs were like bishops in their own constituencies, surrounded by people they could trust, too old and too set in their ways to risk the competition of younger people who they feared were only after their seats.

I did not speak at the Maghery Convention, but I did a lot of networking that proved useful in the future. I met members of the Nationalist Parliamentary party and was able to make an assessment of some of them. I met up again with Paddy Gormley, the MP for Mid-Derry whom I had previously encountered in London, and felt able to confide in him my interest in East Tyrone. I was encouraged by his response. I flew back to London that night (stand-by flight, five guinea fare) enthusiastic, encouraged and hopeful. I was also reassured that the importance I had given to the creation of an organised political structure in my draft manifesto was a winner. Within two weeks of my departure there was a vacancy in the constituency of East Tyrone. The day after hearing the news of Joe Stewart's death, I resigned my two jobs, and three days later I was home.

6: ON MY WAY

A few days after my return from London I purchased a Ford Anglia car for £30. It took only a short time for me to find out my 'bargain' wasn't as good as it appeared to be. The radiator leaked so badly I had to keep a kettle in the boot for regular refills.

Initially, the precise make-up of the Selection Convention for East Tyrone wasn't clear. In some Nationalist-held constituencies, for example, all the priests were entitled to vote. However, one group was certain to be involved: the registration agents. At times called Catholic registration agents, at others national registration agents, their precise title hardly mattered for their function was clear. It was the job of these men to ensure that every Catholic who was entitled to vote was on the electoral register, and that every Protestant who was not entitled was not. Their job was absolutely crucial to non-unionist politicians. It was the function of the rate collector to maintain the register, but since all of the rate collectors in County Tyrone were unionists, they saw their task as that of ensuring all unionists were on the register. Without the efforts of the Catholic registration agents in East Tyrone, who worked in a purely voluntary capacity, there would not have been a nationalist majority on the register.

So that was where I started my campaign for the nomination and that was why I needed my steaming Ford Anglia. I knew my local agent, Tommy McGuigan from Edendork, and from him I got the names and addresses of the other agents. They were all men, mostly Hibernians and small farmers, and I visited all twenty-odd, often walking across fields or into cow byres to meet with them at their work. I soon found that most of the Hibs among them were aware of my grandfather's membership of the AOH, even though he was more than thirty years dead. My father's job, visiting farms to collect pigs for the bacon factory in Cookstown, also proved to be a considerable asset. His judgement on which animals were the optimum weight for market had made him many friends, which was to my advantage. Of course, being the eldest of eleven children from a working-class background with a degree in politics also helped. Above all, I was amazed at the level of negative comment stemming from James O'Reilly's television confrontation with Brian Faulkner just a few weeks earlier. Those who had seen it expressed anger and shame; those who had not seen it had heard about it. My few TV interviews during my time at

Queen's gave me an advantage over other candidates, none of whom had any television experience.

The East Tyrone vacancy occurred at a time when there had been more local political activity than usual, the effect of which was an increased political awareness. In January, the Campaign for Social Justice had been formed, centered on the McCluskeys, and there was speculation about their possible political ambitions. Also in January a branch of the Northern Ireland Labour party had been established in Dungannon and it had been announced that they would fight the local elections. With the certainty that the Westminster election had to be held in 1964, a Republican candidate, Al Molloy, and a Liberal candidate, Giles Fitzherbert, had been selected to contest Fermanagh and South Tyrone. The Maghery Conference and the speculation on the formation of a new Nationalist party had occurred in April. On 21 May local government elections were held with a Mrs McCluskey-led team of independents ousting most of the nationalists in Dungannon Urban Council. The heightened political interest and the feeling that 'the times they are a-changing' worked to the advantage of a twenty-four-year-old with no political baggage.

My 'Manifesto', prepared during the long nights as a security guard in London, was published in summary in the *Dungannon Observer*:

'In the last issue of the *Observer* 26 names were mentioned in connection with the vacant East Tyrone seat at Stormont. None of these people have as yet, to my knowledge, given the nationally minded people of East Tyrone any idea of the policies they would seek to carry out if selected as their standard-bearer.

I have been approached, as one interested in obtaining the nomination, to put forward my policies and I think this is just and right as it is only in comparing the policies and ability of the different candidates that the people of East Tyrone can make up their minds about the question, "Who is the man best qualified to tackle the tough and complicated problems which face us at the present time?"'

I then summarised my position under seven headings:

1. Reunification of Ireland.
2. The commitment to being a full-time MP with a Citizens' Advice Centre.
3. Organisation – The Nationalist party must be organised like any full-scale political party. Only if this is done can we hope to fight the Unionist machine or keep the nationally minded people of the six counties united. It must have a branch in every area of the constituency. It must be an organisation which permits men and women of talent and ability to rise through the ranks, which

gives youth a chance to come forward and which will enable a fresh approach to be made and new thinking to be done on the national and social problems of the present time. In particular such an organisation must make available the money necessary for election campaigns and the payment of registration officials, many of whom have been doing a thankless job for 20 or 30 years. If I become the MP for East Tyrone I would consider the setting up of such an organisation as one of my first tasks and I would attempt to bring it into being in cooperation with the other elected representatives and the registration agents.

4. Discrimination – each case of discrimination in housing, employment, trade and business must be pinpointed and fought. Publicity is the greatest weapon and it is best organised by public representatives who can carry the fight not only to Stormont but to England as well. As I said in a speech in London on May the ninth last – "the cancer of discrimination in Northern Ireland must be shown up at meetings such as this, in the press and TV, through the trade unions and brought to the attention of the British people". If I was the MP for East Tyrone I would fight every single case of discrimination which came to my attention.

5. Employment initiatives.

6. Development of agriculture.

7. A pledge to look after the less fortunate members of the community.

I finished with a challenge to the other candidates to put forward their policies and a ringing declaration that 'the people of East Tyrone deserve the best and surely in the most democratic way they should be allowed to select the best'.

My manifesto gave me the political initiative. I was the one people were talking about. The twenty-six names in the local Press really boiled down to five other contenders, of whom James Donnelly, Paddy Duffy and Paul Stewart seemed to me to be my main opponents. Jimmy Donnelly was a nationalist member of Tyrone County Council and Dungannon Urban Council and a successful, self-made businessman. Paddy Duffy was a young solicitor who practised in both Dungannon and Cookstown, and was deeply involved in the GAA and in community organisations like the co-op movement, the Credit Union and the Dungannon and Coalisland Housing Associations. Paul Stewart was the son of the deceased MP, an auctioneer by trade, born and bred in Dungannon and now living and working in the constituency in Cookstown. Additionally there was Frank Devlin, a publican and former captain in the Irish Army and a member of one of Tyrone's foremost GAA families, and Rory T O'Kelly, solicitor and playwright, whose father had been in charge of the IRA in Coalisland in the 1920s.

The odds seemed stacked against me, and they were. However, I had learned a thing or two from undergraduate politicking and from my study of politics. Where it appeared that a registration agent preferred one of the other candidates, I asked for his second or other preference. And when it became clear that local meetings would be held to select some delegates, I widened my canvass to include those whom the local agents thought of as potential delegates.

I also discovered that while solicitors, by the nature of their job, made friends they also made enemies, and that the latter invariably work harder against you than friends do in your favour. I also realised how unfair but effective a political 'joke' could be. Jimmy Donnelly had built up a successful business from collecting scrap metal and accordingly was known as 'Jimmy Scrap'. PG McQuaid was another Dungannon businessman prepared to try his hand at anything from fowl exporting to smuggling to ballroom proprietor to bookie. He described himself as 'honest PG', a title not universally accepted. He was a colourful character with an engaging personality who raised thousands of pounds for charities and engaged in various publicity strokes, like attempting to break the record for being buried underground, but he was also inclined to the occasional binge during which he was uncontrollable. According to the story, honest PG, Young Currie (as I was known for about thirty years) and Jimmy Scrap died and arrived together at the Pearly Gates to be met by St Peter. He first turned to PG, read out of his black book, gave PG a spoon and told him to come back when he had drained Lough Neagh. He then turned to me and sentenced me to standing on the Old Engine Bridge until Willie Campbell came out of his adjacent pub to invite me in for a drink. St Peter then turned to Jimmy Scrap, but Jimmy had disappeared – and so had the Pearly Gates! Not all of the selection process was fought on this lofty plane, but such scurrility did play a part, as it does in politics.

The intervention of the National Political Front – a combination of the Nationalist Parliamentary members and constituency delegates which had been created at the Maghery meeting – assisted my candidature by broadening the selection procedure through the inclusion of delegates elected at local meetings. The non-sectarian element was not helped by the fact that the two delegates were from each church area and were selected at after-Mass meetings. But, at least priests were not automatically entitled to vote. The delegates elected at local meetings brought an element of democracy to the procedure and widened it beyond the traditional, largely AOH base.

Seventy-one delegates attended the East Tyrone Nationalist Convention on Sunday, 7 June 1964 in Stewartstown. No one referred to the fact, or thought it unfair, that they all were men. The influence of the Nationalist party and the AOH was indicated by the fact that Senator Paddy McGill, secretary of the Nationalist party, and Gerry Conlon, secretary of Tyrone AOH, were joint conveners and that the convention was presided over by Senator Gerry Lennon, Nationalist party and AOH. Despite the Maghery meeting, or possibly because of it, the Nationalist party was determined to control the proceedings.

Things did not start off too well. I was not a public representative or registration agent and neither were two of the other five candidates, and we had not thought it necessary to become delegates through the after-Mass meetings, as a result of which we were initially not admitted. Once this had been rectified, we moved on to the candidates' speeches, which were limited to five minutes – a fact that assisted less articulate and less experienced contenders.

I summarised my 'manifesto', but emphasised that I had television and radio experience, which was an essential qualification for a modern politician. Every delegate present would have seen, or heard of, the James O'Reilly debacle, and since none of the other contenders had any media experience, this gave me an advantage. I also gave a commitment to working as a full-time politician.

The voting on the first count was: James Donnelly, 21; Austin Currie, 19; Paddy Duffy, 15; Paul Stewart, 10; Frank Devlin, 4; and Rory T O' Kelly, 2. I knew at this stage that if I could keep ahead of Paddy Duffy, whose supporters I had assiduously canvassed for their second preferences, I would win. On the elimination of Rory T O'Kelly, the result was: Currie, 21; Donnelly, 21; Duffy, 16; Stewart, 9; and Devlin, 4. On Devlin's elimination the vote was: Currie, 22; Donnelly, 22; Duffy, 18; and Stewart, 9. On Stewart's elimination: Currie, 27; Donnelly, 24; and Duffy, 20. On the final vote I was declared the Nationalist candidate for East Tyrone by 41 votes to 30 and it was made unanimous.

I found out afterwards that 'Honest PG', outside the school where the convention was being held, was busy taking bets on the outcome and had many takers. Before the final count he was offering 2 to 1 against Donnelly and 2 to 1 on Currie.

Two days later, on 9 June, the Nationalist party moved the writ at Stormont for the election on 30 June. Eddie Richardson, MP for South Armagh, was later to claim credit for this unusually quick procedure. He told me that if they had not moved fast, I could not have taken my seat before the summer recess, which would have meant I would not have received any pay over the long summer. Whatever the truth in this, I was, of course, grateful.

On another more important matter, the Nationalist party was not helpful to me. I have already referred to the marginality of the constituency as an asset to the incumbent in terms of the 'split vote'. However, the Stormont constituency of East Tyrone was divided between the Westminster constituencies of Fermanagh–South Tyrone and Mid-Ulster, with eleven electoral areas in the former and nine in the latter. This made the Stormont constituency particularly sensitive and vulnerable to any suggestion of a split vote in the Westminster constituencies.

Early in my campaign a major row erupted when the Nationalist Parliamentary party announced its intention to hold selection conventions in both Fermanagh–South Tyrone and Mid-Ulster. The statement came out of the blue, I was not informed, never mind consulted, and immediately pressure was brought to bear on me by Republicans, who had already selected their candidates in both constituencies. Some of my strong supporters voiced fears of a conspiracy designed to make me lose the election. I couldn't understand how any section of nationalist opinion would be helped by a defeat in the constituency, which had always been nationalist and which had been represented by the leader of the party. Then a statement from Paddy Gormley, MP for Mid-Derry, fanned the controversy further. Paddy had been an early supporter of my candidacy and had turned up at my selection convention along with his brother, Tommy, MP for Mid-Tyrone, to offer his support. As the local unionist paper, the *Tyrone Courier,* somewhat gleefully reported:

'Mr Gormley interpreted the decision of a section of Nationalist MPs and Senators to sponsor candidates in Fermanagh–South Tyrone and Mid-Ulster as a deliberate attempt to provoke republican opposition and thus ensure the defeat of Mr Austin Currie the Nationalist candidate in East Tyrone. "The MPs who issued the statement," he said "know that to win in East Tyrone Austin Currie needs the support and votes of Republicans as well as Nationalists." They were afraid, he said, that if Mr Currie were elected he would try to revitalise nationalist politics. Actions speak louder than words so on Wednesday Mr Gormley gave Mr Currie a cheque for £150, which will cover Mr Currie's election deposit.'

Jim Corrigan, in his 'Candid Comment' column in the *Dungannon Observer,* wrote: 'It is a deliberate move to stir up the Republicans and let them wreck Currie's chances and take the blame for doing so. In two years time there will be a general election and no Currie.' Describing it as 'a rotten trick' he added, 'if there is any justice the anti-Unionist vote in East Tyrone will prove to be stronger than ever, for the people should rally around the man who now faces the strongest opposition ever in this constituency. He is fighting against the Unionist party and the Nationalist Parliamentary party.'

Finally, both papers reported: 'Interviewed on Wednesday Mr Currie said, "I think the Nationalist MPs and senators were singularly ill-advised to issue a statement like this at this time".'

That was my public statement in full on the matter. In private, I was livid. The Nationalist party statement put me on the defensive when all I wanted to do was concentrate on the traditional enemy and on positive proposals for the betterment of my constituents in bread-and-butter terms. Just before I left home to attend my main election rally in Coalisland, I was visited by a Republican delegation demanding assurances that I would not support Nationalist candidates in Fermanagh–South Tyrone and Mid-Ulster. They were not satisfied with my private assurances that I had not been consulted about the Nationalist statement and did not feel myself bound by it. They wanted a public statement in Coalisland that evening that I would oppose any attempt to run Nationalist candidates. I have always reacted negatively to such pressure, even on occasions when my head told me I should give way. So the delegation left in an angry mood, with the promise, only, that I would say something about the matter in Coalisland. That night I referred to the issue in only the broadest terms. The delegates at my convention had made my nomination unanimous; they and the people of East Tyrone had had my policy before them, per my manifesto, for sometime; the election of an MP for East Tyrone was a matter only for the people of East Tyrone and no one else had the right to tell them what to do, and if elected as their MP, no one outside the constituency would tell me what to do. I was in favour of the unity of the country and this would require the unity of the nationally minded people, to which I would always give the highest priority.

I was, of course, sensitive to the fact that Joe Stewart, the MP for more than thirty years, had had a majority of just 815 in the previous election, and as the campaign developed I kept referring to the necessity for every non-Unionist vote to be cast, if the Unionists were to be defeated, and to my detestation of a split vote. I never said I would oppose the selection of Nationalist party candidates in Mid-Ulster and Fermanagh–South Tyrone, but it was of course implicit in what I was saying about the split vote.

The pressure on me in this regard, and the fact that I was forced to commit myself more than I would have liked, had consequences in the future. In the Westminster elections in 1964 and 1966 my hands were effectively tied in relation to the question of support for an attendance candidate over a Republican abstentionist. It was not until the Mid-Ulster by-election in 1969 that I was able to shake off the shackles imposed on me by the announcement of the Nationalist party in 1964.

I had calculated that Republicans would not force the issue so near to the election, and I was right. Indeed, the controversy helped me at the polls. The 'dirty trick', as Jim Corrigan described it, gained me sympathy. The idea of 'Young Currie' being stabbed in the back by outsiders was a vote-catcher in East Tyrone, and for some republicans their distaste for a Nationalist candidate was offset by the welcome sight of a Nationalist candidate who was apparently not to the liking of the Nationalist Parliamentary party. However, the affair did not help my relationship with the parliamentarians. No member of the Parliamentary party, not even the Gormleys, was invited to speak from my platform and no messages of support were requested.

I never got an acceptable explanation of the Nationalist party statement or, more importantly, of its timing during my campaign. It was issued to harm me, or without any consideration of its effect on my candidacy. Either way, the effect was to introduce at the very beginning a coolness and a questioning which was to exist throughout my relationship with the Nationalist party.

Apart from this crisis I enjoyed tremendously my first campaign. I liked being on the back of a lorry with a microphone in my hand and found I was good at it. Even without the mike I had a voice that carried and sometimes dispensed with the mike for effect. My Unionist opponent was Alexander Blevins, a retired RUC sergeant who had been MP for Mid-Tyrone from 1958 to 1962 as a result of the dreaded Nationalist 'split vote'. His brother had been convicted some years previously of forging £5 notes and I amused myself, and my audiences, with cheap references to the suggested Unionist slogan, 'Forge ahead with Blevins'.

I was duly elected as the honourable member for East Tyrone in the early hours of 1 July 1964, increasing the majority from 815 to 1,296, the largest ever in the constituency, in a poll of 89.99%. Thus I became, at twenty-four, the youngest member of the Stormont Parliament.

7: A NATIONALIST AT STORMONT

It was difficult to feel any sense of identity with Stormont. Granted, it was a magnificent building, standing atop a hill and approached by a wide main avenue, a mile long. I could understand unionists being proud of it and why, in the early 1930s, it had been built as a symbol of their determination to hold power in Northern Ireland.

For a nationalist, however, the opposite applied. This striking symbol of unionist power and domination was also the symbol of our powerlessness and second-class status. The huge statue of Carson, 'erected by the loyalists of Ulster', dominating the approach, the Union Jack flying and, on entering the building, the prominence of the Craigavon statue all underlined who was in charge. A visitor from outside Northern Ireland could look at all the portraits and statues and the symbols of Britishness and unionism and never guess that there existed a section of the population, numbering more than one-third, which did not accept or identify with those symbols. It truly was an alien place for a nationalist. Is it any wonder that when, on my first day, I took the oath of allegiance to 'Her Gracious Majesty Queen Elizabeth the second, her heirs and successors', I did so with my fingers crossed behind my back and told the media afterwards that I had taken the oath as if in a play on the stage.

And yet, the Unionists were friendly and welcoming. It was inevitable in a House of only fifty-two members, not all of whom were regular attenders, that we would be thrown into close proximity with one another. On my first day, accompanied by my father and mother and some of my constituents, we met Lord Brookeborough, now the former Prime Minister, on the stairs to the dining-room. To my disgust he did not remember our encounter at Queen's, but when I reminded him of it and thanked him for his help in launching my political career, he laughed heartily. He told us of his great respect for my predecessor, Joe Stewart, and how well they got on. It was hard to believe, as one of my company said afterwards, that 'This was the same ould bastard who kept us second-class citizens.'

I was lucky to have arrived at a by-election as it meant that I served in the same Parliament with, and was able to talk to some historic figures, such as Brookeborough, who was stepping down at the next general election, and

Cahir Healy (South Fermanagh), Joe Connellan (South Down), Fred McCoy (South Tyrone) and Edmund Warnock (St Anne's, Belfast).

Cahir Healy I had long admired as a politician and as a reviewer of historical and political books. Cahir was a convert from Sinn Féin abstentionism to Nationalist attendance and constitutionalism. Representing South Fermanagh at Stormont, he had on a number of occasions held a Westminster seat. He had been interned on the prison ship *Argenta*, moored in Belfast Lough, and during the Second World War, despite being an MP at Westminster, had been interned by the British government in Brixton prison. He had spent a long and frustrating career, from 1918 to the 1960s, first of all coming to terms with the reality of Partition and then trying to find a nationalist response to it. How much easier and personally rewarding for him would have been a political career in his native County Donegal.

Eddie McAteer had succeeded Joe Stewart as leader of the Nationalist party. 'Big Eddie' had written a pamphlet in 1948 in which he had advocated forms of civil disobedience to supplement the efforts of the Anti-Partition League. He had suggested that ridicule could be every bit as effective as rifles. 'Laughs are not banned yet under the Special Powers Act, chuckle your way to freedom. It is still a bit risky to twist the British Lion's tail. Just tickle it.' Predictably enough, the pamphlet was derided – and not just by the unionists. However, it did contain other, more substantial suggestions, including non-payment of rates, claiming maximum benefits, clogging up the administrative machine and a boycott of pro-British functions. 'Be guided by the golden principle that if it pays you, co-operate; if it doesn't pay, don't co-operate. Write and ask for detailed explanations of anything you can think of – and do it as often as possible, of course.'

When I myself began advocating civil disobedience in 1967 and 1968, Eddie sent me a copy of his pamphlet with a note, 'from the master to the disciple'. Eddie did not believe in long speeches, but his short contributions were well-prepared, pithy and witty. Nor did he believe in hanging around Stormont. The taxi to take him to the Derry train was pre-arranged to collect him at 5.00pm, and only a very important development was allowed to upset that arrangement.

It was an indictment of public life in Northern Ireland that someone with the ability of Eddie McAteer was prevented from making the contribution he could have made. He would undoubtedly have been an effective minister. His ability to rise above the party political, to see the wider picture and to look for the positive in political opponents were attributes that the times required.

His misfortune was to have spent a career in nationalist politics at a time when there was no mobility, no chance of change, a period of frustration and hopelessness. When change eventually did come, he found himself a victim of that change he had hoped for and worked towards during the barren years – a terrible irony for a man who deserved much more.

The Gormley brothers, Paddy and Tommy, I had met previously and they had been present as observers at my selection convention. Tommy, his wife, Gertie, and their daughters were to become good personal friends. Paddy had already identified himself before the Maghery meeting, in a speech at Enniskillen the previous February, as a supporter of a properly organised Nationalist party with left-of-centre policies, and had been a supporter since my name was first mentioned for the nomination. It was a serious blow to the possibility of advance on that front when Paddy was seriously injured in a car crash the following year. He did return to Stormont after lengthy convalescence, but he never fully recovered.

James O'Reilly, the member for Mourne, I have already mentioned as a victim of the infamous TV debate with Brian Faulkner. Roddy O'Connor, the MP for West Tyrone and Chief Whip at the time the Nationalist party accepted the role of official opposition, could have been a member of the old Irish Parliamentary party. Joe Connellan, the member for South Down, was coming close to retirement after twenty-two years' service, stretching back to 1929. Like Cahir Healy, Connellan's political career had started with Sinn Féin.

The member for South Armagh was one of the characters of the Parliament. Eddie Richardson first came to prominence as a champion cyclist and was intensely proud of that achievement and of the physique that had made it possible. On my first day at Stormont I was introduced to him in the Nationalist party room. The first thing he did was to lie down on the floor and invite me to jump on his stomach. When I declined he insisted, and eventually I had to do so. This was Eddie's party piece and most visitors received the same welcome. South Armagh was a traditional abstentionist constituency and maybe it took a character like Eddie, and his prodigious constituency work record, to hold the seat.

One bond uniting a number of the Nationalists was The North West of Ireland Printing and Publishing Company, based in Omagh, but with newspapers also in Fermanagh, South Down, Strabane and Donegal. The founder of the company, Michael Lynch, had played a prominent part in nationalist politics in the years before and after Ppartition and the newspapers were an important source of political influence. Roddy O'Connor MP was a director and Joe Connellan and his successor, Michael Keogh, were editors of the *Frontier Sentinel* in Newry. Senator Paddy McGill was editor of the *Ulster Herald* and Senator Paddy O'Hare editor of the *Fermanagh Herald*. I will later recount my own connection with the group.

And then there was Gerry Fitt. I had first met Gerry back in Queen's when he had addressed the New Ireland Society in 1962, at my invitation as President, and he and I had hit it off from the beginning. He joined the Merchant Navy, at the age of sixteen, during the war and had served on the ships in the North Sea, travelling in convoys to bring supplies to Russia. He married Ann from Castlederg in County Tyrone, settled in Belfast and they reared five daughters he affectionately called 'The Miss Fitts'. He was elected to Belfast Corporation in 1958 and then to Stormont as a Dock Irish Labour candidate in 1962.

From the beginning at Stormont I found myself closer to Gerry than to members of the Nationalist party. My suspicion of some of the Nationalists resulting from the announcement of holding conventions in Mid-Ulster and Fermanagh–South Tyrone during my election campaign was a partial explanation, but additionally I was more attracted to his left-of-centre identification. Gerry called it socialist, but there was nothing ideological about his position that I could discern. Gerry was pragmatic and his politics developed from the personal circumstances in which he was reared and lived. And, of course, his sensitivity to the marginal constituency to which he had been elected.

He was an engaging character and great company, with an endless supply of jokes, some of them certainly unparliamentary, which he would vary to suit the occasion or the political personalities involved. Gerry was the main reason for me dallying too long on occasion in the Stormont bar, and I wasn't the only one. Phelim O'Neill, cousin of the Prime Minister and later Minister of Agriculture, was also a great raconteur and he enjoyed Fitt's company immensely. They made quite a contrast. Fitt with his Belfast accent and Merchant Navy background, O'Neill with his upper-class accent and 'country' background, one drinking gin and tonic, no ice, no lemon, the other drinking gin and tonic, plenty of ice and lemon.

When Gerry was elected to Westminster in 1966 a new form of cooperation developed between the two Parliaments of a kind not dreamed of by the respective Prime Ministers, Harold Wilson and Terence O'Neill, or indeed by the electorate that had put Gerry in both Houses. Gerry would tell his Stormont-based jokes at Westminster, collect new ones there, which he would then tell at Stormont and so the cycle would continue. So popular were Gerry's jokes that on his return from Westminster it was not unusual for Brian McConnell, the Unionist Minister for Home Affairs, to cross the floor to sit for a few minutes in the seat behind and ask, 'What's the latest, Gerry?'

Gerry was a quick learner and his native intelligence, speaking ability and experience gained at Westminster made him a formidable political animal. On one occasion, after a visit to the Stormont bar, I was insensitive enough to criticise his grammar during a TV appearance, particularly his misuse of 'seen' and 'done'. I tried to explain that the use of such expressions went largely unnoticed in ordinary speech but came across badly on television. Gerry didn't like my advice, called me 'a fucking snob' and slammed the door behind him as he stormed out. The next day he sought me out, did not apologise, but asked me to repeat what I had said to him. I never again heard him, on TV or radio, use those words in the wrong context. In those early years at Stormont a popular TV programme featured Sergeant Bilko, an intelligent, quick thinking, loquacious, chance-his-arm type of character who was also extremely likeable; I often made the comparison.

When I first arrived at Stormont there were thirty-four Unionist members, thirteen Nationalists of different shades, four Northern Ireland Labour and one Liberal (Sheelagh Murnaghan). Among the thirty-four Unionists there was one Viscount (Brookeborough), one heir to a Lordship (Phelim O'Neill), one Knight (Norman Stronge), two majors (James Chichester-Clark and Ivan Neill) and three captains (Terence O'Neill, William Long and Norman Stronge). There were four QCs, indicating the attraction of Stormont, and its power to appoint judges, to the legal profession. The Speaker was Captain the Right Honourable Sir Charles Norman Lockhart Stronge, Bart; MC; HML; MP. Among the non-Unionist members, we had one solitary QC (Charlie Stewart).

So we were divided by more than politics. These people believed they had a Divine Right to rule, and some of them were contemptuous not just of the nationalists but of some of their own as well. Thirty-two of the thirty-four had one strong bond that united them across the social barrier – they were all Orangemen. The other two Unionist MPs were women and therefore not entitled to membership. The mode of address, as at Westminster, reflected the class structure. People like me were Honourable Members, Ministers were Right Honourable Members, barristers were Learned Members and former military officers were Gallant Members. Luckily, we had no one who combined all of the qualifications. 'The Right Honourable, Learned and Gallant member for …' would have made a long speech out of a short one! You might have risked your life in the North Sea convoys bringing vital supplies to Russia as a member of the Merchant Navy, as Gerry Fitt had done, but you still were only entitled to be called Honourable Member unless you became a Minister and a member of the Privy Council, or became a barrister, or had been an officer in the forces. Johnny McQuade, the Unionist member for Woodvale, had served in the British Army and had had a distinguished career, but Johnny had been a Private and Privates did not qualify for additional terminology. In Johnny's case it didn't matter too much as his contributions were limited to interjections.

Another demarcation of a different type was the Stormont bar. In the old Stormont it was a small room on the first floor presided over by Alfie, an ex-serviceman who had served with the Eighth Army and who regularly regaled us with the story of how he had been run over by a tank, but escaped injury because of the softness of the sand. Alfie wasn't overburdened with work; it was rare for the House to sit late, and drinking during the day was frowned upon. Indeed, drinking at any time was frowned upon and not only by Unionists. Most of the Nationalists didn't drink there and the four members of the Northern Ireland Labour party, all of whom were involved to some extent in Gospel preaching, never darkened its doors. Terence O'Neill would drop in occasionally, particularly at times when there were rumours about his political survival. When he did so the Unionists present would stand to welcome him and soon his distinctive laugh, more due to nervousness than the amount he imbibed, would be heard halfway down the corridor. In 1969 the arrival of MPs identified with the civil rights campaign and the increased number of late sittings meant the bar became more popular. I came to the conclusion that a man who was prepared to have a drink with you couldn't be all bad, and that it was those who didn't take a drink who were invariably the problem. Had Ian Paisley been willing to take a pint the whole history of Northern Ireland might have been different!

The night before Chichester-Clark and Faulkner contested the leadership of the Unionist party in 1969 was the most interesting time I ever spent in the Stormont bar. All of those later to form the SDLP were there, more for gossip than drink. Chichester-Clark's main supporters were also there, most of them Cabinet Ministers. The conversation was pretty uninhibited. One Cabinet Minister was heard to remark about Faulkner, 'If that bastard gets it, we won't even be allowed to come in here'. Faulkner lost the leadership election by one vote, although I can't say if the bar clinched it for Chichester-Clark.

Stormont was a devolved institution, but it was not short of parliamentary pretensions. The magnificence of the building and its setting, the terminology, the modelling on Westminster, the bewigged Speaker and Clerks, the ushers in their tails, Black Rod, the Queen's speech, the mace – all were employed to create the impression of a meaningful Parliamentary Assembly. The Nationalists derided it. We would refer to it as 'a glorified county council', which in many respects it was. Section 75 of the Government of Ireland Act 1920, which established the Parliament and government of Northern Ireland and effectively partitioned Ireland, was quite clear on the authority of the sovereign parliament at Westminster: 'Notwithstanding the establishment of the Parliament of Northern Ireland or anything contained in this act, the supreme authority of the parliament of the United Kingdom shall remain unaffected and undiminished over all persons, matters and things in Northern Ireland and every part thereof.'

As a devolved parliament, Stormont had no control over foreign affairs and no capacity to raise taxes. It did, however, exercise control over many matters affecting the day-to-day life of the citizens, particularly in relation to education, housing, job creation, agriculture, environment, etc. And, of course, through the Minister of Home Affairs it had control of policing, exercised through the RUC and B Specials. There had grown up a convention that, despite Section 75, Westminster did not interfere with the exercise of those particular functions.

And since the boundaries of the State of Northern Ireland were drawn primarily with the aim of maintaining a majority favourable to continued union with Great Britain, the result was that these governmental functions remained permanently in the control of the Unionist party. Historically, when it became clear that Britain could not hold on to the whole island of Ireland, unionists aimed for control of Ulster, all nine counties of the historic Province, but the sectarian majority was too narrow to ensure such control. So the unionist demand for all of Ireland to remain within the Empire, then for Ulster to remain, became finally, on grounds of maintenance of a Protestant unionist majority, a six-county Northern Ireland.

That majority had to be maintained at all costs and so from top to bottom, at central and local government level, the whole power and influence of government was engaged to enforce and maximise unionist control. Within ten years of Partition local government boundaries were redrawn; proportional representation as the method of election was abolished; the oath of allegiance to the British monarch was introduced for even the most menial jobs at central and local government level; a Special Powers Act was passed that was so draconian, that over thirty years later a South African justice minister introducing apartheid legislation compared it unfavourably with the Northern Ireland legislation. Thus Lord Craigavon, first Prime Minister, could honestly say in the Stormont Parliament in April 1934: 'all I can boast is that we are a Protestant parliament and Protestant state.' Even now, although we might poke fun at Stormont's pretensions, its power to influence the lives of our constituents was certainly no laughing matter. Further, in terms of being an opposition MP and trying to contribute to policy development or influencing government, membership of Stormont was a most frustrating and depressing experience. In the history of the Stormont Parliament, from 1920 to 1972, the only amendment accepted by the government was one to the Wild Birds Act 1931. Such a situation led to arrogance on the one hand and irresponsibility on the other.

The accession of O'Neill in 1963 generated hope of change and, along with the Maghery Conference and the O'Neill–Lemass meetings, helped to create a climate, among nationalists, for greater cooperation and involvement with the Stormont system. Many nationalists had reservations regarding the Lemass–O'Neill meeting on the grounds that it was a recognition of Partition by the Irish government. Since Partition had been in existence for forty-five years and we actually sat in the Parliament that symbolised it, this struck me as a particularly ostrich-like stance. I sent Lemass a telegram congratulating him on his realism. On 2 February 1965 the Nationalist party responded positively to O'Neill–Lemass by accepting the position of official opposition. As Opposition leader, Eddie McAteer appointed a team of Shadow Ministers; I was appointed to the Department of Development.

Accepting the role of official opposition was a major decision for the Nationalist party and one that was taken after much agonising. It was highly symbolic in that it represented a degree of acceptance of Partition and its institutions, which nationalists had up to then refused to give. Republicans reacted predictably: the Nationalist party had 'forfeited the right to the title nationalist'. Even David Bleakley of the Northern Ireland Labour party, displaced as the official opposition, made a sneering reference to 'Her Majesty's loyal opposition'. More than any other argument the possibility of being described in such terms had delayed Nationalist acceptance of the title. My own view was that the sneering references had to be tolerated for the greater good. If we were to demand our full rights as citizens, we could not be diverted by such emotive sloganising.

The workload increased substantially as a result of our new role. Indeed, as at Dáil Éireann and Westminster, the role of a responsible opposition spokesperson, without civil service or adequate research back-up, is more difficult than that of a Minister. To do justice to ourselves and to the party, and at the very least to avoid criticism and perhaps even get some credit from a media judging us according to the new criteria of Official Opposition, increased presence in the House and responsible criticism of Ministerial statements, some at short notice, was required. When I first attended Stormont I was amused by the door attendants who would greet me, when I arrived for Question Time at 2.30pm, with a cheery, 'Good morning, Sir', and when I was leaving when the House adjourned around 5.00pm would bid me, 'Goodnight, Sir'. The role of Official Opposition greatly reduced this opportunity for hilarity.

Around the same time, as a result of concomitant increases at Westminster and not, as some cynics on the republican side alleged, as a bribe for becoming the Official Opposition, the salary was increased from £1,050 per annum to £1,450. I was delighted, and meeting Eddie Richardson, MP for South Armagh, in the corridor, I was amused at his reaction: 'They're making this job too attractive. Everyone will be after it now.'

Unfortunately, the role of Official Opposition served only to increase my frustration. The carefully prepared speeches, proposals for legislation and amendments had no better response than previously. No matter how well argued, the process ended with Ministerial rejection and the inevitable result of trooping through the voting lobbies.

The arrogance of the government was particularly well illustrated in the spring of 1965 by its decision to situate a proposed new university at Coleraine, rather than at Derry. Instead of proceeding by the normal parliamentary route, ie, a general discussion on the *Lockwood Report on Higher Education*, followed by a consideration of the views expressed in the House, before proceeding to a decision on the location, a motion was tabled to take the Report into consideration and endorse the government's decision to locate it at Coleraine. This effectively made the issue of the location of the new university a vote of confidence in the government. The reason for this unusual action was the fear that, given a free vote, sufficient numbers of the Unionist party might have joined with the opposition to put the government decision in doubt. Despite the Whip, two members of the party voted against, while others abstained. On the Unionist side, the way in which O'Neill forced the decision through was almost as divisive a factor as the decision itself. This, coming shortly after his decision to meet with Sean Lemass without informing his Cabinet colleagues in advance, confirmed the view of many unionists that the Prime Minister's arrogance was not acceptable. The decision on the new university and the example of how the Prime Minister treated his own party colleagues made us in opposition feel even more strongly that our views were not being taken into account.

We did not know it then, but the decision to reject Derry as the site of the new university was a watershed in the history of Northern Ireland. It confirmed the widespread feeling among nationalists, and indeed among some unionists, that there was a policy being pursued of deliberate neglect of the area west of the River Bann. The Derry decision came on top of the decision to abandon the railway to Fermanagh and Tyrone, and the controversial siting of a new city, 'a counter-magnet to Belfast', between Lurgan and Portadown. The protests in favour of Derry, particularly a motorcade to Stormont and the heightened political awareness it generated, created in Derry itself a determination for change that was a catalyst in terms of events in the near future. The motorcade also brought to prominence a young man who was to play an important role in those coming events: John Hume.

For my own part, I began to concentrate more and more on constituency issues, on radio and television appearances and speeches outside Stormont. Being the youngest MP I had a certain novelty attraction and this, along with my frequent appearances on television and radio, resulted in a considerable number of speaking engagements in the South and in Britain, as well as throughout the North. My association with the McCluskeys and my support for their Campaign for Social Justice gave me a ready-made theme, which I expounded everywhere I could with enthusiasm.

In circumstances where there was no hope of government and where even minor proposed adjustments to government policy were not accepted, I derived satisfaction from serving my constituents. The Parliamentary Question was of great assistance in this regard, although even in this the practice of Ministers answering all supplementary questions together minimised its usefulness. Unlike Westminster, where Ministers answered each supplementary immediately after it was asked, the Stormont Ministers could pick and choose from the collated questions, enabling inefficient Ministers to avoid the hook. But in terms of drawing attention to constituency problems and, nearly as important, drawing the attention of my constituents to my interest in their problems, the PQ was extremely useful.

Almost on a weekly basis my questions returned to the theme of the records of Dungannon Urban and Rural Council and Cookstown Urban and Rural Council in relation to house allocations.

When I became MP for East Tyrone on 1 July 1964, housing allocation had already been a source of controversy locally. Despite imaginative drawing of the boundaries, in the 1960s three of the five Stormont constituencies in County Tyrone returned Nationalist MPs on an almost universal franchise. However, at local government level the County Council, the six Rural Councils and all but one (Strabane) of the four Urban Councils were unionist controlled. In turn, all of the committees of the unionist-dominated councils dealing with such matters as roads, finance and education were, of course, also unionist controlled. And unionist control meant all of the top jobs and as many as possible of the less well-paid ones went to unionist supporters. In 1970, of the twenty top jobs in the gift of Tyrone County Council, only one was held by a Catholic. The control of the allocation of public authority houses was an essential part of the unionist power mechanism, particularly at local government level. In a situation where the franchise at local government level was restricted to those who owned or rented property and their spouses and where the ward boundaries had been carefully drawn to ensure maximum unionist control, the allocation of a council house effectively meant the allocation of two votes.

This property restriction clearly discriminated against the Catholic community where families were invariably larger. As a Member of the Stormont Parliament who was also entitled to vote and to stand for the Westminster Parliament, I did not have a vote for my local council while I lived in the family home before purchasing my own house.

There was, of course, the human dimension to housing allocation as well as the political dimension. Few human conditions contribute more to unhappiness than the lack of adequate housing. It can wreck a marriage and lead to serious disharmony between parents and grown-up children. It can create moral problems where sleeping accommodation is limited. Official figures confirm the relationship between inadequate housing and illness. Given a choice between unemployment and poor housing conditions, most people would choose unemployment. Unfortunately, in the prevailing conditions of Northern Ireland in the early 1960s, too many suffered from both.

There was another useful extension of my parliamentary role, especially in support of my less privileged constituents: fighting local tribunal appeals against the disallowance of social security benefits, such as unemployment, sickness and invalidity benefits. I gained considerable personal satisfaction from winning a high percentage of these cases, especially in instances where families had no other income or where a considerable amount of back-money was involved. Additionally, of course, many of the successful applicants became some of my strongest supporters, while most of the unsuccessful applicants gave me credit for doing my best. Occasionally there were moments of humour. For example, a surprising number of my constituents confused invalidity benefit with 'infertility benefit'. It was sometimes necessary to bluff. One woman was a regular visitor to my Advice Centre in Cookstown. Her problem, which she wished me to solve, was that she continually had temptations, such as throwing a brick through the parish priest's window. As a good Catholic she couldn't explain this particular temptation, except to say that there was a machine in the Cookstown area that was putting this and other bad thoughts into her head. This, mind you, before anyone except scientists had heard of computers. I became fed up with her wild ramblings Saturday after Saturday, until one day I heard that Harold Wilson had created a new appointment, Minister of Technology, and that gave me an idea. I told her of this appointment and that I would refer her case to the new Minister. The following Saturday she was not in the queue. The next Saturday she was back again – to thank me. My representations had been successful and the messages had stopped.

On another occasion, in the aftermath of an announcement that legal aid would henceforth be made available for couples wishing to divorce, a couple, not married to each other, sought my intervention. He had married during the war and, being unable to afford a honeymoon, he and his newly acquired wife had spent the wedding day drinking in the local hostelry. At a certain stage of the evening she had confided that she was pregnant, but the child wasn't his. As he explained to me, 'That was the end of it. I went home to my place and she went home to hers. I took up with this woman here and my wife found her own consolation.' The problem was that he and his new partner now had eight children, and his wife and her partner had seven. He had applied for legal aid for divorce, but had been turned down on the grounds that the new arrangements applied only from the date of the new regulation coming into force and that his position had not changed before or after the change in the regulations. 'They say I have no good reason for getting divorced now,' he told me balefully. I managed to convince the authorities that there were two very good reasons for getting divorced, maybe two further reasons if the other couple were to apply and possibly fifteen more if the position of the children were to be regularised. Following the successful outcome I was told I was assured of 'two good Protestant votes'.

O'Neill called a general election in November 1965, unexpectedly, as he was not obliged to do so until mid-1967. His decision was related to internal difficulties, particularly over his meetings with Lemass, but he also saw an opportunity for undermining the Northern Ireland Labour party in the Belfast area. In the latter aim he was successful, cutting their representation from four to two seats.

I was re-elected unopposed. I wasn't the only one. Due to the first-past-the-post electoral system, the efficiency of the gerrymander and the almost total lack of a swing vote, most constituencies were uncontested and the few changes resulted from the Labour party defeats and retirement. There were, in total, only six changes of personnel in the new Parliament. For me the most significant change was the election of John D Taylor to replace the elderly Fred McCoy in the adjoining constituency of South Tyrone. I knew Taylor reasonably well as we had been students together at Queen's and later, when he was a leader of the Young Unionist movement, we had crossed swords at a number of debates and conferences. His selection as Unionist candidate was partially due to the feeling in South Tyrone that I had been getting away with too much, especially in relation to Dungannon Urban Council, and that a young Unionist MP, also educated at Queen's, would put a stop to my political gallop.

There was no doubt about Taylor's ability, or his ambition, in a party not oversubscribed with talent. What also came across very quickly was his arrogance, which made him unpopular not only with the opposition but with some of his own too, an unpopularity which increased as he began to be identified as an opponent of Terence O'Neill. His election led to competition between him and me, particularly in the Dungannon area where he stoutly defended the actions of the two unionist councils. However, this did not stop us cooperating, when necessary, for the mutual advantage of our constituents. In particular, we put pressure on the government to ensure the motorway to Dungannon was to the specified high standard, and in one exceptional instance he signed a motion tabled by me critical of the cost of providing rural electrification. Such was our reputation that the Liberal MP Sheelagh Murnaghan took to referring to us as 'the terrible twins'. Unfortunately, as my efforts to expose discrimination intensified and as he became more identified with those in opposition to O'Neill's policies, cooperation soon diminished and, with the development of the 'Caledon Affair', was replaced by hostility.

8: THE ACHILLES HEEL OF UNIONISM

Where 1965 was a year of hope, 1966 was one of increasing despair and frustration. The commemoration of the 50th anniversary of the Easter Rising was the focal point, not so much because of the commemoration itself but because of unionist reaction to it. Within the North the events were much more low-key than might have been expected. I participated in a march in Coalisland, not as MP but as Chairman of my local GAA Club, Edendork St Malachy's, though as John Taylor wryly commented, I was much more identified in the public mind as a politician than as an athlete. Undoubtedly the commemorations North and South did raise the patriotic consciousness among nationalists and also emphasised the extent to which 1916, once an event of considerable divisiveness between the two strands of northern nationalism, had now become common to both. It was on the unionist side, however, among the more extreme sections of the Protestant community, that militancy reared its head. It wasn't just a reaction to the republican commemorations, though the alleged threat from the IRA was often cited, but rather a general feeling of insecurity among the Protestant population in the aftermath of O'Neill's meetings with Lemass and persistent suspicion of the Prime Minister and his motives. The Ulster Volunteer Force (UVF) was reformed by Gusty Spence in the early 1960s and initiated a campaign ostensibly aimed at republicans but effectively against Catholics, which culminated in the murder of a barman, Peter Ward, as he left a pub in Malvern Street, Belfast, on 27 May. O'Neill's government was forced to put the UVF in the same category as the IRA: an illegal organisation.

That year also saw the rise and rise of Ian Paisley. I had first encountered him when he spoke at a meeting at Queen's in 1961. He had all the attributes of a mob orator: a towering physique, a stentorian voice, a command of timing, a sense of humour and a message that was an explosive mixture of fundamental religion and radical politics. Even on that occasion, when I first witnessed him in action, I could see from the effect he was having on the women supporters present that there was also a strong sexual element. He went out of his way to exploit and enforce this aspect of his performance. Whenever possible in his main message, and particularly in his jokes, he made reference to sex, fornication, to the Whore of Babylon, to the alleged sexual misbehaviour of priests and nuns.

I have observed Ian Paisley for more than forty years and I am of the belief that he has contributed more to the intensity and the duration of the Troubles, and therefore to the deaths of so many people, than any other individual. I accept that there has always been an element of Ulster Protestantism – long before unionism became an issue and represented by such figures as Henry Cooke and 'Roaring' Hanna – whose energetic fundamentalism was always going to be a problem when even the slightest compromise with Catholicism was suggested. It was our bad luck that when there was the possibility of movement towards better relationships between the two traditions in the North, history threw up a man whose talents and abilities were so attuned to that strand of Ulster Protestantism, and thereby so suited to hinder the progress that was possible. He responded strongly when at that time, in 1966, I described him as 'a bigoted hangover from the seventeenth century', but the passage of time has not given me any reason to change my mind. From the beginning, Paisley was involved at least on the fringe of illegality, through organisations like the Ulster Constitution Defence Committee and the Ulster Protestant Volunteers, which he founded, and by his association with men who were convicted terrorists.

On 8 June 1966 I alleged in Stormont that Paisley was involved with the formation of the First East Tyrone division of the Ulster Volunteer Force near Pomeroy, County Tyrone. The Minister for Home Affairs, Brian McConnell, did not deny my allegation. Over the next three years, as the Paisley-led campaign for the removal of O'Neill intensified, I became more specific in my allegations.

However, I had other, more pressing, concerns to attend to because 1966 was also the year of a British general election. As I have earlier explained, the fact that my Stormont constituency straddled two Westminster constituencies invariably meant that Westminster elections caused me problems, and the 1966 election was no exception.

In the 1964 election in Fermanagh–South Tyrone the seat had been won by the Unionist Marquis of Hamilton with 30,010 votes, with Al Molloy (Republican), 16,138 votes, Giles Fitzherbert (Liberal), 6,006 and Gamble (Labour), 2,339. Significantly, in a seat with a Catholic majority and a traditionally high voter turnout, there were at least 6,000 Catholics who didn't vote. This was interpreted, rightly in my opinion, as a protest against abstentionism, which effectively handed the seat to the Unionists. In Mid-Ulster the result was Forrest (Unionist), 29,715; Mitchell (Republican), 22,810; and

McGarvey (Labour), 5,053. Again, at least 6,000 Catholics did not vote.

Between the two elections the pressure had intensified to end the split vote/abstentionism situation. Further impetus was lent by the belief, particularly among those who supported the Campaign for Social Justice, that with the Labour party in power in Britain, an MP could do a useful job in coordinating and leading a group in the Westminster Parliament to expose Unionist injustice and demand British pressure on the Unionist government. Such a group, the Campaign for Democracy in Ulster, had been formed in 1965, led by Paul Rose MP. Since Labour had come to power under Harold Wilson almost four years earlier, Rose and his campaign colleagues had hoped that the Labour government could exert sufficient pressure on the Unionist government to bring about reforms to remove discrimination against Catholics and nationalists in Northern Ireland. It followed that for an MP to carry out this coordinating role, he or she would have to attend at Westminster.

Largely under the influence of the McCluskeys, a series of meetings was held throughout the constituency, to culminate in a 'Unity Convention' to select a unity candidate. The aim was that Republicans would join in this exercise and accept the majority decision, which the organisers hoped would be in favour of an attendance candidate.

I was approached by a number of individuals to allow my name to go forward as the unity candidate. I would have liked to have gone to Westminster and believed I could have done an effective job there – I had studied the Westminster system and British history and I knew a number of Westminster Labour and Liberal members. However, I had been a Stormont MP for just over two years and was concerned about an impression of 'overweening ambition'. More importantly, I did not believe that the Republicans would step down, no matter how many meetings were held and no matter how large the support for an attendance candidate, and at that stage I was not prepared to take on the dirty job of fighting the election in order to beat the Republican candidate into third place. I felt that the time was not right for me, though I had some qualms of conscience about leaving the job to others. I countered that anxiety with the thought that if others were willing to carry the cross, then I should give them their wish.

So I did not enter the lists and indeed was not present at the convention, which eventually selected James Donnelly from Enniskillen. I did not absent myself deliberately. Some time previously, before the date of the convention had been decided, I had agreed to speak at an anti-discrimination rally in Birmingham. I did not regret the prior engagement. Political events in

Fermanagh–South Tyrone, and particularly the selection of candidates, were red meat affairs. In his book, *Up off their Knees*, Conn McCluskey described what happened in Enniskillen that day: 'Voting took place and Desmond Wright was chosen. He was a Protestant, an old boy of Dungannon Royal School who had previously been interned for his Republican views. There were strong protests from the floor by Republicans. The meeting then adjourned. Whilst we were relaxing we noticed that Desmond Wright had been called into an adjoining room by a group of men. After an interval he reappeared, white and shaking. He announced to the convention he was withdrawing.'

I strongly admired the courage of JJ Donnelly in accepting the poisoned chalice, worked for him behind the scenes and, at a later stage, when Minister, was pleased to appoint him to the Board of the Housing Executive.

In Mid-Ulster the unity candidate process didn't even get off the starter's blocks. I attended the selection convention in Omagh, where it was made crystal clear that Tom Mitchell was again to be the Republican candidate and that he would again be standing on an abstentionist platform. The extent to which Republicans were not for moving was made clear by one of their leaders, Kevin Agnew, when he emphatically said, 'I would prefer to see the children of Cookstown and Magherafelt running around starving and naked under the Tricolour, than see them clothed, fed and prosperous under the Union Jack.'

The Marquis of Hamilton duly won again in 1966 in Fermanagh–South Tyrone with 29,352 votes, but JJ Donnelly, with 14,645, beat Ruairí Ó Brádaigh into third place with 10,270. George Forrest had the expected victory over Mitchell in Mid-Ulster. Again there was a small Catholic turnout in both constituencies.

The joy of the 1966 election was the victory of Gerry Fitt in West Belfast. I had played a part in ensuring he had a clear run against the Unionist candidate by publicly calling for the withdrawal of the National Democratic party candidate. Gerry asked me to campaign for him and I did so with alacrity: not only did I have an extremely good personal relationship with him but it helped to explain my public absence from Fermanagh–South Tyrone. An indication of the social and economic make-up of the constituency at the time was Gerry's request that I concentrate on canvassing in Andersonstown. 'Andersonstown is a middle-class area and you appeal to the middle class,' he told me.

Gerry's election gave a much-needed boost to the campaign for equality. His personal style gave him a strong public profile and gained him a level of support that no other individual MP could have achieved. His 'Hiya, boy,' and

'Hiya, love,' greeting and distinctive seaman's gait soon made him a familiar figure in the corridors of Westminster, while his repertoire of stories and anecdotes soon gave him a popularity he used for political gain in the bars of the Palace of Westminster.

Gerry's arrival at Westminster was a watershed – the first presence of a non-unionist voice from Northern Ireland since 1955. His main objective was to break the convention that civil rights issues, which mainly concerned him, could not be raised as they were the responsibility of the devolved Parliament at Stormont. In this challenge he had the support of a number of Labour MPs who expressed their anger that in the previous Parliament, when Labour's majority had been only four, Unionist MPs spoke and voted on matters in England, Scotland and Wales which they, the British MPs, could not even mention in relation to Northern Ireland. Although Gerry was only one MP out of 650, his personality and the issues he identified with, of concern particularly to the left-wing of the Labour party, meant his influence far exceeded that of the eleven Unionist MPs. In Northern Ireland, the Unionist government found itself, for the first time, on the defensive.

Accompanied by Coalisland Silver Band, I met Gerry Fitt and three British Labour MPs on the outskirts of the town one Saturday afternoon in April 1967. For Paul Rose (Blackley, Manchester), Stan Orme (Salford West) and Dr Maurice Millar (Kelvingrove, Glasgow) it was a new experience as cattle, panicked by the noise of the band and the crowd, scattered across the fields, bellowing plaintively, but for me it was an important occasion, central to my emerging thoughts on political strategy. Gerry had invited the MPs on 'a fact-finding tour' with the intention of visiting Belfast and the three areas of highest unemployment, Newry, Strabane and Derry. But I had managed to hijack the delegation so that Coalisland and Dungannon were substituted for Newry and the emphasis shifted to include discrimination. The question on my mind was how their message would play in a traditional Nationalist/Republican area like Coalisland. Their message was that Northern Ireland was part of the United Kingdom and while it continued to be so, the people of Northern Ireland were entitled to the same rights and privileges as every other citizen of the United Kingdom. Nothing about the inevitable reunification of Ireland, or the establishment of a Republic, socialist or otherwise, no flying or waving of Tricolours: just a simple demand for equality.

Coalisland did not let me down. Despite the early hour – for Coalisland – of 6.00pm for an open-air political meeting, the crowd was large and the visitors (and myself!) were given an enthusiastic welcome as we proceeded behind the

Band to the lorry platform in the Square. Paul Rose whispered to me that, for the first time in his life, he felt like a conquering hero; I advised him to wait.

I need not have worried. The message was received and understood. Like me, many in the audience would have grimaced at the reference to 'Ulster', meaning a six-county Ulster, but then the organisation to which the MPs belonged was named the Campaign for Democracy in Ulster. British rights for British citizens were demanded: one man, one vote; a points system for the allocation of housing; fair electoral boundaries; an end to discrimination in jobs; and the abolition of the Special Powers Act. I chaired the meeting and, in concluding, I used the formula with which I and my audience were happy and which was to become a dominant theme in the civil rights campaign: 'If we are British citizens, and the Unionists say we are, then we demand for the citizens of Coalisland the same rights and privileges as the citizens of Coventry, and for the people of Dungannon the same rights as the people of Doncaster.' We had found the Achilles heel of Unionism.

From Coalisland we proceeded to Dungannon where (over a meal in Joe Stewart's pub, recently converted to a restaurant) the MPs met the McCluskeys and members of Dungannon Council. The Unionists had received an invitation but, not surprisingly, did not turn up. John Taylor MP had complained publicly that he had not had an opportunity to meet the visiting delegation, so I invited him to meet them in Dungannon and to attend the meeting in Coalisland. Rather hospitably, I thought, I had even reserved a chair for him on the platform in Coalisland!

As a result of the meal and the discussions it was nearly midnight before we arrived in Strabane to one of the most rapturous welcomes I have ever experienced. The atmosphere was perfect for demagoguery – a crowded Square, a good PA system, surrounding walls, a common theme of hope and opportunity and a common enemy. We all rose to the occasion, but Gerry, in particular, was in his element. He delivered probably the best mob orator speech I have ever heard.

In that same month the Northern Ireland Civil Rights Association (NICRA) was officially established. I had attended a meeting the previous January in the International Hotel in Belfast at which a steering committee was elected to draw up a constitution. The committee was composed mostly of left-wing and Republican elements, such as the Communist party, Republican clubs, the Belfast Wolfe Tone Society and Trade Unions, but also included representatives of the Campaign for Social Justice, the Northern Ireland Labour party, the Ulster Liberal party and Republican Labour party. I was proposed for the committee, but declined on the grounds that I believed that the new organisation should not be identified with a particular MP. NICRA was based on the British National Council for Civil Liberties (NCCL), which had been in existence for many years and on whose platform I had spoken even before I was elected as an MP.

The five objectives of NICRA were:
1. To defend the basic freedom of all citizens.
2. To protect the rights of the individual.
3. To highlight all possible abuses of power.
4. To demand guarantees for freedom of speech, assembly and association.
5. To inform the public of their lawful rights.

In other words, it was hardly a revolutionary organisation. There was no mention of the border nor indeed of discrimination or gerrymandering. Like the NCCL, its emphasis was on the legal and constitutional rights of individuals and proceeded largely through letter-writing and the documentation of abuses. Any form of public protest was far from the mind of those who brought it into existence.

Meanwhile, I continued with my efforts to do something to end discrimination in the allocation of public authority housing. I took seriously the commitment I had made prior to my election three years earlier – 'Each case of discrimination in housing and employment, trade and business must be pinpointed and fought. Publicity is the greatest weapon and it is best organised by public representatives who can carry the fight not only to Stormont but England as well.' The official report (*Hansard*) of debates in the Northern Ireland House of Commons showed just how seriously I took that commitment and I was a regular speaker at conferences and universities in Britain, where I endeavoured to expose the reality of life in Northern Ireland to as wide an audience as possible.

However, the truth of the matter was that I was getting nowhere exposing injustices in the Stormont House of Commons, but I was adept at getting publicity. Indeed, hardly a week went past without at least one appearance on BBC, UTV or RTÉ and often on all three channels. I was young, new, 'good television' and more than a match for Unionists who opposed me. The problem was that the government, while occasionally embarrassed, did not take adverse publicity seriously as long as that publicity was confined to

Northern Ireland and the Republic. It was adverse publicity in Britain that was of concern, and for this reason it paid attention to the activities of Gerry Fitt at Westminster and was extremely critical of the tours to the North he organised for British politicians. I did my best at my speaking engagements in Britain to attract publicity, sometimes successful in getting a few lines into provincial newspapers like the *Birmingham Mail*, but the truth was that the British media just wasn't interested in Northern Ireland.

The condition of the homeless and those living in overcrowded conditions was more than a political issue to me. I was genuinely angry about the injustice involved. Week after week in my constituency advice centres the most common complaints related to social welfare benefits and housing. Complaints about social welfare I usually could do something about. The rules and regulations were made at Westminster, but it was the responsibility of the Stormont Department for Social Services to implement them. I became quite an expert on the regulations and my success rate in appealing to Local Tribunals and to the Commissioner was high. Indeed, my reputation for winning cases was so great that unionists availed of my services, including, on a number of occasions, unionists from the adjoining constituency, advised by their MP, John Taylor, rather patronisingly, that 'Currie is the expert on social welfare'. It was this aspect of my work as a public representative that gave me the greatest satisfaction. Winning the case against a bureaucratic decision and the resulting payment of back-money owed made up for disappointments in other fields. And, of course, in addition to the personal satisfaction there was invariably electoral reward.

Housing, on the other hand, rewarded nothing but frustration. My three local authorities were unionist controlled and, as I have explained earlier, houses meant votes. I became more and more exasperated by my inability to help my deprived constituents. I visited overcrowded houses, condemned as being unfit for human habitation, knowing that it was their religion and politics which condemned the inhabitants to that misery, and I shared their anger and frustration. The abject reality for many Catholic families was living accommodation barely fit for animals – and this in the 1960s, in an age of new-found confidence and burgeoning consumerism. On 8 November 1967, I described for the benefit of the Stormont benches the conditions in which one family was living:

'Might I give the Minister an eyewitness account of the conditions in which this family live? The last time I went to the house was about a month ago. Mrs Mulgrew was about to return from hospital the next day with a new baby. The house has a very small kitchen, which is nothing better than a pig sty. There is one room, which is actually an attic upstairs. To get to that attic it was necessary to walk up not stairs but a ladder through a hole in the ceiling. When one got into that upstairs room I found there five beds and a cot side by side. To get into the middle beds it was necessary to start at the end and crawl over the other beds. There is one small window in the room. Though every effort has been made to keep it tidy and hygienic, I found the darkness and the smell absolutely disgusting and sickening.

These people have been looking for another house for a long time. The house has been condemned yet Dungannon Rural District Council in its wisdom has not yet seen fit to give the family a house despite the fact that the council seems to have a good record of house building. It builds the houses but will not give them to those people who are most in need. This is a refutation of the Minister's argument that all we need to do is to build more houses. That doesn't really help the people in Tyrone and Fermanagh. When these houses are built the people most in need do not get them because of petty political considerations.'

It was bad enough for those who had to live in such circumstances, but the knowledge that people already living in far superior accommodation were getting the newly built houses added to the anger and bitterness. I shared that anger and bitterness, perhaps to some extent because of the experience of my own father and mother twenty years earlier.

The hopes and expectations I had harboured for Terence O'Neill's tenure as PM were fast disappearing. I had been prepared to give him the benefit of the doubt, had sympathised with his problems in dealing with backwoodsmen in his own party and the strident opposition of Paisley, and had felt that as the evidence accumulated of injustice in housing allocations, he would eventually act. However, two further events in 1967 helped me to realise that I was depending on a broken reed. The position in County Fermanagh in relation to housing discrimination was, if anything, worse than in Tyrone. Fermanagh was, of course, the power base of the former Prime Minister, Lord Brookeborough, and it had long been Unionist policy, in the words of a former Unionist MP, 'to liquidate the nationalist majority in the county'. Fermanagh was designated a pilot area for the reform of local government and the three councils in the county were amalgamated into one. It soon became clear that rather than being 'reform', the purpose was to consolidate unionist control, and it was even proposed to bring in a unionist-dominated area of County Tyrone, around Fivemiletown, to assist in that purpose. In terms of the allocation of housing for political control, the new

County Council was as assiduous as its predecessors. The 'reform' process in Fermanagh illustrated the extent to which things had remained unchanged, despite O'Neill's liberal protestations.

I had accepted the personal *bona fides* of the Prime Minister to a fairer Northern Ireland. Okay, his wife had advertised in the Press for a housekeeper insisting that applicants must be Protestant, but that was many years ago and things had changed since then. Hadn't they? On 3 May 1967 the Prime Minister made the following intervention in the House of Commons:

'The main theme of the honourable members remarks today [Harry Diamond, Republican–Labour, Falls] was this old problem about alleged discrimination in Northern Ireland and while he was speaking my honourable and gallant friend the leader of the house [James Chichester-Clark] who was sitting next to me at the time said, "Perhaps you would like to read this letter". I read it and as it comes from the Falls Road I shall read it out to the Honourable Members. It arrived here yesterday from, I presume, one of the Honourable Member's constituents. It says,

> Falls Road
> Belfast
> Northern Ireland
>
> Major Clarke,
> Dear Sir,
> As a loyal Irish Roman Catholic I, with others, do not want into the Irish Republic. Our church is always crying discrimination but it was given out from the pulpit the other Sunday that no Catholic was to buy from a Protestant shop unless the shop was run by a Catholic nor no Catholic was to employ a Protestant. P.S. Do not mention my name.'

I immediately asked the Prime Minister to give way and accused him of irresponsibility in reading out such a scurrilous allegation without any effort to establish its credibility, especially in a social climate where MPs were in receipt of allegations from all manner of cranks. He stood over his comments and so I tabled a Parliamentary Question, asking whether he had checked the authenticity of the letter before using it in the House, to which he replied, on 9 May. O'Neill admitted that he had not checked the authenticity of the letter before using it and that since then an RUC investigation had been unable to trace the writer. 'In the absence of authentication no weight whatever can be attached to the allegations which the writer makes; that I have no evidence from any other source which would support such allegations and that I accept unreservedly the complete denial from responsible quarters of the substance of these allegations'. He added that he regretted his remarks.

In my response I cast doubt on his sincerity regarding attempts to bring about better community relations given that what he had alleged was a slur on the Catholic clergy and had caused ill-will and suspicion within the community. I wondered how anyone in his position, seeing such a letter and the very serious allegations it contained, could give it any credibility by reading it out and putting it on the record of the House. It seemed to me that to use it in the way he did he must have believed such a thing could happen in a Catholic church and, indeed, that it wasn't very unusual for it to happen.

The whole affair helped me to come to the conclusion that O'Neill's liberalism was only skin-deep, and that the commendable sentiments in favour of reconciliation were more likely to be the product of his speech writers, Jim Mallie and Ken Bloomfield, than of the Prime Minister himself. I have no doubt his instincts were those of a decent man who had spent a lot of his life outside Northern Ireland, but I suspected that he did not really understand the Protestant working man, never mind the Catholic and nationalist working man. Yes, he visited Catholic schools and had his photograph taken with the nuns in charge, but what did such PR promotions tell us about Northern Ireland when the visit of the Prime Minister to a school system where half the population was educated created such an impact ,and what did it tell us about him who laid such stress on it?

My reservations about the depth of O'Neill's liberalism and the extent of his knowledge of the problems in the community were later confirmed by an interview he gave to the *Belfast Telegraph* on 10 May 1969, after his resignation as Prime Minister:

'It is frightfully hard to explain to Protestants that if you give Roman Catholics a good job and a good house they will live like Protestants because they will see neighbours with cars and television sets. They will refuse to have 18 children. But if a Roman Catholic is jobless and lives in the most ghastly hovel he will rear 18 children on national assistance. If you treat Roman Catholics with due consideration and kindness, they will live like Protestants, in spite of the authoritarian nature of their Church.'

By mid-1967 I had come to the conclusion that for change to come about, we had to up the ante.

The 1967 local government elections saw the re-election of John Donaghy and the election of Michael McLoughlin to the McCluskey team on Dungannon Urban District Council. I soon developed a close personal and political relationship with them. At that time, I still lived at home with my parents and had built an office onto the house for the convenience of visiting constituents and to reduce disruption of family life by such visits. Whenever John and Michael visited me, that little office became the location of long and animated discussions on possible ways forward, and the tactics that might advance our cause. I must also report that it was rare for anything to be left in a bottle of Power's Gold Label when they left.

John and Michael provided an interesting contrast: John, emotional and instinctive; Michael, laid-back and dogged; together they were a formidable team on behalf of Dungannon Catholics. Most of the facts and figures gathered on housing and planning matters in the Dungannon area were the work of Michael McLoughlin. His job as a primary schoolteacher enabled him to do research during office hours, after school hours and during the holidays and he was almost a permanent fixture in the offices of Dungannon urban and rural councils, much to the annoyance of Unionist councillors and their staff. Michael and John became my closest confidants, the possessors of my hopes and aspirations in a profession where one has many acquaintances but few friends. They shared my frustration and growing disillusionment and anger at the lack of progress under O'Neill.

My public speeches, too, began to reflect these feelings. On 2 August 1967, speaking in the company of Gerry Fitt at Murlough, County Antrim, on the occasion of the annual Casement commemoration, I said:

'How much longer must we – can we – tolerate a situation where a large section of the population of this state is being denied equality, is being deprived of elementary social justice, is being refused 20th-century democratic rights, is being treated as second-class citizens? At a period in history when peoples everywhere are demanding equality and justice, are we to be content with less? There can be no compromise with injustice, no acceptance of inequality. The minority discriminated against in this area cannot wait for ever and if the government here is not prepared to remove the disabilities under which the minority has suffered for more than 40 years, then other tactics and new methods, consistent with our attachment to the ideals we hold will have to be adopted to ensure equality and justice. I hope that in this struggle, as in the past, we will have the support of all lovers of truth and justice, irrespective of the red herring of sectarianism which has been used to keep us divided for so long.'

Gerry had spoken about 'other means' at a rally at Trafalgar Square, London, the previous month and had been attacked by the Prime Minister for doing so. Part of O'Neill's criticism had been based on a misreporting or misinterpretation of Gerry's speech, which had been construed by the Prime Minister as an incitement to violence. My scripted reference to 'other tactics and new methods' was carefully written to avoid such an allegation. Nevertheless, O'Neill's wrath came down on my head. His attack and our response to it received much media exposure, particularly on television. Whatever the merits of the controversy, O'Neill could not say he had not been warned that opinion in the nationalist community was hardening.

On 12 September I returned to the attack in a speech at Meenagh, Coalisland, comparing what opposition politicians in Britain were describing as 'the national scandal of unemployment' of 2.6% with 19.5% unemployment in Strabane, 17.8% in Derry and 11.4% in Dungannon, and pointing to the continuation and intensification of discrimination in housing and jobs.

'In fact, in Northern Ireland at the present time we have all the elements for a social and economic revolution and in any other country that is what we would have. The people of Britain have a long history of constitutional government, but I am sure if they found themselves in the same situation as we do here, living under similar injustice, they would not tolerate it. Why do we? The tragedy is that a large section of the population of this state has become so used to injustice that it now accepts it as a way of life, as natural, as inevitable. Others who know better remain silent in the face of human tragedy and human degradation and exploitation. Many professional and business people who have ideas and talents which could be used for the benefit of the whole community adopt the "I'm all right, Jack" mentality and are content to accept everything and contribute nothing to the amelioration of the problems of those less fortunate than themselves. Such complacency and apathy is a sickening feature of our life here in 1967.

I can understand Unionist acceptance of the present situation. Unionism is, after all, the party of privilege, the party of the "haves" which uses sectarianism to distract the attention of ordinary people from their real problems and to enable a small clique to keep their hands on the throats of the "have-nots". It is much more difficult to explain the apparent lack of concern of many who would be affronted if termed "unionist" or "Tory".

Is it not time we had real anger in Northern Ireland politics? Not the assumed anger at "old forgotten far off things" but real anger at social, economic and political injustice? Is it not time for a union of all those people who really care about the wrongs being inflicted on their fellow man, irrespective of political, social or religious backgrounds? In the face of such a union, the type of union dreamed about by men like Tone and Henry Joy, in the face of such anger and concern, surely the politicians responsible would have to face the alternative of doing something or being consigned to the political limbo they deserve.'

On 23 October I spoke to the Economic and Political Studies Society in Magee University College, Derry, on the theme of 'O'Neillism'. I referred to the hopes and expectations he had aroused, particularly when he had met Lemass. But despite all the promise and the liberal speeches, nothing had changed. Indeed, there was growing evidence of Unionist retrenchment. The hopes raised and then dashed would lead to greater frustration and anger. People disappointed and frustrated with the apparent failure of constitutionalism and parliamentary action to remove grievances tend to try and solve the problems in their own way. O'Neill still had a chance to leave an indelible impression on history.

'The sands of time have not yet run out for him and if he takes the steps necessary, "O'Neillism" will be a record of real achievement ... However, if he does not take action quickly, certainly within the next twelve months, the ever-growing frustration and anger to which I have already referred must make a real impact on politics in this area. I foresee a growing militancy. There will be more squatting, more acts of civil disobedience, more emphasis on "other means" and less on traditional parliamentary methods. And Terence O'Neill and his government must carry the responsibility.'

The prediction could hardly have been more accurate. Twelve months from 23 October 1967 incorporated 5 October 1968 – the date when history caught up with unionism.

It was not, however, a period of my life entirely dominated by politics. I found out that there was something – rather someone – more important than the speeches, the media appearances and the constituency problems. I had first met Annita Lynch at a Saturday night hop in Queen's in 1961. On our first date, in a cinema queue (for *GI Blues*, starring Elvis, if I remember right), we discovered politics to be a shared interest. Her father had been a Nationalist Senator, indeed a member of the 'Herald Group'. I was immensely proud of her when she became Rag Queen that year. Unfortunately, that led indirectly to my first brush with the law. On Rag Day I added to the customary high jinks, including visits to licenced premises, by boarding the Domestic College float where the Rag Queen was installed in all her glory, surrounded by her princesses. A bag of flour proved too much of a temptation and so, as the procession passed the Black Man monument, flour billowed on the wind and rain. Unfortunately, an RUC man was on duty on the corner and a white man soon accompanied the black one. The incident was reported to the Student Representative Council and the culprit had no option but to own up; I was duly fined £5, most of it to cover the cost of dry-cleaning the RUC uniform.

We had been going out together for just over a year when Annita made an unexpected and shattering announcement. She had decided to enter a convent and become a nun. I responded in the only way I felt I could, 'Who am I to stand between you and God?' It was only then, and in the days and weeks and months that followed, that I realised just how much I loved her.

Annita remained in the convent for three years. She has often said her experience in Strabane Convent gave her an outlook on life that enabled her to cope with the trauma of later years. She required those qualities almost immediately. The day after I heard she had left her novitiate studies, I called at her parents' home in Omagh. Shortly after that, we resumed our relationship.

When we got engaged, in 1967, we shared the moment with rather more people than we had intended – including my political sparring partner, John Taylor. On 16 December 1967, the *Belfast Telegraph* ran a report headed, 'No politics at Currie's engagement', and the introduction read:

'Politics were forgotten and champagne corks popped when the youngest member at Stormont, Mr. Austin Currie, MP for East Tyrone, announced his engagement. For, toasting him at a celebration in a Dublin hotel last night was the youngest Unionist member, John Taylor, MP for South Tyrone.'

Unknown to each other, we had both been invited to the Annual Dinner of Dublin Junior Chamber of Commerce by the organising Chairman, Jim Deegan. Annita and I had bought the ring earlier that day and, naturally, it was noticed. Another guest at the dinner was Andy Hamilton, then the *Telegraph*'s man in Dublin, and he couldn't resist the temptation to publicise the event. I am sure it must have caused some political embarrassment for John Taylor, especially as the event occurred in Dublin and fraternisation with the enemy might have been suspected. For me the consequence was to keep me honest; customs duty was payable on the ring, a fact which, without publicity, I would have ignored.

I suppose our story is a romantic one, and I can still say, almost forty years later, that I am one of the luckiest men in the world.

9: CALEDON

In January 1968, Annita and I had visited the House of Commons where we met Paul Rose, the Labour MP for Blackley, Manchester, who was Chairman of the group of MPs who had formed the Campaign for Democracy in Ulster (CDU), as referred to earlier. Paul was an old friend who had proved his commitment to the cause of social justice in Northern Ireland and I trusted his judgement. Since Labour had come to power under Harold Wilson almost four years earlier, he and his colleagues in the CDU had been urging the Labour government to put pressure on the Unionist government to bring about much-needed social and political reforms. He and I had a long discussion on the lack of progress. Despite Gerry Fitt's efforts, supported by the CDU, the convention preventing Northern Ireland issues being raised in the House of Commons still remained in place, and British Ministers replying to letters from the Campaign for Social Justice were responding, almost word for word, as previous Tory Ministers had. Paul was aware of the increasing militancy of my speeches, particularly the one in Derry the previous October when I had thrown down the gauntlet to O'Neill, and he approved. He now quite bluntly said to me, 'Austin, I have lost hope that this or any other British government will put pressure on the Unionists unless it is forced to do so. Unless you and others like you can create a situation where this government will be forced to intervene in Northern Ireland nothing will happen and the position will remain unchanged.' Paul's judgement confirmed my own belief, which I had expressed in a number of speeches over the previous two years. But the strength of his conviction on the subject, and similar views expressed by other stalwarts of the Campaign for Democracy, like Stan Orme and Kevin McNamara, made a compelling case. Creating the circumstances which would force the British government to intervene in Northern Ireland became central to my political thinking and strategy.

I first met Jimmy and Annie Gildernew on a Saturday afternoon in late October 1964. I was cutting the lawn at my parents' home in Mullaghmarget when they arrived. They were a fine-looking couple, tall and well-built. On the papers he showed me about his sickness benefit problem he was described as 'handyman', but I was not surprised to find out subsequently that he had been a blacksmith. Annie did most of the talking. They wished me to represent him at a Local Tribunal Appeal case against his disallowance of benefit. They were not my constituents, being from Crievelough, Brantry, near Caledon, in the constituency of South Tyrone, and therefore represented by John Taylor, but having listened to Annie's story, I agreed to fight the case. I was successful and over the next three years or so I got to know them well because they came to me whenever Jimmy was in trouble with the Department over benefit, usually sickness benefit.

The village of Caledon is located on the Tyrone/Armagh/Monaghan border, in Tyrone and about twelve miles from Dungannon. It developed around a castle, originally an O'Neill castle, called Kinnard, whose most famous occupant was Phelim O'Neill, leader of the 1641 rebellion. After the rebellion was quashed the property was confiscated and granted initially to the Hamilton family and then, in 1776, sold to the Alexanders, who became Earls of Caledon in 1880. Field Marshal, Lord Alexander of Tunis, the third son of the fourth Earl, was born in the castle in 1891. The estate was one of the largest in Ulster – over 30,000 acres in 1860 – and the Earl of Caledon enjoyed an influential position, politically and socially, in 'society'. My first involvement with the noble Earl came indirectly through Matt Hegarty, the local Catholic registration agent in Caledon. Shortly after my marriage, Matt presented me with a lovely big pheasant. When I enquired as to its origin, he replied, 'with the compliments of Lord Caledon'. I had tasted poached salmon on a number of occasions, but this was my first experience of poached pheasant!

When I first took an interest in Caledon in the 1960s, the population of the village was about 350. The political/religious breakdown on the electoral register for Caledon and the adjoining electoral area of Minterburn was three unionists to one nationalist. It was an area where unionists were securely in control and they did things their way.

On Wednesday, 18 October 1967, I raised in Stormont, on the Adjournment Debate, the question of the allocation of houses in a new housing estate at Kinnard Park, Caledon. I started by quoting from an article that had appeared in the previous week's issue of the *Armagh Democrat*, written by their staff reporter, Sean Hughes:

'On Thursday last I attended the monthly public meeting of Dungannon Rural District Council. Part of the business of the meeting was the allocation of 17 houses in the Caledon division which is represented by Councillor W. R. Scott, Unionist. Along with other press representatives I waited for the list of the proposed new tenants to be read out but this did not take place. Councillor Scott handed in a list and these were apparently the successful applicants. No discussion as to the relative merits of different applicants took place and no one (apart from Councillor Scott) seemed to know who had been given the tenancies. The only audible comment at the press table was one from Councillor Scott himself, to the effect that he would "need another 12 houses", but no decision of any kind was taken on this comment.

Following the meeting I approached the secretary, who was taking notes of the meeting, in order to obtain the names of the persons submitted by Councillor Scott and was informed that I would obtain these by ringing the Council offices the next day. This method of house allocation is said to be a recognised procedure by councillors in the Dungannon Rural District Council. The custom seems to be that in each division the councillor for the area is the entire housing committee and his word is final.'

In such a casual way, virtually unnoticed except by a vigilant young journalist, did the process begin which was to rock the Northern Ireland State to its foundations and end the hegemony of the Unionist party. For of the fifteen new houses allocated in Kinnard Park (there were two allocations elsewhere in Caledon, which were re-lets), only one was allocated to a Catholic despite the fact that a number of Catholic applicants were clearly the most in need.

The housing conditions of one of the unsuccessful applicants were described by the family doctor (a man from a unionist background) as follows: 'the house of the above named is damp, the doors and windows ill fitting and the gable positively dangerous. The approach lane is very rough and wet even in the driest of weather and it would be a very simple matter for one to break an ankle by traversing it. It is impossible to believe that a young married couple with no family already housed in a very sound and relatively new house should receive priority in allocation of the recently erected council houses in Caledon while this family lives in circumstances more suitable for housing pigs. It is time the whole question of housing in this area was investigated by an independent body.'

Another unsuccessful applicant and his wife had a family of eight living in a house with one room, located less than two miles from Caledon. Another with three children lived in one room in an exceedingly damp dwelling. These three unsuccessful applicants had all been on the waiting list for houses, one of them for seven years, and all resided in close proximity to Caledon. Of course there were many more among the waiting list of 269 who were also in serious need and were living elsewhere in the rural area.

Among the successful candidates was one who had returned from England only a month earlier, another had sold his house and farm only two weeks before he was allocated a house; another had not actually applied for a house, but was approached by Councillor Scott to take it in order 'to keep a Papish out' and others from outside the area.

My initial interest in housing in Caledon resulted from representations made to me by a Mrs McQuade, who lived in a house condemned by the Health Authority as unfit for human habitation. She told me she had approached Councillor Scott about one of the new houses and alleged that he had replied, 'you will never sit your backside in a house in Caledon'. I had taken her case up with some vigour and much hope as there was a statutory requirement on the council to rehouse those living in condemned accommodation. The only individual under the law of the land who had a legal right to be rehoused was one who was living in a condemned property. Of course, the law did not specify when such a person had to be rehoused. I took the matter up with the council and pointed out the legal position and Mrs McQuade's entitlement. I went further and brought the case to the attention of the Stormont Minister concerned and told him that I expected the statutory obligation to be discharged in respect of Mrs McQuade and her family. He promised to raise the matter with Dungannon Council.

Mrs McQuade was allocated a house in Kinnard Park, the only Catholic to be successful. In view of Councillor Scott's attitude to Mrs McQuade's application, I felt it was pressure from Stormont that had secured the desired outcome. However, my obvious interest in Caledon housing and the fact that I had been recognised visiting the site and calling with Mrs McQuade led, in the aftermath of developments, to the accusation by John Taylor, in a later debate in Stormont, that I was more deeply involved at this time than was the case. He accused me of organising squatting.

In the early hours of the morning, after the council meeting, two families entered and occupied No. 9 and No. 11 Kinnard Park. The 'squatters' in No. 9 were Brian McKenna, his wife and child (I had previously received representations from Brian McKenna, who was living with his father and mother, wife, baby, grown-up sister and brother in a three-bedroom house in Caledon). In No. 11 were Mr and Mrs Francis Goodfellow and their two children. Mrs Goodfellow was the daughter of my old friends, the Gildernews. I had made representations to the council on behalf of the McKennas, but I had not been approached on behalf of the Goodfellows, nonetheless I gave both families my support and provided political cover. It was not that either family was the most deserving of a house. There were others on the waiting list, including the three families I have mentioned, who were more in need, and if the recent lettings had not been so outrageous I might have been accused of supporting 'queue-jumping'. But as I was later to explain in Stormont, these squattings were a protest and the young couples who engaged in it, while not the most entitled to the houses, were certainly more in need than those to whom the houses had been allocated.

If I may, at this juncture, say something briefly about squatting in general terms, as this form of civil disobedience was starting to become more frequently employed at that time. The squatters, usually a couple with children, required physical courage as the house they occupied had invariably been allocated to a unionist and some form of retaliation or intimidation could be anticipated. Additionally, the circumstances in which they lived, including the fear of being evicted, imposed strains on the relationship which could affect the marriage. These practical considerations meant that only the most determined actually engaged in it and these factors limited the use of squatting as a widespread form of civil disobedience. Yet the incidents of it which did occur received much publicity in the local media and successfully drew attention to allocation injustices.

Dungannon Council cut off the water supply to the houses, but when legal action was threatened, on health grounds, decided instead to proceed through the courts to have the illegal residents evicted. The court case provided an opportunity for more adverse publicity for the council, which was compounded by the Judge's decision, while agreeing to eviction, to grant a six-month stay of execution. It was a moral victory.

While all this was going on I endeavoured to give what political support I could to the two families. I visited them regularly and sought, by getting publicity, to ensure that they were not forgotten. I enlisted the support of Senator Gerry Lennon who, in addition to his political accomplishments, was a vastly experienced lawyer and in this instance he gave his advice and court appearances free of charge. As leader of the Nationalist party in the Northern Ireland Senate and as a National Vice-President of the AOH, Senator Lennon was able to lend an air of responsibility and respectability to what was, of course, an illegality.

John Taylor, MP for the Caledon area, could not, of course, accept my interference in his constituency without response. He did, however, find himself on the defensive from the beginning. The *Tyrone Democrat* reported that I was on the scene visiting the squatters and giving media interviews, while, it was noted, 'Mr Taylor did not make his appearance during the day nor did he interview the two families who are his constituents. Although Mr Taylor was in Caledon that morning I was not able to interview him. (The nearest I got to contacting him was when I observed him drive his car from the backyard of Mr Scott's residence.)' Later, Taylor tabled a motion of censure in Stormont, deploring 'the policy of civil disobedience as manifested in the spectacle of the recent squatting in Caledon, County Tyrone, and particularly deploring the tacit and even express approval afforded to such expedients by the Nationalist members of this House'. It was passed, of course.

The next development in 'the Caledon affair', as it had become known, was the departure of the McKenna family. I have already described the stressful conditions in which squatters lived. Mrs McKenna was English and not used to the unique circumstances in which she found herself, with the Sword of Damocles of eviction hanging over her family. The departure of the McKennas, and the loss of solidarity it represented, put additional pressure on the Goodfellows, but they remained determined.

The tenancy of No. 9, vacated by the McKennas, had now to be awarded by the council and there was considerable speculation in the Caledon area as to who would be the successful applicant; the person who had originally been allocated the house was no longer interested in living there. In view of all the publicity the council and the local councillor had received, I assumed they would be careful to allocate the house to someone clearly in need and that a Catholic family in this category might even have a chance.

I had great difficulty believing the news when I heard it. The house was allocated to a nineteen-year-old, unmarried girl, of all the 269 people on the waiting list, probably the least deserving. Emily Beattie entered into occupation of her new house on 13 June. Five days later, the Goodfellows were evicted from the house next door. The council bailiffs arrived, forced their way into the house and dragged Mrs Goodfellow and her mother out onto the street. Mrs Goodfellow clutched her nine-week-old baby to her as she was pulled along the ground. The whole sorry episode was caught by the TV cameras and Press photographers, and had a major impact on public opinion, particularly when attention was drawn to the occupant of the house next door.

The allocation of a house to Emily Beattie, in these circumstances, was the ultimate two-fingered insult to all who had been campaigning for fairer housing procedures. It was an assertion by Councillor Scott that he would allocate public authority housing in his area as he pleased and to whom he pleased. Undoubtedly the insult had me in mind, but it was also aimed at the Minister responsible for housing, William Fitzsimons, and his Parliamentary

Secretary, Nat Minford, who had been working behind the scenes to secure a reasonable outcome. Minford and Gerry Fitt were utilising facilities in the Stormont toilet when the Junior Minister said to Fitt, 'those bloody madmen in Dungannon are trying to destroy us'. A photograph of O'Neill visiting a convent was one thing; South Tyrone unionists represented the reality.

I was surprised and deeply angered at the arrogance and stupidity of Councillor Scott and those who supported him in his action. I immediately recognised the propaganda weapon provided by Caledon and Councillor Scott and the unique opportunity it presented to strike a blow, possibly a fatal blow, at the unjust system of housing allocation not only in Dungannon but throughout Northern Ireland. As I said at the time, I could have waited for years and not have found a better example. There was no way the allocation could be justified. It was time to go for broke.

The following day, 19 June, I raised the affair on the Adjournment Debate and spoke for thirty minutes. I did not expect any redress. My intention was to put certain matters on the record in anticipation of what I had already decided to do. I described the disgraceful scene as the family was evicted. The squatting had been a protest against the corrupt system, not against individual allegations. The commitment of the Prime Minister to better community relations should be judged not by pious platitudes but by action on the ground. I challenged the Minister to justify the allocation to Emily Beattie and alleged that she worked as a secretary in the office of Brian McRoberts, solicitor, Armagh, who was the prospective Unionist candidate for West Belfast, and that this was a possible reason for her preferment. I also reminded the House of the many occasions when I had raised this and other examples of injustice.

'I believe I have used all the traditional parliamentary methods open to me. Representations have been made to the local councillor, the local council, the Minister, the Prime Minister and today to Parliament itself. I have made use of all the procedural moves which it is possible for me to use. I have made representations to the local authorities, representations direct to the Minister, I have asked parliamentary questions, have raised the matter on a private members' motion, on Adjournment Debates and I have asked the Prime Minister to intervene. As to tactics and moves on this issue in Caledon, I have come to the end of the road from the strictly parliamentary point of view.'

And I concluded by saying that if no remedy was forthcoming for what I considered to be a blatant case of injustice:

'... it will not be possible for me to stop fighting for justice in this case because this is something about which I feel much too strongly to give up. I will not cease my efforts because to do so would neither be fair to myself, nor the people I represent. But let me say that if I do not get a satisfactory reply today I will accept that this is a failure of traditional parliamentary representation and I will continue this fight in other ways until all public authority houses in my area are allocated only on the basis of need.'

There was a time limit on Adjournment Debates of one hour, so there were only two more speakers, Harry Diamond (Republican Labour) and John Taylor. Harry supported me fully and said that the government, through toleration of maladministration, had created an explosive situation and that experience showed 'that where unjust law is operated there will be a violent reaction to it'. John Taylor spoke next and alleged that the only reason I was raising the Caledon issue was so that 'misleading statements [would] be printed in *Hansard*, sent over to London and distributed among various anti-Ulster Labour members in the Westminster House.' He praised the record of Dungannon RDC in housing and accused me of doing my utmost to imperil and destroy community relations in Tyrone. In response to repeated challenges from Gerry Fitt, Harry Diamond and myself, amid an increasingly unruly House, to justify the Emily Beattie allocation, he said, 'This house was then allocated to Miss Beattie. It was not, as has been said today by the Honourable Member for East Tyrone, let to one person. This house has gone to four grown-ups. I called there last night and there were indeed four–'. At this stage I interjected, 'It is a damned lie', and despite repeated requests from the Speaker to withdraw that unparliamentary expression I kept repeating it and, predictably, the Speaker ordered me out of the House.

By this stage the House was in uproar, with members shouting at each other and the Unionists jeering at me as I began my walk towards the door. I threw my notes in the direction of the Unionist benches and shouted above the uproar, 'All hell will break loose, and by God I will lead it.'

I have described earlier how I was escorted from Stormont by the RUC, arrived home to tell Annita of my intentions and then, in our front room, informed an invited group from Caledon of what I intended to do and asked them for their assistance.

The following morning, Thursday, 20 June 1968, I drove the twelve miles to Caledon in my Volkswagen Beetle, accompanied by Annita. We did so with some trepidation for we both knew there might be people in the Caledon and wider area who would respond in a physical way to my presence in Caledon. I had contacted Mrs McQuade the previous evening and she opened the door immediately I knocked. Annita then departed for Dungannon with instructions to inform the media and then Eddie McAteer, my party Leader, and Gerry Fitt, my closest political associate. Unfortunately, she was unable to contact McAteer directly – apparently he was already on the train on his way to Stormont – and she did not think it would be appropriate to leave a message. This led to some slight unpleasantness later as some considered it a deliberate snub to Eddie, which it was not.

The arrangement with the Caledon people was that as many as possible would meet me at McQuades' at 11.30am. By 12.15 I was beginning to panic: no one had arrived; Annita would have completed the journey home and would be contacting the media and one of them might ring the RUC in Caledon to confirm the story. What if the RUC arrived prematurely? I had decided to proceed on my own when two men arrived, Patsy Gildernew, brother of Mrs Goodfellow, and Joe Campbell, whom, to my knowledge, I had never met before. I was disappointed there were not more, but three of us was enough. We borrowed Mrs McQuade's poker and proceeded to the rear of No. 9, Emily Beattie's house, where, in an act of solidarity, the three of us used the poker to break a window and enter the house. We then barricaded ourselves in by placing the few items of furniture available against the front and back doors. As time passed, my concern grew that no action would be taken against us, by the council or whoever, and that we would have to stay overnight, during the hours of darkness when anything might happen. I later learned that there was a rumour, referred to by McAteer and Fitt in the Stormont debate while I was still in the house, that the UVF was threatening to march on Caledon.

Anyway, it was some small comfort to observe that Patsy Gildernew had much the same physique as his blacksmith father. Joe Campbell voiced concerns at the delay – his father was elderly and he feared he might not be home in time to milk the cows.

Shortly, we observed the arrival of photographers, then a TV crew, followed by another; Annita had done her work well. Then an RUC Sergeant arrived and I recognised him as the local Sergeant, Ivan Duncan, whom I knew from enquiries I had made earlier in the year about the diversion of an AOH church parade in the village. I considered him to be a fair man. He inquired the reason for our presence in the house and I replied that it was a non-violent protest against the system of house allocation. The Sergeant replied it was a civil matter and he was there to make sure there was no breach of the peace. Soon after that other police arrived, including a District Inspector (Supt) and a Head Constable (Inspector). The RUC was clearly taking the matter seriously.

When we had been in occupation about two-and-a-half hours, a man and a good-looking young girl approached the door. 'That's Emily and her brother,' Joe Campbell said. The brother, Samuel, I later found out, was a serving RUC man in Armagh, but he was not wearing uniform when he approached the house. He tried the front and back doors, and when he could not gain access he came to the window and demanded we leave the house. I told him it was a non-violent protest and he would have to put us out. He went away and returned with a sledgehammer, with which he forced an entry. Once in, he came straight towards me with the intention, I assumed, of laying hands on me. I said, 'Wait a minute, we are not resisting. This is a non-violent protest.' I then walked out the front door, followed by Joe and Patsy, and straight into a crowd of photographers and TV cameramen.

That night I sat in my own front room and watched myself being interviewed on the news from London. It was the first time, as far as I knew, that any interview had ever taken place on British national television on the subject of discrimination against the minority in Northern Ireland. The phone started to ring: all congratulations apart from one abusive call. The call I appreciated most was from Paul Rose MP. He said, 'Austin, the message is at long last getting through to those the Unionists fear – British politicians and British public opinion. Keep it up.' I told him I remembered vividly what he had said to me at the House of Commons the previous January about forcing the British government to put pressure on the Unionists. I added, 'Paul, I have other ideas in mind.'

10: THE CIVIL RIGHTS MOVEMENT

About a week after the 'sit-in' at Caledon, which had, as hoped, received wide publicity, John Donaghy, Michael McLoughlin and I held a *post-mortem*. I put to the two councillors an idea that had been lurking at the back of my mind for some time, namely that we should organise a civil rights march. As part of my degree course I had specialised in American history and the US Supreme Court. I had identified with the struggle of African-Americans for emancipation and equal treatment and had observed with keen interest the development of the civil rights campaign in America. I had read some of the speeches of Martin Luther King and had occasionally quoted from them. Media comparisons between the condition of black people in the USA and 'Ireland's white negroes' struck a responsive chord.

I was of the opinion that civil rights marches, if properly organised and controlled, could make a major contribution to publicising the true state of affairs in Northern Ireland, both in Britain and internationally, and thereby result in the necessary British government pressure on the Stormont government. I had also been considering how anti-unionist opinion might be better mobilised and what specific courses of action I was prepared to initiate or support when I spoke of 'other means'.

In April and May 1968 public meetings had been held in Armagh protesting against the banning of the annual Easter commemoration parade and the organisers had been arrested, allegedly at the behest of Ian Paisley, who had threatened a counter-demonstration. Anger at the ban, and the circumstances in which it had been imposed, was indicated by the breadth of political opinion on the platform, which included Eddie McAteer MP, Eddie Richardson MP, and myself of the Nationalist party, Gerry Fitt MP (Republican Labour), Tom Mitchell and Kevin Agnew (Republicans), Reverend Albert McElroy (Northern Ireland Liberal party), John McCann (National Democratic party) and Fred Heatley (NICRA). The unity displayed on the platform encouraged me to call for 'a twentieth-century New Departure' that would promote unity and create:

'... a new alliance in a cohesive movement which will embrace the existing progressive nationally minded groups and which will reflect the concerns, ideas and aspirations of the ordinary people from the grassroots up. Such a movement would not confine itself to "constitutional methods" if by these words is meant the type of political activity we have been involved in over the years but would use all the weapons in the arsenal of non-violent civil disobedience ... We will have justice or we will make a governmental system based on injustice unworkable.'

By 'New Departure' I had been invoking the development, under Charles Stewart Parnell, of a national movement involving the Land League, the Irish Parliamentary party and elements of the Fenian movement in Ireland and the United States. However, I am afraid I had taken for granted a knowledge of history which did not exist among many of my listeners or those who read reports of my speech, and I had not elaborated, so only three or four people made reference to it afterwards. I had not yet learned that for a message to be understood and remembered it was necessary to repeat it nearly *ad nauseum* and to brief political correspondents and other opinion-formers. Nonetheless, I had already illustrated what I meant by 'weapons in the arsenal of non-violent civil disobedience' by my activity in Caledon, and my proposal to John and Michael for a civil rights march was yet another illustration.

They were enthusiastic and we explored in some detail how it should be implemented. We decided that the broadest spectrum of opinion as possible should be mobilised. It was Michael who suggested that, since discrimination in housing was a central abuse and was topical post-Caledon, we should carry out a housing survey and involve as many in this work as possible. Housing statistics were Michael's forte so we knew the necessary research could and would be done, but the involvement of others would both spread the workload and give the survey greater credibility. In the end, the survey was carried out by a group consisting of me, as Chairman, John Donaghy and Michael McLoughlin (Independent Councillors), Jack Hassard (Northern Ireland Labour Councillor) and Tommy O'Connor and Brian Quinn (Tyrone Republican Clubs). The survey, which was completed on 8 August and published in the *Irish News*, provided an up-to-date picture of housing allocations in the Dungannon area, which buttressed the allegations of discrimination.

On Saturday, 27 July, Michael McLoughlin and I travelled to Maghera, County Derry, to meet members of the NICRA executive. We travelled in Michael's car, a Hillman Minx, registration number 2009 HZ. This was the first of many journeys in that vehicle to marches, meetings and demonstrations, to such an extent we began to call it 'the staff car'. The meeting in Maghera had been arranged by Dr Conn McCluskey and Fred Heatley, members of the NICRA executive. The proposal I put was a simple one: we intended to organise a march, before the end of August, between Coalisland and Dungannon, a distance of four miles, ending with a rally in the Square in Dungannon, and we would be describing it as a civil rights march. We would look after the organisation of the march locally and would provide stewards to ensure it was properly marshalled and non-violent. We were going to do this anyway, but we would prefer to do it under the auspices of NICRA and under their banner. We appreciated that our proposal represented a considerable departure from the way NICRA had been operating up to then and was a radical change of direction, but we believed it was time for such a change in the aftermath of Caledon.

It was clear from the questions and comments that there were mixed feelings among members of the executive and reservations were expressed, particularly by Betty Sinclair, a member of the Communist party, who was Chairperson of NICRA. She felt that the proposal was too radical a change from the role envisaged for NICRA when it was established. But when Michael and I withdrew to allow them to discuss it amongst themselves, we were confident of the result. The march was scheduled for Saturday, 24 August, the date we had requested.

(Incidentally, the meeting had been held in the house of Kevin Agnew, Chairperson of the Republican Clubs and a member of the NICRA executive. This was the same Kevin Agnew who, at a selection convention in Omagh four years earlier, had advocated a policy of abstentionism by saying he would prefer to see the children of Cookstown and Magherafelt running around starving and naked under the Tricolour than see them well-fed and clothed under the Union Jack. He showed Michael and me around his magnificent house, particularly his private oratory where, he said, he prayed every day. It was clear to us that no one belonging to him would ever run around starving and naked under any flag!)

The preparations for the march were coordinated locally by the same team that had carried out the housing survey, with me again acting as Chairman. We were determined to do everything above board, and so the RUC was informed of the route well before the time legally required.

We had no idea how many might participate in the march. The *Irish News* was predicting 30,000, but there was no precedent. We were determined that the march would be disciplined, dignified and orderly, and at the crowded public meeting in St Patrick's Hall, Coalisland, on the Wednesday night before the march, we received a boost from the attendance of Fr Austin Eustace, the senior curate in Dungannon parish. Fr Eustace was no ordinary priest. He had shown his commitment to social and economic as well as political justice by creating a local agriculture co-op, a housing association and a credit union, and he had denounced the local councils for discrimination in planning. Fr Eustace told the meeting: 'the powers-that-be must realise that as long as the dictates of social and distributive justice are being deliberately flouted by those people acting in their name and in virtue of their authority, so long will the present unrest grow in intensity, not only in Dungannon but throughout the Province.'

Most of the meeting focussed on the creation of a body of stewards to ensure that discipline and good order would be preserved at all times. There was comment afterwards that a number of the stewards were republicans. That was inevitable. The march would not have been representative of the area if this had not been the case. It should be remembered, too, that this was prior to the split in the republican movement, at a time when 'the Armed Struggle' had been abandoned and the emphasis was on non-violent agitation. Equally, there were quite a number who were clearly not republican, for example, nationalists and AOH, individual GAA members and men who did not belong to any organisation. The meeting decided that armbands would be necessary to distinguish the stewards and Pat Hughes was given the job of providing them. He approached Jim 'the tailor' Morgan and for two shillings each forty-seven armbands were made for a total outlay of £4/14s. We got very good value for when, after the Derry march, there was renewed appreciation of the need for effective stewarding, the Coalisland stewards and their armbands were welcome, and sometimes very necessary, features of other marches.

On the evening before the march a second meeting was held in St Patrick's Hall to brief the stewards, and afterwards John, Michael and I returned to my home at about a quarter to midnight. Annita was not there as she was expecting our first child and due to complications she was in hospital for observation. As we came through the door the telephone was ringing. It was Det. Sgt Harry McCrum of the RUC Special Branch in Dungannon, asking if he and a colleague could visit me. The 'colleague' turned out to be the top RUC man in Dungannon, District Inspector Ivan Sterritt, and the purpose of the unexpected midnight visit was to inform us that that day's march was banned from entering the Square in Dungannon and would instead be diverted to Ann

Street, in the Catholic end of the town. The DI duly served each of us with a document to this effect, which also stated that he had 'reasonable grounds for apprehending that the entry of that procession into certain parts of the town of Dungannon may occasion a breach of the peace or serious public disorder.' The DI informed us that a counter-demonstration was being organised by the Ulster Protestant volunteers in the Square, and a large crowd of Paisleyites was expected to be bussed in from Armagh and other areas of Tyrone and, as a result, he had no alternative but to re-route our march away from the Square.

John, Michael and I took a hard line. A civil rights march was non-sectarian and we were not going to besmirch it by diverting it into the Catholic ghetto. We had complied with regulations and cooperated with the RUC from the outset. No objection had been raised until now, the very day of the march. The counter-demonstration organisers had not complied with the law, yet their demonstration was to be allowed in the Square and ours diverted. It was the responsibility of the RUC to ensure that the lawful march was allowed and its participants protected. Our arguments were all to no avail. The decision to re-route had been taken and that was that.

As the argument raged, the phone rang. It was a nurse at the hospital. Annita's complications had become more serious: did they have my permission to carry out whatever medical intervention might prove necessary? Suddenly the right of access to Dungannon Square seemed of less importance. I got rid of the RUC and my two colleagues as quickly as possible and spent a sleepless night until the phone rang again. Congratulations! I had a baby daughter and she – though premature and in an incubator – and her mother were fine. The media, looking for comments on the re-route, had to wait as I visited my wife and new daughter. And thus was a precedent established: all my children, five in all, were born on occasions of political crisis. My first was named Estelle. She might have been Marcia!

The RUC diversion was not the only problem. Three days before the march the Soviet Union invaded Czechoslovakia. Since a major purpose of the march was to attract British and international media attention to civil rights abuses in Northern Ireland, the invasion was a major setback: the presence of Russian tanks on the streets of Prague was of more interest to the media than anything that was likely to happen in Coalisland or Dungannon. When criticism was levelled at the civil rights movement on the basis that communists like Betty Sinclair were on the executive, I often retorted that if communist influence had been as great as was alleged, the Russians should have told us of their intentions.

Not unexpectedly the march was late leaving Coalisland; there is time and there is Coalisland time. We were pleased with the turnout, however. The media, as is always the case when calculating numbers at public demonstrations, estimated between 5000 and 15,000. I thought about 7,000, although John Taylor, according to the local unionist paper, had counted just 580 marchers!

We left Coalisland preceded by the Coalisland Silver Band, with two other bands, Clonoe Pipe Band and Carnan AOH, also participating. I was at the front along with a number of MPs, including Eddie McAteer, Gerry Fitt, James O'Reilly and Eddie Richardson, and Stormont Senators Gerry Lennon, Patrick McGill and Paud Mallon and members of NICRA executive, including Betty Sinclair, Frank Gogarty, Conn McCluskey, Kevin Agnew, Fred Heatley and Derek Peters. Only the blue NICRA banner, newly made for the occasion, was allowed to be carried. The Belfast Young Socialists tried to dispute this ruling, and as a result the removal of their banner became the first symbol of the stewards' determination. There were hundreds of placards, most of them testifying to the hard work of Jim McGarvey and his wife, Margaret, and Denis Haughey.

I was reassured to see a large turnout from the Nationalist party. Two days after Caledon I had proposed a motion at the Nationalist party conference, which had been tabled some time in advance, advocating 'a policy of non-violent civil disobedience to wreck a system which has at its basis, a deliberate policy of denying equal treatment and equal opportunity for all'. The conference had supported my action in Caledon, but had declined to support the motion, preferring to ask the executive committee to study the implications and report back to a Special Conference within six months. This had been generally interpreted as a setback for me, so I was pleased to see such widespread support within the party for this particular form of extra-parliamentary activity.

About a mile from Coalisland, at Gilmore's Crossroads, the RUC stopped the march to serve the leaders with the Diversion Order already served on Michael, John and me. Service was refused, with Gerry Fitt responding, 'take that pornographic literature out of my sight'.

It was a pleasant late August evening and despite the tension caused by the RUC presence and the knowledge that a confrontation was likely to occur, our spirits were high and the band music helped the marching, most of it uphill. Bernadette Devlin wrote about the march in *The Price of my Soul* in such terms as to make me wonder whether she had actually been in attendance at all. According to her version, men 'dropped in at every pub along the way' and 'drunk men [were] lolloping in and out'. There was only one pub on the road between Coalisland and Dungannon, and Willie Campbell's Ye Olde Stagger Inn was closed. I know this for certain because Derek Peters, a Communist member of the NICRA executive, was walking beside me and was forced to depart the march in some discomfort to answer the call of nature. He went to the pub, but it was closed and he returned to the march having had to make alternative arrangements. More importantly, Devlin's allegation that the crowd roared in support of the IRA was untrue: it simply did not happen.

On the outskirts of Dungannon we were met by the town's Brass and Reed Band, led by Paddy Hughes, his stiff back, as he led us up the hill towards the hospital corner and confrontation with the RUC, seeming to symbolise our determination. The band peeled off to the left as we approached the RUC, lined across the road with two police tenders and a rope stretched in front of them. The lorry that had travelled from Coalisland with us, equipped with a PR system for the dual purpose of acting as a platform and as a command post for the stewards, was driven to the front and the stewards ran forward to link arms and prevent a confrontation.

On the other side of the police cordon a crowd of extreme Protestants had been allowed to congregate, estimated at about 1,500 in number. Some of these people sang 'The Sash' and chanted sectarian slogans. It was irresponsible of the RUC to allow this crowd to assemble so close to the line of our march, a march that was, after all, legal, while the crowd which had congregated in opposition to it had no legal approval.

In August 1969 the Cameron Commission, which had been established the previous March by the government to investigate the reasons for and nature of 'disturbances' in Northern Ireland, commented as follows on the Coalisland–Dungannon march:

'After the march had been announced at the end of July the police originally raised no objection in principle. The route was to be from Coalisland to Market Square, Dungannon. However there was soon a move in extreme Unionist circles to oppose the march on the grounds that Market Square was unionist territory. Senator Stewart (Chairman of the Urban Council and a prominent resident) told police that there would be trouble if the march entered the Square and proposed a reroute by Quarry Lane to Ann Street. Mr John Taylor MP also told the police that there would be trouble if the procession entered the Square. We think it to be inferred from their own evidence that whether these local unionist leaders would have organised, they at least would not have discouraged the organisation of a counter-demonstration if the march had been allowed to enter Market Square. Such a counter-demonstration, if organised, would almost certainly have led to an outbreak of violence as persons occupying positions of such public responsibility cannot have failed to appreciate. Faced with these representations the police decided that the threat of counter-demonstrations should be taken seriously, the more so as the Ulster Protestant Volunteers advertised a public meeting to be held in the Market Square on the evening of the 24th August.'

In the tense atmosphere, with the RUC blocking the road in order to force us down the Quarry Lane and the Paisleyite crowd baying for blood behind them, there were some irresponsibles who wished to force their way through. The group of Young Socialists from Belfast, who had already caused a problem by attempting to carry their own banner, now had to be prevented by the stewards from engaging in confrontation with the police. A statement issued afterwards in the name of their secretary, David A Graham, condemned the speakers 'who without exception accepted the police decision instead of continuing with the march. Had they not sold their principles and continued leading the parade into Dungannon, something could have been achieved in the name of civil rights.' Clearly some people still had a lot to learn about non-violent protest. The necessity for stewards to maintain discipline was underlined.

Gerry Fitt and I both spoke, as did Betty Sinclair and Jack Hassard NILP, member of Dungannon Urban Council, and Erskine Holmes of the Northern Ireland Labour party and Joe McCann of the NDP. *Cameron* was later critical of Gerry for a reference to 'black bastards' in relation to the RUC. He drew parallels with what had happened in Prague during the week, and from the height of the lorry I said I could identify with Jack Kennedy and his feelings when he looked across the Berlin Wall. Notwithstanding such strong statements, our theme was strongly that of non-violent resistance in the face of provocation, and apart from the Young Socialists the meeting passed off peacefully. Betty Sinclair, as Chairperson, concluded by leading us in singing, 'We Shall Overcome', the first time, to my knowledge, that the American civil rights anthem had been sung on any public platform in Northern Ireland. It was significant that the editorial in the next day's issue of the *Irish News* was headed, 'We Shall Overcome': the message was getting through.

The Cameron Commission would conclude that, 'It is significant that the first civil rights march, unaccompanied by any provocative display of weapons, banners or symbols, was carried out without any breach of the peace. It attracted considerable public attention and was also regarded as proof in certain circles that many elements in the society of Northern Ireland whose ultimate political purpose differed in very marked degree could co-operate in peaceful and lawful demonstration in favour of certain common and limited objectives.'

With the singing of 'We Shall Overcome' the crowd began to disperse and a number of us were invited to the McCluskey home nearby. It was an appropriate place to gather and discuss the day's events in view of the part Conn and Patricia had played in bringing about this day. It was a happy and hopeful gathering: we felt we had made history. Despite extreme provocation by the Paisleyites, the arrogance of the unionist public representatives and the partiality of the RUC, it had been non-violent, no small achievement and one to be proud of. Granted, the lack of international media coverage was a disappointment. If only the Russians had stayed at home ... Still, it would be different in Derry.

In the run-up to the Coalisland march I had found myself back in Caledon, this time in the courthouse. The day the summons was delivered I arrived home to find Annita in tears. 'I never thought I'd be married to a jailbird,' she sobbed. In the months and years ahead, she got used to the idea.

When I arrived at the courthouse I was pleased to see a number of people with placards bearing supportive messages, such as 'Dungannon RDC in dock' and 'Convict Dungannon RDC'. Members of the picket included Tommy O'Connor, Chairman of Tyrone Republican Clubs. Tommy, whom I had known at the Academy and got to know better when I invited him to join the housing study afterwards, later told me that local republicans in Tyrone got a ticking-off from Sinn Féin headquarters in Dublin for allowing me to make the running and get publicity on an issue republicans should have been leading. That day outside Caledon courthouse was the first I heard of the existence of a Republican Club in Brantry, near Caledon. In recent times, with the attempted rewriting of history which has coincided with the provisional republican movement attempting to claim ownership of the peace process, the Brantry Republican Club has been given credit for the Caledon squatting. That is a distortion of history.

The court case was valuable publicity and it served to remind people of what the civil rights movement was about. The evidence helped to clarify certain issues which had been disputed, particularly the statement of John Taylor, which I had described in Stormont as 'a damned lie'. Senator Gerry Lennon was the solicitor representing me, Patsy Gildernew and Joe Campbell. He was a very experienced lawyer, but was also adept at bringing out points he knew to be politically important. When Emily Beattie's brother, the RUC officer, said the house had been allocated to the Beattie family and not just to his sister, Gerry was able to expose it as the attempted cover-up it was by producing the original application. He then went on to suggest that Constable Beattie would have been an illegal sub-tenant had he, in fact, taken up residence in the house.

I wasn't even called to give evidence. The magistrate dismissed the case and awarded costs on the basis that, while we had undoubtedly trespassed and did not deny that fact, we were making a political protest and did not intend to remain permanently in the house. Therefore, the Act under which we had been charged did not apply. Our celebrations did not last long, however. The government was determined to have its pound of flesh and appealed to the High Court via the 'case stated' procedure. There, the case was heard before three judges who decided that the local magistrate in Caledon had erred in law and instructed that the case be returned to him for conviction. The worrying thing to me was not the order to convict, which in the circumstances was not unexpected, but the awarding of costs against us. Gerry Lennon and his legal team did not present a bill, but the government lawyers did and it was a hefty imposition on a full-time politician with a wife and child. My fellow convicts did not offer to pay, and I felt I could not ask them to do so.

There was a lighter side to this development. We duly appeared in Caledon courthouse, with attendant publicity. The magistrate stated he was left with no alternative but to convict, and fined us a derisory £5 each. As I left the courthouse I was, of course, asked for my reaction. My comment took into consideration the events that had occurred since the squatting, which included the civil rights marches, the abolition of Derry Corporation, the sacking of Bill Craig, the imposition of a points system for the allocation of housing and exposure around the world of discriminatory practices. I was told later that, in preparation for the evening bulletin, the BBC reporter was rehearsing what he would say on air: 'Mr Austin Currie, twenty-eight-year-old MP for East Tyrone, on leaving Caledon courthouse after being fined five pounds for entering a house occupied by a nineteen-year-old girl said, "It was the best fiver's worth I ever got".' The bulletin did not go out in that form.

11: DEMONSTRATIONS AND COUNTER-DEMONSTRATIONS

I do not know whether I was ever officially co-opted to the executive of NICRA, but after the Coalisland–Dungannon march I became a regular at executive meetings. It had been announced in Dungannon that the next civil rights March would be in Derry, but it soon transpired that due to local differences the march might not be as easy to organise as anticipated. The militants in Derry were in the Derry Housing Action Committee, which had been active in organising squats and sit-ins. One activist in the organisation was Eamon McCann, known to me from our time at Queen's as an extremely able debater in the Literific and a member of the Northern Ireland Labour party. But his views appeared to me to be closer to Trotsky than members of the rather staid Labour party would have liked.

I deliberately kept out of Derry and did not accompany Conn McCluskey, John Donaghy and Michael McLoughlin when they visited the city prior to the march. My relationship with Eddie McAteer was not sufficiently good to risk allegations of interference in his city. I was, however, kept updated by my Dungannon colleagues, on the local tensions in Derry and the lack of local unity, the presence of which had contributed so much to the success of the Dungannon march.

The fact is that the NICRA executive never had a controlling influence over the civil rights campaign. The major decisions were taken locally, as had been the case in relation to the first march. The strength of the movement lay in the local organisation and much of it was built on individuals who had come through the Eleven-Plus process, particularly teachers. Many of the same people would, at a later stage, form the nucleus of the SDLP.

Annita and I spent the week before 5 October in Birmingham, where three of my uncles lived. There, by appointment, I met Mary Holland of the *Observer*, who travelled from London to meet me. She intended being in Derry for the march and I briefed her on the situation. Her reports from Derry, and then on Northern Ireland generally, in the influential *Observer* newspaper made considerable impact on decisions taken in Britain.

We had an enjoyable week in Birmingham and it was with some reluctance, and despite efforts by my relatives to get us to stay on longer, that we caught the early morning flight back to Belfast on Saturday, 5 October. I dropped Annita off at her parents' home in Omagh and then I proceeded to Derry with Michael McLoughlin and John Donaghy. I don't need to elaborate in detail on the events in Derry that day. It has gone down in history and was well recorded in the media, particularly the Telefís Éireann film that was broadcast around the world.

I was disappointed when we arrived at the starting point, at Waterside Railway Station, because the crowd was far below expectations. Nor was there any sign of stewards. The Minister for Home Affairs, Bill Craig, had banned all marches and processions east of the River Foyle, or within the city's walls, citing likely confrontation with a counter-demonstration by the Apprentice Boys. The latter was an entirely bogus assertion, made for the purpose of having the civil rights march banned. I thought to myself, as I looked at the small turnout, that if Craig had not intervened the attendance would have been very small indeed. Craig's decision was deeply resented by Derry nationalists with the result that the attendance was added to by people who would not have identified with the organisers had the ban not been imposed. Unlike the Coalisland march, the organisers here, who were mostly left-wing or republican, were representative of only a minority of Derry Catholics.

Eddie McAteer and his main lieutenants in Derry were there. Gerry Fitt had worked hard to secure the attendance of three Westminster Labour MPs, Anne Kerr, Russell Kerr and John Ryan, and local and foreign media was well represented.

Betty Sinclair and other members of NICRA had not arrived by the appointed time and the crowd swelled slightly in number. The RUC then announced, by loudhailer, that any march would be in contravention of the Ministerial Order and, ominously, that women and children should leave the scene. It was clear that the RUC meant business. Furthermore, the trouble some of the organisers took to ensure that Eddie McAteer, Gerry Fitt and I were in the front row indicated to me that they knew the RUC meant business. But what sort of business? I soon found out. The march started off, but the road ahead was blocked by two police tenders with RUC personnel standing in front of and between them. I couldn't see any way of getting through, so I assumed that we would process as far as we could and then there would be a stand-off. Suddenly, the policeman in front of me had a baton in his hand and was moving forward. I ducked and felt a blow on my shoulder that was presumably aimed at my head. The Telefís Éireann film shows me, with my hand up to protect my head, actually getting through the police cordon and then coming back again. After being hit I had just kept going until stopped by a tender, and then came back to rejoin the marchers from the other side. I was extremely lucky not to be clobbered again, but I preferred that chance to being caught on my own between the tenders and the police. All was, of course, utter confusion at this stage, but I did see Gerry Fitt with blood running down his face being half carried away.

The organisers appeared not to have made any contingency plans. People were milling around not knowing what to do. Unlike Dungannon, there was no mobile platform and no instructions were being given that I could hear. Eventually a chair was produced and a number of us spoke. All of the speeches were angry, particularly when we heard that Gerry had been taken to hospital, but no one was irresponsible enough to suggest taking on the RUC. The speeches ended with Betty Sinclair advising people to go home. I was expecting us to conclude with 'We Shall Overcome' when people started shouting that the police were attacking again. I couldn't believe what then happened. A number of police came running with batons drawn, striking at anyone in their way. I joined the others who were retreating as quickly as possible, only to find there was no escape: the RUC had blocked the exit. One policeman, whom I was later to meet in another confrontation in Irish Street in Dungannon, seemed to take a personal interest in my welfare and came at me with raised baton. Ivan Cooper got in the way and, to my relief, he followed him – maybe he disliked 'turncoats' more than Fenians! Somehow or other I got away from the action and was huddled in a shop doorway when the water cannon was brought into action. The water was not only wet, it smelled.

Back in Omagh, at my in-laws' house, John, Michael and I were received with relief as news of the confrontation was already on radio and TV. Annita echoed my sentiments when she said, 'Thanks be to God we came home from Birmingham.'

The news on television that night, and every news bulletin over the weekend, showed the extent of the violence inflicted by the RUC. Two characters stood out: County Inspector Meharg with his blackthorn stick striking a protester while he lay on the ground, and a marcher appealing for restraint and then doubling up with pain as an RUC man drove his baton into his stomach. I recognised the victim as Paddy Douglas, a neighbour in Donaghmore, and the following day visited him at his home. His wife told me the family doctor had seen him and he was in bed. I was shown to the bedroom and entered with some trepidation, unsure as to what sight would greet me. I need not have worried. He had seen the film and was in great form; I wondered whether to commiserate or congratulate.

In one afternoon the whole political situation in Northern Ireland was transformed and 'a terrible beauty was born'. The actions of the RUC created a Catherine wheel out of a damp squib. Because of the brutality of the RUC and its exposure on TV and in the Press, a small (probably numbering 400 marchers, at most), badly organised and relatively undisciplined demonstration became the instrument that would help destroy monolithic unionism.

The 'paper wall' I had been complaining about even before my election, and which had sheltered unionism from adverse publicity about its 'un-British' practices, was well and truly breached. Harold Wilson could say to Unionists in the House of Commons, 'I saw it myself on TV'. *The Times* and *Manchester Guardian* called for inquiries into Bill Craig's handling of the Derry march, and comparisons were made with the brutality of the Chicago police, under Mayor Daley, outside the Democratic Convention a month earlier. In a number of interviews given outside his house and on the BBC's 'The World this Weekend' programme, Bill Craig was so inept and blustering that some listeners came to the conclusion he had been drinking.

The good publicity continued for weeks as the civil rights campaign was judged to have been reasonable and responsible. In Derry there was rioting in the aftermath of the march but this was seen largely as a result of the RUC's overreaction. As civil rights activity in the city came under the control of the Derry Citizens Action Committee and John Hume and Ivan Cooper came to prominence, unionist allegations of Communist and IRA control were seen to be bogus. Students at Queen's, organised as People's Democracy (PD), attempted to march from the university to Belfast City Hall and were seen as reasonable and responsible in contrast to Paisley and his followers, who organised counter-demonstrations and threatened, and in some instances used, violence against them.

Civil rights branches mushroomed in many areas, and I found myself much in demand as a speaker at meetings and on TV and radio. The other leaders and I found ourselves as likely to be interviewed by David Frost, or William Hardcastle, or some anchorman from CBS as by Billy Flackes of BBC Northern Ireland, or Mike Burns of Radio Éireann. Those were wonderful days of progress on the political front, which I will recount later, of popularity, enthusiasm, standing ovations, even of euphoria. And also of the heightened sensitivity which comes from an awareness of personal danger.

Dungannon continued to be a centre of confrontation with extreme Protestants. On 23 November a group from People's Democracy decided to visit the town to hold a meeting in the Dunowen Restaurant in the Square. They did so without informing anyone locally of their intentions, with the result that when they started to announce their arrival over a PA system in the Square, a Protestant crowd soon gathered to protect the Holy of Holies (ie, the Square) from defilement. Some PD supporters were attacked and the Dunowen Restaurant was badly damaged. Councillor Jack Hassard, who worked in the post office in the Square, came under attack. Despite the lack of prior notice I was soon on the scene demanding protection, but the RUC could truthfully say they had no prior warning.

On 30 November a civil rights march took place in Armagh that exposed, to anyone who could have doubted it, the malign influence of Ian Paisley and the threat he represented to any hope for peaceful change in Northern Ireland. I had attended the meeting that had established a civil rights branch in Armagh, and I was confident that the proposed inaugural march would be well-organised and properly stewarded. To make absolutely sure, the Armagh organisers requested the support of the Coalisland/Dungannon stewards and their armbands, which was readily given.

We gathered for the journey to Armagh, but there was an item of unfinished business to be dealt with before we left Dungannon. The nationalist community in Dungannon had never accepted that the Square was a no-go area for them, and so before we departed for Armagh, without any prior notification, a meeting was held in the Square at which I and others asserted our right to hold meetings there. Honour having been satisfied, we then proceeded, without any trouble, to Armagh.

At Armagh we found a disgraceful and frightening situation. During the night Paisley and his followers, many of whom were armed with clubs and cudgels, including Paisley himself who carried a blackthorn stick, had taken over the centre of the town. At roadblocks on the outskirts, police had seized two revolvers as well as over two hundred weapons, such as billhooks and scythes. There was clearly a serious possibility that some of those who had taken over the city centre, including part of the proposed march route, might be carrying firearms.

That day, Armagh provided a powerful symbol of what was at stake. On the one hand, a peaceful civil rights march, the route of which had been agreed with the RUC and which did not propose to process along disputed or contentious territory, not carrying any provocative banners or flags, displaying only the single 'civil rights' banner, with marshals on both sides of the marchers clearly identified by their armbands, and the whole assembly marching for reasons which were certainly not revolutionary, demanding equality rather than proposing inferior status for any section of the community. On the other hand, a crowd, more a mob than demonstrators, whose proposed route, deliberately selected for confrontation, was, in the words of the Cameron Commission, 'provocative in the extreme', a large element of which were armed and determined on violence, and motivated perhaps to some extent by fear, but certainly by bigotry, and displaying many of the characteristics of Fascism.

I had earlier in the year described Paisley as 'a bigoted hangover from the seventeenth century'. On this occasion, he was determined on a trial of strength not only with the civil rights movement but also with the government, and on the level of stopping the march and defying the RUC and the government he was indeed successful. He manipulated a situation where the two crowds were less than one hundred yards apart and we had no alternative but to stop, or face the inevitability of a bloody confrontation and possible injuries, or even deaths.

Of course the RUC should never have allowed the situation to get to that stage. They had ample warning and evidence of Paisley's intentions. Posters distributed in Armagh in the days prior to the march had warned residents to move women and children out of the city on the day of the march and to board up their windows. If action had been taken in time against those clearly intent on violence against legal and approved marchers, then the situation would not have developed to the extent that the RUC had no alternative but to stop the civil rights march. It was a defeat for the RUC, and therefore for the government.

Despite the fact that the march had to be aborted, it was still a victory for the civil rights movement. In very stressful and tense circumstances, in the face of intense provocation, discipline had been held and the commitment to non-violence underlined. And, of course, the raw reality of Northern Ireland politics, the very thing we were campaigning against, had been exposed for all to see. Paisley had sought to intimidate us. He had not succeeded. I was not the only one who asked the question, 'What would life be like for us if Paisley and his ilk were allowed to dominate?' We had to stand up to them. We left Armagh a bit shaken, but with greater confidence and determination. We were not to know, but that Armagh demonstration would turn out to be the high-water mark of civil rights demonstrations.

The next confrontation was on the night of 4 December when a meeting was held in St Patrick's Hall, Dungannon, to elect a civil rights committee. John Hume and I were the main speakers and when we arrived we were given a standing ovation that went on for at least five minutes – a first for both of us. We took the opportunity of spelling out the non-violent message, quoting Ghandi, Martin Luther King and Terence MacSwiney, insisting that it was not only the right and moral way forward but the only way forward. The unionists knew how to deal with violence, they had successfully combatted it before and had the power of the State to do it, but they did not know how to handle non-violence, particularly when we were demanding the rights to which we were entitled as British citizens. Never was the message more strongly put over or more enthusiastically received as that night in Dungannon. We emerged full of hope and confidence and goodwill, and stood face to face with the reality of Northern politics: hundreds of Paisleyites in the Square, howling for our blood, and a police force that had allowed them to congregate and was not prepared to protect us. A number of shots were fired from the unionist crowd, some of whom were off-duty B specials, and Jack Hassard's car was attacked when he attempted to drive through the Square.

By this stage the civil rights movement was almost a mass movement. Most towns with a sizeable Catholic population had a civil rights branch. However the speed of development outstripped the capacity of NICRA to exercise control over the branches, there was no card-bearing membership as such and the NICRA executive had difficulty coordinating activities. It is hard to maintain unity in any mass movement, and the weakness of the central executive compounded the problem. In addition, there were faultlines that, under pressure, would inevitably widen, which they did, and quite soon thereafter.

It was inevitable too that as the Unionist government was forced to respond to the increasing pressure from the British government to introduce reforms, individuals and groups within the broad civil rights movement would respond in different ways.

On 14 November, Harold Wilson met O'Neill, Faulkner and Craig in Downing Street, and on 22 November the Stormont government issued a five-point reform programme, which, had it been announced three months earlier, would have forestalled the need for a civil rights campaign. The five points were:

1. A fairer system for the allocation of council houses;

2. The appointment of an Ombudsman;

3. The replacement of Derry Corporation by a Commission;

4. The ending of the Special Powers Act, as soon as the security situation allowed;

5. The ending of the company vote for elections.

However, in the new circumstances that prevailed since 5 October, these were minimal concessions and pointedly did not promise 'one man, one vote'. While we welcomed the proposed reforms as a step in the right direction, many of us attacked it as being 'too little, too late'. As the Armagh march eight days later illustrated, the concessions did not reduce the need for civil rights pressure, indeed, in my opinion, the evidence of progress, even if limited, reinforced the argument for keeping up the pressure.

Then, on 9 December, O'Neill made his 'Crossroads' speech, appealing to the public over the heads of those in his party, including members of his Cabinet, who were opposed to any concessions. He posed the question, 'What kind of Ulster do you want? A happy and respected province in good standing with the rest of the United Kingdom, or a place continually torn apart by riots and demonstrations and regarded by the rest of Britain as a political outcast?' I remember watching the broadcast and thinking that the very articulation of these questions confirmed the success of the civil rights movement. Wasn't this precisely what Paul Rose had meant when he had given me advice on how to proceed in January of the previous year? And wasn't this exactly what I had been aiming for when squatting in Caledon and initiating the first civil rights march?

O'Neill's speech, supported by a *Belfast Telegraph* campaign of endorsement, made a big impact on public opinion. In an end-of-year poll, the *Sunday Independent* made him 'Man of the Year'. The success of O'Neill's speech encouraged him to sack Bill Craig two days after its delivery. By the end of 1968, O'Neill appeared to be in a strong position and the great majority of those involved in civil rights, myself included, were prepared, warily, to give him a breathing space.

A small minority was not of this mind, however. The PDs decided to organise a 'Selma to Alabama' march and chose an itinerary from Belfast to Derry that was, in Northern Ireland terms, the nearest equivalent to the Deep South. The experience of Armagh in November was ignored and the small group started off through the 'enemy territory', depending on the RUC for protection and without even rudimentary safeguards, such as a body of stewards, or any arrangements for resting and sleeping in safe areas. It was dangerous and irresponsible. It was also a two-fingered gesture to NICRA and the rest of the civil rights movement. The marchers were ambushed at Burntollet Bridge, in circumstances where some of them might have been killed, by a mob including a good number of off-duty B men. To make matters worse there were strong reasons to believe that elements in the RUC may have colluded in leading the marchers into a trap. There was, of course, gathering support and sympathy for the courage and suffering of the mostly young students, whatever might have been thought of their leadership. So by the time they reached Derry they were treated like heroes and welcomed even by those who had initially condemned them.

The Cameron Commission later commented:

'For moderates this march had disastrous effects. It polarised the extreme elements in the communities in each place it entered. It lost sympathy for the civil rights movement and led to serious rioting in Maghera and Londonderry. It divided the civil rights movement and weakened the Derry Citizens Action Committee. We are driven to think that the leaders must have intended that their ventures would weaken the moderate reforming forces in Northern Ireland. We think that their object was to increase tension so that, in the process, a more radical programme could be realised.'

They certainly succeeded in increasing tension, but, like the Paisleyites in Armagh, while they rejoiced at their short-term success, their long-term objectives were harmed. The behaviour of the PD, their increasing emphasis on demands which were not part of the mainstream civil rights programme and their determination to be the tail wagging the movement led many to question the usefulness of further marches. The marches were, after all, a tactic employed primarily to force political change by exerting pressure on the British government and, through them, on the Stormont government. They had been successful in this aim, as O'Neill was now admitting. For those of us who were asking this question, the march in Newry, within a week of Burntollet, gave the answer.

The violence in Newry was all the more shocking for being unexpected. There was controversy over a re-route, but it appeared a compromise had been worked out between the organisers and the RUC. There appeared to be adequate numbers of stewards, including a contingent from Coalisland/Dungannon. However, the organisation was completely inadequate and there was no central control, not even a PA system. The march degenerated into a riot despite the best efforts of the stewards and speakers like John Hume, Michael Farrell and me. Five police tenders were burned or pushed into the canal. I watched with amazement as one professional man from Dungannon beat at the police tender with his rolled umbrella, his face contorted in hate. It was a bad day for the civil rights movement. I could only wonder, along with Gerry Fitt when he said, 'The government was well aware that the eyes of the world, through press and television, were focused on these incidents, and the police, far from taking any action to prevent what happened, appeared to condone the burning of their vehicles.'

There were further civil rights marches and demonstrations, but after Newry there was no longer the same confidence that non-violence could be ensured and control maintained over the more extreme elements. There were marches in Omagh in April and in Strabane in June, and a number of other, smaller marches and demonstrations in Fermanagh and other places in protest against more localised grievances. Bob Purdie, in *Politics of the Streets*, calculated that between the end of January and the end of July there were ten occasions on which civil rights activities led to trouble, and twenty-one such demonstrations which passed off entirely peacefully. However, some of these demonstrations showed the increasing disunity within the movement, particularly at Strabane on 29 June. It was a period when the political landscape was changing dramatically, and the pace of that change accelerated when Terence O'Neill called a general election for 24 February 1969.

12: CONSPIRACY AND CONTROVERSY

The period between Caledon in June 1968 and the fall of the Power-Sharing Executive in May 1974 was the most satisfying and fulfilling in my whole political career. Things were happening and I was helping to make them happen. Changes took place that, only a few weeks earlier, had seemed unlikely, if not impossible. Within just a few months, the civil rights movement had achieved what had proved impossible for conventional politics to achieve over a period of almost fifty years.

My frustration and impotence as a member at Stormont prior to Caledon gave me great sympathy for my predecessors, like Joe Devlin, Cahir Healy and Joe Stewart, trying so hard to represent their people in a system where unionism was unassailable, and for Eddie McAteer for whom opportunity had come too late. Year after year these men had protested against housing allocation abuses and had demanded a fair points system. Within six weeks of the Derry march the new system for the allocation of houses was granted, and that was only the beginning.

These were also stressful and dangerous years when, on a number of occasions, I was lucky to survive. The same is true of those close to me, my wife and children, father and mother, brothers and sisters and members of their families. It was only afterwards that I learned of the suffering endured by some of them, and I am sure I still do not know the whole of it.

The Stormont general election of 1969 was the first where there was doubt about the outcome. The Unionist party was split into pro- and anti-O'Neill factions and Terence O'Neill, in the aftermath of his 'Crossroads' speech, was attempting to mobilise moderate support, both Protestant and Catholic. A number of individuals who had risen to prominence through the civil rights movement, particularly John Hume and Ivan Cooper, decided to stand against sitting Nationalist MPs. In a further stirring of the political pot, the People's Democracy, originally based in Queen's University, decided to nominate candidates in a number of constituencies, both unionist-held and nationalist-held.

I might have had an unopposed return, as had happened in the general election of 1965, except for the intervention of the PDs. A constituent,

Thomas R McGurk from Brockagh, on the shore of Lough Neagh, announced his intention to contest the seat. I had no worry about the outcome in view of my prominence, especially since Caledon, and I had been building up a constituency organisation since 1964. McGurk soon realised he was on a hiding to nothing and withdrew, but his intervention had encouraged elements in the Unionist party to hope I might be beaten on a split vote and accordingly they nominated a candidate. My only regret was that in having to defend my own seat, I was prevented from mobilising nationalist support in South Tyrone where John Taylor was being challenged by a moderate, pro-O'Neill candidate.

My nomination as the Nationalist candidate was unanimous. I took the opportunity to present to the delegates firm proposals for the creation of a left-of-centre democratically organised political party, which I committed myself to organising as soon as possible after the election, and this proposal was endorsed by the delegates.

My Unionist opponent was Edmund Curran, a native of Dungannon, who was working as a journalist with the *Belfast Telegraph*. Ed and I had known each other since Queen's and we had a good personal relationship. Politically, he was in an awkward position as he was personally pro-O'Neill in a constituency where the unionist electorate was, at best, equally divided. He sought to overcome this problem by attacking me as an extremist in the hope of mobilising anti-Currie sentiment among unionists and also of attracting support from the more conservative Catholic voters. I was determined not to let him off the hook and all of my speeches contained a challenge to him to come off the fence and declare his allegiance. Tiny Tim had a song in the Top Twenty at the time called 'Tiptoe through the Tulips'. Ed's journalistic colleagues loved my description of him, 'Like Tiny Tim, tiptoeing round the Orange Halls of East Tyrone, fearful of stepping on pro- or anti-O'Neill corns.'

The result was a triumph. I won by 2,564, an increase from 1,296 in 1964, which had been the largest majority ever in East Tyrone. The turnout was 89.9%.

In South Tyrone, John Taylor was returned against Reverend Eakins, an unofficial Unionist, with a slashed majority of 1,150 on a turnout of 83.6%. Had I been free to mobilise nationalist support in the constituency, he might have been defeated. The turnout in East Tyrone was the highest in the entire election and, considering that some unionists did not vote because of the O'Neill controversy, was a considerable tribute to my organisation. Annita had acted as my election agent and had done a superb job. In returning thanks at the count, I caused considerable amusement by remarking that I was possibly the first candidate to admit that I had slept with my agent.

Ed Curran's occupation as a journalist led to increased interest among members of that profession in the election, particularly among the 'Insight' team in the *Sunday Times*, with the result that certain practices, indeed to call them by their proper name, abuses, in relation to Northern Ireland elections came under the investigative microscope. The 'Insight' team focussed on the abuse of postal votes. I will expand on this, and related matters, at a later stage, so all I will say now is that I had succeeded in building up an election machine in East Tyrone that surpassed that of the Unionists in all respects – no mean feat considering the patronage at their disposal and the influence of the Orange Order.

The 'Crossroads' election did not have the result O'Neill had anticipated. Of the thirty-nine Unionist MPs, twenty-four were official (pro-O'Neill) and three were unofficial (pro-O'Neill), while ten were official (anti-O'Neill) and another two official but ambivalent in their attitude to O'Neill. The Prime Minister clearly still had the monkey on his back.

The election, called by O'Neill to sort out his enemies in the Unionist party, had been more successful in sorting out his traditional opponents on the Nationalist benches. John Hume defeated Eddie McAteer; Ivan Cooper defeated Paddy Gormley; and Paddy O'Hanlon, who had also come to prominence through the civil rights movement, displaced Eddie Richardson. I was personally sorry to see the political demise of old colleagues, but encouraged by the fact that the three new MPs were publicly committed to the formation of a new party. The People's Democracy candidates did relatively well, with one of them coming within 224 votes of taking the nationalist seat in South Down. For the future, a significant result was the good showing made by a twenty-one-year-old psychology student called Bernadette Devlin in a contest with the future Prime Minister, James Chichester-Clark. Other important results were Paddy Devlin's defeat of Harry Diamond in Falls, and the election of Paddy Kennedy in Belfast Central to join Gerry Fitt in the Republican Labour party.

For Nationalists, Stormont became, for the first time, an interesting, even on occasions an exciting place to be. I had a feeling I had never had before, that I was participating in something that was meaningful to the entire community. The presence of so many MPs identified with civil rights meant that there was a link between parliamentary and extra-parliamentary activity, although the former had increased in relevance. I was also interested to see how the new MPs would relate to Fitt and me, and what progress could be made towards setting up a new party. The extent of cooperation at Stormont would clearly be one strong indication. The first opportunity arose when the government introduced a Public Order Bill we considered draconian. The result was gratifying: a cohesive and effective opposition could be organised at Stormont level. But in view of traditional party, geographical and personality differences, could this be translated into an organised party in the constituencies?

Events inside and outside Stormont were to distract us from this task for some time. Prior to the election I had accepted an invitation to participate in the St Patrick's Day parade in New York, to appear on a number of TV and radio shows there and to speak at a 'Truth Rally' in the Sunnyside Gardens Arena, organised by the American-Irish Action Committee. This was my first visit to the United States and I was soon to find out, like so many Irish politicians before and after me, that the Irish-American political scene was akin to walking through a minefield, and even comparatively minor political differences at home were magnified across the Atlantic.

It was not a major problem on this occasion, at a time when the civil rights campaign was still on the crest of a wave, but was to cause serious difficulties at a later stage, especially after the Provisional IRA came into existence. But even in March 1969 there were mines to be skirted. For example, I had no hesitation in joining a picket, organised by the Action Committee, at the British Embassy in New York, but demurred when it was suggested we move from there to the Irish Embassy. I had to explain that it was not my policy, or the policy of NICRA, to attack the Irish government, and if events developed in the way I anticipated, the minority in the North would require all the assistance we could get from all quarters.

At the 'Truth Rally' I was the main speaker and was preceded by, among others, Conor Cruise O'Brien, then a Professor at a New York university, but soon to return to Dublin to be elected to the Dáil as a Labour TD. In the course of his speech, Conor praised the civil rights movement in Ireland and declared that anyone who supported that struggle would be a hypocrite if he didn't also support the similar struggle in the United States. About a quarter of the audience walked out. In my speech, parts of which were enthusiastically received, I supported Conor, though in slightly more diplomatic language. Nevertheless, the audience again thinned out.

However, it was a successful occasion overall and I was confident I had managed to explain, to potentially influential Irish-Americans, that there was now a new dimension to the Irish problem, that non-violence was the way forward and that there was a new leadership with which they were invited to identify and to support. At the end of the meeting I was invited to spend the night at the home of the Chairman of the organising committee. There was not even time to stop for a drink to celebrate my endeavours. On the way to his house, travelling on the subway, he told me we had to hurry because his wife would not retire for the night until he was home and the Rosary had been said. So we had a cup of tea, the Rosary was recited and I went to bed – with my tongue hanging out! Still, he seemed a nice old man. I was not to know that Michael J Flannery was to become one of the top Provo supporters in the United States, heading up an organisation, Noraid, that would contribute millions of dollars and give other, more lethal material assistance, which would terminate the lives of hundreds of people in the North.

On my return home I learned that, on the same night as my speech in New York, the opposition in Stormont had staged a sit-down on the floor of the Parliament in protest against the guillotine being imposed on the Public Order Bill debate. Even Vivian Simpson had sat on the floor of the House and joined in the singing of 'We Shall overcome'. It was an early sign of the new militancy and I was sorry to have missed it.

The second item of interest was that the by-election for the Mid-Ulster constituency, caused by the death of George Forrest, was to be held within a month and that a convention to select a candidate to fight the election for the anti-unionist cause was being organised. I had already expressed an interest in the nomination, but my main focus was on Fermanagh–South Tyrone in the general election due the following year, where I felt I would have a better chance and where there was not as much nationalist–republican antipathy as in Mid-Ulster. I was, however, determined to do what I could to ensure that the two constituencies would be cut loose from the abstentionist baggage and I knew my involvement in Mid-Ulster could help to bring this about.

Prior to the Coalisland–Dungannon march, a number of republicans had been involved in the compilation of the Housing Survey that had provided part of the justification for the march, and I had maintained informal contacts with them. I knew from these contacts that there was considerable opposition to the abstentionist policy and to the declared candidature of Kevin Agnew, who would be standing on that policy. Indeed, the very fact that Agnew was a candidate instead of Tom Mitchell, who had held the seat back in 1956 and had contested it in every election since, indicated division in Republican ranks on the issue.

At the beginning of February six prominent Tyrone members, including Tommy O'Connor, who had been a member of the Housing Survey group and a member of the Sinn Féin Árd Comhairle, and Kevin Mallon resigned from Sinn Féin. In a statement they said, 'We are convinced of the immediate necessity for the formation of a new political organisation which will embrace and unite all the progressive elements in the country.' This development encouraged me in the belief that the Republican decision to fight the seat on an abstentionist ticket might not be irrevocable.

The McCluskeys had again been instrumental in organising a 'unity candidate' campaign, which had at its centre the holding of meetings in different parts of the constituency at which prospective candidates could speak. The process would culminate in a 'Unity Convention'. Due to my trip to America, I had missed some of the meetings, but when I joined the 'unity circus', as it was described, I soon came to certain conclusions: I had substantial support, indeed a poll organised by the Liberal party had shown me to be well out in front; there was no way Agnew would stand down in my favour nor would he accept a convention decision in my favour; on the other hand, Agnew would not relish fighting me in an election where there was a good chance he would finish third. Clearly, he and I were cancelling each other out and the way was open for a compromise candidate on an attendance ticket.

At the Selection Convention a letter from Kevin Agnew was read out, which declared that he was withdrawing his candidature in the interest of unity, and I quickly followed suit, also in the interest of unity. Bernadette Devlin was then unanimously selected to oppose Mrs Forrest, the Unionist candidate and widow of the deceased MP. I had not won the nomination, but I had helped in the selection of a candidate who would attend Westminster and when this could happen in Mid-Ulster it was a certainty it would also happen in Fermanagh–South Tyrone.

'Wee Bernie' had the support of every shade of anti-unionist opinion in the constituency and her election was assured. I described her during the campaign as 'not the size of two turf, but there is enough heat in those two turf to burn them in the House of Commons'. Well, she didn't burn Reggie Maudling, the British Home Secretary, she only slapped his face and pulled his hair. Was it, in the end, worth all the effort to get her elected? I gave my view in a *Guardian* article in May 1975 when I posed the question, 'What went wrong?'

'It certainly was not lack of courage, physical or moral. She showed her courage not only on the barricades but at the level of personal decision ... Bernadette Devlin is the George Best of politics. The stability and balance just weren't there. As the pressures increased, she didn't cope, for all her courage and idealism. But would any of us have done any better considering the exceptional nature of those pressures on one so young? A totally new lifestyle lived mostly away from home; the darling, then the devil of the media, whose only consistency was to treat her with levity – especially? – when she went out of her way to be serious; the personal and political crisis against the background of a community whose lives rather than votes were the main concern.

Yet, Bernadette Devlin was given the greatest opportunity of any Irish politician this century of being a force for reform and reconciliation. In the British Parliament, Gerry Fitt and others had for years battered their heads against the convention that Northern Ireland could not be discussed. But Bernadette had the good luck of being able to make her maiden speech on Ireland on her very first day in the House. The media had for years ignored conditions in "John Bull's political slum". The 22-year-old girl could easily have become the articulate voice of a frustrated and angry people; this phenomenon of Ulster, by emphasis on social and economic problems, common to Catholics and Protestants alike, could have been a bridge-builder in a community where such bridges were nearly non-existent. The tragedy of Bernadette Devlin is that she threw all these chances away. She polarised rather than united and became the equivalent of Paisley on the other side. She played for Celtic, he for Rangers.'

Almost thirty years later, I feel no need to revise these opinions. Indeed, her total irrelevancy over this long period in a number of changing political scenarios suggests strongly that a considerable talent had been misused. At the time, however, Bernadette's victory and the unity that had brought it about, did give a substantial boost to the anti-unionist cause.

Terence O'Neill's position as Prime Minister was quickly eroding. It was not helped by a series of explosions that disrupted water and electricity supplies in the Belfast area, seven in the month of April alone. The immediate assumption among most commentators and politicians was that the explosions were the work of the IRA. The B Specials were mobilised and 1,500 British soldiers were sent to provide security for vital installations. I alleged in the Stormont House of Commons that the explosions had been caused by Protestant extremists with the objective of ousting O'Neill, and I provided to the Minister of Home Affairs the names and addresses of two men I held were responsible. Unionist MPs and sections of the unionist Press demanded I reveal my source, which of course I refused to do. To name my informant would have put his life at risk and, a very secondary consideration, would have meant no more information from that or any other source. So I had no alternative but to suffer the abuse and the smears. More importantly, the names were leaked to those against whom I had made the allegations, almost certainly by members of the RUC, and for some time I had good reason to fear that violent retribution might be taken against me, or members of my family. Now, more than thirty years later, I feel it is safe to disclose the circumstances in which I obtained the information that I know to have been accurate.

A friend of mine told me that an Armagh Catholic had informed him that a Protestant he had known for a number of years, and whom he believed to be an honest man, had approached him about contacting me. He had not told him what he wanted to speak to me about, but said that it was confidential and important. Would I be prepared to meet him? We met by arrangement at a private house outside Coalisland, nominated by me for I feared a set-up, and I soon accepted his *bona fides*. He told me a relative had a boyfriend whom he described as a 'Paisley man' and that he had confided in her that he was one of the men responsible for the explosions at an electricity pylon at Kilmore, County Armagh, and that one of the men with him had been involved, with others, in the other explosions. The motive behind the explosions was to undermine Prime Minister O'Neill by causing the Protestant community to fear that law and order had broken down and that republicans were attempting a *coup*.

Though derided when I first made the allegations, within a short time, particularly when the explosions stopped after the resignation of O'Neill, there was almost universal acceptance that extremist Protestants had been responsible and for the purpose I had alleged. Lord Scarman, in his 1972 report, stated, 'at the time it was widely thought the explosions were the work of the IRA, though it is quite clear now that they were not'.

Later that year, in October, I was the recipient of more information which, if it had been acted upon, could have prevented a tragedy. Samuel Stevenson, a close associate of Ian Paisley who had been involved with him in the Ulster Constitution Defence Committee and the Ulster Protestant Volunteers, made contact with me to say he had information he would like me to have. Again, I took precautions and arranged to meet him in Dungannon, at the office of Paddy Duffy, a solicitor who was deeply involved in civil rights and would later be an SDLP Assemblyman. Paddy arranged for one of his secretaries to be present to take notes. I also felt it necessary to inform the local Special Branch Sergeant, Harry McCrum, to whom I will refer again later, to keep the premises under surveillance. We were living in risky times and I had received a number of death threats, by letter and phone, from loyalists.

Stevenson told me that loyalists were responsible for the acts of sabotage, as I had alleged, that he knew this because he himself had participated in some of them, and that they had been carried out to bring down O'Neill and to secure prison releases for Paisley and his right-hand man, Bunting. He supplied me with a number of names of those responsible, which included the names I had previously given to the Minister for Home Affairs. He said he was giving me this information because his conscience was troubling him and he was more involved than he had ever wished to be and now wished to get out.

However, his most startling disclosure was that they intended to attack targets in the Republic, and that he and a Thomas McDowell from Kilkeel, County Down, had already reconnoitred an electricity power station at Ballyshannon, County Donegal, which he thought would be blown up the following weekend. I had no way of knowing what credence to give to this information. Stevenson did not ask for money – though I gave him £10 to cover his costs of travelling from Belfast – so money was not the motive. After discussing the matter with Paddy Duffy, I decided I had no alternative but to treat the matter seriously and to pass on the information. Accordingly, I informed Detective Sergeant McCrum of what I had been told and he said he would give the information to his authorities and would request that the information concerning Ballyshannon be passed on to the Garda Síochána. To be doubly sure, I also spoke to Councillor Michael McLoughlin and he travelled to County Monaghan and gave the information to a member of Irish Army intelligence whom he and I had met the previous August.

The following Sunday night/Monday morning there was an explosion at the Ballyshannon power station and Thomas McDowell was found at the scene, suffering from injuries from which he later died. He had touched a 110,000-volt wire and had been thrown onto the roof of the transformer. More than a hundred-weight of gelignite had been wired up around the building, which would have been destroyed had McDowell not electrocuted himself. A car was heard speeding towards the border after the incident.

I do not know what action, if any, had been taken on the information provided by me. One newspaper said, 'One report stated that the area was sealed off within minutes, which would indicate that the Gardaí was in a state of readiness.' Unfortunately, not in sufficient readiness to prevent the loss of a life and to capture the bomber's fellow saboteurs.

Stevenson was later charged and sentenced to twelve years' imprisonment for his involvement with explosions at Castlereagh, Kilmore and Templepatrick. Five other men were found not guilty by juries in three separate trials. The result of these trials, indicating how difficult it was to obtain convictions against alleged loyalist terrorists, was largely responsible for the decision to abolish trial by jury for this type of offence. However, Lord Scarman, in his *Report of Tribunal of Inquiry*, without mentioning my name reached conclusions which supported my original allegations. He said:

'All five explosions were the work of Protestant extremists among whom must be included Mr. Stevenson. Their purpose was to strengthen the campaign to topple the then Prime Minister, Captain O'Neill, from power and to secure the release from gaol of Dr. Paisley and Major Bunting.'

Shortly before these events the Dungannon-based priest, Fr Denis Faul, had run into a storm of controversy when he attacked aspects of the legal and judicial system and alleged that the jury system, with its inbuilt Protestant bias, was unfair to Catholics. Cardinal Conway, probably at the behest of Catholic lawyers, issued a statement saying that Fr Faul's comments were 'both unfortunate and unwarranted'. Shortly after the Cardinal's unprecedented public rebuke, I was a participant in a TV panel discussion where the issue came up and I defended Fr Faul. The following morning, at two minutes past nine, my phone rang. It was Cardinal Conway to say he had watched the TV discussion the previous evening and he would be issuing a statement later that day. A statement, issued for 'purposes of clarification', denied that the Cardinal intended to give blanket approval to the judicial system. The outcome of the trials I have referred to fully justified Fr Faul's criticisms, certainly in relation to the jury system.

13: ESCALATING VIOLENCE

In August 1969 the British government was forced to commit its Army to the streets of Northern Ireland at the request of the Stormont government, which had to admit its inability to maintain law and order from its own resources. The decision had far-reaching constitutional and political implications because no British government could commit its Army, under its direct command, without that military presence being accompanied by a political presence. It was clearly unrealistic that a government should allow control of its Army to be transferred to another government, particularly a government that was devolved and subservient. The responsibility the British government and Parliament had under Section 75 of the Government of Ireland Act 1920 was reinforced by the practical considerations which now arose as a result of the direct involvement of the Army. When the Army was involved, there could be no dodging of the question of who was in control.

Events had been moving in this direction for some time, even before Terence O'Neill had been forced to resign and was succeeded by James Chichester-Clark. In April, in the aftermath of the explosions at water and electricity installations, 1,500 soldiers were given responsibility for the guarding of public utilities. These troops were part of the normal garrison in Northern Ireland, were committed for a specific purpose and were not involved in direct contact with the public or the hands-on political decision-making that the maintenance of law and order on the streets would necessitate.

When I had returned from the United States in March, I had predicted 'a long hot summer'. The campaign in Stormont against the Public Order legislation, the Mid-Ulster by-election, the acts of sabotage and the resignation of O'Neill had all helped to increase the political temperature. There were steps forward, such as announcements by the O'Neill government of one man, one vote legislation and by the Chichester-Clark government conceding an independent commission to redraw local government boundaries and an amnesty for all offences connected with demonstrations since 5 October (which applied to me and other civil rights leaders, but also enabled the government to release Paisley, who was serving a sentence for his behaviour at Armagh). But there were also a number of examples of increasing sectarianism and rioting, for example, in Derry, Dungiven, Lurgan, Belfast's Ardoyne at the beginning of May, and at Unity Flats and the Crumlin Road in July and early August. Both sections of the community were involved in this rioting. The attempt by a Protestant mob to attack Unity Flats at the beginning of August was particularly ominous. Two deaths attributable to police action, Sam Devenney in Derry and Francis McCluskey in Dungiven, did not increase Catholic confidence in the RUC.

Civil rights agitation was continuing in the Coalisland–Dungannon area, with increasing frustration on one side and increasing militancy among Protestant extremists on the other. On 20 April an attempt to march to the RUC station in the Square in Dungannon to hand in a petition was prevented by the police and a sit-down took place, followed by the issuing of summons for obstructing the Queen's highway. The Urban Council continued with its discriminatory housing allocation policy despite the issuing of new guidelines by the Department. On two occasions at the end of July there were squattings and well-publicised evictions. One of these, by the Hurle family, which I supported, was particularly emotive. On 4 August I arranged for a deputation to Stormont to meet with Minister Brian Faulkner to discuss Catholic grievances, which included housing, planning, employment by the local councils and the need for an accelerated house-building programme. Members of the delegation had put considerable preparation into the meeting and they made their points well, with detailed supporting information. They ought not have bothered; Faulkner was polite, but he did not concede an inch. He defended the record of the two Dungannon councils and then left for another appointment. It was a bad error of judgement on his part. The delegation was representative of all of those in the Dungannon area who had real concerns about the deteriorating situation in their town. It included the McCluskeys, Councillors Donaghy, Hassard and McLoughlin, as well as members of the local civil rights committee. Additionally, it included Fr Austin Eustace, the highly respected and influential senior curate. The deputation left Stormont in an angry mood, convinced that no amelioration of their position was likely to come from Faulkner.

The effect was that members of the delegation returned to Dungannon in militant mood, united by Faulkner's intransigence. The first sign of the new militancy was a decision to continue and increase the numbers involved in a picket that had been placed on the Urban Council offices during the monthly council meeting in May, June and July. And, of course, the council office was located in the Square, the no-go area for Papists unless they were shopping in the Protestant shops. A picket was organised for Monday, 11 August. Almost inevitably there would be trouble, possibly serious trouble. I had continued to meet with Michael McLoughlin and John Donaghy since the Coalisland–Dungannon march and we travelled to civil rights demonstrations and meetings together. We talked not only about the local situation but attempted an overall view of the political situation. We came to certain conclusions.

I arranged a meeting with Neal Blaney TD, the Minister for Agriculture in Jack Lynch's government, and on Friday, 8 August, Michael and I met him in his Department in Dublin. As Minister for Agriculture, Blaney had, of course, no direct, official responsibility for Northern Ireland, however I had met him on a number of occasions and we got on well on a personal level. More importantly, he was the one member of the Irish government who had shown a real interest in Northern Ireland, or the Six Counties, as he and most nationalists described the Northern State. A fair bit of cynicism attached to this interest, which was interpreted by many as a ploy by an unsuccessful contender for the leadership of Fianna Fáil to use republicanism as a means to embarrass Taoiseach Lynch, and as a stepping stone to the party leadership at the next opportunity. However, I, and most northern nationalists, did not share these sentiments. He was a Donegal man, a fellow Ulster man and entitled to be more nationalist or republican than the others, most of whom, including Jack Lynch, had shown little interest in our situation in the North.

Michael and I made it clear to Blaney from the outset that we were speaking to him as a member of the government, for the information of the government, and that we were giving him our personal assessment of the developing situation in the North and how the Irish government should respond to it. We were of the opinion that the situation in the North was deteriorating and that there could be serious trouble in Derry if the Apprentice Boys' march went ahead on 12 August. We also described how this trouble was highly likely to spread to other areas, and we specifically mentioned Dungannon, Coalisland, Armagh, Lurgan and Enniskillen. Indeed, trouble in Dungannon was likely to precede Derry as a result of loyalist opposition to the picket at the council offices, which would take place the night before the Derry march. I told him that the previous week, at a meeting of opposition MPs with Chichester-Clark and his Minister for Home Affairs, Bertie Porter, I had warned of this possibility if the Derry march went ahead, but apparently they did not give my view any credence.

I also told Blaney that if there were trouble in a number of separate areas, the RUC would not be able to handle it. The strength of the RUC was only 3,200, and a percentage of those could not be used for riot-control duties, either because they were needed for administrative duties or were physically unable. It had been obvious in July and at the beginning of August that the RUC was having difficulty coping with demonstrations in areas of potential trouble when its strength was dispersed.

Michael and I warned of the dangerous situation that could arise if the B Specials were called up. They were lacking in discipline at the best of times and there was no knowing what they might do in a riotous situation when passions were inflamed. At any rate, their presence on the streets, where they would inevitably identify with Protestant extremists, would anger Catholics. The Catholic community would be under grave threat. However, if the Stormont government was unable to control the situation with its own resources, then the British government would be forced to intervene and, in the circumstances we had postulated, the quicker that intervention occurred the better it would be for Catholics. Additionally, there were political and constitutional advantages which would accrue from this scenario for the nationalist population of the North, and indeed for nationalism on the entire island. The British military presence would have to be accompanied by British political presence and the political price would be paid by Stormont, possibly by its abolition. The whole political, and possibly constitutional, situation would be transformed, and we wished the Irish government to be ready to deal with such a situation.

Blaney listened to us, puffing on his pipe, interrupting our narrative only once to ask a question about the situation in Dungannon. It was a relevant question, indicating to me that, as we had expected, he had been briefed on the situation there; a Donegal man based in Dungannon was a well-known member of the 'Donegal Mafia'. When Michael and I had finished he thanked us and said he had only one reservation. As a republican, he wished to see the end of British influence in Ireland because the British had never had a right to be in any part of Ireland, so how could an Irish government support more British troops and more British influence in the North? Surely in these circumstances, where law and order had broken down, it was the United Nations that should be asked to intervene?

I responded that while this was undoubtedly preferable, we had to be realistic. How long would it take, even if the UN agreed, to have UN forces on the ground in circumstances where Catholics might be getting massacred? Furthermore, the UN would not intervene without British agreement, which would be unlikely. Whether we liked it or not, where the saving of lives might be the paramount consideration, there was no alternative to the British Army.

At this juncture the Minister said he was already late for another appointment at the show-jumping arena at the RDS in Ballsbridge where, as Minister for Agriculture, he had to be present for the Nations Cup. He wished to continue the conversation and invited us to accompany him. We thanked him, but no, we had to return North.

Events developed as we had predicted, only more dangerously so. There was rioting in Dungannon on Monday night, 11 August, with RUC baton charges against the Catholic crowd. Civil rights stewards had the situation under control when a car was driven at speed through the Catholic crowd, forcing pedestrians and at least one policeman to jump out of the way to avoid being run over. This car proceeded to the Square, where it was greeted by sustained applause from the Protestant crowd. The driver, a Protestant, was subsequently found guilty of careless driving, a charge substituted for dangerous driving. The action provoked the Catholic crowd and the rioting became intense.

The Scarman Tribunal of Inquiry was later to find that members of the RUC behaved in a way which was 'wholly unjustified' when, in the early hours of the morning, they moved into the small Catholic housing estate of Fairmount Park, shouting and banging their batons on their shields, frightening residents. The *Scarman Report* was also critical of the presence of a number of B Specials in civilian clothes among the Protestant crowd. Lord Justice Scarman added:

'There is nothing in the evidence to suggest that the rioting of the 11th August was planned or organised ahead. It arose out of existing tension exacerbated by certain quite trivial incidents in the Market Square. Unfortunately, it escalated so as to have a very serious effect upon the minds and attitudes of both sections of the community. The Catholics set their minds on 'defence' – by which they meant the use of barricades and violence to keep the Protestants and police out of their areas; the Protestants became hostile and watchful, ready to strike hard at the Catholic rioters if the police did not deal with the situation to their satisfaction. There is no doubt that the tensions aroused by the events of 11th August contributed to the serious riots in both Dungannon and Coalisland on 12th and 13th August.'

I had been in Dungannon on Monday night, and on Tuesday morning, along with John Donaghy, Michael McLoughlin and Plunkett O'Donnell of the civil rights branch, had visited the Catholic housing estates. We found the residents fearful and angry, particularly in Fairmount Park. Rumours abounded that Protestants, accompanied by B men, planned to burn down Fairmount Park and the Ballygawley Road housing estates that night. Barricades were erected at the entrances to the estates. I sent a telegram that morning to the British Home Secretary, Jim Callaghan, saying that the powder keg was likely to explode and demanding immediate British intervention.

In the event, no attack by loyalists took place. At least some of the credit for this was due to Sergeant McCrum, who sent word to known Protestant extremists that they would be dealt with if an attack took place and then followed this up by patrolling the two Catholic estates during the night in the company of another policeman, a Catholic, both of them armed with sterling sub-machine-guns.

The scene of the action shifted to Coalisland, four miles away, where residents were acutely aware of what had happened in Dungannon and then, as the day advanced, of events occurring in Derry. In the afternoon the Coalisland Citizens Action Committee (CCAC) picketed the RUC station in protest. This went off peacefully, but later in the evening a crowd began to gather in the Square and stones were thrown at the RUC station. I arrived in Coalisland and, along with members of the CCAC, managed to calm the crowd, most of whom dispersed, leaving a hard-core of potential troublemakers. Word began to spread of what was happening in Derry, where serious trouble had started. Men began to gather with transistor radios. Police reinforcements arrived, accompanied by an armoured vehicle. The situation began to deteriorate seriously, despite the best efforts of members of the Action Committee, led by the Chairman, Patsy O'Neill, and the Secretary, Denis Haughey. The RUC station came under attack, not only with stones but with petrol bombs. This was the first time I had seen this potentially lethal weapon and it occurred to me they had not materialised out of thin air; obviously there had been some element of preparation. Rioting went on until after 2.00am, with charge and counter-charge and the building and dismantling of barricades.

When things had quietened down I returned to my house outside Donaghmore, two miles away. Annita asked me to telephone my mother, who was aware I was in Coalisland and was worried for my safety. As I spoke to her on the telephone in the hallway, I saw, through the glass-fronted doorway, the lights of a car as it pulled into the driveway. I saw a flash, followed by the sound of something whizzing past my ear. I hit the ground quickly and lay there on my stomach as two more shots were fired, watching the phone dangle on its lead from side to side and listening to my mother becoming more and more hysterical. That was the first of more than thirty attacks on the house over the next few years, and not the most serious of them.

The following day, 13 August, there was trouble in both Coalisland and Dungannon. After the events of the previous two nights it was almost inevitable, but an added factor was NICRA's call for diversionary demonstrations 'to take the heat off Derry'. The Dungannon civil rights committee decided it was too dangerous to hold a meeting in view of the recent occurrences. I decided to spend my time in Coalisland. However, members of Dungannon CRA changed their minds and a meeting was held in Ann Street, in the Catholic end of the town. The chairman, Aidan Corrigan, told the crowd of about two hundred people that the meeting had been called to show solidarity with the people of the Bogside and to help draw the police away from there. When the meeting was over the crowd dispersed, helped by a heavy shower of rain, but some continued to add to the barricades already erected. It was when the police moved in to remove these barricades that serious rioting began.

The police officer in charge, County Inspector Landale, attempted to obtain reinforcements, but none were available because of the situations in Derry and Coalisland, so he bolstered his troop numbers with about forty B Specials. Despite the assurance that B men would not be used in riotous situations, repeated in a TV broadcast that very evening by the Prime Minister, the County Inspector now proceeded to do just that and compounded his culpability by allowing them to carry their weapons. Some of the Catholic crowd disgraced themselves by burning down the offices of the local unionist newspaper, the *Tyrone Courier*, and by attacking the firemen who arrived to put out the fire, but even these gross stupidities did not justify what the B Specials proceeded to do. They fired into the Catholic crowd, hitting Gregory Willoughby, Ann Hughes and Eugene Faloon, mercifully only injuring them.

The conclusion of Lord Scarman was 'that contrary to orders, at least four members of the USC opened fire on an unarmed Catholic crowd, injuring three of them. Even though some of the civilians in the Catholic crowd may have been taunting the USC [B Specials] and throwing missiles, there can be no justification for the shooting, which occurred at a time when there was no effective RUC leadership in Ann Street.' Even though the four members of the

B Specials, from the Kilnaslee platoon, were identified through their weapons, no action was ever taken against them.

I was invited to speak at a meeting in Coalisland at 9.00pm, but because of a broadcast on TV and radio by Taoiseach Jack Lynch, the meeting was delayed until it was over. I listened to it on the radio in my car and most of those gathered for the meeting did likewise, in local pubs and houses, or on their car radios or transistors. The Taoiseach said it was evident that the Stormont government was no longer in control of the situation: 'Indeed, the present situation is the inevitable outcome of the policies pursued for decades by successive Stormont governments. It is clear also that the Irish government can no longer stand by and see innocent people injured and perhaps worse.' He called for a UN peacekeeping force and said he had asked the British government to ensure that police attacks on the people of Derry should cease immediately. He announced that Army field hospitals would be set up at points along the border to treat people who did not wish to go to hospitals in Northern Ireland. I was pleased at the statement. There was no reference to the deployment of British troops, only, predictably, to the UN. However the request to the British government to ensure that police attacks on the people of Derry ceased could be interpreted as the nod to the British to take whatever steps were necessary to secure that end, including the commitment of troops.

Our meeting was held at the far end of Main Street, away from the Square and the police station. Denis Haughey, Aidan Corrigan, Plunkett O'Donnell and I spoke and we all praised the Lynch speech and advised non-violence. I expressed an opinion of the speech, which I later circulated in a press release, to the effect that Jack Lynch had said as much as he could and as little as he could: as much as he could given the political and military realities, and as little as he could in view of the pressures on him as a result of what was happening in Derry, Dungannon, Coalisland and elsewhere. I advised the crowd to go home quietly as there was no point in risking death or injury and wrecking their own town. For those who were there in response to the NICRA call to take the heat off Derry, this end had already been achieved as due to the previous night and that night's meeting, policemen who would otherwise have been in Derry were confined to the Coalisland and Dungannon areas. But the other speakers and I might just as well have kept our breath to cool our porridge. There were those in Coalisland that night who were determined to have a go at the RUC and had made preparations to that end.

Afterwards, there were allegations that the 'Lynch speech' had fired up people in Coalisland and other areas. This was not my impression in Coalisland, indeed the opposite seemed the case. People were pleased that the Irish government was taking a stand in their defence, even if it was more verbal than anything else. Pressure was being put on the British to put the boot into the hated Unionist government, so things were going in the right direction.

Unfortunately, that night in Coalisland the hot-heads took over. From the offices of the *Tyrone Democrat* I was a close observer of the scene and in the right place to know what was going on and to make judgements. Following the initial stone and petrol-bomb attacks on the RUC station, the District Inspector in charge requested reinforcements and these arrived in the form of a few RUC officers and a party of B men armed with rifles, revolvers and a Sterling sub-machine-gun, and accompanied by an armoured car. The Specials did not have riot gear, just their weapons. Suddenly a JCB appeared with its shovel raised to protect the driver and proceeded towards the station, providing cover for those behind it throwing bricks and petrol bombs. Depending on your point of view, it was either a very foolhardy or a very courageous thing to do. It did, however, precipitate a response from the B men who, contrary to the orders of the RUC officer in command and the direction of the Prime Minister, opened fire on the crowd. A number of men were injured, including Kevin Teague, a man well-known to me, who was shot in the leg.

Following the shooting I tried to contact 'Beezer' Porter, the Minister for Home Affairs, a man too liberal in his views to have held a position in that right-wing government, but he was unavailable. I was able to speak to his Permanent Secretary, a Mr Greaves, who was in the incident centre at Police Headquarters and denied any knowledge of the shooting. About forty-five minutes later he rang me back to confirm the shooting, but he denied B men were involved. I did not believe that he did not, at that stage, know the truth, so it was not a terribly amicable discussion. There were no more attempted assaults on the station. Barricades were erected and a stand-off developed. At about 3.30am I felt able to leave Coalisland – but not to return home.

Around midnight I had received a phone call to the *Democrat* offices from a person well-known to me whom I considered reliable. He told me that he and another man were walking towards Donaghmore from the village of Castlecaulfield when they saw a party of B Specials stopping traffic on the road. Rightly suspecting that the B men were members of the Castlecaulfield platoon, and not wishing to have to endure the usual indignity of having to identify themselves to their neighbours and possibly be searched, they took to the adjacent field to avoid the roadblock. Hiding behind the hedge they overheard a conversation between members of the platoon, some of whose voices they recognised. Their conversation was about shooting up my home that night.

I immediately rang Annita, told her I believed my informant and that I was making arrangements for her and Estelle, just under a year old at the time, to be collected so she could stay the night at my parents' home. She refused to move; it was our house and they weren't driving her out. I didn't argue. I rang my brother, Brian, told him I could not get out of Coalisland, explained the position and asked him and whatever other brothers were available to take Annita and Estelle out of the house. If she resisted, he had my full permission to carry her out if necessary. When my brothers arrived Annita accepted the reality without too much resistance. The following morning I visited our home. The windows had been shot through and there were bulletmarks on the brickwork. The brave men of the Castlecaulfield platoon had done their work, believing, and not caring, that a woman and young child were in that house.

The previous day representations had been made to me that residents of the Fairmount Park and Ballygawley Road housing estates were fearful for their lives and that the women and children were finding the uncertain situation extremely stressful. Could I make arrangements for them to be brought across the border to safety? Similar requests were being made to the Irish government from other areas, and a decision was taken to use the Army camp at Gormanston, County Meath, as a refugee centre. In making arrangements for the Dungannon people, I now included my own wife and child.

That evening I drove Annita and Estelle to Monaghan for transportation to Gormanston. It was an emotional farewell. My wife confided to me afterwards that she thought there was a good chance she would not see me alive again. If pressed, I would not have disagreed with her. It is about twelve miles from the border at Aughnacloy to Dungannon and I was stopped by B men at no less than five roadblocks along that route. They, of course, recognised me and subjected me to abuse and intimidation, including clicking their weapons threateningly and prodding me with them. At three of these roadblocks I was made open the car boot, remove the spare wheel and bounce it on the road. I couldn't see any point in this practice, except to show me who was in charge. When I reached Dungannon, I found B men everywhere, gathered in groups every hundred yards or so. As I passed the courthouse, a number of them raised their rifles and pointed them in my direction. Among them I recognised Sammy Price, from my own village of Donaghmore. That night, and for some time after, I did not sleep in my own home. I remain grateful to a number of friends and relations for their kindness in accommodating me at that time.

The B Specials and I had never been friends, but that evening, 14 August 1969, they had particular reason to loathe me, and others like me. At 5.00pm a company of 400 soldiers from the Princess of Wales' Own Regiment took up positions in Derry and the RUC and the Specials were ordered to withdraw. The following day British troops took up duty in Belfast and within a few days they were in Dungannon. The more intelligent of the Specials – a limited number, I agree – as they were raising their rifles to me, would have suspected their days were numbered.

It was a miracle no one had been killed in Coalisland or Dungannon. But they were not so lucky elsewhere. Circumstances similar to the way the B men had behaved in Dungannon resulted in the death of John Gallagher in Armagh. It was in Belfast, however, that the irresponsibility of those in charge of the RUC and the Specials and the enormity of community division was most appalling. Ten people lost their lives – eight Catholics and two Protestants. A process was begun whereby, as estimated by the Community Relations Commission, 60,000 people, more than 10% of the city's population, would be forced to move between then and 1973: the biggest forced migration anywhere in Europe since the end of the Second World War.

A major political change had indeed taken place, but at a very high price. Unfortunately, even given that high price, the value of the end product was diminished. I have long believed that in 1969, by not abolishing or suspending the Stormont Parliament and government, the British government made probably its most serious mistake since the creation of Stormont in 1920. The Stormont Parliament and government effectively ended on 14 August when British troops moved into Derry. It was, however, to take another two years and seven months, a major escalation of violence, many needless deaths, internment, Bloody Sunday and the alienation of almost the entire Catholic community before the death of Stormont was officially confirmed. The British government intervened in August 1969 only because it had no alternative, and when it did so its involvement was the minimum possible in the circumstances.

The presence of the British Army had, of course, to be accompanied by the British political presence, just as Michael McLoughlin and I had predicted to Blaney. A senior British official, Oliver Wright, was appointed United

Kingdom Representative, with an office in Stormont Castle, and the General Officer Commanding (GOC) Northern Ireland was given overall responsibility for security. But the British failed to face the ultimate logic of these actions, which would have meant the abolition of the Northern Ireland Parliament and government. Instead, they declared that the Army was 'in aid of the civil power', and that civil power was Stormont.

The abolition or suspension of Stormont, based on its obvious inability to enforce its remit and maintain law and order, would have been greeted with joy in the nationalist community and surly acceptance in the unionist community. To try and maintain the pretence that the Stormont government still ruled led, almost inevitably, to the alienation of a large section of the Catholic community from Britain and its Army, because they saw Britain as being tarred with the unionist brush. In the Protestant community, the failure of the hybrid to enforce law and order in the no-go areas which had developed, and the disbandment of the B Specials, increased feelings of insecurity and fuelled support for extremists.

There were some in the nationalist community who saw the direct involvement of the British Army on the streets as a welcome beginning of a new phase in the age-old struggle against the traditional enemy, but they were very few. The founding of the Provisional IRA and its violent campaign to force the British to withdraw was not inevitable.

The events of August 1969, particularly in Belfast, aroused very real fear for the safety of Catholics in many areas of the North, but the emphasis was on protection and defence. It was not until February 1971, eighteen months later, that the first British soldier was killed.

The change in the relationship between the Army and sections of the Catholic population began with the election of the Heath government in June 1970. Within three weeks, at the beginning of July, when the major nationalist concern was the imminent Orange parades, the Falls Road curfew occurred when, for thirty-four hours, local Catholics were confined to their homes as the Army carried out house-to-house searches.

A few days before the British Army first appeared on the streets I was representing a constituent before a sickness benefit Local Tribunal when the Chairman asked to speak to me privately. He was a staunch unionist but had a distinguished war record, having been awarded the Military Cross for valour. He said to me he had noticed that I and my associates had been demanding the intervention of the British Army to replace the RUC and the B Specials. He advised me strongly that I was making a mistake. 'The British Army is the best in the world, but like any army it is trained to kill. It will be a very blunt instrument for peacekeeping purposes,' he said. My reply was to the effect that as far as the nationalist community was concerned the Russians or the Nazis would be preferable to the RUC and the B men and that the arrival of the Army would be an important political development. We were both right. The Falls Road curfew showed how blunt an instrument the Army was. Additionally, the presence in the Falls of John Brooke, the Unionist Minister for Information, with the Army only helped to underline, for most nationalists, the new direction of British policy under the Tories. The Army was on the other side. The Provisionals would soon be in business.

Shortly after the dramatic events of mid-August, James O'Reilly MP and I met Taoiseach Jack Lynch. The press release issued afterwards said that the protection of Irish men and women in the northern part of the country was the main theme of the discussion. There was no reference to another part of the hour-long meeting, which was of even greater significance. In the course of his assessment of developments, the Taoiseach said that part of the problem for his government was that the crisis had occurred so unexpectedly and without warning. I interjected to say this should not have been the case because I had correctly predicted to Minister Blaney in advance what was likely to happen. Jack Lynch immediately questioned me on the date and then rose from his desk to go over to the telephone in the corner of his office. I heard part of the conversation, which I presumed was with the Cabinet Secretary, asking that the record be checked whether Minister Blaney had reported on his discussions with me. He then returned to his desk and the meeting continued. Shortly before our meeting ended the phone went again, there was a short discussion and on his return to his desk the Taoiseach said, 'I do not remember such a report being made to me and there is no record of it.' At a further meeting some weeks later when I asked him privately if further enquiries had altered the position, he confirmed that no report had been made to the government of Blaney's meeting with Michael McLoughlin and I. I was not, therefore, so surprised as most other people when I learned of some of the circumstances surrounding the sacking of Mr Blaney in May of the following year.

14: FALLOUT FROM *HUNT*

The days following the events of mid-August 1969 were full of fear and tension. My wife and daughter were in Gormanston camp, it was too dangerous for me to live at home, but staying with friends meant that they too might become targets. I was invited to speak at a public meeting in Monaghan and decided to stay in a hotel there and make that town my base until things settled down. It was a mistake.

At that time, Monaghan had more than its fair share of head-bangers. There were, of course, some like myself who wished to avoid intimidation or worse. There were some who, having been forced out of their homes, had fled to the safety of Monaghan or Dundalk. The great majority were genuine, but there were, of course, some chancers exploiting the opportunity of a week or two at someone else's expense. And there were also those with a political agenda, opportunistic and anxious to capitalise on a condition of instability. Monaghan became a centre of conspiracy and intrigue, often fuelled by late-night drinking.

A civil rights office was established in the town to act as a contact point for those coming over the border and also as a centre for the collection and distribution of aid for refugees. I do not know the full circumstances, but before long NICRA found it necessary to issue a public statement disassociating itself from this office.

It was impossible for me to avoid getting involved in discussions on the current situation and its opportunities and challenges. In particular, there were strong advocates of Irish Army intervention in the North in order to create 'an international incident' which would increase the pressure on the United Nations to intervene. The theory was that if the Irish Army entered Newry, or Strabane, or the West Bank of Derry, it would be welcomed by the local Catholic population and the area could be held while the Southern government entered into discussions on the political and constitutional future with the British government. The danger of that proposed course of action should have been apparent in circumstances where refugees were already streaming out of Belfast and other areas. Who would protect innocent Catholics in the hundreds of areas of Northern Ireland where they were vulnerable while these bridgeheads were being established and conditions brought about where negotiations could take place? And apart from these scenarios, with widespread deaths and civil war as a likely outcome, what about the practical considerations of an Irish Army of less than 6,500 men, poorly equipped? That 'initiatives' of this nature were being discussed at all is a good indication of the atmosphere prevailing in places like Monaghan in August 1969

On the morning of 22 August, I was awakened by knocking on my hotel room door and someone shouting that there was a telephone call for me. There was no telephone in my room, so I took the call in the corridor. It was Charles Haughey TD, Minister for Finance. He told me that the previous day the government had taken a decision to make money available for the relief of distress in the North. Did my area require assistance? I wondered how he had known where to contact me, but, overcoming my surprise, I informed him of the situation in Dungannon, where people had fled the housing estates and some were already in Gormanston camp. Would they qualify? He indicated that he thought they would. I then pushed him a bit further – what did he mean by 'distress'? The reply was, 'Anything you want it to mean, Austin.' There was something in the way he said it that made me cautious. I said I would get back to him. I never did, nor did I have anything to do with the fund. I had reason to be glad of that later when a Dáil Committee was established to inquire into the handling of the fund monies, amid allegations that some of the money had been used to arm what would later become the Provisional IRA.

Annita and Estelle had been in the refugee centre at Gormanston Camp for about three weeks. She had been among the first to arrive there and found the Army unprepared for refugees, mostly women and children, in a male environment. At the beginning, Estelle had to sleep in a drawer. However, she found the Army authorities extremely welcoming and they quickly made the necessary adjustments. Annita was soon acting as a liaison, and was also in demand for TV and radio interviews. A number of people contacted her to offer the hospitality of their homes, but she felt that she was performing a useful and necessary role, and that it would not help morale among the women if it was thought she was being singled out for special attention. So, at the beginning she declined all the offers. Eventually, she was visited by Michael Viney, whom I had met on a number of occasions, and his wife, Ethna, also a journalist, who very kindly invited her to stay with them. We will always be grateful to people like the Vineys who came to our assistance so generously over the years whenever we were in trouble.

Thankfully, politics began to take over from the violence. On 19 August the British and Stormont governments issued the Downing Street Declaration, which, while repeating the mandatory British commitment to Northern Ireland remaining British, also declared, 'the determination of the Northern Ireland government that there shall be full equality of treatment for all citizens'. As an indication of British commitment to the process two senior British civil servants, Oliver Wright and Alex Baker, took up residence at Stormont, in a watchdog capacity, as I observed publicly.

On 27 August the British Home Secretary visited the North. I found it easy to like 'Sunny' Jim Callaghan. As Chancellor of the Exchequer, Callaghan's political reputation had taken a dive with the devaluation of the pound. But now, as Home Secretary with responsibility for the North, he had bipartisan support in the House of Commons, and when Northern Ireland was debated he dominated the House. His visits to the North provided 'good' television and while there he acted almost in the role of a proconsul. Northern Ireland made him once again the heir-presumptive to Harold Wilson.

Along with other opposition MPs, I met him on the morning before the *Hunt Report* was officially published. He gave us a preview of the Report's findings, which recommended sweeping changes to the RUC though not, unfortunately, a change of name or uniform. They included the disarming of the force, the setting up of a Police Authority and 'vigorous efforts' to recruit Catholics. Even more controversially, the Report proposed a locally recruited, part-time force under the control of the British Army, while a new Police Volunteer Reserve would replace the B specials. The discontinuance of the B men led to two nights of rioting on the Shankill Road, during which the first policeman to be killed in the Troubles, Constable Victor Arbuckle, was shot by the UVF.

The decision to establish the Ulster Defence Regiment (UDR) and my response to it was to have a significant effect on my political career. I did not agree that any new military force was necessary. The British Army had now clearly been given responsibility for security, as distinct from the policing function, a fact that had been obscured by the paramilitary roles of the RUC and the B Specials. The *Hunt Report* had recommended that the RUC should be relieved of all duties of a military nature.

I felt it important, in line with what I had been arguing since I first came into politics, that the British responsibility under Section 75 of the Government of Ireland Act should be fully recognised and the ultimate responsibility of the UK government and Parliament underlined. This could best be assured by direct UK responsibility for security, exercised through the British Army, rather than through a locally recruited military force.

It could be argued, and was, that the UDR would be part of the British Army, under the control of the GOC Northern Ireland and, ultimately, of the Secretary for Defence in the UK government. That remained to be seen, but the name 'Ulster' and local recruitment strongly suggested a unionist bias. I, and other opposition MPs, argued with Callaghan that the new force was not necessary, that it was a sop to the unionists for the loss of their B men and that it could end up as a new B Special force.

Callaghan denied it was a sop while implicitly admitting his opinion that the unionist government could not survive a situation where the B men were disbanded and there was no local force to replace them. He contended that British control and effective vetting procedures would prevent another B Special force emerging and we, the opposition MPs, could help in this regard by advising Catholics to join the new force.

I recognised that Callaghan would not be moved on this issue. The UDR would come into existence; in fact, it was probably part of the deal with the Chichester-Clark government for its acceptance of the *Hunt* recommendations and other reform proposals, and that even the 'phasing out', as it was being described, of the B men would probably be Chichester-Clark's political memorial. In circumstances where the new force was going to be set up whether we liked it or not, surely our priority as opposition MPs was to ensure that everything possible was done to ensure it would not become a new B Specials?

This, I felt, could best be brought about in two ways: by Catholics joining the UDR, and by assuring, through the vetting procedures, that Protestant extremists would not be allowed to join. Protestant extremists would be unlikely to join the new force if they felt that the presence of Catholics would prevent it from developing in a way acceptable to them.

There was another consideration, albeit one which could not be voiced publicly. The events of August 1969, particularly in Belfast, had aroused fears that a situation could develop where large sections of the Catholic community might be under threat. This was to become known as a 'Doomsday situation'. In such a situation, surely the presence of Catholics, trained in the use of arms and disciplined, might be prudent? This consideration was certainly given weight by the Catholic Ex-Servicemen's Association, a body of veterans of the Irish, British and other armies, and accordingly it called for Catholic enrolment in the new defence force.

On leaving the meeting with Callaghan, I told the media I would be prepared to encourage Catholics to join both the new unarmed police service and the still un-named, locally recruited part-time force.

Over the next few days most opinion-formers expressed their views. The *Hunt Report* was, almost unanimously, welcomed by nationalists, but unionists expressed deep reservations. While some Catholics expressed regret that the name RUC and the colour of the uniform would not be changed, almost all who expressed a view were of the opinion that Catholics should be encouraged to join. Cardinal Conway said , 'I imagine that many of the police themselves will welcome these changes and I anticipate that Catholics will be willing to join the new force in considerable numbers.' The fact that the Cardinal, for the most part conservative and careful in his statements, expressed his view in such terms was a good indication of how widespread the opinion was.

Support for Catholics joining the new part-time defence force, under the control of the GOC, was also widespread among Catholic spokespersons. Frank Gogarty, Chairman of NICRA, said he had no objection to it as it was 'in no way controlled by the Ministry of Home Affairs'. Even in circumstances where the Unionist government emphasised the necessity for an oath of allegiance for members of the UDR in an effort to discourage Catholics from joining, a number of opposition MPs continued to advocate Catholic enlistment. In Stormont on 11 November, John Hume said:

'The Minister has mentioned the test of loyalty for service in this force and the oath of allegiance is being played up once again by the government and the honourable members opposite. May I remind them that it is my belief that the oath of allegiance has always been used by the honourable members opposite, not for what an oath should be, but as an obstacle placed in the way of a section of the community and deliberately done so to prevent people taking part in anything. I would point out to them that just as members of Parliament have done, just as civil servants have done, and just as teachers have done, we will jump over the obstacle once again and I will encourage all sections of the community to join this new force.'

During the same debate Ivan Cooper said, 'I too would urge all sections of the community to come forward and support both the reserve police force and the new defence force.' Paddy Kennedy, who would be identified with a pro-Provisional approach only a few months later, also supported Catholics joining: '... like the honourable members for East Tyrone and Foyle I welcome the establishment of these two forces as it leads to the dismantling and disbandment of the B special force. Like the honourable member for Foyle I feel that members of the minority should be encouraged to join this force and that no obstacles, particularly in the nature of a security check, should be put upon them just because they are opposed to the Unionist Government.'

Developing events would change perspectives, and I found myself more under attack for my advice on the RUC and the UDR than any of my political colleagues. I regret to say that I did not receive the support from some of them that our common endorsement would have suggested. When Hume, Cooper and I were being described as 'recruiting sergeants for the UDR', we were left on our own to defend a position others had previously occupied with us.

An event in Coalisland the previous January had given me some confidence that my position on the UDR would be understood. At a meeting of the local civil rights organisation, the Coalisland Citizens Action Committee, it was decided to draw attention to the sectarian bias of the B specials – largely for the benefit of the British government and public. As the *Tyrone Democrat* reported in its issue of 17 January 1969, 'more than 600 people, headed by members of Coalisland Citizens Action Committee, converged on the local RUC station last Thursday night with a view to enlisting in the B specials.' The report added that the march to the barracks followed a resolution passed at a public meeting in the Square – 'If the mobilisation of the Specials is to be anything other than provocation and if the government is sincere in their desire to ensure law and order, then we, who have proved our dedication to non-violence despite intense provocation demand our right to be members of the B Specials or any other force which has the alleged aim of promoting law and order.' 'Any other force' would clearly apply to the proposed UDR. The accompanying photograph in the *Democrat* of those marching to the RUC station showed well-known local republican Kevin Mallon in the front row!

The task of getting enough Catholic UDR members to prevent it from developing as a sectarian force was always going to be an uphill struggle. The heart invariably ruled the head, and the idea of donning a British uniform to serve beside former B men in defence of Northern Ireland could only hope to have support in a rational atmosphere. Any chance of that was effectively ended within three months of *Hunt*, when the Provisional Republican movement came into existence. The nail in the coffin was the Lower Falls curfew, which alienated the local Catholic community from the British Army.

Despite the ammunition it gave to my political opponents, I have never regretted the position I took in relation to Catholic membership of the RUC and UDR, except in one respect. As the IRA campaign developed, directed at the post-*Hunt* RUC as well as at the UDR, I agonised that some of those being murdered or intimidated were in that position because they had followed my advice. In the circumstances, I was more than willing to provide references to a number of young Catholics who, because of personal and family pressures, wished to transfer to the Gardaí or to police forces in Britain, the USA and elsewhere.

Shortly after the *Hunt Report* a civil servant from the British Ministry of Defence started to visit me at my home and continued to do so on a monthly basis. He was an archetypal British civil servant: pinstripe suit, rolled umbrella, even a bowler hat on his first visit. He explained that he was part of the vetting operation of applicants for the UDR and asked for my opinion of the suitability of named applicants. One of them was Sammy Clarke, later to be mentioned in the *Scarman Report* as the Sergeant instructor of the B Specials who shot at and injured Catholics in Dungannon in August 1969, and also known to me as the Sergeant in charge of the group of B Specials who shot up my house in Donaghmore. Clarke was not admitted to the UDR, despite strong support from his constituency MP, John Taylor. However, as the Police Reserve was under the control of the Ministry of Home Affairs and Taylor was a Minister of State in that Department, Clarke soon became a Reserve Constable. He was murdered by the IRA in 1975, and I will recount later the circumstances in which I attended his funeral. When the Tories came to power my friend in the MoD stopped calling; it seemed my opinion on UDR applicants was no longer required.

In 1970 I experienced a setback in my political career. I sought the 'unity' nomination for Fermanagh–South Tyrone. Based on the McCluskeys' model of 1966 in the constituency and of 1969 in Mid-Ulster, this involved a series of meetings throughout the constituency at which the candidates presented themselves, followed by a convention where delegates selected at local meetings elected the candidate. Some of my friends advised me to stay out of the 'unity circus', nominate as a candidate and then put it up to the other potential candidates whether they wished to enter the contest with the probability of coming third and earning the odium of having split the vote. However, I had always supported the McCluskeys in their efforts to get a single candidate, plus if I wilfully ignored the unity convention, it would give an excuse for republicans to do likewise. My opponents were Andy Boyd, a Belfast-based journalist, Aidan Corrigan, Chairman of the Dungannon civil rights branch, JJ Donnelly, who had courageously fought the previous election, Thomas R McGurk who had threatened to fight me in East Tyrone as a member of the People's Democracy, Frank McIlvanna, a teacher who was later to serve on the SDLP Executive, and Frank McManus, Chairman of Fermanagh civil rights. Ruairí Ó Brádaigh, the defeated Republican candidate in 1966, did not participate, preferring to wait in the wings to see how things would unfold.

It was a bruising but enjoyable contest. The public meetings were well attended, the exchanges sometimes too personal, but still very much democracy in action. Churchill may have considered the steeples of Fermanagh and Tyrone to be 'dreary', but no such epithet could be levelled at our public meetings. As perceived front-runner, I came under pressure and, of course, the UDR issue was used against me, though not to any worrying extent. It had its lighter moments, too. At the Coalisland meeting the terms 'recruiting sergeant' and 'Redmondite' were being thrown about by some members of the platform party. A note was passed to me from a member of the audience: 'Ask Thomas R McGurk what 'R' stands for.' McGurk's mother, apparently, was from Waterford where the Redmonites were still revered by a section of the community. Unfortunately, in view of future events, I was too gentlemanly to put the question to him.

I had arranged for the results from local meetings at which delegates were being selected to be phoned in, and as the figures showed me with 103 votes out of 180 I left for the convention in Enniskillen in confident mood. The first questionmark came into my head as I observed Ruairí Ó Brádaigh chatting to delegates as they entered the convention hall. I was told he was telling delegates he would fight the election if Currie were the candidate. Then the convention chairman announced that there would be a secret ballot of delegates. This made nonsense of the delegate selection procedure, where delegates had been mandated to vote for specific candidates. Aidan Corrigan announced he was withdrawing in favour of Frank McManus. A number of delegates objected to these announcements, but were ruled out of order by the Chairman. Then Paddy Donnelly, a delegate from Mountjoy in East Tyrone, complained to me that his fellow delegate, also pledged to vote for me, was refusing to show him his vote. I did not need the declaration of the count to tell me that a determined effort was being made to fiddle me out of the nomination. McManus had 90 votes, my 103 had fallen to 80 and McGurk, who had not received a single vote at the delegate selection meetings, got 10 and on the second count, predictably, all of McGurk's votes went to McManus. I loyally supported the successful candidate and campaigned for him. Ó Brádaigh did not contest. McManus defeated the Unionist candidate, the Marquis of Hamilton, by 1,442 in a 92% poll.

Frank McManus became the 'unity' MP for Fermanagh–South Tyrone. Rarely has there been such a misnomer. His divisive activities included being Chairman of the Northern Resistance Movement (a Provo- and Blaney-supported breakaway from NICRA), Chairman of Comhairle Uladh (a Provo-backed nine-county Ulster organisation) and a founder member of the Irish Independence party, which flourished briefly until supporters of Sinn Féin decided they preferred the organ-grinder to the monkey. He opposed the Power-Sharing Executive just as strongly as any of the extreme unionists and quite deservedly lost his seat in the following election. As Conn McCluskey, one of the strongest advocates of unity candidates, concluded in his book, *Up off their Knees*, 'all these activities suggested that the idea of Unity candidates was no longer attainable'.

At the same time the civil rights movement, which had done so much to bring about the transformation of the Northern Ireland political scene, was beginning to split and lose its relevance. It was, of course, inevitable that a movement which had come into existence to redress specific grievances should lose momentum and support as its demands were conceded. The nature and make-up of the coalition contributed to this process: we all had our own agendas, but some of us were more committed to submerging our own to the common good.

The separate structure and organisation of the People's Democracy and its insistence on taking its own (sometimes contradictory) decisions created a problem from the start, for example, its determination to press ahead with the Belfast to Derry march in January 1969, despite the moratorium declared by NICRA. Its emergence as a political party in the 1969 election meant that other politicians had to judge the organisation by different standards. Principally, its determination to widen the civil rights agenda to embrace socialist and even Trotskyite demands and to pursue a policy of demanding changes in the South, 'Tories out, north and south', was certain to split the civil rights movement sooner or later.

As one who, from the beginning, had seen the civil rights movement as an umbrella bringing together people and organisations in a broadly based movement campaigning to eliminate civil rights abuses in Northern Ireland, I was deeply concerned about these developments, but in the interest of unity I bit my tongue. Others did not. The first open split occurred at the civil rights march in Strabane at the end of June 1969 when Eamon McCann and

Bernadette Devlin attacked me and others from the platform. This was the first public show of disunity, but the previous March, Betty Sinclair, John McInerney and Fred Heatley had resigned from the NICRA executive over a PD proposal to march through the almost entirely Protestant East Belfast area. Further differences and internal convulsions followed, and many of the original leaders found themselves either voted out or felt compelled to withdraw from participation because they could no longer stomach what was happening. Before the 1970 AGM, Conn McCluskey, John Donaghy and Bríd Rogers announced they would not be standing for the executive because 'the Civil Rights movement had ceased to be what it originally was … a broadly based movement commanding widespread support. It had lost its sense of unity and wide support.'

The People's Democracy was not the only organisation to contribute to this situation. Since the split in the Republican movement, the differences between the Officials and the Provos were having an effect on NICRA. The 'Stickies' were determined to exert maximum control and did so in alliance with the Communist party. The 'Pinheads', as the Provos were called in the early days (because they used a pin to attach the Easter Lily to their lapels, while the Officials used an adhesive), focussed their campaign on taking over, or setting up branches which eventually were coordinated in a civil resistance movement.

The problem with NICRA from the beginning was that it was unrepresentative of the movement. The strength of the civil rights movement was in the local branches and indeed some of the areas of most successful activity, such as Derry, where the Derry Citizens Action Committee was in charge, were not even affiliated to NICRA. So no effective discipline could be applied to branches or individuals who got out of line. An example of this was the Armagh branch which, after a largely PD takeover, insisted on flying the Red Flag and singing 'The Internationale' at its meetings. I did not bite my tongue on this occasion and a sharp verbal altercation ensued.

Unfortunate as such illustrations of disunity and lack of direction were, they served to illustrate the even greater necessity for cohesion on the political level among the Stormont parliamentarians. It was time for a sustained effort to create the new left-of-centre party so often and so long promised.

15: THE SDLP

The SDLP is probably the only political party anywhere born on a radio programme. *The Irish Times* carried the story in August 1970 that the only obstacle to the launch of a new Northern political party was disagreement over who should lead it. I arranged to be interviewed on Radio Éireann's lunchtime news programme and in the course of my recorded remarks said, 'the only person with the necessary experience and ability is Gerry Fitt'. I then telephoned John Hume, left a message for Fitt to ring me, told them what I had done and later had the satisfaction of hearing Gerry, live in the Belfast studio after listening to the recorded interviews with John and I, accepting the leadership of the new party. The SDLP was in business.

Of course, it wasn't as easy as that. Indeed it had proved more difficult than expected. The idea of establishing a party similar to the SDLP had been around for a long time. Six years earlier the Maghery Conference had resulted in agreement in principle. The National Democratic party (NDP) had been formed and the Nationalist party had been holding annual conferences since 1965. The main problem was the nationalist dilemma since Partition: the need for strong representation to fight discrimination versus the fear of buttressing Partition by active participation in its institutions. That dilemma was compounded by personality politics and the lack of effective leadership.

The civil rights campaign had exposed the Achilles heel of unionists. They professed adherence to British standards while refusing to implement them. They had no answer to the question: 'If we are British subjects, why can't the citizens of Belfast and Coalisland have the same rights as the citizens of Birmingham and Coventry?' A modern, democratically organised political party was essential to put maximum pressure on the Unionist and British governments and to solidify and build upon, through political action, what had been achieved on the streets.

The new Parliament, elected in February 1969, provided the best opportunity for progress to a new party. Four of us, Independents Ivan Cooper, John Hume and Paddy O'Hanlon, and myself, a Nationalist, had been elected on manifestos – Hume and I in particular – which committed us to the formation of a new left-of-centre party. Since Maghery, the Nationalist party, with six members, had made considerable progress towards annual conferences and policy formation, but was organised only in those constituencies where it had MPs, and even then it didn't have a card-carrying membership. The defeat of Eddie McAteer, in particular, had been a devastating blow to the party's morale and placed a questionmark over its future existence.

Clearly, I was awaiting the opportunity to defect. Fitt and Paddy Kennedy were members of the Republican Labour party, but it soon became evident that there were personality differences between the two. Kennedy was determined to be his own man, and as political developments unfolded he moved closer to 'Republican' in his party title and away from 'Labour'. Paddy Devlin and Vivian Simpson represented the Northern Ireland Labour party, which by its constitution was pledged to the maintenance of Northern Ireland within the United Kingdom. Devlin represented Falls, had played and continued to play an important role in the civil rights campaign, and his activities and public utterances during the crisis of August 1969 strongly suggested he was not in the pro-unionist tradition of the Northern Ireland Labour party. We were a disparate bunch with a number of strong personalities, used to being big fish in a small pool and without experience of the discipline required in an organised political party. It was going to take time.

United opposition to the Public Order (Amendment) Bill gave us experience of working with each other and illustrated to the electorate what we meant by vigorous opposition. Then, in December, we took a further step when the Parliamentary Alliance was created and spokesmen were appointed to shadow government ministers. As an indication of the importance we attached to housing and local government reform, John Hume and I became joint Spokespersons on Development. Significantly for the future, Roddy O'Connor, the new Nationalist leader, and Vivian Simpson, NILP leader, opted out. Obviously they would not be interested in the new party. However, the rest of the Nationalists joined and James O'Reilly became Chief Whip with the job of shadowing the Prime Minister.

While we were slowly beginning to get our parliamentary act together, other, more dramatic developments were taking place, some of which I have already referred to, which distracted us from the job of party-building. These developments included: the new situation created by the increased British government involvement in the North's affairs and the hands-on approach of Callaghan; the controversy over the *Hunt Report*; the split in the republican movement and the creation of the Provisionals in January 1970; three nights of rioting in Ballymurphy in April, which saw the first major confrontation between the Catholic community and the British Army, the use of CS gas and a warning from the GOC that petrol-bombers would be shot; the growth of Catholic sectarianism exemplified by the expulsion of Protestants from the New Barnsley estate in the same month; the election of Paisley and Beattie in by-elections to Stormont; the formation of the Alliance party; the sackings of Haughey and Blaney from the Southern government and the Arms Trial; the election of a Tory government in June; the Lower Falls curfew; and the escalation of the Provo bombing campaign.

The parliamentary Alliance operated at the level of the lowest common denominator and so it was not a vehicle for major or dramatic developments. Issues such as Catholic participation in the UDR, or the emphasis which ought to be placed on street politics or parliamentary politics, or indeed participation in the Stormont assembly at all, were not issues for the Alliance, but rather for its constituent parties. The elected politicians were not providing leadership in circumstances where we were the only people who could provide it. Our procrastination was becoming irresponsibility. This view was shared by members of the Labour party at Westminster, who had the best interests of the nationalist community at heart. Along with old friends like Paul Rose, Stan Orme and Kevin McNamara, others became interested in helping to bring about the new political alignment. Chief among them was Maurice Foley, a Junior Minister in the Wilson administration. In December 1969, Maurice arranged for a number of us to meet Arthur Skeffington, the chairman of the Labour party, to discuss the possibility of a new party which might have trade union links. This was at a time when the Northern Ireland Labour party and the British Labour party were having discussions about integration and it was significant that Paddy Devlin, chairman of the NILP, was seeking an alternative. The London meeting was also important because it confirmed that Fitt was under pressure from people he paid attention to at Westminster to become involved in a new political alignment. It was becoming clearer who among the Stormont MPs was likely to be involved, apart from the three Independents and myself who had mandates from the February 1969 Stormont election.

Gerry Fitt, conscious of an upcoming Westminster election (it occurred in June 1970), would not wish to rock the boat in advance. He was having problems with his party colleague, Paddy Kennedy, who seemed determined to assert his independence of his mentor and was paying more and more attention to the newly formed Provisional Sinn Féin. In the circumstances, Fitt's caution was understandable, while his dependence on the support of his other party colleague, Senator Paddy Wilson, a close personal as well as political ally, was crucial. As always, Gerry relied heavily on the intuition of his wife, Ann, and she had taken a dislike to John Hume. I kept telling him he was a big fish in a small pool and that it was time to be a big fish in a bigger pool.

Fitt could not have made the move without the support of Devlin, whose Stormont constituency of Falls was central to Fitt's Westminster constituency. Devlin had narrowly beaten Fitt's parliamentary colleague, Harry Diamond, in 1969 and might, in certain circumstances, decide to contest West Belfast. However, by the end of 1969 Paddy was finding himself out on a limb and amenable to leaving the Labour party. His activities in August 1969 had not endeared him to the NILP. He had issued a statement, in the company of Kennedy and Paddy O'Hanlon, urging the Irish government to help 'the beleaguered areas' of the North and the NILP had subsequently distanced itself from its Chairman, stating he spoke 'in a personal capacity, not on behalf of the party'. When Paddy announced his intention to boycott Stormont as a protest against the events of August 1969, the NILP announced that if he did not return to Stormont he would be breaching his endorsement as a Labour MP. Clearly, Paddy and the NILP were running on different tracks.

The only Nationalist MP we really wanted was James O'Reilly, though if some of the others had decided to join us we would, of course, have accepted them. The one exception was Roderick H O'Connor, whom it would have been impossible to market as a left-of-centre radical. To be fair, he didn't see himself in that context either and had made his position clear by refusing to participate in the opposition alliance at Stormont. James O'Reilly, despite our approaches, decided not to join us: 'I came into politics as a Nationalist and that's the way I will leave politics.' As events evolved, he could have obtained a SDLP nomination for the 1973 Assembly election and, had he accepted, would almost certainly have won a seat. However, he insisted on running as an Independent Nationalist and lost. In 1974, as Minister in charge of housing, I asked James to become a member of the Board of the Housing Executive. He thanked me, said he appreciated that his efforts on behalf of the homeless were remembered, but no, he was out of politics and that was that. He would have made a major contribution to the Housing Executive.

So, we were six – Cooper, Currie, Devlin, Fitt, Hume and O'Hanlon – and we started to meet at Gweedore in the Donegal Gaeltacht, beginning a practice that would last for a number of years. Considerable political business was done at these gatherings, including some crucial decisions, but politics was only part of the agenda. Wives, girlfriends and children often joined us and from an early stage the group that was to become the SDLP took seriously the paraphrasing of the Rosary Crusade slogan, 'The party that drinks together stays together'. We found it useful, particularly at times when difficulties arose politically or personally, to head for Bunbeg. We would have formal discussions around a table, but sometimes more would be accomplished walking on the wonderful Magheragallen strand, or late into the night at the Errigal, or, in later years, at Óstan Gweedore. This camaraderie helped us to overcome difficulties in stressful times. We all enjoyed the *craic*. Fitt told his stories, played the mouth organ and drank his gin and tonic 'no ice, no lemon'; Hume sang *'Plaisir d'amour'*, did his Orangemen's walk and drank whiskey; Cooper told stories, mimicked nearly everyone and drank beer; Devlin sang 'Carrickfergus', drank brandy and sometimes Liebfraumilch (by the bottle); O'Hanlon sang 'The Boys from Mullaghbawn', strummed the guitar and drank his vodka. I just drank!

At our first meeting in Gweedore despite, and maybe because of, the socialising, considerable progress was made. We agreed in principle to set up a new party, that it should be democratically organised, be left-of-centre and committed to the reunification of Ireland by peaceful means and by consent of the majority in the North as well as in the South. This latter issue was a matter of long discussion for it was contrary to the traditional nationalist view that unification was a matter for the Irish people as a unit to decide.

We ran into disagreement over the name. The Belfast men, Fitt and Devlin, were insistent on 'Labour' being in the title, while the rest of us wanted 'Social Democratic'.

On Friday, 13 February 1970 we held discussions in the hotel in Toome, on the shores of Lough Neagh. At my suggestion, as it was a constituency issue for me, the cover story we gave to the media was that we were investigating the eel industry with a view to its nationalisation. Public ownership of fishing rights on inland waters was included in the original policy statement of the new party. We resumed our discussion of the name of the proposed new party and quickly agreed that both Labour and Social Democratic should feature. The question then, which should come first? The Belfast men were adamant on Labour and said they could not fight an election in Belfast which did not give priority to that word. Hume, Cooper, O'Hanlon and I argued that since we were a new party, a different sort of name was required and Social Democrat would project a new image in the context of the new Europe, which was just beginning to emerge. Willy Brandt, the leader of the Social Democrats in West Germany, had just taken over as Chancellor and with his background and policies he was, for me, the very personification of social democracy. Fitt and Devlin were so determined on the issue and the rest of us so anxious for progress that eventually we conceded that Labour should come first. About two minutes later Devlin, apparently tired after the discussion and lying back on the couch with his eyes closed, suddenly sat up. 'Fuck,' he said, 'the fucking LSD fucking party.' The connection with drugs and pre-decimalisation money won the argument that all of the idealistic Europeanism of Hume and I could not. So, Social Democratic and Labour (SDLP) the new party became.

The Lough Neagh eels cover story did not entirely stand up. That very evening the *Belfast Telegraph* reported, 'New party – opposition MPs in shock move'. The story had the by-line of the highly respected *Telegraph* political correspondent, John Wallace, and since he and Gerry were extremely good personal friends the rest of us strongly suspected where the leak had sprung. But at least the new name had not been leaked. We had agreed among ourselves that the name was not to be disclosed and I, for one, had decided that the implementation of this decision would be a good test of our new partnership and trust in one another. On 1 March a conference was organised by the NDP for the purpose of 'giving the radical elements in northern politics … an opportunity to discuss any points of difference and visible areas of co-operation.' The leadership of the NDP had naturally become very frustrated at the apparent lack of progress in establishing the new party, to which they were committed. It was tempting to report to them the actual progress made, including the name, as a wildly enthusiastic reception would have been guaranteed. The temptation was resisted and I was delighted that our mutual trust and confidence in each other had been vindicated.

It took thirty years for me to discover there had been disclosure, albeit under condition of confidentiality. When documents from 1970 were released to the National Archives under the thirty-year rule, included was a note marked 'Secret', written by Eamonn Gallagher, the Department of Foreign Affairs official who, in the aftermath of the dramatic events of August 1969, had been appointed as a roving ambassador to Northern Ireland. This note was written on 16 February 1970, three days after our meeting in Toome, where we had taken the confidential decision regarding the name SDLP:

'John Hume MP informed me in strict confidence yesterday that plans are going ahead for the creation of a new opposition party in the six counties. The founding members are ………… If this succeeds it will be a most important political development as a coalition including Hume, Fitt and Currie will be very strong indeed and should eventually attract other opposition MPs. The general colouration of the new party is left of centre. It will be called the Social Democratic and Labour Party -- the latter word in deference to Fitt and Devlin. Hume asked me to convey to the Taoiseach and the Minister his assurance that, notwithstanding the necessary inclusion of the word Labour in the name of the party, there will be no connection between it and the British, Irish and Northern Ireland Labour Parties. He is anxious that the Taoiseach and the Minister should know this in advance of the announcement of the formation of the new party, but he is very anxious that no word of the creation should leak out in advance.'

At the first opportunity, during the Stormont Easter recess in April, we went back to Bunbeg, this time joined by Senator Paddy Wilson. We reached agreement on all matters except the one that wasn't discussed: leadership. This subject and the launch date were left to await developments, particularly Gerry's sensitive position in relation to the Republican Labour party. John and I were deputed to draw up a document based on our agreements and this we proceeded to do when the Bunbeg discussions ended. He returned with me to my home in Donaghmore where, at about two o'clock in the morning, we dictated the first policy and founding document of the SDLP to Annita, who typed it on her portable typewriter. Two days later I brought it to Stormont to be signed by the six MPs. I still have that original document (see picture section 2), with the changes suggested by our colleagues in John's handwriting and mine.

As Harold MacMillan had said a few years earlier in a different context, 'events, dear boy' intervened to delay our launch even longer than anticipated. The Alliance party was announced shortly after we had signed up in April, and in May the Westminster election was declared for 18 June resulting in a Conservative government led by Edward Heath. At the beginning of July the new government authorised the Falls curfew, and by August I was beginning to despair that conditions would never be right for the launch of the new party.

Early on the morning of Monday, 17 August I received a phone call from Sean Hughes, a journalist with the *Tyrone Democrat* who acted as a stringer for a number of media outlets. He enquired if I had read in *The Irish Times* a story about a new party being formed. On being told I hadn't collected my newspapers yet, Sean called at my home with them. The story, by Michael McInerney the paper's political correspondent, was headed, 'North's opposition seeking one voice', and the introduction stated, 'a new form of organisation may be started in the North during the coming week and, in time, could hope to represent broadly non-unionist or even progressive peace voices in the North'. There was also an editorial headed 'Missing Piece', which said, 'one of the missing pieces in the northern pattern of events is a concerted viewpoint and guiding line from the opposition MPs ... Westminster obviously has some changes in mind for the North. One of the important factors in any decision they make will be the attitude of the opposition. If the British government wishes to sound out that opposition, where does it turn? To whom does it speak? It is a question of practical politics, not of ideological differences.'

No source for McInerney's information was mentioned, but my strong suspicion became a certainty when I read, on the very same page, a piece also by McInerney headed, 'Hume sees big test in Northern Ireland's legislation,' and began, 'Mr John Hume MP in an interview yesterday in Dublin said ...' I didn't need the assistance of Sherlock Holmes!

Too much time had already been wasted, so I decided to take the bull by the horns and asked Sean to ring the Radio Éireann 'One-Thirty News' programme to say that I would be prepared to do an interview on *The Irish Times'* story. As arranged, the interviewer, I think it was Mike Burns, asked me whether it was true that the only factors holding up the formation of the new party were failure to agree on the name and on the leader. I replied that the name had already been agreed, though I declined to say what it was, and as far as a leader was concerned, 'the only person with the necessary experience and ability to lead the new party is Gerry Fitt'. I then phoned John, told him what I had done and got his agreement to Gerry as leader. Finding Gerry was a bit more difficult, however. The holiday home he rented at Murlough on the North Antrim coast did not have a telephone. I rang his local pub, Hunters, and arranged for Gerry to be given a message to phone me urgently. When he did, within the hour, I told him it was a *fait accompli*: John and I were supporting him for leader and although I had not spoken to the other three, I was absolutely confident it would be unanimous. Gerry got a lift to Belfast, listened to John and I in the RTÉ studio and accepted the leadership on air. Four days later, at a press conference in the Grand Central Hotel, Belfast, the party was officially launched by the six MPs and Senator Paddy Wilson.

In his autobiography, *Straight Left*, published in 1993, sixteen years after he had left the SDLP, largely because of differences with John Hume, Paddy Devlin alleged that prior to the launch of the SDLP, Hume was involved in an effort to create a 'Catholic political party'. Paddy alleged that John had organised a weekend meeting in Donegal, attended by middle-class Catholics, for the purpose of promoting his new party and that 'Austin Currie must have received the same word from the Donegal meeting as I did for we independently issued separate statements that Monday morning saying we were forming a new political party immediately and that Gerry Fitt would be leader of it'. I have to say categorically that I had not received any word about a Donegal meeting. I have already described the circumstances and the context in which I set up the radio interviews that led Gerry to accept the leadership and got the party off the ground. I was frustrated by the delay and I seized the opportunity presented by *The Irish Times'* article, there was no other motivation. I did not have then, nor have I seen since, any evidence of John Hume attempting to establish a Catholic party and, frankly, I don't believe it. Even apart from his long-held commitment to the idea of a left-of-centre, non-sectarian party, the evidence of the Eamonn Gallagher report to Jack Lynch and Paddy Hillery, whereby Hume had informed him of the proposed formation of the SDLP and his justification of 'Labour' in the title, would indicate that Hume fully accepted the policy of the new party and had no alternative in mind. For John to have been involved as alleged would have been the basest of hypocrisy and double-dealing. Furthermore, I do not remember any indication from Paddy at the time that he believed this to be the case.

The building of a new political party, centrally and locally, added greatly to my workload, particularly at a time when so many political developments were taking place. Premises were rented for Party Headquarters at College Park North in Central Belfast. An indication of the financial standing of the individuals concerned and the confidence the Munster and Leinster Bank had in the future of our party is the fact that the signatures of all six founding MPs were required to obtain the overdraft to rent the premises. In fact, finance was always a problem for the SDLP. Those who supported us in the North were not monied people, certainly not in the early days, and we relied on our friends south of the border. Paddy Duffy, the party Treasurer, and I spoke at a meeting in the South County Hotel in Dublin shortly after the party was launched and at that meeting a support group was formed. The Chairman was Dr John Kelly, a Newry man and lecturer at UCD. Initially, Fianna Fáil people were reluctant to get involved, despite John Hume's assurances, and it took a lunch with Jack Lynch and Brian Lenihan in the Dáil, which John Kelly and I attended, before they came on board.

Throughout the SDLP's existence the Dublin group has been a major contributor and members like Mackie and Marjorie Moyna, Phil Rooney, Paddy McKillion and Sean Kelleher have deservedly received standing ovations at annual conferences down the years. We were extremely lucky that the

National Democratic party came over to the SDLP *en masse*, providing much of the manpower and the know-how for setting up the party structure. Fortunately, the new party did not have to rely on the organisational capacities of the six founders, and we were lucky to have the commitment of some outstanding general secretaries, like John Duffy, Dan McAreavey, Eamon Hanna, Bríd Rodgers and Gerry Cosgrove.

The six of us were the largest group in the opposition at Stormont and we took over the leadership, dominating to a greater extent than our number would have suggested. We punched above our weight; effectively, the SDLP was the opposition. And we were even more than that. As Ken Bloomfield, then assistant secretary to the Cabinet, later recorded in his memoir, *Stormont in Crisis*, 'From the outset the new SDLP ran rings around the Unionist party in the game of making friends and influencing people.' It was necessary that this be the case for we had to justify our presence in the Parliament in circumstances where the question was increasingly being asked, not only about our involvement in Stormont, but whether Stormont itself should exist. Would the interests of the minority community not be better served by the abolition of Stormont and Direct Rule from Westminster? After all, that was the logic behind the appeal for greater British involvement in 1969.

As long as the reform programme was going through Stormont, the issue was not an urgent one. In particular, the 'civil rights' MPs elected in 1969 – Cooper, Hume and O'Hanlon – had argued that the civil rights gains on the streets had to be consolidated by political action in Parliament. That this was what was happening during the premiership of Chichester-Clark meant the presence of the SDLP in Stormont was justified on that level. But as the political situation developed and long-term judgements had to be made, the question of the adaptability of the Stormont system to our political needs became more and more relevant.

Even before the formation of the SDLP I was turning my mind to the long term. In the same issue of *The Irish Times,* on 17 August, in which Michael McInerney had flown Hume's kite on the new party, there was another report headed, 'Constitutional talks urged by Currie'. I was reported as having said in a speech in Cookstown that 'the only possible solution to the Northern Ireland problem must be in the context of a revised constitutional relationship between Britain and Ireland, North and South. Discussion should now be taking place ... between Westminster, Dublin and representatives of both unionists and anti-unionists in the North on the form of a new constitutional relationship.' It was clear, in advance of the formation of the SDLP, the role I envisaged for the new party.

In the interim, the prime task was to get as much of the reform programme through Stormont as possible. James Chichester-Clark was in an almost impossible situation. He would always be identified in the unionist mind with the abolition of the B Specials. The continuation of no-go areas in circumstances where republican violence was escalating left him vulnerable to a 'law and order' campaign, and 'Chi Chi' didn't impress by his eloquence. In fact, he stammered and stuttered and on television, in particular, he was hopeless. However, he came across as honest, especially in comparison with the deviousness of the man he had defeated by one vote, Brian Faulkner. Honest, but not very bright. He also seemed to have an identity problem. We had great fun with an interview he gave to the German magazine *Der Spiegel*. Asked if an Ulsterman was an Irishman, he replied, 'Well now, he lives on the same island, I don't know.' As the *Belfast Telegraph* editorial commented, 'His ancestors take up an entire page of *Burke's Landed Gentry of Ireland*. He is descended from Clarks (settled in County Londonderry in 1690), from Dawson (settled in Drogheda in 1611) and the Chichesters.'

The civil rights movement had demanded various reforms, such as an Ombudsman, the reorganisation of local government, one man, one vote and, that which gave me the greatest personal satisfaction, the establishment of a Housing Executive to take housing allocation out of the hands of local councillors and effectively end discrimination in housing. Although these reforms were going through Stormont, in other respects the situation was deteriorating. The Provisional IRA was gaining strength. In February 1971 the first British soldier to be killed in action, Gunner Curtis, died on the New Lodge Road. That same month, two unarmed RUC men were gunned down, beginning the process whereby the RUC would again be an armed force and thereby negating one of the most welcome of the *Hunt Report* proposals. In March, in one of the most inhumane actions of the whole Troubles and one which shocked people like myself into a realisation of the barbarism that might be expected from our 'freedom fighters', three young Scottish soldiers, two of them brothers, were lured from a bar with the promise of drink and sex and cold-bloodedly shot as they relieved themselves at the side of the road. Chichester-Clark and his government came under more and more pressure from the right wing of the party and from Ian Paisley, now a Stormont and Westminster MP.

I too had come under pressure, and not just politically. At 3.30am on

Sunday, 8 March 1970, Annita and I were awakened by a loud bang. Our immediate fear was for Estelle, aged just over eighteen months, who was sleeping in her cot in the front room. The bomb had been placed at the gable wall and had blown in the window of the spare room, showering the room with glass and damaging the roof. Had anyone been in the room, he or she certainly would have been injured. What made matters worse was that the birth of our second child was imminent; Caitríona was born seven days later. Thankfully no physical harm was done to Annita, Estelle, or Caitríona, but once again I was reminded of the effect of my political involvement on my family.

The attack on my home coincided with the trial of men accused of causing the explosions designed to bring down O'Neill as Premier. The RUC believed my accusations at that time were the reason for the present outrage. I received a phone call within minutes of the bomb going off which supported that belief. The anonymous caller said, 'Maybe you will keep your mouth shut now.' It was an anxious time, not helped by a statement from John Taylor, Parliamentary Secretary to the Minister for Home Affairs who, while condemning the attack, went on to say that those responsible for the explosion should bear in mind that such events helped me politically. It was a wounding comment as it inferred, as was pointed out by John Hume in the Stormont debate on the issue, that I was prepared to put considerations of political advantage before the safety of my wife and children. One of Taylor's colleagues, Robin Bailie MP, described the remarks as 'uncalled for and that for someone in a responsible position for the administration of justice they were indeed quite irresponsible'. Certainly, Taylor's comments did not help our personal relations, or indeed community relations in County Tyrone. Despite, or possibly because of Taylor's comments, the government took the bombing sufficiently seriously to offer a reward of £5,000 for conviction of the perpetrators.

In early 1972 John Taylor, then a Minister of State for Home Affairs, was seriously wounded in an attempted assassination by the Official IRA. I immediately condemned the murder attempt without reservation and, while there was still hope of his survival, refused to participate in the preparation of an obituary programme for the BBC. Politics can be a tough game and, in the circumstances in Northern Ireland in the 1970s, even brutal. But that is no excuse for lack of basic human instincts.

16: FAULKNER'S STORMONT

Few have disputed the ability of Brian Faulkner. In his memoirs, *Stormont in Crisis*, Ken Bloomfield, his key advisor and speechwriter, wrote, 'Everyone knew that he was clever, energetic, ambitious. Some thought he was shallow, devious and unprincipled.' For most of his political career, I was in the 'some' category.

Faulkner was one of the first full-time politicians, and his professionalism was like a shaft of light in the Stormont mausoleum: an able platform speaker, on many occasions at the Dispatch Box a brilliant parliamentarian, mentally agile and articulate on TV and radio, an expert at using the media to his own advantage and an able minister in six positions in government. Following his first contribution to the House as Prime Minister, on 23 March 1971, as the following speaker I congratulated him on his election and said, 'There are some of us who have told him in the past that the highest tribute we could pay to him was, that if he were at Westminster, he is probably the only member of the frontbench here who would be on the frontbench at Westminster.' After this sincere compliment to him, if not to his Right Honourable friends sitting beside him, I went on to warn of his weakness. He had spoken about trust and confidence:

'I would say to the Prime Minister, without there being anything whatever personal in it, that it is possibly more necessary for him to emphasise those two matters than for anyone else who might have been put in the position in which he now finds himself. I say that to him in a friendly way – that he should put more emphasis on confidence and trust in the future because there are many people in both sections of this community who do not have that confidence and that trust in him.'

I did not exaggerate. He was trusted by very few, certainly not by the Catholic community, and not by Terence O'Neill. Nor indeed by Harold Wilson, or Ted Heath. As the years went by, hardly by anyone. To a large extent the suspicion arose from his performance under O'Neill, which gave the impression of power-hungry opportunism. The 'I am concerned with policies, not with personalities' line was so transparent that it aroused cynicism, even in those who preferred him to O'Neill. Not that O'Neill was free from blame either. He displayed a petty vindictiveness on occasions, in office and out of it, which was sadly at variance with the good relations he preached. Faulkner's attitude, however, built up a mountain of suspicion and bitterness that was not easy to surmount. And if his colleagues in his own party felt this way about him, it is easy to imagine how the Catholic community felt. Very few in Northern Ireland at the time thought of Richard Nixon when 'Tricky Dicky' was mentioned.

At the time of his accession, nothing had done him more harm in the eyes of the Catholic community than his close identification with the Orange Order and his zeal in cultivating and defending the organisation. In particular, his famous forced march along the Longstone Road, in the face of huge opposition from the local Catholic community, had never been forgotten or forgiven. The modern-day comparison is with the Garvaghy Road.

Faulkner's other misfortune was to become leader of the Unionist party and Prime Minister of Northern Ireland at a time when history was about to deliver its judgement on fifty years of unionist rule. Given his ability and the fact that he had a unionist power base more secure than O'Neill's, it is just possible, had he succeeded Brookeborough – as well he might if the Unionist Parliamentary party had been allowed to decide – that he might have been able to change unionism sufficiently to ride the storm. He was certainly in a better position to take on Paisley, and his business background would have made it easier to sell North–South cooperation. However, by 1971 when he at last became Prime Minister, his options were running out. Northern Ireland and the Unionist party had changed beyond all recognition in the eight years since O'Neill had held the reins.

Our hero made two efforts to bound free: an attempt to involve the opposition more fully in the Stormont system, and internment.

When Faulkner stood up in the Stormont House of Commons on 27 June 1971, the 50th anniversary of the opening of the Parliament, the proposals he made would have been enthusiastically welcomed by the Opposition at any other time over the fifty years as an indication of unionist willingness to reach out to the minority community and to take their views into account in the running of the State. He proposed setting up three functional committees covering social, environmental and industrial services, at least two of which would have Opposition MPs as chairmen and for which service they would be paid. The purpose of the committees would be the consideration of major proposals of policy, review of performance and consideration of legislation. 'I consider it to be the task of my government to reach out beyond the bounds of any ordinary legislative programme; to be ready to propose quite exceptional measures to break out of the mould of fear and mutual suspicion.' He invited Opposition MPs to get involved with him in 'a serious attempt to bring the various political interests represented here together for frank and wide-ranging discussions … to seek some measure of common ground in restoring peace and stability and resuming social and economic advance.' At a press briefing afterwards he said, 'Short of asking the Opposition to run the country, this is the best means of participation for them.'

It was a magnificent performance, and to an Opposition with only the Wild Bird Act 1931 to its legislative credit in fifty years, the new proposals represented a major, even revolutionary, advance. But things had changed radically since 1968. We noted the number of times Faulkner used the word 'participation'. It was a keyword, even a code word, which I had first heard in a new context in October 1969, employed by a Callaghan civil servant during the Home Secretary's second visit to the North. As the meaning of the word evolved in further discussions with other British officials, it became clear it meant more than participation in parliamentary committees, it meant participation in government itself. The devious Faulkner was attempting not only to involve us more closely in the Stormont system to bolster it but also to use our involvement at this minimum level to fend off British pressure for real participation in government by the opposition.

For the SDLP it was a tricky situation. We had received no advance notice of Faulkner's proposals and therefore had had no opportunity to agree on the party line. The Prime Minister had made an impressive speech, which was bound to be welcomed by the media. He would undoubtedly be attacked by Paisley and the right wing of his own party for appeasement, and attacks from those quarters would increase support among our supporters. If we attacked him we would appear churlish and negative, and possibly even irresponsible considering the continuing escalation in Provo violence and the increasing fear of a right-wing takeover. And, of course, his offer of paid chairmanships further complicated matters – we could not appear to have been bought.

In his immediate response, Gerry Fitt was cautious, '… we will read his remarks with great care and we hope we shall be able to cooperate with him in the new departures he has announced, provided that these new avenues of approach would be to the benefit of the whole community. We have been tricked too many times in the past and we have very real reasons for all of the fears and suspicions shown by the opposition side of the House since the inception of the state.'

John Hume spoke on the second day of the debate when we had had an opportunity to read Faulkner's proposals and discuss them. The centrepiece of his remarks was an attack on the men of violence and he too was cautious regarding the PM's proposals:

'We must view this problem – and I think we will be excused for viewing it – against the whole background of caution: against the background of having heard a lot of the words before and no results produced; against the background of knowing the Prime Minister and his government are dependent upon the support of a party which only last week found itself unable to break the links with a body which is in no way in favour of civil and religious liberty or freedom and equality in this society.'

I had been given the job of drafting the SDLP amendment to the government motion and of proposing it in my speech on the third and final day of the debate. I had become concerned by what I considered to be the 'over the top' response to Faulkner's speech in the media. The words and the performance were being widely praised and a certain euphoria was building up which I believed to be wildly unrealistic. I met Gerry in the corridor and quickly found that he shared my concerns, with the additional worry that some phone calls he had already received indicated that some members of the party had become over-enthusiastic. We decided that the party amendment, and my speech proposing it, should seek to provide a more balanced and realistic approach, but that it should also be forward-looking and positive.

Accordingly, I proposed the following amendment:

'… and while welcoming the expressed intention of the Prime Minister to ensure in the future genuine and constructive participation in the work of Parliament by all its members, and to initiate consultations with members of opposition parties, humbly regrets that the government proposals represent only a tinkering with a system which is not relevant to the exceptional conditions of political life in Northern Ireland and calls for the setting up of a Select Committee representative of the House, which would have available to it the necessary expertise and secretariat, for the purpose of recommending the necessary institutional and procedural changes.'

'Humbly' was added by the Parliamentary clerk – the amendment was, after all, to 'the humble address to his Excellency the Governor' standing in for the Queen!

I praised Faulkner for his speech, which I said encouraged other MPs to contribute to the best Queen's Speech debate I could remember. He had used the word 'participation' which was a key SDLP concept, and he had expressed his intention to promote 'genuine and constructive participation', a phrase I myself could not have bettered. I explained why it would be necessary to have changes in view of the *MacCrory Report*, which had proposed major new functions for central government at the expense of local government. 'We are prepared to give the Prime Minister's proposals a guarded welcome, but we have not yet had an opportunity to study them in detail. Bearing in mind – and let us be realistic about it – what might be described as the confidence gap between the Prime Minister and ourselves on the opposition side of the House, then I think the Prime Minister could not reasonably expect more from us at this stage in time.' I then went on to spell out what I saw as the job of the Select Committee I was proposing, but I did so in terms which made it clear that the changes the SDLP was thinking of went far beyond what Faulkner had in mind. I concluded with more prescience than I knew:

'The month of June, coming as it does just before July, is not usually a good time for serious consideration of issues such as those in the Prime Minister's speech. I hope that other events will not overtake us. It is recognised that the Prime Minister and the government will face considerable challenge during this summer. Their political lives depend more on what happens or what could happen on the streets this summer than on the speeches they make in Parliament, no matter how good those speeches are. I hope that these proposals will not be pigeon-holed and then, if the Prime Minister is still in office and this House is still in existence at the end of the summer, they will be taken out again and seriously considered.'

It was a good speech, which stated the SDLP position in realistic terms, although a later contribution by Paddy Devlin that gave rather extravagant praise to Faulkner provided some quotable quotes for our opponents on the republican side. It had been a good three days for Faulkner, and indeed a good three days for Parliament, even the Stormont Parliament. Taken on the level of good speeches, of expressed good intentions and of hope, but divorced from the actuality of what was happening on the streets, the level of confidence that things might be starting to improve was certainly higher after the debate.

The icy douche of cold reality came four days later. Faulkner and half his Cabinet, all Orangemen, met leaders of the Orange Order, Royal Black Preceptory and Apprentice Boys at Orange Headquarters in Lurgan. Faulkner afterwards explained that the meeting had been held to explain the government policy on parades to those responsible for organising parades. But if that was the intention, why did it require the Prime Minister and half his Cabinet to attend? And why was the meeting held at Orange Headquarters rather than at Stormont? And why no public announcement? To the SDLP it seemed that Faulkner the zealous Orangeman was displaying his true colours, and that what I dubbed 'the Lurgan Parliament' was more important to him and more relevant than the one on Stormont Hill. My kinder feelings towards Faulkner were further dissipated when, as Minister for Home Affairs, he allowed the Orangemen to march through Coalisland, a 90%-plus Catholic town in the heart of my constituency. Only the efforts of the local Citizens Action Committee, assisted by me, prevented serious violence in the town. The spectacle of the Orangemen marching through Coalisland, despite my direct appeals to Faulkner, put in context his triumphant speech given just three days earlier. Once again, it was the reality of the streets that mattered.

Stormont went into recess for the summer on Thursday, 8 July. Two days earlier I had said, 'If we are forced to accept legislation like this, which is completely unsuitable in Northern Ireland conditions, then what is the justification for this Parliament and what is the justification for us coming here and discussing the matter?' This, however, was in a debate on a Social Security Bill, a 'step by step with Britain' measure passed at Westminster by the Tory government, which was opposed by the SDLP, clause by clause, as an attack on the welfare state. As we left Stormont for the summer recess that Thursday, shortly after six o'clock, we had just listened to Faulkner report on serious rioting in Derry and the news that two men had been shot by the Army. He concluded, 'we are living in trying times'. Neither he nor I knew just how much more trying the times would quickly become. Nor did I know that this was to be my last attendance in the old Stormont Parliament.

The deaths of Desmond Beattie and Seamus Cusack escalated the process that led to the fall of Stormont. The British Army alleged that Cusack had been shot while aiming a rifle and Beattie while preparing to throw a petrol bomb; both claims were hotly disputed by Derry Catholics. The day after the shootings John Hume demanded a public inquiry, saying that such an inquiry would prove the Army was telling lies. On the following day, John phoned me to say we needed a party meeting, but as he could not leave Derry because of the high tension there, would I attend a meeting in his home the following Sunday.

When I arrived at John's house, Ivan Cooper and Paddy O'Hanlon were already there, as well as, unexpectedly, Michael O'Leary TD, a prominent front bencher and later leader of the Irish Labour party, who was on a visit to Derry. John explained that Fitt and Devlin had been unavailable to travel to Derry, but that he had spoken to them by telephone and they were willing to agree to anything the rest of us might decide. We were in Derry, John and, to a lesser extent, Ivan were in the eye of the storm, they knew Derry and their judgements in relation to Derry had been right in the past, so when John proposed that we issue an ultimatum to the British government to announce a public inquiry into the killings by the following Thursday or else the SDLP would withdraw from Stormont, I found little difficulty in agreeing. My concern was not about the ultimatum or the threat, but the possible response of Fitt and Devlin to the proposal. Abstentionism had always come easier to West of the Bann nationalists than to Belfast representatives – a feature of Northern nationalism since the foundation of the Northern Ireland State. Moreover, Gerry had always been particularly strong on the importance of regular attendance at Stormont and Paddy, prior to his involvement in the SDLP, had been a member of the Northern Ireland Labour party, where any proposal not to attend Stormont would not even have merited discussion. Additionally, Gerry would be concerned about his Westminster seat, since a proposal to boycott Stormont over actions of the British Army under the control of the British government was bound to lead to the question of boycotting the Westminster Parliament as well. I was assured that no statement would be issued until approval of the two Belfast men had been obtained.

We decided to issue the ultimatum, subject to the approval of Fitt and Devlin, and the meeting then moved on to a discussion of how we could fill the vacuum likely to be created by the SDLP leaving Stormont. We certainly could not allow the growing Provisionals to fill the vacuum. This had always been the weakness of abstentionist politics in the past: the lack of a political forum and a lessening of the importance of the letters 'MP' after one's name. It was Michael O'Leary who suggested some form of an alternative assembly to fill the gap. A cursory discussion followed, but a seed had been planted in fertile ground.

I returned home, not unduly concerned about our decision. There was a good chance a formula would be found to satisfy our demand for an inquiry. A telephone conversation with Gerry later that night confirmed this feeling. He was angry about the ultimatum, had some choice phrases to describe those of us who had taken the decision, but said he felt he could bring sufficient pressure to bear on Maudling, the Home Secretary, to achieve a face-saving formula. He and I were wrong. The British government was not prepared to go further than an inquest and there was no way the SDLP could accept that. Not for the first, or last, time we ran into the brick wall of British obduracy when actions of their Army were questioned. 'Our Army, right or wrong.'

Serious thinking and discussion quickly followed, and by the time the SDLP's ultimatum expired, we had put together a document that would prove to be historic. It put the Cusack and Beattie killings in their proper context 'as a final but important straw' which had forced us:

'... to the point when we have been faced with a clear choice: either to continue to give credibility to the system which in itself is basically unstable and from which derives the unrest that is destroying our community or take a stand in order to bring home to those in authority the need for strong political action to solve our problems and to prevent any further tragic loss of life which derives from the instability of our political institutions.'

There had been legislative reform, yes, but there had been no change of heart and right-wing forces were increasing their grip, as had been illustrated by the displacing of two Prime Ministers while a third, just recently, along with half his Cabinet had bowed the knee to a secret, sectarian organisation at Lurgan. We had to question British policy and we indicted it as 'still governed as it always has been, except for a few short months in 1969, by the threat of a right-wing backlash. There can be no solution until the right wing is confronted.' Our statement went on to condemn violence in the strongest terms and to say to our supporters 'stay off the streets and give no support whatever to the violence or the perpetrators of it'.

The SDLP statement was issued at a press conference the day after the expiry of our ultimatum. By then we had the support of all the opposition MPs, except the NILP member, Vivian Simpson. More importantly, our six MPs and two Senators (Claude Wilton, a former Liberal, had joined us in November 1970) were united in favour of the new departure, despite initial misgivings.

To some observers, particularly those who had been euphoric over Faulkner's committees offer, the apparently new SDLP position represented a major and unwelcome change. They had not paid sufficient attention to the amendment I had proposed, which had described the committees as representing 'only a tinkering with a system which is not relevant to the exceptional conditions of political life in Northern Ireland'. However, there was no doubt that our position had hardened. Our statement indicated another reason for this new direction, apart from our fears of the growth of the unionist right wing, namely our suspicion of the Tory administration in London. We had had a good relationship with Callaghan and we naturally identified more with the left-of-centre Labour government than with the Tories, traditional allies of the unionists in the 'Conservative and Unionist party'. Maudling's visits to the North had been a disaster, and we found it difficult to believe that Ted Heath would be sympathetic to our cause. We had also noticed a change in the Army since the Tories had taken over, illustrated particularly by the Falls Road curfew.

Other developments, some of them directly the responsibility of the Westminster government – such as the proposals for a full-time battalion, or battalions, of the UDR, which undermined our efforts to get Catholics to join the organisation, and the 'shoot to kill on suspicion' statements from Faulkner, which had not been fully disowned – were clearly inimical to the interests of the SDLP. I had noted the change locally in my own constituency, where new Army commanders no longer sought my advice. In all areas of the North the party detected decreasing consultation at all levels and an insensitivity, at least, to our political positions. The failure to try to meet our needs over the Cusack–Beattie shootings was just another illustration of the way things had been moving.

In another respect the Derry killings were politically important. In our statement we had asked the British government to face the logic of its presence in Northern Ireland. We also, as a party, were forced to face the logic of that presence, a factor about which we had been ambivalent since 1969. The *Belfast Telegraph* of 22 October 1969 reported a speech I gave at Trinity College: 'Mr. Currie said he was opposed to permanent Direct Rule from Westminster. He did not favour abolishing the Stormont government but he would agree as an interim to its suspension "while the stable was being cleaned out". Stormont could not be replaced by Westminster permanently because Stormont was an Irish Parliament and Westminster was not.'

At the launch of the SDLP, Gerry Fitt had stated, as official party policy, that we did not favour the abolition of Stormont. Accordingly, until the Cusack–Beattie killings we had seen our position as driving the civil rights reforms and supporting O'Neill and Chichester-Clark, and then Faulkner in implementing those commitments. Even our statement withdrawing from Stormont was not a full-blooded demand for its abolition, instead making references to 'within the present system' and 'the present Parliamentary system'. Clearly, in a situation where the Direct Rule government had been responsible for the Derry killings and the other wrongs of which we complained, logic would have been affronted by a full-blooded demand for Direct Rule by the government responsible. All-out political war on Stormont was not to be long delayed, however, when Faulkner played his last, desperate card.

The benefit of hindsight makes it possible to see that our withdrawal from Stormont over the Cusack–Beattie killings was a mistake. It had one consequence to which we had not given sufficient consideration: it removed from Faulkner one concern which might have prevented him from introducing internment, at least in the short term, and which made it easier for the London government to agree to support him in its introduction. Faulkner knew we would not stomach internment, and that any hope of the 'participation' he considered necessary for the continuation of Stormont would be wrecked by our threatened withdrawal if it were introduced. Our boycott of Stormont relieved him of that disincentive. On the other hand, the continued escalation of the Provos' campaign, the demands of his party and his own inclination given the success of internment during the 1950s' IRA campaign when he was Minister of Home Affairs, made it likely that internment would come at some stage.

Shortly before nine o'clock on the morning of 9 August 1971, my phone started ringing and it hardly ceased over the next few days. A 'dry run' a week previously had alerted the more politically conscious and experienced candidates for internment and most were not at home when the police and Army arrived. Of the 452 names on the list, only 342 were arrested and a number of those turned out to be the wrong people – fathers instead of sons, sons instead of fathers, while others were the only males at the address at the time. The violent reaction followed within hours, indicating IRA leadership still at large and plans already prepared. Within three days twenty-two people were dead and up to 7,000 homeless. For the two governments, internment was a political disaster; for the community, particularly for the ordinary, working-class people, it was a catastrophe. Northern Ireland hovered on the brink of civil war.

I found it hard to believe the authorities were so stupid to 'lift' some of those they did. To my almost certain knowledge (someone in my position could never be 100% sure) the majority of those arrested in the Coalisland/Dungannon area were not members of the IRA. The authorities compounded their stupidity by interning only Catholics, and this in a situation where Protestant extremists had been involved in violence since 1966 and the UVF was an illegal organisation. This one-sidedness gave credence to those who alleged that Faulkner was only interested in stamping out violence in the Catholic community and intent on restoring Orange hegemony.

Within days allegations of ill-treatment, brutality and torture were in circulation. Statements from prisoners, witnessed by priests and solicitors, were made available to the media. One statement in particular, from PJ McClean, a NICRA activist and primary schoolteacher in mid-Tyrone, enumerated sixteen different 'forms of punishment', including having a bag over his head at all times, standing against a wall for hours on end, sleep deprivation and physical beatings. He and others alleged they were thrown from helicopters in the belief they were high in the air, instead of feet from the ground.

The British and international media was so busy reporting violence that the brutality allegations went unreported except in the local press. Then John Whale of the 'Insight' team in the *Sunday Times* rang me to enquire about another aspect of the internment story. I told him about the brutality allegations and put him in touch with Fr Denis Faul. The following Sunday there was an exposé that was the start of serious adverse publicity for the British government, in Britain and internationally.

What with the phone ringing and relatives of the interned visiting my house at all hours of the day and night, family life was seriously disrupted at this time, especially as I was away from home so often organising opposition to internment, visiting relatives and making representations on behalf of the detained. Annita had to cope on her own, and with three children under three, one (Dualta) just two weeks old, it was a nightmare for her, dealing with distressed and anxious mothers and wives in circumstances where her own home was vulnerable to attack.

A number of my constituents were released before Internment Orders were signed by Faulkner, whether due to my intervention or the realisation that there was no evidence against them, I do not know. By the end of August, when I visited constituents on the prison ship *Maidstone* berthed in Belfast Lough, there were still fourteen men for me to meet over a five-hour period in a caravan adjacent to the ship.

From the beginning of internment I knew what the political reality was and what had to be done and I was determined to do all in my power to bring it about. By introducing internment, Faulkner had thrown down the gauntlet, not only to the SDLP but to the whole Catholic community. I accept that he had to do something to try to stop the escalating Provo campaign, which had reached a stage in deaths and destruction he could not tolerate, but we had warned him of the consequences of internment without trial. We opposed it on principle and we would have left Stormont upon its introduction, if we had not already done so. If the right people had been taken out of circulation and if loyalists had also been interned, it might have been tacitly accepted as a *fait accompli* if it had been successful in reducing the level of violence, which was unacceptable to the majority of Catholics as well as Protestants. But 'lifting' innocent Catholics while guilty Protestants remained at large, plus the brutality that accompanied the exercise, made it a 'him or us' situation where no compromise was possible. I was determined this was the issue on which the whole Stormont system would be brought down.

Within hours of the dawn raids the SDLP MPs were meeting in Dungannon with the Nationalist party, Republican Labour party and the executive of the Civil Rights Association. The statement issued afterwards was largely ours:

'We express our total opposition to internment and regard it as further proof of the total failure of the system of government in Northern Ireland. We also outrightly condemn the British government's action in clearly taking a course of repression and support for the discredited Unionist regime, a course that had failed before and will fail again.'

We called for

'–all who held public positions in Northern Ireland whether elected or appointed to express their opposition to internment by immediate withdrawal from their positions

–the general public to immediately withhold all rent and rates'

and called on,

'–the Westminster government to suspend immediately the system of government in operation in N. Ireland in view of its absolute failure to provide peace, justice and stability and to initiate immediate talks on new political and constitutional arrangements ... At this time of grave crisis, in order to prevent any further serious loss of life, we call on all who support us to stand firm and disciplined behind us. We emphasise the need for absolute unity in all areas and we pledge ourselves to firm and determined leadership in order to provide, once and for all, a political solution to the problems of this country.'

175

The SDLP opposition to internment was intensified by our attitude to the man who had initiated it. Certainly, in my case there was a high degree of personal animosity. A year later I put my feelings on record in an interview in *SDLP News*:

'It was one of those occasions when personal inclination, public opinion and political judgement absolutely and completely coincided. By refusing to talk to Faulkner or the British, by initiating a civil disobedience campaign and by symbolising our rejection of the system through the alternative assembly, we could end internment, end Faulkner and end the system.'

Reference to 'Tricky Dicky', with its comparison with Richard Nixon, always got a favourable response. I described him as 'twisting and turning like a Lough Neagh eel caught in a net' and nearly every anti-internment speech made by me and my colleagues had some barbed and often personal reference to him. On another occasion I said, 'The trouble with Brian Faulkner is that if the Catholics asked him to stand on his head for them and he agreed, they would still say "Rat".' It was clear this was a fight to the political death, his or ours.

The period from the introduction of internment to the dissolution of Stormont was one of frenetic political activity when family considerations came a bad second. Party and political meetings were held almost daily as I sought to maximise the opposition to internment and to build on the alienation of almost the entire Catholic population in order to hammer home the message that Stormont, as it had existed for fifty years, was no longer acceptable.

On the Sunday following internment I organised a meeting, in Coalisland, of opposition councillors to initiate a withdrawal from councils as a protest against internment. On 15 August I attended a meeting of all opposition MPs (except Vivian Simpson) in Belfast, which decided that 'the purpose of the campaign (civil disobedience and withdrawal) is to demonstrate clearly that a large section of this community has withdrawn its consent from the system of government. No system of government can survive if a significant section of the population is determined that it will not be governed under the system.' The insertion of the second sentence was from one of my speeches and it was to become a recurrent theme of the campaign. Two days later, at a rally in Coalisland during a one-day protest shut-down, I said, 'We want to make it perfectly clear that we are not prepared to be governed under the present system of government in Northern Ireland.'

On 18 August I was again back in Belfast, this time addressing a meeting of Catholic members and ex-members of the UDR and telling them that I was no longer prepared to advise Catholics to join the UDR because of the role of the Army in internment and the ill-treatment of detainees. A number of Catholic members promptly resigned. On 22 August, along with Hume and others, I spoke at a rally in Derry City's football ground at Brandywell where, in a strong attack on the use of violence, I said:

'The Unionist government had their B men and their armed policemen. We did not have their resources and yet we beat them. We can also beat the British army and the British government to force a political solution but we would be very silly to think we can do it by the methods they are using to oppress us. We stand on civil disobedience, non-violence and passive resistance. If we stand on them in unity and discipline, this time we will overcome.'

On 27 August, following a meeting I participated in, the *Irish News* carried an advertisement inserted jointly by the SDLP and NICRA on implementation of the rent and rates strike. The advertisement advised on two matters and, unknown to me then, would later cause me serious political difficulty:

'The campaign of civil disobedience began on Monday 9th August when over 300 men were taken from their homes under the Special Powers Act. It will end when the last detainee has been released.
Every supporter of the campaign is asked to pay no rent or rates for the duration of internment. The money is being withheld from a repressive regime and no arrears will be paid for the period internment is in operation.'

There has been serious criticism of the SDLP, even from commentators without a political axe to grind, that in impaling ourselves so securely on these two hooks of internment and rent and rates, we were seriously lacking in judgement and indeed were irresponsible. Certainly, for the party, and for me personally, as events developed we found our commitments on these two matters to be a source of political inconvenience and embarrassment. I will refer to these difficulties at a later stage, but I have to say that despite the seriousness of the later political difficulties, particularly to me as an individual, our decisions in the context of the political needs of the time were correct.

We were playing for high stakes: the ending of a system of government that had been in operation for over fifty years and had denied equality of treatment to more than one-third of its citizens. Faulkner had chosen this battleground. If he was successful, the unionist system and unionist control would have been re-entrenched and, as in the past, British governments would have accepted the *fait accompli*. Furthermore, this victory would have been achieved through the use of internment – part of the draconian legislation which had brought the civil rights movement into being in the first place. People like me were against internment on principle, and against the one-sided way in which it had been implemented, and we felt fully justified in including its ending in the original civil rights demands.

We felt we had no alternative but to oppose it with every non-violent weapon at our disposal. Not only that, the anger and resentment at internment, the hatred of Faulkner for introducing it, somehow had to be channelled by the SDLP and the civil rights movement in a non-violent direction, if that were possible. We had to find a non-violent alternative to the Provos and the Official IRA. It was an uneven struggle, but a party founded on the civil rights movement and a philosophy of non-violence had to attempt it. And the future of the SDLP was also at stake. There were siren voices everywhere, from Sinn Féin with its proposed Dáil Uladh, to the Provo–Blaney front of Northern Resistance, to the increasingly official republican dominance of NICRA, to Bernadette Devlin and Frank McManus and the People's Democracy. Only strong leadership, with no 'ifs' or 'buts', would prevent us from being submerged.

Consideration was given to setting up a fund, or funds, where participants in the rent and rates strike could lodge their unpaid money. This possibility was referred to in the joint SDLP–NICRA advertisement and the suggestion was put forward that where adequate organisation existed in a local area, rents could be collected and lodged in local accounts. I had serious reservations about this suggestion. Collections could lead to intimidation and the handling of public money would inevitably lead to problems, accusations and suspicions. Bernadette Devlin had just completed a tour of the United States, during which she had collected money for relief of distress and that was already a cause of controversy. Anyway, I argued, if the organisers of the rent and rates strike were making provision for the unpaid monies to be saved, did this not suggest they had in mind eventual payment? Did such a measure not detract from the seriousness of the campaign? What was the point of telling people, 'no arrears will ever be paid for the period internment is in operation', and at the same time making provision for the saving of arrears? Of course, as Minister for Housing the hens came home to roost on my desk!

At a meeting in Keady, County Armagh, on 31 August, I spelled out the four-point SDLP position:

'Firstly the SDLP is not prepared to enter into negotiations with anyone in government until the last detainee and internee has been released or has been charged with a specific offence.

Secondly, when this necessary pre-requisite has been met we are prepared to negotiate on the basis of the suspension of Stormont.

Thirdly, the appointment of a Commission representative of the two sections of opinion in the North as an interim measure.

Fourthly, quadripartite talks embracing Westminster and Dublin in order to establish a long-term solution to the Northern Ireland problem.'

We soon came under sustained pressure to renege on our commitment. The British Home Secretary, Reginald Maudling, tried to start discussions at the beginning of September. The SDLP response was blunt:

'... the present serious situation underlines the failure of the policies of the British Government. The tragic mess that this community finds itself in has resulted from those policies and in particular from internment. We are being asked to help to sort out the mess without any effort being made to reverse the policies which created it. Put more crudely, the British Government decided through internment to put the boot in and when the disastrous reaction which we forecast occurred, they are asking us to help them sort it out, but are refusing to take out the boot ... we are extremely anxious to talk but only when the last man detained without trial has been released. To do otherwise would be to build false hopes in the community.'

That did not mean we would not talk to others. In August and September I attended three meetings with the Dublin government in the company of most of the opposition MPs. The discussions revolved around internment, the alternative assembly and the political way forward. As the largest political grouping, the SDLP MPs took the lead, although we would have done so anyway in terms of ability and attitude. Gone were the days when the old Nationalist party went to Dublin to seek advice and to be patted on the head in consolation for the injustices being inflicted. We were our own men, taking our own decisions, informing the Irish government of those decisions and asking for its help in implementing them. We didn't always, in the privacy of the meeting, get the wholehearted support we required on the issue of internment. For example, no Irish government was going to oppose internment in the full-blooded way the SDLP did because the power to intern was on the Statute Book in the South as part of the Offences against the State legislation. No Irish government has ever been prepared to rule out internment in all circumstances, and the Jack Lynch-led government we met at that time was particularly conscious of its recent difficulties in relation to the Arms Trial and related circumstances. We had to be sensitive to the government's problem in this respect and the government had to be sensitive to ours. A formula was found whereby one-sided internment could be condemned in the context of an overall disastrous policy based on an unjust Partition settlement.

In effect, the Dublin government had no alternative but to support us. Public opinion in the South was overwhelmingly on our side and we were the people on the ground at the coalface. On a personal level, we got on well. Jack Lynch and Paddy Hillery, his Minister for Foreign Affairs, were both quiet-spoken, but from my meetings with them, official and unofficial, I felt confident they could be relied on to support us.

We also met with the opposition parties, to keep them informed of our position. In September, in Virginia in County Cavan, Cooper, Hume, O'Hanlon and I met Liam Cosgrave, the Fine Gael Leader, and a number of his frontbenchers, at the initiative of Paddy Harte, the TD for Donegal North East. We had a long and constructive discussion and the fact that we took them into our confidence stood us in good stead when Fine Gael went into government in 1973. We also, of course, had meetings with the Labour party, with whom we had a fraternal relationship in the Labour Council of Ireland and later in the Socialist International.

From that time I was strongly of the view that the SDLP should strive to have the best possible relationships with all of the political parties in the South. As Chief Whip, at a later stage, I always insisted that when we visited Dublin for meetings with the government we would also meet the opposition parties. This policy was clearly to our advantage when, in 1973, the Fine Gael–Labour coalition succeeded Fianna Fáil and again in 1977 when, surprisingly, Fianna Fáil took over from them. As Chief Whip I had another rule of thumb: if at all possible, meet the government last. The Opposition was always keen to know what the government had said to us and it wasn't always politic to be forthcoming. Of only slightly lesser importance to members of a delegation under considerable political and personal stress and staying overnight in Dublin was the fact that to be wined and dined by the government was much preferable to what an opposition party could offer!

We also entered into talks with the British Labour party and when, in November, Harold Wilson announced a new Labour party policy, based on fifteen points, for a solution to the Irish problem, the SDLP received credit for his conversion to a policy of progress towards a united Ireland. Although I had always supported the British Labour party – my uncle Jimmy was a Labour councillor and Chairman of his Constituency party, and the SDLP was left-of-centre and Labour was a fraternal member of the Socialist International – I didn't like or trust Harold Wilson. The first time I met him, shortly after he went into opposition in 1970, I was seated beside him for a luncheon, during which he spent most of the time taking credit for all the things he thought I agreed with and blaming Jim Callaghan for what he thought I disapproved of. On another occasion, when we met in his room at the House of Commons, we enquired why the meeting was delayed, as it was well after the appointed time. He replied, 'Oh, we're waiting on Shirley [Williams]. She's a Catholic, like yourselves.' Four years after Northern Ireland had pushed itself to the top of the agenda in British politics, the former Prime Minister had still not caught on to how little the religion of a British politician meant to us. We soon told him.

The SDLP was not participating in talks with the British and Unionist governments, yet our concerns were dominating the agenda. In early September, Jack Lynch travelled to Chequers, the British Prime Minister's country home. Only a few weeks earlier, in response to a telegram from Lynch, Heath had described his intervention as 'unwarranted, unhelpful and in no way a contribution towards peace'. Northern Ireland was no business of Lynch's, yet now the Taoiseach was at Chequers, the first time an Irish leader had been invited there, and before the end of the month he was back again to attend a tripartite meeting with Faulkner. By 22 September, Maudling was talking in the House of Commons about 'agreed ways whereby there can be assured to the majority and minority communities alike an active permanent and guaranteed part in the life of public affairs in Northern Ireland'. In late October, James Downey, the London editor of *The Irish Times*, wrote that Direct Rule was being considered by the British government. Leaks began to appear in the British media in the aftermath of Maudling's 'active, permanent and guaranteed' role for the minority, speculating on PR government, a Council of Ireland, a Catholic Deputy Prime Minister, a Secretary of State for Northern Ireland, and other suggestions from fertile and informed minds.

The reality on the streets was terrifying. Since internment the IRA campaign had intensified day after day, week after week. They operated in an environment where the Catholic community was so alienated by internment that no information was forthcoming to the security forces. I attended a public anti-internment meeting in Andersonstown, described by Gerry Fitt only four years earlier as 'the middle class, respectable part of my constituency', and was appalled at the sectarianism. I began to understand why so many civil rights campaigners had been so reluctant to agitate in Belfast. In part it was due to folk memory of the pogroms of the past, reinforced by the events of 1969, particularly the burning of Bombay Street by Protestant extremists. I abhorred the sectarianism, but could understand the fear, the suspicion and the desperation which underlay it. Unfortunately, it meant that these people were easy prey to those who put themselves forward as their defenders.

In the prevailing atmosphere it wasn't easy to preach the gospel of non-violence, of turning the other cheek. Indeed it required courage and commitment to do so. The plain truth is that in the aftermath of internment many Catholics, particularly those in the ghettos, were cheering on the IRA as it proved, day after unremitting day, that internment had been a failure, indeed a disaster. Additionally, every bomb, every shooting was seen as a two-finger salute to the hated Faulkner, who was regularly seen on TV assuring viewers, against all the evidence of their own eyes and ears, that internment was succeeding. Events like internees escaping from the prison ship *Maidstone*, celebrated in song and verse, did not make it easier for those of us who condemned what the comrades of those heroes were doing and, presumably, what some of the escapees would soon be involved in.

There were, however, enough IRA operations to make some of these supporters worry about where they were being led, and what type of people were now in charge. On 25 August, just over two weeks after internment, a bomb exploded at the headquarters of the Northern Ireland Electricity Board, killing one and injuring thirty-five, most of them typists and secretaries. Only one of the two bombs planted had exploded; if the other had gone off, there would have been a massacre among the 600 employees. The telephone warning had given no timescale and the evacuation had only begun when the bomb went off.

Four days later, at the Four Step Inn on the Shankill Road, two men were killed and twenty-seven were injured when a bomb exploded at a bar thronged with Linfield soccer supporters. Fifty thousand people attended the funerals. The SDLP condemned the attack as 'a callous, murderous and inhuman attempt to stir up sectarian strife'. On 2 November, three people were killed, all Protestants, and more than thirty injured when an IRA bomb exploded at the Red Lion Pub on the Ormeau Road, six seconds after it had been placed with a ten-second warning. On 11 December two men and two small children were killed and nineteen injured in a no-warning bomb attack at a furniture showroom on the Shankill Road. The attack took place at lunchtime on Saturday when the road was packed with people doing their Christmas shopping. The two children, aged two and seventeen months, were in their pram when a wall collapsed on them.

To this day, Republican leaders continue to tell us that the Provisional IRA never targeted innocent civilians and that great efforts were made to minimise civilian casualties. Some of these defenders were not only active in the IRA at the time of such atrocities on civilians but were in leadership positions. Not only were civilians deliberately targeted, most obviously in the Abercorn explosion, but the selection of bars and a furniture showroom on the Shankill Road testifies to the fact that the Provo leadership was as sectarian as their opposite numbers in the Protestant paramilitaries, who were targeting Catholic pubs.

According to the RUC Press Office: 'In the six months preceding internment there were 288 explosions; in the succeeding six months this increased threefold. In the same two periods shooting incidents multiplied sixfold, security force deaths fourfold and civilian deaths over eightfold, respectively.' Operating in a political vacuum, with no political forum apart from Gerry Fitt at Westminster, it was quite an achievement for the SDLP to remain politically relevant at all, never mind increasing its relevance and credibility. I remember on a number of occasions privately comparing our position to that of the Irish Parliamentary party during the campaign against conscription, a political struggle which the Irish party decisively lost. Anti-internment feeling compared with that against conscription and SDLP speakers had similar competition on public platforms as had their MP predecessors. It was another good reason for keeping the message simple – 'no talks until the last internee is released' – even though the slogan created a political hostage for the future.

The alternative assembly promised in the statement of the opposition MPs on departing Stormont in July eventually met in October under the grandiose title of 'The Assembly of the Northern Irish people'. Efforts to find a location in line with its title, first in the Guildhall in Derry and then in the council offices in Strabane, were unsuccessful and eventually we met in The Castle in

Dungiven, County Derry, which turned out to be a ballroom. John Hume was elected President, Senator Gerry Lennon of the Nationalist party Chairman, and all of the MPs, senators and councillors who had withdrawn from their elected offices were entitled to attend. We met with as much dignity as we could muster: John Hume made an opening address and the MPs in attendance took questions. But, of course, the Assembly had no means to implement its decisions. That was beside the point, however. Whatever comparisons might be made with the First Dáil of 1919, the purpose of the Assembly was to symbolise the alienation of a large section of the Catholic community from the Stormont institutions of government. In the words of John's opening address, the purpose was 'to demonstrate clearly that a large section of the community had withdrawn its consent from the system of government. No system of government can survive if a significant section of the population is determined that it will not be governed.' That was the central message: the alienation of almost an entire community. This was what the Assembly symbolised, it was what the withdrawal from Stormont, the local councils and boards meant and what the refusal to pay rents and rates was all about. And ultimately, as Ted Heath confirmed to me later, it was that alienation and the certainty that it could only be remedied by radical action that was to topple Stormont. The Alternative Assembly met only twice before other events overtook it, but it made its contribution to the campaign to end internment and Stormont by non-violent means.

What with private and public meetings to decide tactics, discuss policy, fight internment, establish SDLP branches, coordinate rent and rate strikers, media interviews and travelling to Dublin, Britain and America, there was not much time left for ordinary constituency work, or indeed for that which ought to have been a priority even in exceptional times, family life. Internment was the great preoccupation, not just with the campaign against it but with the practical consequences of men, often the breadwinner in the family, being imprisoned. When a house was raided, usually in the early hours of the morning, the first requirement of relatives was to find out where the detainee had been taken. In the Dungannon area, this usually meant phone calls to me, or Fr Denis Faul, or both. A whole day could be taken up trying to establish at which detention centre the man in question was being held, and in making representations for his release. At the beginning, relatives of nearly everyone interned contacted me, usually at four or five in the morning, but as the IRA campaign developed and my condemnation of IRA actions intensified, invariably only those relatives who believed their menfolk to be innocent contacted me. By this stage I had my contacts in the security forces, and the fact that I made representations on behalf of individual prisoners was seen as a presumption of innocence. My greatest satisfaction was to be able to inform a wife or mother that her husband or son was coming home.

On 21 October, at short notice, Hume, O'Hanlon and I began a forty-eight-hour hunger strike outside No. 10 Downing Street, to highlight the injustices of internment and the allegations of torture, which we believed required greater publicity. Without any invitation to do so, Bernadette Devlin joined us on the second day. We found the policemen outside No. 10 to be extremely cooperative, allowing us to sit on the steps for a period while photographs were taken. We then moved directly across the road from No. 10 where two camp-beds had been provided for us, by whom I can't remember, but certainly not by the residents of No. 10. Unfortunately, sand-blasting work was being carried out on the building and as it rained the first day we were there, the sand was carried by the rain and wind and added to the discomfort of an empty stomach. About 4.00am on our second night a Labour MP, Don Concannon, joined us after a late-night sitting in the Commons. He inquired whether we were on hunger strike, or on an Irish hunger strike. Fortunately, in an interview John had said 'we will take no solid food. All we are allowing ourselves is water and perhaps a little medicinal fluid'. The bottle of brandy certainly helped combat the cold of a late October night! On a number of occasions the Prime Minister, Edward Heath, entered and departed No. 10; at no time did he even appear to glance in our direction. The effect was to intensify our determination that the occasion of our next visit would see us inside the building that was the centre of British power and influence.

Everyday life in the Dungannon/Coalisland area was more convulsed with each passing day. It had got to the stage where people were afraid to go to pubs or restaurants because bombs had become so commonplace. And it wasn't just the activities of the two IRAs and the Protestant paramilitaries my constituents had to worry about. Just before Christmas 1971, Martin McShane, sixteen years old, was shot dead by the British Army in a field adjacent to his home, at the changing rooms of Coalisland Fianna GAA club. I was on the scene within minutes and my enquiries led me to describe the killing as 'murder of the worst kind'. The first Army statement alleged that immediately after the shooting, three people were seen to drive off in two cars and a loaded M1 carbine was thrown from one of them. This was later withdrawn and replaced by another statement to the effect that Martin had

had a gun and was shot when he aimed it at a soldier. It was also alleged, at the subsequent inquest, that the boy had 'vaulted' a fence immediately before the shooting. However, it transpired in evidence given by a RUC constable that the fence varied in height between 2 metres and 2.13 metres: some vault! Other evidence referred to Martin having a toy gun in his possession, but nothing in the intervening years has caused me to vary my original assessment.

On 4 December a bomb went off at McGurk's bar in North Queen Street, Belfast, killing fifteen people, including the owner's wife and his fourteen-year-old daughter, and children and pensioners. It was to be the single biggest loss of life in one incident in Northern Ireland until the Omagh bombing in 1998. No organisation claimed responsibility, but official sources blamed the IRA, saying it was 'an own goal'. Six years later a UVF member received fifteen life sentences for the bombing. This atrocity, along with the shooting of Martin McShane, both events taking place in December, made Christmas 1971 a most dismal and depressing time. The Curries were not the only Catholic family that didn't socialise outside the home, and we didn't feel safe there either. It had been, by far, the worst year of the Troubles; 1972 had to be better, surely?

17 : TROUBLED TIMES

Fortunately or unfortunately, I arrived late in Derry on 30 January 1972, the day that has gone down in history as Bloody Sunday. John Donaghy and I were stopped so many times by the Army and the police on our journey from Dungannon that the civil rights march was already underway when we arrived and we were prevented from proceeding further than Waterloo Place, which adjoins William Street. There were a large number of Army and police at this point, where a barrier had been erected and a water cannon was in position. We were told by a RUC officer that we would not be allowed to proceed further as 'things are happening on the other side'. That soon became obvious from the sounds of shouting voices and what I assumed to be rubber bullets. I spoke to a number of Army and police personnel to try to find out what was going on, but with little success. I was informed later that one Army officer I spoke to was in fact General Ford, Commander of Land Forces, Northern Ireland. He had not been in the North very long and I did not recognise him, except that he was a high-ranking officer. As we were certainly not being allowed through and there was nothing we could do, John and I decided to head for home. It was only when we stopped at a hotel to watch the evening news that we became aware of the outrage that had occurred.

Bloody Sunday and the murder of thirteen unarmed Catholics completed the alienation of the minority community, already well advanced by internment. The action of the Parachute Regiment united Catholic opinion across Northern Ireland and across the island. Even the most moderate, including those who had resolutely opposed the use of force, derived satisfaction from the burning of the British Embassy in Dublin. I was among those who watched the televised images of the flames engulfing the Embassy with satisfaction. It seemed an appropriate symbol of our anger, particularly as no one was killed or injured.

A particular focus of my anger was GB Newe, who had been appointed by Faulkner as his Minister of State two months after internment, the first (and only) Catholic to hold Ministerial Office under the old Stormont system. He had accepted Office at a time when almost the entire Catholic community was in opposition to internment, and when we in the SDLP were asking people in public life to withdraw in order to symbolise alienation from the system and as a means to end it. Now, in the aftermath of Bloody Sunday, when even leading members of the legal profession were withdrawing from cooperation with the State, Mr Newe again made a public statement announcing his intention to stay on in government.

I responded angrily. The *Tyrone Democrat* carried my statement in full:

'If you are a man at all, if you wish to maintain any shred of your reputation, you should resign immediately. The administration of which you are a member is no longer recognised by your co-religionists North or South of the border as having any moral or political right to their allegiance. You are like a Jew in Hitler's cabinet. Get out.'

These were probably the harshest words I have directed at anyone in my whole political career, and I have sometimes wondered whether I was unfair. GB Newe was certainly a man of integrity who had been Regional Organiser of the Northern Ireland Council of Social Services and a founder member of PACE (Protestant and Catholic Encounter). He clearly had a social conscience and was a committed non-sectarian. In the early 1960s he had been consistent in his publicly expressed view that Catholics should play a greater role in the public life of the North and he had advocated that the Nationalist party should become the official opposition. Whatever else might be said of his decision to join Faulkner's government, he was certainly not lacking in courage.

But whatever his good motives and personal qualities, he was politically naive. His appointment by Faulkner at the height of the campaign against internment, when the civil disobedience campaign was beginning to bite, and when the Alternative Assembly had just met, symbolising the determination of so many of Newe's co-religionists to withdraw from the Stormont system, was clearly so opportunistic that anyone living in the real political world would not have accepted. Then, having experienced the antagonism which followed his acceptance, and his inability to moderate the policies being pursued by the right-wing government to which he belonged, he added insult to injury by declaring he intended to continue in government after Bloody Sunday. Looking back, and putting my apparently harsh and less than tolerant criticism in context, I think I was right to spell out to him the reality of his position.

After Bloody Sunday there were no hostages and no agonising. More than ever it was Faulkner, or us. It occurred to me, though of course I never expressed it publicly, that maybe we were a bit unfair to Faulkner, blaming him for actions for which the British government was responsible. We had left

Stormont over the refusal of the British government to order an inquiry into the deaths of Beattie and Cusack in Derry. Now we were demanding the end of Stormont because of the death of thirteen people on Bloody Sunday. The responsibility for both of these actions lay with the British Army, which was directly responsible to the government at Westminster. We had withdrawn from Stormont and were campaigning for its abolition, but Gerry Fitt, our party leader, along with the more extreme MPs Bernadette Devlin and Frank McManus continued to attend the Westminster Parliament. Brian Faulkner may have had a point when he complained there was a lack of fairness in the political life of Northern Ireland.

After Bloody Sunday, too, the IRA received a major boost in support for its demand for British withdrawal. Recruits flooded to the cause and the murderous campaign of both Provisional and Officials intensified. The attempted assassination of John Taylor MP by the Official IRA, a dastardly act in itself, intensified the risk for all politicians and Bill Craig did not diminish that fear when, in launching his Vanguard movement, he spoke about 'liquidating the enemy' without being very specific as to who the enemy was. A bomb at the Dunowen Inn in Dungannon during a meeting of SDLP and Nationalist MPs again reminded me that I should perhaps be careful about planning for the future.

NICRA announced a protest march in Newry for Sunday, 6 February, and I was asked to be one of the main speakers. The proposed march, as well as being a commemoration of the dead and a protest against their deaths, was also a show of defiance as all marches had been banned. It was also an act of courage as no one could be absolutely certain that the British Army would not respond as it had done in Derry. British and Unionist politicians made appeals to the organisers to reconsider, and Prime Minister Heath even asked Cardinal Conway and Cardinal Heenan of Westminster to intervene. Neither Cardinal dignified the request with a reply.

The march was a triumph for the organisers and participants, and especially for Rory McShane, the Newry CRA Chairman, and Sean Hollywood, Chief Marshal. About 100,000 people participated and before the start we were asked to raise our hands to indicate our agreement with the decision of the organisers that it would be a dignified, non-violent march carried out in total silence to commemorate the thirteen killed in Derry. It was a tense occasion, with British Army helicopters flying overhead, but the careful prior planning based on exact local knowledge, the pledge of non-violence and the discipline imposed by the stewards to avoid confrontation points with the

Army and police all contributed to a demonstration I was proud and honoured to be part of. Twelve MPs were near the head of the march, including all six of the SDLP. People from the Republic had been advised by the organisers not to attend, but rather to hold demonstrations of solidarity in their local areas, and most heeded this responsible advice.

It was the largest crowd I had ever spoken to, and though tense and nervous I enjoyed the experience. I told them that the march and rally had sent a message to Heath, Maudling, Carrington and Faulkner that 'these wogs won't lie down', that the dignified and courageous march had symbolised the alienation of an entire community from a system of government they were no longer prepared to accept, that the day's events had shown decisively that non-violence could make a tremendous political impact, that they had proved that bombings and shootings and rioting could obscure a basic position of alienation and that if we stayed united, courageous and dedicated we would overcome. It went down well as did the other speeches from Rory McShane, Michael Keogh, the local Nationalist MP, and Paddy O'Hanlon, SDLP MP for South Armagh, Bernadette Devlin MP, Frank McManus MP, and Frank Gogarty, Vice-Chairman of NICRA. The crowd then dispersed peacefully, confounding both the Jeremiahs and those on the loyalist and republican sides who had hoped for confrontation. It was a magnificent achievement and it received tremendous publicity in Britain and around the world, increasing the pressure on the British government for a political initiative.

There was a sequel. We had participated in an illegal march and the penalty, on conviction, was a mandatory prison sentence of six months. The summonses duly arrived and the six SDLP MPs met to discuss our course of action. Obviously, we were guilty as charged. We could hardly deny our involvement in the march as we had been prominent in the media coverage and two of us had spoken at the rally. The issue we had to decide on was whether we would appeal the sentence and if we would be prepared to be bound to the peace, which might prevent us from participating in future banned marches, or whether we should accept the consequences and serve the mandatory six months in prison. Gerry was of the opinion that if any of us were imprisoned, it would be necessary for him to remain free to raise the unjust incarceration at Westminster. John was of the view that international opinion would have to be mobilised, particularly in the United States, and it would be necessary for him to be free to do so. I, rather cowardly, sheltered behind my wife and children, who needed my presence. The two younger MPs were in favour of doing time. Paddy O'Hanlon came from a republican background and said that one's credentials were never fully accepted until one had spent time in prison, while Ivan felt that a spell behind bars would be in the proud tradition of Protestant patriots. Paddy Devlin sat back and listened to us until we had all finished. Paddy was fond of the expletives and of one in particular. He was the first I heard use it in the middle of a word, as in 'the bus con-fucking-ductor', but he also, as he admitted in his autobiography, *Straight Left*, 'frequently proved the telling effect of basic four letter words especially when there was a dash of menace or passion behind them'. On this occasion he reminded us, with a good dash of both menace and passion, that he was the only one who had experience of prison (he had been interned during the Second World War) and then proceeded, in his own pithy way, to describe the unbearable sexual frustrations that pertained behind bars. That was the end of the discussion.

We left Party Headquarters and went to the Europa Hotel, already gaining a reputation as 'the world's most bombed' hotel, for a meal in the Coffee Dock. There we met the manager, Harpur Brown, who invited us to the hotel penthouse. Despite our reservations, he insisted. It being a Saturday evening there was quite a crowd there and we were introduced to a number of people, including one gentleman whose name I did not hear, but whose company invited us to have drinks with them. It turned out to be an enjoyable and rather late night.

On Monday morning, the six of us were in the dock at Newry courthouse along with the other defendants who had participated in the Newry march. It was a veritable rogues' gallery of prominent opposition politicians. The Clerk of the Court asked us 'to be upstanding for his Honour the Judge'. I could hardly get to my feet with shock. The judge was our drinking companion of the previous Saturday night! The proceedings didn't last long. We all pleaded guilty. His Honour told us he had no alternative but to pronounce the full sentence: 'Six months imprisonment, which is mandatory – suspended for six months.' Our discussion on going to jail hadn't been necessary after all.

I am sorry to have to relate that this liberal and progressive judge, a Protestant and a former member of the Labour party, who, as my experience of him indicated, lived in the real world and knew how to enjoy himself, unlike some of his stuffy and hidebound colleagues, was murdered by the IRA in his own home, just over two years later. On the same morning as Martin McBirney was shot, another judge, Rory Conaghan, was murdered in front of his eight-year-old daughter. Despite the proven impartiality of both judges and their anti-Establishment rulings on a number of occasions, the IRA murdered them 'for collaborating with the British war machine'.

The Dublin government decided to launch an international propaganda campaign to put pressure on the British in the wake of Bloody Sunday, and I was asked to participate in a committee in Dublin, as advisor and coordinator. At the end of February, along with a number of others from Ireland, I travelled to Washington, DC to appear before a subcommittee of the Committee of Foreign Affairs in the House of Representatives. My knowledge of the American political system, and particularly of the committee system, gained from my studies at Queen's, was put to use and I was asked to coordinate the effort of the visiting delegation and the US-based participants. Evidence was given to the subcommittee by Senators Edward Kennedy and Abe Ribicoff, by Governor Hugh Carey of New York and a number of members of the House of Representatives. I was pleased to be asked to assist in the drafting of Senator Kennedy's presentation, and to check the contributions of a number of Congressmen. Father Edward Daly – made famous by the powerful footage that showed him waving his white handkerchief as he tried to help a victim of Bloody Sunday – made a major contribution to the Hearing.

Even though I was in America for just over a week, on my return it was clear from media leaks that events were moving fast towards the suspension or dissolution of Stormont. I was invited to participate in a panel organised by the *Sunday Times* to discuss the political future of the North. Reverend Martin Smyth, not yet an MP but a leader of the Orange Order and prominent in the Unionist party, was a fellow panellist. In a private conversation with him I predicted that Stormont wouldn't last another month. His response was one of genuine disbelief: Ted Heath was leader of the Conservative and Unionist party and he would not betray the Unionist government. I wondered, and not for the first time, whether it was naivete or just downright stupidity that explained the deficiency in so many Unionist politicians.

Direct rule was announced on 24 March. In anticipation of an announcement, and knowing we would have to respond to it, the SDLP Parliamentary party met in Lifford, County Donegal. Fearful of a violent loyalist reaction, I brought Annita and our three children, Estelle, Caitríona and Dualta, with me. When the end of Stormont became official it didn't take us long to reach a unanimous position, but we announced to the media that, due to a prior commitment to consult with the Party Executive, we were reserving our statement for the press conference the following day. After a short meeting with the Executive we began to celebrate what was a major political victory. In the early hours of the

Above: At mother's Aunt Charlotte's, Derry, Coalisland.

Above: St Patrick's Academy Gaelic Football team, Dungannon, Rannafast cup, 1955. Austin is fourth from left, back row. Extreme left, back row, is Art McRory, future manager of Tyrone; first on left, front row, is Edmund Haughey; third from left, back row, is Tommy O'Connor.

Left: Rag Day, Queen's University Belfast, 1961. Austin is second from right, back row; Phil Coulter is front right.

Left: Bournemouth's best bus conductor, 1961.

Below: Austin with his father and mother on Graduation day, Queen's University, 1963.

Above: Austin with Councillor Harry Campbell, Frank Mooney and Master Slevin, delegates from Donaghmore to the Selection Convention, 1964.

Below: Caledon squatters, June 1968, with Patsy Gildernew, and Joe Campbell (obscured, on left).

Right: Wedding day, January 1968.

No. 4

PUBLIC ORDER ACT (NORTHERN IRELAND) 1951.

Whereas I have reason to believe that it is intended to hold a public procession from Coalisland to Dungannon in the County of Tyrone on Saturday the 24th. day of August, 1968, and I have reasonable grounds for apprehending that the entry of that procession into certain parts of the town of Dungannon may occasion a breach of the peace or serious public disorder, either immediately or at any time thereafter, I, George Ivan Sterritt, District Inspector of the Royal Ulster Constabulary, by virtue of the powers vested in me by Section 2 of the Public Order Act (N.I.) 1951 for the preservation of public order, hereby direct that, as a condition upon which the said procession may take place, the said procession shall not enter or use any part of the town of Dungannon other than Oaks Road, Quarry Lane, Donaghmore Road, and Ann Street, on Saturday the 24th August, 1968.

(Signed)_____Sterritt___
District Inspector of
the R.U.C.

Dated at Dungannon this 23rd day of August, 1968.

TO:_____

Above: Public Order Act 1951, prohibiting entry to the Square in Dungannon to the first civil rights march, 24 August 1968.

Above: Speaking during street protest in Coalisland, 1969.

Below: John Hume and Austin Currie on hunger strike in Downing Street, opposite No.10, in October 1971. Behind the hoardings workmen were sandblasting a building.

Above: Start of Newry march protesting at Bloody Sunday, February 1972. Marchers include (*from front*): Paddy Devlin MP, Frank Gogarty (Chairman NICRA), John O'Connell TD, Hugh Logue, Paddy O'Hanlon MP, Michael O'Leary TD, John Hume MP, Austin Currie MP, Gerry Fitt MP, Ivan Cooper MP, Paddy Kennedy MP, Bernadette Devlin MP, Frank McManus MP, Michael Keogh MP, Senator Paddy Wilson, Kevin Boland TD.

Right: Austin with Ted Kennedy, 1972.

morning such was the euphoria, I attempted a rendition. Some of my colleagues voiced the opinion that even the fall of Stormont was not sufficient excuse for me to sing!

At the press conference the following day, we welcomed the Heath initiative, but said that internment remained an obstacle to talks. We also called for the IRA to cease its campaign in order to save lives, to highlight the loyalist backlash threat and enable the British to better deal with it if and when it came and, of course, to enable the discontinuation of internment. A cessation at that stage, even a ceasefire, I believed, would have enabled the Provos to gain credit in the nationalist community for the end of Stormont. Even a temporary ceasefire would have marked, in IRA terms, the successful conclusion of phase one of their campaign, with a later resumption of violence marking the start of phase two. The decision not to do so indicated political incompetence, which was to be proven within four months.

A cessation would also, of course, have put enormous pressure on Willie Whitelaw, the newly appointed Secretary of State, to end internment. However, even taking into consideration the continuation of Provo (and Official IRA) violence, I was disappointed with the lack of progress in ending internment. When Whitelaw took over, in March 1972, he announced his intention to review, personally, the cases of all internees, at that stage numbering 924. Within a week he had released forty-seven men and announced that they would no longer be required to take an oath regarding their future conduct. In May, a new advisory committee was established to consider applications for release. By August a combination of SDLP pressure, Whitelaw's efforts to involve the Provos in the political process and the Official IRA ceasefire had reduced the number of internees to 243. That was as good as it got, and the SDLP, anxious to enter into political dialogue but pledged to a 'no talks until internment ends' position, was in difficulty.

On 26 May the SDLP felt it necessary to update its position on internment.

'It is now being said in some quarters that one of the reasons for the continuation of the campaign of violence is the party political objective of preventing elected representatives from engaging in political talks by providing an excuse for the continuation of internment. We want to make it abundantly and positively clear that we have no intention of being held as hostages by anyone and should we become convinced that this is the case then we will have no hesitation in taking whatever steps we consider necessary to achieve our aims.'

This warning to the Provos was reinforced by the announcement that, as an indication of our confidence that meaningful peaceful progress could be made, we were asking those who had withdrawn from public life under Stormont to return to their positions and to give full cooperation to the Whitelaw administration.

In late May an IRA murder occurred in my constituency, at Moortown, that fuelled the growing demands for a ceasefire – even in an area like Moortown, where the Provos had considerable support. The IRA had fired on a car parked at the Parochial House in the belief that it was a police car. William Hughes, a fifty-six-year-old Catholic from Dungannon, was shot dead and his daughter injured. I was informed of the atrocity within minutes and, acting on local information, issued a statement that was widely quoted nationally and internationally. I said, 'For many in my constituency this cowardly, vicious murder must be the last straw. On behalf of them I demand of both wings of the IRA: Get off our backs. You are at least as bad as those from whom you hypocritically pretend to defend us.' Both wings of the IRA denied responsibility and my judgement was questioned in some quarters, even by mourners at the funeral, which I attended. A few nights later, while attending a meeting of the Dungannon branch of the SDLP in the Dunowen Inn, I was informed that my presence was required at the door by a number of men. With some trepidation I went out to speak to them. One of them introduced himself as Brendan Hughes, son of the murdered man, returned from New York for the funeral. In view of the IRA denial, he challenged me for proof of my statement. I could, of course, only answer that this was the information I had received from a person in the local area who had been reliable in the past. He and his companions said they believed the IRA's denial as they had admitted their mistakes in the past and things became a little heated. I had sympathy for him in his bereavement and coming home from New York, where there was considerable support for the IRA, he might have found it difficult to believe that the IRA could be responsible for such an act. It took ten years for me to be vindicated: an IRA man from Coalisland was convicted of the murder, partially on the basis of his own confession.

Events then developed in a way that enabled us to loosen the shackles we had placed upon ourselves in relation to internment. On 13 June the Chief of Staff of the Provisional IRA, Seán Mac Stíofáin, offered to meet Whitelaw in 'Free Derry' to discuss conditions for a ceasefire. Predictably Whitelaw refused, but the SDLP noticed there had been no reference by Mac Stíofáin to the ending of internment as a pre-condition, and Devlin and Hume moved in to facilitate the development of the process by meeting Whitelaw in London. Whitelaw indicated that the ending of violence would be followed by the ending of internment, possibly as early as two weeks thereafter. This meeting began a period of toing and froing between my two colleagues, Whitelaw and the IRA, which culminated in the announcement of a ceasefire and an IRA–Whitelaw meeting in London on 7 July. The IRA delegation included Gerry Adams and Martin McGuinness. Adams had been released from internment on the insistence of the IRA leadership and, ironically, a condition of his release was that he was to be in the custody of Paddy Devlin. The Provos blew their opportunity. They proved their political incompetence by making fundamental demands that were impossible for the British to concede. The ceasefire lasted only two weeks and shortly afterwards, on 21 July, on what became known as Bloody Friday, the IRA perpetrated one of the greatest atrocities of the Troubles when it exploded twenty bombs within an hour, killing nine people and injuring 130. Whitelaw had no choice but to respond to such an atrocity, and within days he moved to remove the barricades in Belfast and Derry in an operation codenamed 'Motorman'.

Political developments followed on the heels of this latest upheaval. On 1 August, Annita and I were on holiday in Galway when I received a phone call from the Department of Foreign Affairs asking me to attend a meeting with the Taoiseach and the Minister that night. It almost caused a family row since we had only just arrived in Galway and politics was again intervening to disrupt the much anticipated holiday and to leave Annita, yet again, on her own with the children. So my mood was not too pleasant as I drove to Dublin. Nor was it improved when I heard that a helicopter had been sent to Lifford to collect my SDLP colleagues, that the Taoiseach would not be attending and that the meeting would be delayed. George Colley, Minister for Finance, stood in for Jack Lynch, accompanied by Paddy Hillery, Minister for Foreign Affairs. Our discussions lasted until after midnight.

I could not understand the urgency. The helicopter flight hyped the meeting so that it had the top priority on the news next morning. My colleagues and I decided the urgency might not be divorced from the fact that a by-election was being held the following day in Mid-Cork, a constituency vital for the government; losing that seat could have precipitated a general election. Maybe we were unfair in our assumption as the government won easily, and there was one item on the agenda of our meeting that was highly relevant. It became clear from the two ministers that the Dublin government was strongly in favour, and would be very supportive of us entering discussions with Whitelaw, irrespective of our commitment on internment. Whether organised between Dublin and Whitelaw or not, I do not know, but almost immediately we received an invitation to meet Whitelaw, with a suggested date of Monday, 7 August.

On Sunday the MPs met at Party Headquarters in Belfast to consider Whitelaw's invitation. We were very conscious of our commitment not to talk to him while internment lasted. Also, we were within three days of the first anniversary of internment and protest rallies were being organised in many areas. If we were going to break our word, it was hardly the most politic of times to do so. On the other hand, the Provo leadership, to which the majority of internees now gave allegiance, had met the British government without even a mention of internment. Allegations of 'sell-out' would be widespread, but at least could have no credibility from that quarter. Additionally, after a meeting with the Dublin government the Nationalist party MPs had announced that they were prepared to talk to Whitelaw, but only about the release of internees. The SDLP's refusal to enter into talks with the British government had become a barrier to political progress. The issue for us was not whether we would meet Whitelaw while internment lasted, but when we would meet him and in what circumstances. Paddy Devlin, as Chief Whip, was instructed to arrange the meeting for the following day and we agreed to meet at Headquarters beforehand.

When I arrived early the following afternoon I was surprised to find that the meeting with Whitelaw was not yet organised. Paddy had decided to arrange it at very short notice to minimise leaks because we wanted it to be a surprise political development. Unfortunately, when the date had originally been suggested Whitelaw's officials had pencilled in a morning meeting and he had other commitments for the afternoon and evening. Devlin's colourful expletives won the day, however, and we found ourselves on the way to Laneside, a British-owned residence near Hollywood, County Down, a secluded spot often used for meetings of a confidential or secret nature.

I had not met William Whitelaw previously, but found him impressive and likeable. He was a big man physically, with a personality to match, and he did his best to radiate bonhomie when he entered the room. He was one of those upper-class Englishmen whose stammering and apparent inability to complete a sentence partially disguised a sharp mind. It was easy to believe that Willie represented a compassionate conservatism and his boss, Heath, the harder variety. In my dealings with Whitelaw over the next year I would also find him shrewd, cunning and, on one occasion, devious.

On this occasion he was at his affable best, delighted to meet us at last, but sorry that he had a dinner engagement he could not get out of, so our time was severely limited. We told him that since this was our first meeting, one that required considerable political courage on our part because of his failure to deliver on internment, he would have to delay his dinner engagement, or preferably put it off. There followed about ninety minutes of intense engagement on internment and related security matters, such as military occupation of community centres and Casement Park, before the Secretary of State, at the persistent prompting of his officials, said he was already an hour late for his dinner engagement at the nearby Culloden Hotel and had to leave. We extracted a promise that he would return as soon as he could.

As Whitelaw left an official brought into the room a large silver tray laden with bottles and glasses. I noted that Paddy and Powers were included, as well as Bushmills and Scotch, which had been provided at pre-Direct Rule receptions; someone was making an effort to be sensitive. However, we had a strict rule for such occasions: no drinking until business was concluded. It was a lovely August evening and we repaired to the garden, which overlooked Belfast Lough, to discuss our meeting, wondering how long it would take for the Secretary of State to return. Paddy O'Hanlon found a long bamboo cane and we amused ourselves by holding an impromptu javelin competition, which Ivan Cooper won. Still no sign of Whitelaw returning. It was after eleven o'clock, over two-and-a-half hours since he had left, when he reappeared. We recognised immediately that further discussion was unlikely to be productive. Willie had arrived at the dinner towards the end of the main course, had eaten little and drank a lot. His officials were clearly disappointed to see the tray with its untouched bottles, but they had no alternative but to procure black coffee for their boss and arrange for the meeting to reconvene the following afternoon.

When we met again he graciously apologised for his 'tiredness' of the previous evening, said he had had a good night's sleep and was now, to use one of his favourite words, feeling 'splendid'. He told us he had just signed more Release Orders for internees, but as this meant that around 250 remained in prison, we were less than effusive in our response. We had already decided that the intervention of the Prime Minister would be necessary to end internment and that Whitelaw might indeed welcome us putting our case to Heath personally. Our opinion in this respect was confirmed by the official statement released by Whitelaw after the meeting: 'The Secretary of State took note of the SDLP's views and undertook to convey them to Mr. Heath as soon as possible.'

On 11 September the six MPs, Party Chairman Eddie McGrady and General Secretary Julian Jacottet travelled to London to meet with Heath the following day. In the course of the evening the two Paddys and Ivan came to me with a request that I lead off at the meeting with Heath. They figured that the PM knew Gerry from the House of Commons and might have a bias against him, and Gerry was unlikely to stand down for John. I had time to prepare my case, but I didn't sleep very well that night.

As we were driven up the avenue to Chequers, I couldn't help thinking that less than twelve months previously the Taoiseach had been invited here for the first time. Now here we were, six former Stormont MPs whose political party had been in existence for just two years, involved in talks with the British government at the highest level.

Heath was accompanied by Whitelaw and a number of high-ranking civil servants from both London and Belfast. Seated opposite him, I made the SDLP presentation: the alienation of the Catholic community from the system he had suspended; the role internment had played and continued to play in that alienation; how any new system of government must involve minority representatives at the highest level; the legitimacy of the nationalist aspiration to a United Ireland brought about by consent, the necessity for the involvement of the Irish government in any conference; and then back to the ending of internment as the key to opening up the whole process. Throughout my presentation and that of my colleagues, Heath just sat there, slumped in his chair, not taking notes, neither indicating approval nor disapproval, utterly impassive. I had only brief notes, but I had prepared well and I was glad of that. There are few things more disconcerting to a speaker than absolutely no reaction from the person to whom the case is being directed.

When we had made our case, concluding with Gerry, Heath straightened up in his chair and over a period of about thirty minutes replied to the points we had made without any reference to Whitelaw or the civil servants. On the immediate issue of the ending of internment, he told us he was committed to doing so and gave us his word it would be done at the first opportunity the security situation permitted. He reminded us that despite the risks his government had taken in meeting the IRA leadership they had resumed the violence and that since most of the internees were giving allegiance to the IRA, most people in Britain were opposed to their release. He accepted most of the other points we had made, including a role for the Irish government, but hoped that, as a first step, we would attend the conference being organised by Whitelaw at Darlington.

When the Prime Minister had concluded, tea and scones were brought in. Paddy Devlin, always with an eye for the quotable quote, joked, 'Since it looks as if we are not getting anything else, I might as well have the last scone.' Amazingly, there weren't any expletives! Paddy's intervention helped ease the atmosphere and for the next hour or so we batted the issues back and forth across the table. Whitelaw and the civil servants just looked on. Nothing was held back on either side. My colleagues and I left Chequers satisfied with our performance and confident that we had made a favourable impression on Heath. Whatever course of action he took, positive or negative from our point of view, it could not be said he had taken it ignorant of the SDLP viewpoint. The encounter was a valuable experience and would stand us in good stead at Sunningdale, just over a year later.

We refused to attend the Darlington conference two weeks later because of internment and the absence of the Irish government, but in order to ensure that we kept the political initiative we produced a policy document, *Towards a New Ireland*, which was based on proposals for Joint Sovereignty (condominium) over Northern Ireland by the British and Irish governments, comprising a power-sharing government, a declaration by the British government to work towards Irish unity and a treaty between Britain and Ireland incorporating a fifty-member, all-Ireland senate with equal representation from North and South to harmonise the structures, laws and services, North and South. In launching the document we emphasised that our proposals had to be considered as a whole, that they were interlocking and designed to provide solutions to several aspects of the Northern Ireland problem. Nearly everyone admired our ingenuity; not everyone accepted the practicality. The main usefulness of *Towards a New Ireland* was in outlining the basic problems which had to be accommodated in any settlement, and challenging those who did not agree with the model put forward to produce an alternative that would accommodate those problems. It also had the great advantage for constitutional politicians of containing a set of proposals that was entirely different from anything the Provos had put forward.

Some responses were surprising. As part of our campaign to promote full understanding of the principles underlying the condominium proposals, we offered to discuss them with any group willing to meet us. We were pleased when our invitation was accepted by a group representing the Protestant Churches. I was confident we had taken into consideration and catered for all possible areas of difficulty. Imagine my surprise when an eminent Bishop demanded assurances that the SDLP did not intend to overthrow the

Williamite land settlement!

The pace of political developments increased in the last few months of 1972. Only the UUP, Alliance and Northern Ireland Labour parties attended the Darlington conference at the end of September, but it produced a discussion paper, *The Future of Northern Ireland*, which progressed the political process. The condominium proposal was rejected, but the discussion paper approved of the two elements upon which the SDLP proposals were based: 'Real participation should be achieved by giving minority interests a share in the exercise of executive power' and 'whatever arrangements are made for the future administration of Northern Ireland must take account of the province's relationship with the Republic of Ireland'. In the *White Paper* which followed five weeks later, the requirements of power-sharing and 'an Irish dimension' were firmed up and became central to any future agreement.

In November, at the SDLP annual conference, a motion proposed by Ivan Cooper finally freed the party 'to enter into immediate discussions with the British Secretary of State and all interested political parties'. Ivan did not dodge the issue of internment. By deciding to enter into talks we 'were engaged in a sell-out of internees', but that 'no political party can afford to remain inflexible in the face of continuing death and destruction. We have a duty to provide vision, leadership and hope and the British government must be left in no doubt about where this party stands.' I voted for the motion, as did the great majority of delegates, but I did so with a heavy heart. We had entered into a commitment of 'no talks until internment ends' and now we were reneging on that pledge. It was not our fault that internment still existed, and we had done all in our power to end it. The blame lay fairly evenly between the British government and the Provos, but as a political party our main responsibility was to advance the political process, which we could only do through dialogue. I might not feel good about it but it had to be done.

At that time, however, something had happened in my personal life that was far more important to me than what was happening politically. The previous week I had travelled to Cork with John Hume, Ivan Cooper and Paddy Duffy, a member of the Executive, to attend a fundraiser for the SDLP at the Imperial Hotel. We drove to Dublin, parked our cars in the Dáil car park and proceeded to Cork by train. The function was very successful, but ran very late, and it was around 2.00am when a number of us adjourned to the residents' lounge for a nightcap and a chat about the evening's proceedings. Shortly before 3.00am I received a phone call from our family doctor, Tommy Campbell, to tell me Annita had been beaten up by two men who had forced their way into the house. She was 'not in good shape', but I was not to worry. He had telephoned to prevent me hearing it on the news first, or from some other source. He was not very forthcoming over the phone and I feared she had been more seriously injured than he was telling me. I determined to get home as quickly as possible and John, Ivan and Paddy said they would go with me. At first we had hoped a helicopter might be available, but eventually we got a taxi to Dublin. There was more frustration at the Dáil where we had to wait for the car park gates to be opened.

Arriving home, I was shocked to see my poor wife's face with her blackened eyes and swollen lips, and livid when I heard what had happened. She had been awakened at 2.00am by the dog barking and knocking at the door. She thought it might be some constituent whose relative had been arrested, or some similar emergency. After some hesitation she went down to the hallway to enquire who was knocking. She was asked, 'Is Austin in?' and she replied that I was away. The male voice replied that it was urgent he saw me. She could see two figures silhouetted outside the glass doorway. On being told again that I was not at home, one of the men said he would shoot her through the door if she didn't open it. When she did so they entered, one pointing a gun at her, carried out a search of the house and demanded to know when I would be returning. They then physically and sexually assaulted her. One of the men said they would make sure there would be no more 'Currie bastards born' and while one kicked her legs apart the second man began kicking her on the lower part of her body. As Annita lay on the floor one of her assailants produced a knife and as he started to use it on her breasts, she fainted. When she came to, she found that 'UVF' had been carved onto her breasts, the men were gone and Estelle, aged four, was standing staring at her.

Thankfully, Annita suffered no long-term physical effects, although the psychological after-effects of the ordeal remained for a long time.

My wife had suffered this degrading treatment because of me and my involvement in politics. It was the seventh attack on our home, though by far the worst, and unlikely to be the last. My family was in the front line and as a responsible father and husband I had to seriously consider the situation. The immediate public response from Annita and I was that we would not be forced out of our home and I would not be intimidated out of politics. But privately there was a lot of soul-searching and considerable feelings of guilt. Had I the right to inflict these dangers on my wife and family? And did Annita and I, as parents, not have a primary responsibility to protect our three young children?

We were helped at this terrible time by the support of family and friends and the hundreds of messages of sympathy we received from all over Ireland, Britain and elsewhere. We were particularly grateful to Dr John Kelly, a Newry man, to whom I have already referred, and his wife Nora, who arranged for us to stay at the Glenview Hotel in County Wicklow, where we were comforted by a number of well-wishers who visited us, including old friends from Queen's, Seamus and Marie Heaney. Annita and I, and our children, will always be grateful to the kind friends who, on occasions like this, enabled us to escape from the stressful conditions in which we lived, sometimes at considerable inconvenience to themselves. I have already mentioned the Vineys and the Kellys, but I would also like to record my gratitude to Donal and Eileen Barrington, Eoin and Joan Ryan, Donal and Mary Daly and Jack and Mary O'Toole from Lettermore in Connemara, where the peace and tranquility could not have provided a greater contrast to the environment we had left. Also to Tony and Susan O'Reilly for their invitation to stay at their house in the beautiful village of Glandore in West Cork and to Estrid, Catherine Mary and the others who made our time there so wonderful. 'A friend in need is a friend indeed.'

Annita insisted there was no way I could, or should give up politics. We were not the only ones who had suffered. Around the same time Plunkett O'Donnell, a leading civil rights activist in the Dungannon area, was shot at his home by loyalists and was lucky to survive. Hundreds had lost their lives. I had a contribution to make to solving the problem I myself had contributed to prioritising, so it would be an abdication of responsibility and an act of cowardice for me to attempt to get out of politics. So, was there something else we could do? It was suggested that we move house to a less vulnerable location. But was there any safe place in Northern Ireland any longer? The attacks on our home had been perpetrated by Protestant extremists, but that might change. There had been threats from republican sources, particularly after my 'Get off our backs' condemnation of the Moortown murder. Moving into a Catholic ghetto would increase the opportunity for attacks from that source. Anyway, we couldn't afford to move and none of those suggesting we move were offering to help on that level.

We had no alternative but to accept the offer of RUC protection. It was, of course, their responsibility and duty to do so, but despite the *Hunt* reforms (and my support of them) and the fact that the unionist regime, of which they had been the upholders, was now gone, I still had serious reservations on a personal and political level about the RUC. But what else could I do? The police believed that the men who attacked Annita had been looking for me and had I been at home I would have been murdered. Not finding me they released their frustration on my wife. That meant she and I and our children continued to be under threat.

After a previous attack on the house the police had recommended that I carry a weapon for personal protection. Now they insisted on twenty-four-hour police protection on me and on my home. For me, it meant advising them of my itinerary and being trailed by officers in an unmarked car. However, the car was identifiable by its radio aerial, Belfast number plates and sometimes bullet-proof glass windows, and I often dispensed with the service, particularly in nationalist areas of my constituency where the threat to my protectors was greater than to me. At my home measures had to be taken to satisfy the security needs of the police. A concrete block wall, 7 feet high (2.13 metres), was built along the back of the house, leaving a path for patrolling, with look-out sangers at each end. The garage, attached to the bungalow, was the base for two officers operating in three eight-hour shifts. The front of the garage was protected by concrete blocks, bullet-proof glass and sandbags. Bullet-proof protective glass was installed at all of the windows and powerful lights erected in the garden. All of this at a 1,050 sq. ft bungalow!

These living conditions put a heavy strain on Annita, who had given up her teaching job to look after the children and was there most of the time. It was like having lodgers in the house, but lodgers who continually changed and who were armed. The situation became almost intolerable when the IRA began to shoot at the police. At that time a new house was being constructed directly across the road. The IRA would shoot from behind the half-built walls, particularly when the RUC shift was being changed and they were most vulnerable. On one occasion they seriously wounded an officer in his car in the driveway. On another, a sergeant on inspection duties was shot dead after leaving our house. Sometimes stray shots went through our windows, causing great fear and danger to our children. On one awful occasion, Annita heard a sound from the garage and found one hysterical young policeman, who, while cleaning his weapon, had accidentally shot his colleague in the head. Annita did the best she could until the ambulance arrived, but the young policeman died. We were in a position where the police were there to protect us from loyalists, and now the IRA were shooting at our protectors, in a house with a woman and three young children. We were in a no-win situation.

From the beginning, Annita and I did our best to have friendly relations with our guards. Some of them had joined the RUC post-*Hunt* expecting to be doing a normal police job. With one or two exceptions, we had a good relationship with the older members, too. It is amazing, but one can become used to anything. On one occasion, as I drove away from home with my family in the car and the police car behind, Dualta, referring to a neighbour's son, asked, 'Daddy, why doesn't Richard Hughes' daddy have policemen with him?' A sense of humour was necessary for survival. The four years these conditions lasted imposed a terrible strain on the Currie family. I will explain later the circumstances in which this period ended.

The following February, Frank Aiken TD rang to ask me if he could come to see me and could I arrange for John Hume to be present also. He did not elaborate, but I immediately agreed. Aiken was highly respected as a South Armagh man, Commander of the Fourth Northern Brigade old IRA, a founder member of Fianna Fáil with de Valera and the Leader's close confidante, holder of many Offices of State, the most recent of which was Minister for Foreign Affairs. His daughter drove him to my home on his seventy-fifth birthday, where he put a simple proposition to me and John. A general election was due shortly in the South and he would like one of us to run in his place, as an Independent. He would support and campaign for whichever of us was prepared to stand, and he felt confident of the result. The only condition was that he be allowed to campaign for Padraig Faulkner as well, the other sitting Fianna Fáil TD. He gave me a signed document outlining his proposal. He explained that he was concerned about the lack of realistic knowledge of Northern Ireland in the Dáil, and that either John or I could fill the void and provide leadership. At the time, I suspected that this was not the full story, and disclosures since then strongly suggest that his approach to us was motivated primarily by his suspicions of Charles Haughey and his fear of him again becoming a major force within Fianna Fáil. He wanted the Dáil to take its lead from me or John rather than from Haughey.

We thanked him, but explained that there was no way we could leave Northern politics, particularly at a crucial time when major political developments were about to occur. The North required our undivided attention. Nevertheless, I couldn't help thinking to myself, in the aftermath of Annita's ordeal, how much nicer, and safer, for my family and I it would be, south of the border.

18: OPENING GAMBITS

In 1972, 496 people lost their lives, of whom 279 were killed by republicans, 121 by loyalists, and seventy-nine by the British Army and RUC. In 1973, fatalities decreased to 263, of whom 124 were killed by republicans, seventy-eight by loyalists, thirty by the British Army and three by the RUC/UDR.

Among the dead were: Senator Paddy Wilson, my SDLP colleague and friend and Gerry Fitt's confidante and election agent, shot and stabbed thirty-two times by his loyalist killers; Francis and Bernadette Mullan, constituents, murdered in front of their two-year-old son, who was shot in the leg, at their home outside Moy, in the area that would become known as the 'Murder Triangle'; and Kevin Kilpatrick, described as 'the officer commanding East Tyrone brigade IRA'. I attended the Wilson and Mullan funerals, but, knowing it would be a military funeral, not the Kilpatrick one. However, since I knew members of the Kilpatrick family I visited the family home on the evening of the funeral. I did so with some trepidation, not knowing what reception I would get because of my severe criticisms of the IRA. I need not have worried. The dead man's mother, in full view of a number of people, some of whom I knew to be IRA supporters and possibly members, threw her arms around me. She confided that while she grieved for her son, his death was, in a way, a relief. She had for some time had difficulty sleeping, praying not only for Kevin but for those he might be responsible for killing or maiming. At least now she knew where he was, and she did not have to worry about his possible victims. A truly Christian woman.

By 1973, the six MPs who formed the nucleus of the SDLP had become an effective and formidable team, steeled by our experiences and confident of our ability to take on and beat the best our opposition had to offer. Increasingly, we were also able to rely on members of the SDLP organisation, particularly men like John Duffy, who became General Secretary in early 1973, Ben Carragher and Denis Haughey, who provided ideas and position papers.

Most of the time, we six founder members got on extremely well together on a personal level. There were occasional flare-ups, of course, usually involving 'big Paddy' (to distinguish him from the other Paddy, O'Hanlon), who was, on occasion, irascible, a trait he later suggested was caused by undiagnosed diabetes. I must admit that this possibility had not occurred to me when, at a party meeting in Headquarters, he had tried to hit me over the head with a chair. Nor, I am sure, had it occurred to Gerry when he was punched in the face in a corridor at Stormont following a difference on political tactics. But that was Paddy Devlin, part of the temperament one factored into the equation when dealing with him. And they were but small imperfections when compared to his big, generous, caring heart, his commitment to equality and social justice and his sensitive political antennae.

Gerry Fitt was an unusual party leader. He rarely used a script. Even on important occasions, such as his annual speech to the party conference, he relied only on notes, sometimes scribbled on the back of an envelope – literally. On one occasion he quoted from John Donne, nearly causing me to fall off my chair in shock. I found out afterwards that the quote had been given to him by Conor Cruise O'Brien. He did not perform a traditional leader's function at party meetings either. He did not try to impose any discipline or order, nor did he try to sum up or bring matters to a conclusion. Indeed he was invariably the worst offender in terms of digressions, interrupting to tell jokes that rarely had anything to do with the subject under discussion. His strength was in his judgement of individuals, his predictions of how someone was likely to respond to particular circumstances, and the amount of information he was able to collect from all quarters on which such judgements could be based.

John Hume initially made his mark at our meetings because of his capacity to quickly write a statement expressing the consensus of our discussions. Paddy Devlin could write a statement and so could I, but neither of us could do it as well as John. He had to be watched, however, as he had a tendency to introduce certain words, Hume-speak, easily identifiable as his and which gave the impression that he was responsible for the proposal or idea. Sometimes he was, and sometimes not. The ability to quickly write a statement is a valuable facility for a politician or civil servant, as the author of a working draft is in a strong position to influence the eventual outcome. John was the best draft-writer I ever experienced. He had a formidable capacity to analyse a situation and present it as part of a consistent line of argument. He was an original thinker, but also extremely good at picking up points made by others and presenting them as his own. In the early days, John did not have the primacy he was later to achieve within the SDLP, then, he was very much one among equals.

Ivan Cooper came from a unionist background and provided a different perspective from the rest of us, which it was essential for us to take into consideration. Due to his background and his former membership of the Young Unionist organisation, he was reviled by unionist extremists even more than the rest of us, but there was none of the extremism in Ivan that one often finds in converts. In the intense sectarian cauldron that was Northern Ireland in the 1970s, it took substantial physical courage to participate politically to the extent which he did.

Paddy O'Hanlon, with his beard and open shirt, guitar and ballads, did not immediately strike one as an intellectual. From a family in South Armagh that was steeped in the traditional republican tradition, Paddy thought deeply about handed-down concepts and his utilitarian approach provided a necessary counterbalance to emotional and romantic notions.

I must add that the four of us who were married were deeply indebted to our wives. Ann Fitt, Theresa Devlin, Pat Hume and Annita were not only brave and committed, they were politically astute and tolerant of their spouses' imperfections. Without their unselfish support, their husbands could not have contributed to public life in the way they did.

The statistics for 1973 were an abysmal fact, but at least it was more than two hundred fewer deaths than the previous year. Also, in 1973 the political process got back on track. In March, there was the Border Poll and the publication of the *White Paper: Northern Ireland Constitutional Proposals*. In May, elections were held to the new councils. In June, we had the elections to the new Assembly. In October, talks began at Stormont Castle on future arrangements for government. In November, the talks ended with agreement on a Northern Ireland Executive Designate, and at the beginning of December, agreement was reached at Sunningdale between the British and Irish governments and the Unionist party, Alliance party and the SDLP. Despite the killings and the worst the IRA and loyalists could do, 1973 was an *annus miraculous* for the political process. Despite the pressures, the almost intolerable conditions in which we were living at home – relieved occasionally by Hugh Mooney, one of the few willing to babysit for us, at a time when he was fullback on the All-Ireland-winning Tyrone minor team! – and the fears I had not only for my wife and children but for my parents and my brothers and sisters, I revelled in the new challenges, the opportunity to help make history and the responsibility for finding a solution that would replace the disaster of the 1920 settlement.

Already, in advance of the September 1972 party document *Towards a New Ireland* and the British discussion paper *The Future of Northern Ireland*, in an interview in *Fortnight* magazine in June 1972 I had put forward some proposals for a settlement, in a personal initiative that the review highlighted as, 'When is the talking going to start – Austin Currie opens the bidding'. I suggested a quadripartite conference, a Power-sharing Executive elected on a proportional basis by an Assembly itself elected by proportional representation, and a Council of Ireland with real powers in the economic and harmonisation areas which, I suggested, would be particularly effective when both Britain and Ireland joined the EEC. At a time when the party was receiving criticism for not coming forward with positive suggestions, my proposals were welcomed as a serious contribution.

The *White Paper* published by the British government on 20 March 1973, which elaborated on power-sharing and the Irish dimension, became the centre around which the debate revolved. The SDLP MPs and Executive reserved judgement until the paper had been discussed in detail at a meeting in Altmore House Hotel, in my constituency. We extended a guarded welcome, but expressed reservations about the absence of proposals for police reform and called for amplification of the Council of Ireland, the proposed Executive and, of course, the ending of internment.

In May we had our first electoral test as a party in the local government elections. It was the first election since the 1920s to be fought on the proportional representation system, a development I had strongly urged to the authors of the *MacCrory Report*, which had proposed the reorganisation of local government. We did well, but not quite as well as I had hoped, obtaining 13.4% of the first-preference votes. However, we won 83 of the 103 anti-Partitionist seats, and thereby clearly established ourselves as representatives of the great majority of the non-unionist electorate. The council elections were also important in providing the first opportunity for new SDLP candidates to prove their vote-drawing capacity, an opportunity that such future luminaries as Seamus Mallon, Paddy Duffy, Hugh Logue, Frank Feely and Tom Daly grasped with both hands. Eddie McGrady had already distinguished himself as chairman of Downpatrick Council and as a parliamentary candidate against Brian Faulkner.

I have never believed in a dual mandate and therefore did not stand for election to the new Dungannon Council. I did, however, act as Director of Elections for the SDLP team. We won five of the nine non-unionist seats, which was satisfactory in an election where participating at all while internment was still in existence was an issue, but I was disappointed that the unionists still maintained control, albeit by a margin of 11 to 9. Better transfers could have achieved a historic victory in the cradle of civil rights.

The first meeting of the new council indicated that the local Unionists, like the Bourbons, had learnt nothing and forgotten nothing. They used their two-vote majority to take every single position, even the two representatives on the Board of Building Control Inspectors. Councillor Joe Higgins SDLP alleged, with reference to the author of the report that had indicted the old Council, 'If Lord Cameron came back we would find him holding his nose as he would find that Dungannon Council still stinks.' It was hardly a good augury for the new era of power-sharing recommended in the *White Paper*.

The Assembly elections followed less than a month later and this time the SDLP triumphed. Party candidates gained 22.1% of the first-preference votes and we won nineteen seats, which with the twenty-three for the Faulkner Unionists, eight for Alliance and 1 for NILP gave the pro-power-sharing parties a majority of twenty-four over the Unionists and Loyalists who were opposed to the *White Paper*. Republican club candidates received only 1.8% and the Nationalist party 1.4%, leaving the SDLP as the only nationalist representation in the assembly. Not bad for a party only three years in existence! I topped the poll in Fermanagh–South Tyrone and was elected on the first count. Tom Daly was also elected for the SDLP, but Fergus McQuillan finished sixth in the five-seat constituency. This was a disappointment as we had hoped to take three seats, but again nationalist abstention over internment wrecked that possibility.

Suddenly, instead of six of us there were nineteen, including a number with outstanding ability. The new SDLP men (no one commented in those days on the lack of women!) were Michael Canavan, Tom Daly, Paddy Duffy, Frank Feely, Des Gillespie, Aidan Larkin, Hugh Logue, Vincent McCluskey, Eddie McGrady, Seamus Mallon, Hugh News, Paddy O'Donoghue and John O'Hagan. All of them were known to me, but their party Leader, who had not spent as much time on the constituency circuit, did not recognise some of them. He and I were in the Members' bar when one, whose complexion was even more florid than mine, entered. Gerry enquired, *sotto voce*, 'Is he one of ours?' and then added, 'Doesn't he look like a gin and tonic?' He had guessed correctly, that was the newcomer's drink.

The twenty-four majority in favour of the Westminster government's *White Paper* proposals wasn't quite as good as it looked on paper. There was disunity in the ranks, even among the so-called pledged Unionists who were supposedly committed to the *White Paper*, but some of whom appeared not to support it, either because of confusion or because they were against participation in the Executive by the SDLP. The Unionist manifesto dictated by Faulkner had committed his party not to 'participate in government with those whose primary objective is to break the union with Great Britain'. His shrewd use of the word 'primary', while it sufficed during the election, did not seem quite as wise when negotiations became a reality.

The new Assembly met for the first time on 31 July and the tactics of the Democratic Unionists (8), Vanguard Unionists (7), anti-*White Paper* Unionists (10) and non-aligned Unionists (2) soon became clear. They were determined to obstruct proceedings and prevent the formation of an Executive until March 1974, at which time the Constitution Act would lapse and a new election might change the balance of power. The obstructionists were aided by the venue for the first meeting: the Great Hall at Stormont, which had dreadful acoustics. We in the SDLP were partially to blame. We wished to make a symbolic break with the past by not meeting in the old Stormont Commons, had advocated Armagh as an alternative venue, and then had to accept the Great Hall as a compromise. There were other factors, too. Few of the new Assembly members had any Parliamentary experience, and indeed most of them had only eight weeks' council experience. The Speaker, Nat Minford, was weak and unable to maintain control, particularly when confronted by the bullying tactics of Ian Paisley. Nat had made a certain reputation for himself in the old Parliament by calling Paisley a 'big, bloated bullfrog'. Now, he was paying the price. The first day was bad enough, but when talks got under way between Faulkner Unionists, Alliance and ourselves, and particularly when speculation grew that there might be a successful outcome, the frustration and desperation of the Loyalists led not just to obstruction but to disorder, and on a number of occasions the police had to be called in to clear the chamber.

The SDLP took the initiative that led to the commencement of talks. We had been preparing for some time. In September, the Assembly party had decided to establish ten subcommittees, involving all Assemblymen, to examine every aspect of policy, from finance to housing and from community relations to prices and incomes policy, with final drafts to be completed by 3 October. We held meetings with British government officials. I reported on one such meeting as follows: 'The talks were heated because of the devious behaviour displayed by the "Brits" on the forming of a Council of Ireland, policing arrangements, internment and military presence and behaviour.' We had also been meeting with the Irish government and officials. On 20 September we were given a report by the Taoiseach, Liam Cosgrave, on his recent meeting with Ted Heath and were able to report back to our Assembly party that the two Premiers had reached agreement, in principle, on a Council of Ireland. On 19 September, Irish government officials briefed our Assembly party on aspects of the Council of Ireland and brought us up-to-date with the thinking of the two sovereign governments.

By early October we considered ourselves ready for negotiations, and indeed we were in a much better position than the Unionists or Alliance party. We initially proposed talks on the social and economic policies which might be implemented by an Executive, and our initiative received positive responses from Whitelaw, Faulkner and Oliver Napier, the leader of the Alliance party.

On 5 October 1973, the fifth anniversary of the march in Derry which first catapulted Northern Ireland into the world's headlines, we entered Stormont Castle to begin negotiations on the future government of the North. As we walked in, Gerry Fitt said to me, 'We could come out of here as Ministers.' I didn't quite believe it, particularly as that outcome would have meant we had reached agreement with the architect of internment, Brian Faulkner. This was the man I had excoriated from dozens of platforms all over Ireland, and indeed Britain and the United States, as 'Tricky Dicky', as 'slippery as a barrel full of Lough Neagh eels'. It had occurred to me that he might have similar reservations about dealing with me. After all, he had been the recipient of my personal jibes and many in the unionist community blamed me for starting the Troubles. Recently, with the publication of documents under the thirty-year rule, it was confirmed that Faulkner's reservations about me were as great as mine about him. However, that October morning I resolved to put all such personal considerations out of my mind and I hoped he would do likewise. The job of finding a resolution to the political problems afflicting our common people had to be the paramount consideration.

The SDLP had six negotiators: Gerry, John, Paddy (Devlin), Ivan, Eddie McGrady and myself; the Unionists had six also: Brian Faulkner, Herbie Kirk, Roy Bradford, Basil McIvor, Leslie Morrell and John Baxter; and the Alliance party had three: Oliver Napier, Bob Cooper and Basil Glass. In selecting the team, Gerry felt he ought to include a representative of the new members of the Assembly party, and Eddie McGrady had the advantage of being Chairman of the Assembly group as well as a former Party Chairman. Unfortunately, as our delegation was restricted to six this meant that one of the six founder MPs had to be left out, and Paddy O'Hanlon was the casualty. (Worse was to follow for Paddy, as not being part of the successful negotiating team was a disadvantage when it came to selection of the Ministerial team.) Faulkner, in terms of ability and professionalism, dominated his team. It was obvious from an early stage that he and Bradford were not always singing from the same hymn book, never mind sheet. I did not find this surprising. Bradford had made approaches to me and others in the SDLP suggesting that we might prefer to deal with him rather than Faulkner. Annita and I had even been invited to dinner at his home. It was so transparently a shafting exercise that it had the opposite effect on me.

Whitelaw proved to be a superb chairman. He jollied us along, reacting like a startled horse at signs of trouble, then moving quickly to forestall it with a jocose remark, or even by deliberately changing the subject. He found variable lunchtimes particularly useful. From twelve o'clock onwards, as difficulty threatened, he was quite likely to say, 'Time for lunch'. On a number of occasions the caterers were caught on the hop. Willie wouldn't be in the least embarrassed. He would simply announce, 'Time for a G&T – a large one', and before and during lunch he would have two or three. He drank gin and tonic during the day and whisky in the evenings; I learned to recognise the signs, the rheumy eyes and the habit of knawing his knuckles. His personality and sensitive political brain contributed enormously to the success of the talks.

The preparatory work stood us in good stead and created an impression of professionalism. Three of Faulkner's team were former Ministers who had fallen into the bad habit of relying on civil service back-up and scripts, so when we produced a draft social and economic programme they were caught off-guard. Bradford attempted to retrieve some ground at a later stage of the talks by trying to amend the draft and Faulkner had to use his authority to stop the first of many slanging matches between Bradford and Devlin, who had seen the adoption of the SDLP-proposed programme as a victory of socialism over capitalism.

That confrontation occurred later in the talks, however. The initial agreement gave us confidence to go on to deal with some of the more controversial issues. In his opening remarks the Secretary of State reminded us that we were meeting under the terms of the Northern Ireland Constitution Act, which provided 'the statutory basis of a constitutional settlement' and which was the law of the land, not a negotiating document. The Act also established that Northern Ireland would remain part of the United Kingdom unless, in a Border Poll, the people indicated they desired otherwise, and it also contained the initial legislative authority that provided for consultation, agreements and arrangements with the Republic. He and his government would do all they could to help, but it was up to us to agree among ourselves.

Next, Faulkner took the opportunity of putting on the record the conditions which had been agreed by his Assembly group for sharing power with the SDLP: there had to be a clear commitment to the terms of the Constitution Act, particularly the section dealing with a Border Poll; the SDLP would have to call off the rent and rates strike and give firm backing to the security forces, including the RUC; there would have to be a Unionist majority on the Executive and any Council of Ireland would have to contain safeguards and limitations against absorption of Northern Ireland into an Irish Republic.

In his contribution, Gerry proposed that we adopt the principle that nothing was agreed until everything had been agreed, ie, anything agreed at any stage must be subject to final agreement. He outlined the SDLP's position on the key points: the Constitution Act was not an issue, otherwise we would not have been present; the very first document produced by the SDLP, and the Constitution of the party itself, committed the party to no change in the constitutional position except with the consent of a majority in Northern Ireland; the rent and rate strike was a peaceful protest against internment, therefore when internment ended, as he hoped it would as a result of the negotiations, the rent and rate strike would also end immediately. At this stage Paddy interjected, with some levity but also with much logic, 'It would be incongruous for me to hold the office of Chief Executive and at the same time to be on rent strike.' Gerry concluded his remarks by emphasising the importance the SDLP attached to a police service with which all sections of the community could identify, the Council of Ireland and the ending of internment.

Oliver Napier put forward the Alliance party's position which, predictably, was not a cause of concern to the rest of us. The agreed statement at the end of our five-hour meeting said that the parties had agreed in principle 'that they should work together with the aim of forming an Executive', referred to the progress made on a social and economic programme and that the 'outstanding issues, such as policing, detention and a Council of Ireland, would be discussed by the parties both individually and collectively with the Secretary of State'.

For us, the statement was a better start than the most optimistic of us had dared to expect. At the same time, it was also clear that there were difficulties, possibly very serious difficulties, which we would have to confront and overcome. In his deliberately bumbling way, Whitelaw had referred to these difficulties towards the end of the meeting. First, policing. Faulkner had clearly said that 'the RUC must be accepted as the police force of the land'. Whitelaw warned, 'Don't destroy what you've got.' Clearly the SDLP would not find it easy to achieve the major policing changes we thought necessary, including a change of name, in order to ensure minority participation and cross-community identification with the police force.

On internment, or 'detention', as the British ministers insisted on calling it, Whitelaw was tying it to the reduction and ending of violence and Faulkner, while not taking as strong a line as might have been expected, was adamant that political considerations should not be the determining factor. We, of course, pushed for the ending of internment, or, if we could not achieve that, substantial releases. It was not strictly an issue for a multi-party conference, but rather for bilateral discussions between us and the British government; Whitelaw indicated he was prepared to discuss it with us on a confidential basis.

On the Council of Ireland, Whitelaw reiterated the *White Paper* position that the British government would facilitate the formation of a Council and, of course, the project would not proceed without discussion and agreement with the South, but it would be useful to have the views of the parties represented in Stormont Castle on the structure and the functions. Clearly, the battle here would be between the Unionists and the SDLP. And finally, if we were able to surmount the other hurdles, we would have to face the thorny question of who would hold which positions on the Executive and, in particular, the Unionist demand for a majority. These were the crunch issues which were to dominate our discussions in sessions of the conference and in bilaterals with Whitelaw for the next seven weeks.

At our next meetings, on 8 and 9 October, the two subjects that dominated the discussion were policing and internment. We argued that policing had to be viewed in the wider context of Catholic and nationalist identification with the structures of a State with which we had never before identified, and that identification with the police service whose duty it was to defend those structures was a necessity. Some of us, Hume and I in particular, had supported the *Hunt* reforms and had asked Catholics to join the RUC, but this had not happened and now it was obvious that something more than a tinkering was required. The minimum would be a change of name, to the Northern Ireland Police Service, and a change in uniform, which we had demanded in 1969. Faulkner was implacably opposed to both these proposals: 'Changing the name would destroy the RUC.' On internment we argued that its ending, at the very least, 'would have to be seen to be in sight' and Faulkner agreed that 'some formula will have to be found in this sphere'. Whitelaw reminded us that both subjects were the direct responsibility of the UK government. Whitelaw also informed us that he had ordered his office to start making preparations for a possible conference involving the Irish government, and he hoped to have papers on the subject for the following week. He indicated that one subject for discussion with the Republic would be extradition, where the position was 'wholly intolerable'.

On 16 October we again discussed policing, again with no sign of progress. Indeed, Faulkner said that as far as he and his delegation were concerned the change he wished to see was 'the government in Dublin and the British government [ordering] their police forces to co-operate, especially the Special Branches'. Roy Bradford suggested that changes could be made to the Police Authority to obtain 'a stronger political voice' on the Authority. SDLP agreed and Alliance demurred. For the first time a possible policing link with the Council of Ireland was mentioned when I referred to 'devising a mechanism to formalise co-operation between the police, North and South, and the Council of Ireland'. No one pursued the suggestion, and I did not wish to elaborate at that time.

By this stage we had come to terms with each other on the level of personal relationships, which were surprisingly good. We addressed each other in first-name terms and at the buffet lunches we mingled more than might have been expected. It was clear that Gerry and Brian were getting on well, though I think Faulkner was having some difficulty in understanding, and certainly in appreciating, some of Gerry's jokes. Despite my initial reservations, the architect of internment and I were developing a good relationship based, for my part, on a recognition that he was a professional politician who was committed to securing an agreement and expressed his views in moderate, non-partisan terms and, for his part, I think, out of a recognition that I too was committed to agreement and expressed my views succinctly, contributed only when I had something to say and was controlling my tendency to partisanship.

This welcome state of affairs came under serious pressure at the meeting of 29 October when a slanging match erupted between Bradford and Devlin over the draft *Social and Economic Programme*. The subcommittee dealing with the programme, chaired by David Howell, one of Whitelaw's ministers, had had few meetings but had apparently reached the position where it could recommend endorsement at the plenary sitting. It was at this stage that Bradford attempted to introduce amendments. Devlin lost his temper, accusing Bradford of trying to turn the document into a capitalist programme. The row was defused when Faulkner, at the request of Fitt, agreed to take over the Unionist handling of the document and Bradford was bypassed. This was the first indication of the animosity between Devlin and Bradford and it was to become a permanent feature of their relationship.

The meeting of 30 October was devoted almost entirely to internment. The SDLP delegation took a hardline, led off by Ivan Cooper who emphasised that opposition to internment was as strong as ever and that it had radicalised a large section of young nationalists. As long as internment lasted, there would be opposition to the structures of government, even if they were power-sharing structures. Faulkner agreed on a Declaration of Intent to end internment, when the security situation allowed it. However, he did not want a link between the ending of internment and the creation of an Executive, so if it were possible to release them on security grounds, it ought to be done now. Oliver Napier supported the SDLP position: internment undermined the rule of law and releases were required. John Hume provided facts and figures to illustrate the effect of internment on the Catholic community. I tried to move the argument on. I recognised that the ending of internment would be a gamble because we could not guarantee that some of those released would not get involved in violence. It was also clear that the Provos did not want an end to internment because of the alienation it was causing, which boosted their support. The nettle would have to be grasped. Again, Whitelaw gave a commitment to discuss the issue in confidence with us, promising to be as forthcoming as he could.

On the following day, 31 October, we had our final discussion on the Council of Ireland. Brian Faulkner took the initiative, stating that he was in favour of a Council, indeed he claimed that the proposal had originated with the Unionists, before Direct Rule, at the Darlington conference. He put forward three reasons for supporting a Council: first and foremost, security considerations, the need to prevent any part of the island being a haven for terrorists; a need for coordination of government activities on social and economic matters because of our geographical situation; and thirdly, the necessity to promote mutual understanding and tolerance of the different Irish traditions. However, the Council could not be an All-Ireland Parliament nor should it be seen as a step along the road to one. Decisions should be taken by unanimity, to protect the position of the unionist minority. A single-tier intergovernmental Council would provide a forum for discussion of practical matters, such as tourism, electricity, and regional development, which could then be implemented by the two governments separately.

John took the lead in putting forward our proposals. We accepted that unification could only come about with the consent of the majority in Northern Ireland. However, it must be acknowledged that a large section of the Catholic population believed in the ideal of a united Ireland and that this was a perfectly acceptable political aspiration, as equally valid as the unionist one. For this reason, and also for practical economic reasons, a Council of Ireland to increase cooperation between North and South had to be a strong component of the political package we were negotiating. It would be essential for nationalists to identify with the new institutions and the Council, for which the evolving European institutions provided a good working model, could facilitate that identification. The Council should be two-tier, intergovernmental and interparliamentary, so that Ministers would not only get to know each other and contribute to the solution of common problems but ordinary members of the Dáil and Assembly could also play an active, contributory role. The Council should have a Secretariat independent of the two governments, and the Council, in addition, should have executive and harmonising roles.

There were two surprises. Bob Cooper, deputy leader of the Alliance party, indicated that he had changed his mind since the Darlington conference and now thought there might be a case for a second tier. And Faulkner, in a short contribution near the end, indicated there might be a case for an interparliamentary body similar to the association the old Stormont had had with other Parliaments in the Commonwealth. It wasn't nearly good enough, but at least the usefulness of some sort of other tier had been accepted and could be built upon. I left Stormont Castle that night more hopeful than I had expected to be. Faulkner's openness to the Council of Ireland, albeit largely for security reasons, had been a pleasant surprise.

My impressions were confirmed at the next meeting on 5 November. While Faulkner continued to describe the proposed second tier as 'a mischievous talking shop', he did not rule it out and indeed agreed to give it further consideration. A month into the talks and we were still around the table and making progress, if slowly.

Whitelaw and his officials had decided that the contentious matters of internment and the Council of Ireland should be put to one side for the moment, and on 6 November we began to discuss what administrative changes would be required to conform to the *White Paper* stipulation that there be twelve Executive positions. With their experience of government, the

Unionists clearly had the advantage in these discussions, but the issue was non-party political and we had the advantage of a paper prepared by the Northern Ireland Office (NIO). However, there were two political sensitivities: the functions of existing Departments which might be transferred to the Council of Ireland; and the positions to be held by the parties in the Executive, what became known as 'the numbers game'. Towards the end of our discussions, Paddy Devlin momentarily forgot his commitment to sensitivity by attempting to raise the latter issue, prompting Whitelaw's quick decision of adjournment and drinks. It was clear, however, that the issue could not be avoided for much longer.

Faulkner's weakness in the numbers game was the arithmetic of the Assembly. He had twenty-one members pledged to support him, SDLP had nineteen and Alliance had eight. In the Assembly two members of his team, James Strong and Herbie Whitten, had made it clear they would not support SDLP participation in government, which meant Faulkner had only nineteen votes to support an Executive – the same as we had. He argued that the Border Poll had shown conclusively that there was a unionist majority in Northern Ireland and that the Constitution Act, with its emphasis on the Executive being 'widely accepted', required a Unionist majority. It was one of the conditions agreed by his Assembly party for entering into talks and was non-negotiable.

On 12 November we met again, with the Council of Ireland on the agenda for the morning session and the numbers game in the afternoon. Whitelaw began proceedings by announcing the banning of the Ulster Freedom Fighters and the Red Hand Commandos, which had claimed responsibility for explosions a few days previously. We could all agree on this at least. Faulkner again expressed his reservations about the second tier, but suggested an Inter-Parliamentary Union on either British Isles or all-island basis. He also raised another matter of division: if we were successful in forming an Executive, it should come into formal existence before any conference involving the Irish government in order to avoid any suggestion that the Republic had a say in the internal affairs of Northern Ireland. The SDLP strongly resisted this proposal. From the beginning we had insisted, and the parties to the talks had agreed with us, that nothing could be agreed until everything had been agreed. We were not prepared to risk a situation where the Executive would be formed without the Council of Ireland having been agreed.

In the afternoon the gloves came off. Fitt lacerated Faulkner for demanding a majority on the Executive. In a twelve-minute onslaught he described Faulkner as 'the weakest man in the room'. It was numbers that could support an Executive that counted, and Faulkner had the same numbers as the SDLP. The situation in Northern Ireland had changed and Faulkner had to recognise the new reality: he could be the Chief Executive presiding over an Executive which would include Alliance, which was a Unionist party, but he was not entitled to more members than the SDLP. 'It has to be 5, 5, 2.' Brian came back strongly, 'Yes, I am the weakest but if there wasn't a requirement for power-sharing I would have no difficulty in forming an Executive from among fifty-nine Unionist members.'

Oliver Napier strongly supported Fitt. The numbers on the Executive should be proportional to each party's backing for the government. 'It is a proportional game, not a numbers game,' he said and insisted on 5, 5, 2. I questioned Faulkner on his claim that he represented the 'unpledged' Unionists ('They are members of my party') and unionists generally. Did he claim to represent Craig and his group, who favoured a Unilateral Declaration of Independence (UDI), or Paisley, who was supporting integration with Britain, or other unionists, like Hugh Smith, who was associated with the UVF? I went on to suggest a referendum on the final package of agreement, an idea supported by Oliver Napier but which Faulkner opposed on the grounds, 'it would open the sluice gates'. I have long regretted that I did not push the suggestion harder. Eventually, Whitelaw brought the rather acrimonious discussion to a close, saying he was reserving his own position and would consult with the parties separately. Just as we broke up Faulkner said, 'if we get a majority on the Executive you might be surprised on the amount of agreement on other matters.' It was the only small ray of hope that day.

The centre of activity shifted from the conference room at Stormont Castle to meetings on a bilateral basis with Whitelaw. It did not take long for the word to spread to the media that the talks were in difficulty, and to make matters worse some of the speculation gave a 'jobs for the boys' slant to our problem. There was also speculation, which I refused to believe at the beginning, that Heath was planning to transfer Whitelaw back to Britain to sort out the industrial relations problems with the miners. I could not believe that at this juncture, when progress towards the solution of the Northern Ireland problem was so dependent on Whitelaw, that the actions of the Prime Minister would be motivated by party political considerations. At that stage of my political career, I think I was not sufficiently cynical for my own good.

On Monday, 19 November talks were still ongoing with Whitelaw and the conference meeting of that day made no progress. It began late and ended early to avoid a total breakdown. However, Whitelaw produced a document which indicated considerable progress on the other issues and which became the basis for negotiation.

The crucial meeting between the SDLP and Whitelaw occurred on Tuesday, 20 November. His demeanour and attitude suggested to me that he was under considerable pressure; his knuckles were in danger of being gnawed away. The speculation regarding his imminent transfer was obviously correct. We went through the agenda, with the assistance of the document of the previous day. On internment, he voiced his concern that about 30% of internees released had become involved, or re-involved, with the IRA. However, he was hopeful that the political progress being made and the possible creation of new power-sharing institutions would result in the men of violence being isolated. In these circumstances, he hoped that internment would speedily come to an end. The SDLP delegation pressed him again to release as many as possible before Christmas.

On policing, Whitelaw reiterated his belief that effective policing could only come about by public support for, and identification with, 'the RUC, which is the police service for Northern Ireland'. No joy there for the SDLP. We again made the point that unless changes were made, there would not be the necessary identification with the police service.

On the Council of Ireland, he was pleased with the progress already made and the British government was encouraged to put forward proposals that would also be discussed with the Irish government at a tripartite conference, which he hoped could be held in early December. His government accepted the key points: that the Council of Ireland should be confined to the North and South of Ireland, though arrangements would be necessary to protect British interests in the area of finance and other reserved subjects; that the Council should be two-tier and consist not only of representatives of the two governments on the island but representatives of the parties in the Dáil and Assembly; that the council would have its own Secretariat and would have executive functions as well as a consultative role; that the Council should operate on the basis of unanimity; and that the Council should play a useful role in relation to certain subjects, such as extradition and the common law-enforcement area.

What Whitelaw was saying to us represented more of an advance on the Council of Ireland than we had expected by that stage. We had anticipated a harder fight, supported by the Irish government at the tripartite conference, to achieve some of what was now being offered. The only immediately obvious deficiency was the lack of any mention of a harmonising function, but when we brought it to his attention, Whitelaw promised to look at this again.

Of course, there was a price to be paid for progress on this front: Faulkner must have a majority on the Executive, otherwise he could not deliver his party. And Faulkner was essential to the whole project, as Whitelaw pointed out: 'I have gone as far as I possibly can to deliver power-sharing. But I recognise that if Brian Faulkner cannot do it, nobody can.' He proposed six Executive positions for the Unionists, four for the SDLP and one for Alliance. Additionally, a member of the SDLP would be appointed as Chief Whip and a member of the Alliance party would become legal advisor, but neither would be members of the Executive.

Gerry had already, the previous day, described a 6, 4, 1 proposal as 'an insult to the SDLP', and there was no way we were going to accept it. But we knew we were on weak ground. That very day, Faulkner was battling for his political life at a meeting of the Ulster Unionist Council and we knew that one of his commitments to the party would be an overall unionist majority on the Executive. However, we took a strong line, repeated all the arguments, but found Whitelaw unyielding. Then, just as I was coming to the conclusion that we were impaled on the horns of a dilemma from which there would be no escape, Whitelaw said, in a rather off-handed way, 'Well, Brian must have his majority on the Executive, but it may be possible to give more positions to you and to Alliance outside the Executive.' This would require an amendment to the Constitution Act but he would, if necessary, see what could be done in this regard.

The following morning the newspapers were full of speculation that this day, Wednesday, 21 November, would be 'crunch day'. The *Irish News* had two front-page stories. One headline was, 'Faulkner wins party vote on power-sharing'. The report showed how narrow his victory was, with a majority of ten out of 750 delegates, and also stated that, 'The undertakings spelled out by Mr Faulkner are understood to have included condemnation by the SDLP of the rent and rates strike; full SDLP support for the RUC; and an overall Executive majority for the Unionists.' The other story, headed 'Loyalist put out feelers to the SDLP', reported 'the sensational development of an approach from within the DUP–Vanguard Loyalist coalition for a conference with the SDLP to discuss power-sharing on a new basis.' It was the first I had heard of this sensational development. It turned out to be a product of the fertile mind of Paddy Devlin, concocted to put pressure on Faulkner.

When we met at Stormont Castle at 10.00am the paper circulated by the NIO made it clear that Whitelaw's officials, like our delegation, had worked late. The paper on E.R. headed notepaper ('Elizabeth Regina', not much sensitivity for our republican credentials) had been changed in certain important ways from the draft we had discussed with Whitelaw. The harmonisation function had been added to the Council of Ireland, as well as a possible role 'in the law and order field'. The latter was added, we assumed, because of the case we had made for a policing function for the Council. The section on internees had been strengthened: 'The Secretary of State hopes to be able to bring into use his statutory powers of selective release. It is his intention, if the security situation permits, to do so in time for a number of detainees to be released before Christmas.' There was no mention at all of the make-up of the Executive. The section headed 'Formation of the Executive' in the previous position paper of 19 November had been entirely deleted.

We discussed the document first. On internment, Whitelaw said he couldn't promise the release of more than one hundred men before Christmas. What he envisaged in terms of a common law-enforcement area was the pursuit of terrorists in both directions across the border. When Faulkner asked for an assurance that the Council of Ireland would not have a policing function, he did not receive it.

After lunch we got down to the numbers game once again. Whitelaw repeated his position of two days previously, 6, 4, 1. Fitt and Napier reiterated 5, 5, 2. Faulkner said that his experience of the Unionist Council had confirmed his belief that he must have a majority. The 'unpledged' were members of his party and in four years time, when we would have to face the electorate, the majority of Unionists would be in the one party again. In the notes I made on the occasion I wrote, 'All restating positions – and waiting for Whitelaw compromise' and 'Shadow boxing for one hour' . The SDLP certainly was. However, I could not be sure to what extent Faulkner and Alliance were privy to the same knowledge as we were. Eventually, Willie pulled the rabbit out of the hat: the Constitution Act could be amended to change the numbers on the Executive and extra positions could be created outside the Executive. The Unionists would have the necessary overall majority, but within the administration as a whole the SDLP and Alliance would gain. He added, 'I have the agreement of the Prime Minister that if this is the only way in which the Executive can be formed, then the necessary changes can be made to the Act.'

We had already decided that, in view of our gains on other matters, particularly on the Council, we could not allow a breakdown on this issue in circumstances where the whole agreement would come crashing down and Faulkner would have credibility for his position. So all that remained was to get the right mixture of Executive and non-Executive posts in the proportions which had been agreed, and to achieve those ministerial positions which could best transform Northern Ireland society in the way we wanted. The civil servants had recommended nine Departments, but the functions of some kept changing and different combinations were suggested. Fitt, who as Deputy Chief Executive had been suggested, in the draft of 19 November, as Head of the Department of Manpower Services, decided – wisely, I thought, because Gerry's talents were not in bossing a department – not to take a Department, but instead to play an overall role. Oliver Napier, who had been slotted in as Head of Department of Local Government and Community Relations, opted instead, and to my surprise, for Executive Head of Legal Affairs.

Apart from the three party leaders, the occupants-to-be of the other positions were not referred to as such. Appointments were the prerogative of the party leaders, but it was not hard to guess who was destined for what. When Oliver Napier preferred Legal Affairs to Local Government and Community Relations, it was recommended that Local Government be attached to Environment, but when, towards the end of our discussions, it was further linked to Housing and Planning, Brian Faulkner winked at me across the table; either Gerry had been talking, or I had made my interest very obvious. Paddy had made known his interest in the Department of Health and Social Services from an early stage. John surprised some people by opting for Commerce instead of Finance. Finance was the more senior and had, as its most important function, the allocation of resources between the different departments, a function that could be used to boost or curtail Ministers in other departments. It did not, however, have the high profile of similar Ministers in other jurisdictions. Commerce, on the other hand, was high profile and had made Brian Faulkner. John reckoned that the delivery of jobs to areas of high unemployment, which were also nationalist areas, would be a major justification for our joining the Executive. At a later stage I had reason to regret this decision when Herbie Kirk, who then got Finance, caused problems for me in relation to the rent and rate strike. When Gerry announced his appointments in a speech in the House of Commons a few days later he slotted Ivan into Community Relations and Eddie McGrady into Planning and Co-ordination, both positions outside the Executive.

While discussions were going on about the grouping of functions, there was much banter and cross-talk. It was a tremendous relief to have reached agreement, something which had appeared remote at some stages. We had tested each other and, with the exception of the Bradford–Devlin relationship, our respect for each other had grown and we were easy in one another's company. It boded well for cooperation in tackling the immense political, social, economic and other problems which might shortly be our responsibility – if agreement were reached on the outstanding matters at the tripartite conference.

Towards the end of what was becoming a long day – in all, over ten hours – the plenary session was interrupted by the necessity for party discussions, and some of these dragged on a bit. It became clear Whitelaw was becoming impatient. He was due to make his important announcement of the breakthrough to the Commons next afternoon, and he had a Cabinet meeting beforehand. Around six o'clock our discussions were interrupted by the arrival of a helicopter and every fifteen minutes or so the engine was revved up. We had one final point to decide, however. Whitelaw and Faulkner had been insistent that the Executive would come into existence before the talks involving the Irish government, and that we would travel to that conference as members of the Executive. A title was now required to indicate that the SDLP had won that argument. Maybe it was tiredness, but an appropriate description eluded us and the civil servants present. At one stage I suggested, 'something like a putative Executive'; Paisley would have had great fun with that one! Someone else suggested 'The Executive in embryo'. Had the helicopter pilot overheard our discussion, he would have revved his engine even more loudly.

It was 7.05pm before we could resume the final plenary session, and at 8:30pm we were able to celebrate our agreement: Executive Designate. Willie's eyes were more rheumy than usual, Brian and Gerry thumped each other's backs, the new Chief Executive (Designate) shook my hand warmly and congratulated me on my performance during the talks. We went out to meet the media to announce a truly historic achievement.

I was very tired and had seen little of my family during the six weeks of negotiations, but there was no time to celebrate or relax. The job was not yet finished. We were due at Sunningdale in just two weeks' time.

19: SUNNINGDALE AND AGREEMENT

Halfway through the RAF flight from Aldergrove to Northolt, Roy Bradford moved down the plane to sit beside me. I was a bit surprised, for although I had a reasonably good relationship with him, we were certainly not 'buddy, buddy' and I had not given him any encouragement in his efforts to displace Faulkner. After some small talk he came to the point: he believed that it was the turn of the SDLP to be pressurised by Heath as Faulkner had been 'screwed' previously. We landed at the RAF base at Northolt and as we drank coffee in the Royal Lounge, John Baxter, one of Faulkner's new men and Minister for Information (Designate), confided to me that he was fearful the two governments had already cut a deal. At first, I mischievously offered to show him a copy of the final communiqué, but then took pity on him and assured him that, while there had been some understandings, there was still plenty, too much in my view, which could lead to serious disagreement. Both conversations indicated to me that morale in the Unionist camp was not at its highest.

On the coach to Sunningdale, in Berkshire, accompanied by motorcycle outriders, Faulkner and Fitt sat together and conversed animatedly for most of the journey. From the lack of laughter, Fitt wasn't telling jokes, or maybe Faulkner didn't understand them! Sunningdale was a Civil Service Training College and the accommodation was rather spartan. After dinner we had a meeting in Gerry's room, but in case of bugging we took our final decisions in a huddle outside in the garden. Since it was late evening on 5 December, we did not take long to reach conclusions. Gerry, as Leader, was to open our case with a short statement that would be drafted by John along agreed lines. He and I would contribute at the earliest appropriate opportunity. I was asked to include a reference to *Towards a New Ireland*, our policy document of 1972 and still the official policy of the party despite the new emphasis on power-sharing and a Council of Ireland.

My notes, written at 12.45am, show my concerns for the proceedings later that day. The absence of Whitelaw was a serious weakness. Francis Pym, his successor, could not possibly fill the void. Even Heath would have difficulty doing so, but from our experience of him at Chequers we knew he would have mastered the brief. The questions were: how committed was he to the success of the talks? And was it possible that Bradford was right and he would come down hard on the SDLP? My other niggling doubt concerned the Irish government. There was no doubt about their commitment to the settlement, but the major preoccupation of some of the Ministers was not about the North but peaceful conditions South of the border. I wrote, 'My fears that S. government will accept less than us – (maybe accept anything at all). Only SDLP can force good settlement.'

It was an impressive gathering of politicians and civil servants from the two islands. The Prime Minister, Ted Heath, who chaired the conference, was supported by Sir Alec Douglas Hume, Foreign Secretary and former Prime Minister, Francis Pym, the Northern Ireland Secretary, and David Howell, his Minister of State and Sir Peter Rawlinson, the Attorney-General. The Republic's delegation was led by the Taoiseach, Liam Cosgrave, and comprised the Tánaiste, Brendan Corish, the Minister for Finance, Richie Ryan, the Minister for Foreign Affairs, Garret FitzGerald, Minister for Justice, Paddy Cooney, Minister for Posts and Telegraphs, Conor Cruise O'Brien, the Attorney-General, Declan Costello, and Minister for Local Government, James Tully. Brian Faulkner led the Unionist delegation of Herbie Kirk, Roy Bradford, Basil McIvor, Leslie Morrell and John Baxter. Alliance was represented by Oliver Napier, Bob Cooper and Basil Glass. The SDLP delegates were Gerry Fitt, John Hume, Paddy Devlin, Ivan Cooper, Eddie McGrady and Austin Currie. Additionally, we had three advisors, Paddy O'Hanlon, Paddy Duffy and Michael Canavan. Thirty-five British civil servants attended, and there were thirty-seven from the Irish side. As we were merely the Executive Designate, the Northern Ireland parties had to perform without the benefit of officials.

The Prime Minister opened proceedings in a short speech in which he said there was no agreed agenda or programme of work, what we were concerned about was a package that wouldn't fit easily into a formal agenda and the discussions were following on from talks in Northern Ireland where 'it was accepted that there should be agreement on all the main issues before the parties came together in the Executive'. We had to examine a variety of inter-related subjects – the structure of the Council of Ireland, law and order generally, including detention, the security situation and how terrorism might be dealt with on an all-Ireland basis, policing ('provided it is understood that the RUC must continue to provide the police service for Northern Ireland'), and the vital issue of the territorial status of Northern Ireland.

He was followed by the Taoiseach, Faulkner, Fitt and Napier (both of whom spoke for only four minutes each). The Taoiseach, Liam Cosgrave, stressed that what the Irish people needed was institutions which would encourage and promote trust and cooperation, which would provide effective measures to sustain and defend them and would be accepted by all in the island of Ireland. We had to be pragmatic and realistic. Faulkner, speaking without a script, made an impressive contribution. The Stormont Castle talks, he stated, had been a tremendous achievement. 'Apparently incompatible aspirations have been put together in the Executive Designate with no sacrifice of principle ... the Republic must recognise the right of the people of Northern Ireland to order their own constitutional affairs ... the first vital thing is recognition of that right and if that is done the other things will become possible.' He was worried that the Council of Ireland was '100 times more difficult' than power-sharing. On terrorism, he gave credit to the South for helping to end the 1956–1962 campaign and said total cooperation was now necessary to end the present campaign: the Council of Ireland could assist in this regard.

Following the Leaders' contributions we had a short break, and when we came back Heath suggested that between then and lunch we might concentrate on the Council of Ireland, law and order, including extradition and human rights, and thirdly on the question of the status of Northern Ireland.

Declan Costello, the Republic's Attorney-General, made a detailed contribution on Common Law, policing and related matters. The SDLP had discussed these and other matters with the Irish government when we had met in Dublin on 3 December, so I was aware of the government's proposals.

He proposed that, especially in view of the security problem, the achievement, at the earliest possible date, of a combination of a common form of policing and common law-enforcement arrangements for the whole of Ireland under the Council of Ireland was desirable.

It was an important and effective contribution, giving teeth to the Council of Ireland. The proposals would not have come as a surprise to the British side, to which they had been transmitted the previous month, but they appeared to take the Unionists by surprise. But the response of the British Attorney-General, Sir Peter Rawlinson, was the most disconcerting as it was so negative. He appeared to be hearing the proposals for the first time, and not to have done his homework. In fact, his attitude was a problem throughout the conference. In particular, he seemed to have difficulty in understanding the different approach of the Irish government, necessitated by a written constitution. He adopted a superior, condescending attitude that did not go down well with the Irish delegates, including the Unionists. I'm glad to say he was the only one of the British delegation who behaved in this way.

John rescued us from what might have developed into an acrimonious debate by turning the focus onto the Unionists, saying they were getting a guarantee of their position never previously achieved, so what were they going to give in return? My note at this stage reads, 'Faulkner being badly squeezed – tries to get back to status.' He asked the South for a commitment to change the Constitution. In the meantime, all he required was 'a simple declaration' that the people of Northern Ireland had the right to decide their own constitutional future. Heath, like Whitelaw, recognised a good time for the lunch break.

Over lunch I had a short conversation with Ted Heath, who remembered me from Chequers the previous year. I had received my invitation to dinner at NNo. 10 that evening and I told him how much I was looking forward to being inside rather than, as on my previous visit, outside, on hunger strike.

In the afternoon, considerable progress was made on the Council of Ireland and I made my first contribution to the proceedings. Faulkner had expressed reservations about the Executive and harmonisation functions for the Council and, as gently as I could, I reminded him that this matter had already been agreed at Stormont Castle and there was no way we were going to re-open issues already agreed.

As arranged at the party meeting the previous evening, I brought up the question of a Declaration of Intent from the British government along the lines suggested in *Towards a New Ireland*. The SDLP considered such a Declaration important as a British contribution to an eventual solution to the Northern Ireland problem, but also tactically important in order to cover our backs against possible criticism from within and without our own ranks that we were concerned only with a stop-gap interim solution. I now asked the British side to make a Declaration that they believed it would be in the best interests of all sections of the communities, on both islands, if Ireland were to become united on terms acceptable to all the people of Ireland. I stressed that such a Declaration should contain no hint of coercion and that the SDLP was, of course, totally committed to no change in the constitutional position of Northern Ireland without the consent of the majority there. Heath intervened to say that if the people of Northern Ireland wished to change the constitutional relationship with Great Britain, then he believed no British government would stand in their way. That was good, as far as it went, I course what we would have liked him to say was that the British gover would encourage the people of Northern Ireland to think in terms of e unification. However, my raising the issue helped to concentrate mind need for some formulae for future British intentions, which was ev covered in the Joint Declaration on the Status of Northern Ireland in communiqué.

There was agreement on the number of Ministers on the Council an way in which members of the Dáil and the Assembly would be electe Consultative Assembly of the Council, ie, by proportional representa that all parties, including the loyalists, would be represented. The Sec would be independent of both legislatures and would operate Secretary-General.

An unfortunate occurrence in relation to the agreement on the nt Ministers from each side on the Ministerial Council had a surprising One of the ground rules for the conference was that since nothing wou agreed until everything was agreed, there should be no briefing of the Press until the whole package had been agreed. Muiris Mac Conghail, the Irish government Press Officer, inadvertently leaked to the media the agreement regarding the numbers on the Ministerial Council. The following morning there were angry exchanges, emanating largely, and not surprisingly, from the Unionist camp and the Irish government was seriously embarrassed. The upshot was that the previous agreement on five members from each side was withdrawn. The surprising outcome was that when we returned to the subject the Irish government proposed seven from each side, presumably in an effort to scotch the original leak, and the amendment was accepted without demur.

When we took a break for fifteen minutes just before four o'clock things were going well. On resumption, Heath directed our attention to Status, law and order and policing, but he did it in such a way that did not make us feel we were being dictated to: an important consideration when another sovereign government was involved in the discussions. Faulkner queried possible amendment of the Irish Constitution – the possibility of deleting Articles 2 and 3, which claimed jurisdiction over Northern Ireland. The Taoiseach was quite blunt in his response. No amendment was possible, for no such amendment would be likely, in present circumstances, to have sufficient support in a referendum. But, he added, we are prepared to make a formal Declaration that we will register with the United Nations. Faulkner was disposed to argue the case further, but Conor Cruise O'Brien, generally

nised as the most pro-Unionist of the Dublin Ministers, strongly
rted Cosgrave. The present Irish Constitution was de Valera's
tution, the Fianna Fáil opposition would oppose the proposed changes,
re very unlikely to pass and the result would be worse than our present
. Surprisingly, the delegate who was most insistent on pushing the
s Oliver Napier. On this, as on extradition, he was more unionist than
onists themselves.

ssions then moved on to policing, and it soon became evident
wa ely to be the most intractable problem. Heath had made it
re was no question of re-naming the RUC and that the RUC
the support of all who aspired to being in government. We, of
ad had to accept that position at Stormont Castle when Whitelaw
ined the British government's position, but it made the SDLP's
more difficult. A change of name and uniform would be a symbolic
with the past that would have an impact on the nationalist
munity. These changes having been ruled out, we required an
alternative, and some form of link with the Council of Ireland was the only
alternative we could come up with. However, the linking of two matters
which worried the Unionists – the Council of Ireland and changes to RUC
control – made it even more difficult for them to accept.

I attempted to be helpful. Our aim was a permanent end to politically
motivated violence. The proposals we were considering, particularly
power-sharing and the Council of Ireland, were extremely helpful in enabling
nationalists to identify with the State and its institutions to an extent never
before achieved. This would take time, however, and in the meantime there
was a policing job to be done. The SDLP was more conscious of this than any
other party since it was the areas we represented which had suffered most
from lack of acceptable policing. The lack of a police service with which both
communities could identify would be the Achilles heel of the settlement we
were proposing. I went further. It was extremely worrying to consider the
situation that could develop if we entered into an Executive without being
able to enforce law and order. 'We would be in a position of responsibility
without authority.'

At the time, of course, I didn't realise how prescient I was in terms of a
situation I would have to deal with later as a Minister. My comments were
made to push the case that a policing link with the Council of Ireland was
necessary to give nationalists an identification with the RUC, but of course I,
and the others who pressed for such a link, was effectively saying, without

spelling it out at this juncture, that the policing function should be returned from Westminster to Ireland, to the Executive and to the Council of Ireland.

Brian Faulkner questioned the possible effectiveness of the Council of Ireland for policing. Since we had agreed that all decisions on the Council would have to be unanimous, what would be the policing position if we found it impossible to be unanimous in relation to this essential function? Paddy Cooney, the Minister for Justice, had given him this opening by saying safeguards would be required in the event of a deadlock. Roy Bradford said that, above all, policing had to be effective and that the Council of Ireland proposal would not bring that about because a police force responsible to the Council of Ireland would be anathema to Northern Ireland Protestants.

It was now after 6.00pm and the coach to take us to Downing Street was due to depart at 6.45pm. Heath proposed, and it was agreed, that the policing issue be referred to a subcommittee, as had happened with a number of other issues. At 6.20pm the Plenary was adjourned until 11.30am on the following morning, Friday, 7 December.

My thoughts that first night were positive. Heath was showing total commitment; Gerry had asked him about his responsibilities in the Commons and he had responded that he had made alternative arrangements. Bradford's hopes, and my concerns, about the SDLP being 'screwed' were not being realised. In fact, there had been indications that the pressure might be applied to the Unionists. The relationship between Heath and Faulkner was not good. It was nothing that was actually said, but rather a less than full reply, a look, the ignoring of a point, it all added up to the suggestion that there was something just below the surface, being suppressed. The decision to end the old Stormont had caused greater personal antagonism than I had suspected.

Entering No. 10 Downing Street that evening gave me great satisfaction. I was glad Paddy O'Hanlon was there too as he had accompanied John and me on our hunger strike. When Heath was welcoming us, he said to me, 'I hope you will find the hospitality better than on the last occasion'. And indeed it was an excellent meal. It was almost a fitting reward and recompense for the cold and the wet and the indignity of two years previously, although the Champagne Cognac did not compare to the brandy Don Concannon had provided halfway through that very cold night.

At table, I was seated between Sir Geoffrey Arthur, the Deputy Under-Secretary in the Foreign Office, and Michael Murphy, the Assistant Secretary in the Department of Finance, and opposite Sir David Holden, the

Head of the Northern Ireland Civil Service. Whoever made the seating arrangements had anticipated my need for civil service expertise!

After the formal part of the proceedings was concluded and the mingling began, I found myself in conversation with the Prime Minister. Others have described Heath as cold and haughty, but on this occasion, as at Chequers, I did not find him so. He wasn't good at small talk, but I have a certain deficiency in that department myself, and he struck me as being shy rather than haughty. Someone must have told him I had an interest in music because he insisted on bringing me upstairs to his private flat to show me his Steinbeck, which he said he had bought for £450 and was now worth £5,000. I hadn't the honesty to tell him it was my wife who had the musical interest, not me.

On our return downstairs the party had livened up considerably. Paddy Devlin was endeavouring to persuade the Martin Neary Singers, who had provided the background music during dinner, and others, to contribute something more lively to the proceedings. Alec Douglas Hume advised me to run for an English constituency: 'Isn't Gerry combining the two?' Even when I told him that my uncle Jimmy was Chairman of the Perry Barr Labour Constituency party, he still thought it a good idea.

On the coach back to Sunningdale, the SDLP singers had taken over from the Martin Neary Singers, and even Faulkner was induced to give a rendering of 'The Star of the County Down', and a good rendering it was. Arriving back at our quarters, we discovered a problem: Gerry had decided to stay overnight in his usual London abode, the Irish Club, and had taken the keys to our drinks cabinet with him, accidentally, we believed. The Alliance party, for whom we had not much liking because of their performance that day, came to the rescue and a number of us, all with the best intentions of an early night, congregated in their room. Hume, Devlin, O'Hanlon and myself, Oliver Napier, Bob Cooper and Basil Glass of the Alliance party, Philip Woodfield and two other officials from the British delegation and Ken Bloomfield, speechwriter and former advisor and confidante to Terence O'Neill, Chichester-Clark and Faulkner. We all took a nightcap together and talked not about the events of the day or the decisions we would have to take tomorrow, but, with a certain confidence, of the problems we would tackle on taking over government. Ken Bloomfield told me he doubted if the Department could deliver on the 20,000 new houses promised annually; it might be necessary to bring in people from outside. Nevertheless, before going to bed I entered the following in my journal: 'Things falling into line. Whitelaw successful in phase one. Heath is now committed to making talks a success. We have won.' It was far too early to make that judgement, but it had been a good day, and it wasn't just the drink talking!

Day Two had a delayed start because the five subcommittees were conducting meetings prior to the main session. Eddie McGrady and Paddy O'Hanlon were on the Finance Committee; Paddy Devlin on Functions; Ivan Cooper and Paddy Duffy on the Common Law-enforcement Area; John Hume on Status; and Michael Canavan and I were on the Policing subcommittee; Gerry had decided he was best suited for a roving commission. It was decided at the party meeting that policing was likely to be the most intractable issue and that agreement on other matters would exert its own pressure for agreement on policing. Michael and I were instructed to stall, if necessary. I told the others I doubted such a tactic would be required.

Michael Canavan was the party spokesman on security and policing. Steady, reliable and totally committed, he was a running mate of John Hume's and was close to him personally and politically. On top of his brief, he was the ideal partner for me in a tactical exercise where it might be necessary to be uncompromising, even to appear obdurate and intransigent.

A draft communiqué circulated at the plenary session at 6.00pm that day (Friday, 7 December) indicated that considerable progress had been made by a number of subcommittees. On the fundamental issue of the status of Northern Ireland, Solemn Declarations would be registered at the United Nations. The Irish government 'fully accepted and solemnly declared that there could be no change in the status of Northern Ireland until a majority of the people of Northern Ireland desired change in the status.' The British government 'solemnly declared that it was, and would remain, their policy to support the wishes of the majority of the people of Northern Ireland about the status of Northern Ireland', and went on to say, 'If therefore, in the future, the majority of the people of Northern Ireland should indicate a wish to become part of a united Ireland HMG would support that wish.' The Unionists had achieved their primary objective – a Solemn Declaration from the Irish government that the constitutional position of Northern Ireland would not change without the consent of the majority of its people, something which Unionists had demanded since Partition in 1920. And the SDLP, while not getting the positive Declaration of Intent we would have liked, did have a Declaration from the British government, for the first time, that if the situation arose where a majority in Northern Ireland wished to change the constitutional position, British government policy would change accordingly.

In further discussion on status the relevant clauses were appropriately refined. The Irish government had a difficulty in that in the draft, the British Declaration came first, and there was a fear that the form of the Declaration might cause difficulties of a constitutional nature in the context of the Irish written Constitution and Articles 2 and 3, in particular. An ingenious revision to the draft saw the two Declarations printed side-by-side, which in fact later proved important in defeating a legal challenge in the Supreme Court. I was later told by one of the Irish officials that Garret FitzGerald, who had been unusually quiet at the Plenary Sessions, had been instrumental in bringing about this solution.

Substantial agreement was also evident in the draft on the Council of Ireland and its functions and membership. The Council would consist of an equal number of ministers from North and South, operating on the basis of unanimity. It would have a permanent headquarters. On a separate advisory and consultative level there would be a body consisting of members from the Dáil and the Assembly, elected in equal numbers, by proportional representation, from the parties in the Dáil and the Assembly. The Council would have a Secretariat operating under a Secretary-General. Studies would be initiated to identify areas of common interest in relation to which the Council of Ireland would take executive decisions and, in appropriate cases, be responsible for carrying those decisions into effect. These studies would have the purpose of identifying suitable areas of activity for executive action by the Council.

This first draft in relation to the Council of Ireland wasn't acceptable to the SDLP and Irish government delegations, and in subsequent discussions and negotiations it was beefed up. It was agreed the Council of Ministers would have executive and harmonising functions and that the Consultative Assembly would have advisory and review functions. In the context of its harmonising functions and consultative role, the Council of Ireland 'would undertake important work relating, for instance, to the impact of EEC membership'.

From the SDLP point of view, we hoped that in the Council of Ireland, even with its limitations, we had helped to create something which, over a period of time, could develop and evolve to ensure a more united island, on an agreed basis. We felt sure that the opportunity to work together, North and South, in tackling common problems would create a situation where such common activity for mutual advantage would be taken for granted, and would be built upon at all levels. We did not see the Council as a threat to the fundamental interests of unionists. The Status Declaration by the Irish government, supported fully by the SDLP, enshrined unionist consent to change in the constitutional position and besides, decisions taken by the Council of Ministers had to be unanimous. Finally, we placed emphasis on the comparison between the Council and the newly emergent European institutions, and we hoped to achieve for our Council a similar ability to evolve and adapt in a changing political climate.

Even on the most troublesome issue of policing, the first draft communiqué seemed to indicate progress. I immediately noted that the suggestions made owed more to the optimism of the civil service drafters than to anything which had happened on the policing subcommittee. It recommended a Standing Joint Police Authorities Committee with equal membership taken from the two Police Authorities, North and South, which would discuss and report on all matters within the purview of those Police Authorities. The Chief Constable and the Garda Commissioner would form a Standing Police Committee that would consider matters of common interest. Up to one-third of the Northern Ireland Police Authority would be appointed by the Secretary of State, on the nomination of the Council of Ireland, and the Minister of Justice in the Republic would have a similar function in relation to the new Police Authority in his jurisdiction.

These provisions, from the SDLP's point of view, were inadequate, but at least the principle seemed to have been accepted that the Council of Ireland should have some responsibility for policing, which would go some way to offset, for nationalists, the insistence of the British government that there would be no change in the name, or the uniform of the RUC.

The conference had been scheduled to conclude at lunchtime on Saturday, 8 December and save for the policing problem might well have done so. However, as a result of the policing stalemate it over ran by more than thirty hours, until Sunday evening. For those of us directly involved in the policing issue, it was a time of frantic toing and froing from policing committee to party meeting to Plenary, to informal one-to-one discussions with other negotiators, to meetings of party Leaders and interventions by anyone who thought he could break the impasse, to very private *tête-à-têtes* in the gardens watched, but hopefully not heard, by members of the Thames Valley police force, who seemed to be behind every tree.

At Friday night's Plenary Session, which had ended at 11.40pm, the Attorney-General's group dealing with extradition and a common law-enforcement area reported progress and said they would continue their discussions into the night; the Status subcommittee reported 'some progress towards a meeting of minds' and also decided to keep at it; the group considering financial aspects of the Council of Ireland said they had agreed on the document. But on behalf of the policing group, I reported that 'we have disagreed on every section of the draft'. We were, however, able to agree that there was no point in further discussion that night.

The Policing Committee reconvened at 9.15am on Saturday morning, but was so deadlocked that our meeting lasted only twenty minutes. By this time I was becoming annoyed by the performance of Paddy Cooney, the Irish Minister for Justice. While we in the SDLP continually emphasised the importance of a policing link with the Council of Ireland as a means of increasing nationalist support for the police, Cooney continuously minimised the role of the Council and emphasised the need for a police force to be capable of taking quick and decisive action, unimpeded by what he described as 'encumbrances'. This was an understandable attitude for a Minister responsible for law and order and fearing an overflow of IRA violence into his jurisdiction, but IRA violence was an all-island problem and the strengthening of the police service in the North, by attracting nationalist support to it through the link with the Council of Ireland, was in everyone's interest. Even more to the point, what the SDLP was proposing already had the support of his government. This had been agreed at the SDLP–Irish government meeting on 3 December and confirmed only the previous day. So when, at that morning's short meeting, I reiterated the role envisaged for the Council of Ireland in the appointment of the Police Authorities and Cooney said, 'Hedge it about so that the two governments will control', I kicked him under the table. It was certainly no surprise to me that the Irish government in which he was Minister for Justice never did get around to appointing a Police Authority, with or without a Council of Ireland. Indeed, to this very day there is no Police Authority in the South.

As the Saturday lunchtime deadline expired and other committees finished their allotted tasks, the policing subcommittee became the sole focus of attention and attendance widened considerably from the original membership. On Saturday afternoon, in addition to Pym, Faulkner, Bradford, Cooney, Bob Cooper, Michael Canavan and myself, there were also in attendance Garret FitzGerald, Conor Cruise O'Brien, Oliver Napier, John Hume, Paddy Devlin, David Howell and a number of civil servants. Gerry also came in to observe the proceedings.

Faulkner and Napier had obviously discussed a new line of approach, and it was Napier who brought it up first. There could be a policing role for the

Council of Ireland, but the most effective way to bring about identification was through the Assembly and the Power-Sharing Executive, which meant the restoration of what he described as 'normal policing' to the Assembly. By 'normal' policing he meant 'all those powers not involving security'. Faulkner strongly supported him on the return of a policing function, but added, presumably in an attempt to get our support, that a police complaints procedure might be attached to the Council of Ireland.

It was, of course, the decision of this current British government to remove policing and security powers that had led to the suspension of the old Stormont system. As a result, I was not surprised by the strongly negative British reaction to Faulkner's proposal. It came from Sir Frank Cooper, the top civil servant in the Northern Ireland Office, acting as the main advisor to Heath and, in the absence of Whitelaw, the person in the British delegation most conversant with the realities of the politics of Northern Ireland. We knew from experience that he was a ruthless career civil servant who could put the boot in when he thought it expedient. This he now did, with alacrity. The Unionist and Alliance proposal was 'facile'. The RUC was content to be under Westminster Rule and did not wish to see that position changed. It would resent being put back in the political arena and must be kept free from the sort of political control it had laboured under in the old Stormont. Anyhow, how could we possibly separate policing from a security role? The Bobby on the beat was the eyes and ears upon which security decisions were taken. Was riot control, for example, a policing or security role? Cooper was his master's voice on this issue, but the strength of his attack underlined his own conviction. Faulkner attempted a comeback. Special Branch could be excluded from 'normal' policing. If some form of policing were to be devolved to the Executive, it would be easier for the Unionists to consider a meaningful police link to the Council of Ireland. Cooper was having none of it. When we adjourned at 6.00pm, we were no nearer to a solution.

I gave my impression of where we stood to the party meeting that followed. The Northern Ireland parties could find agreement on the return of some form of policing function to the Assembly and the Executive. Any administration that could not implement and enforce its own decisions and relied on another government, in this case the British government, to do so for it would be a political eunuch. But we had to face the reality that Heath was implacably opposed to reversing his decision of 1972. Was there any way of devolving even minor policing functions as a first step that would be related to the Council of Ireland and later, as the Executive proved itself, further

237

steps could be taken? Could we discuss these possibilities with the Unionists and Alliance?

Paddy Devlin was particularly supportive of the suggestion of consultation with the other Northern parties, indeed, I suspected that he had already been involved in such discussions. It soon became clear that we could find an agreed line on devolving some policing functions. Faulkner was now so adamant on this point that I began to suspect there was an element of score-settling with Heath, which would not be helpful to the possibility of success. Garret FitzGerald was particularly supportive of the SDLP position, but when I complained to him about the attitude of his colleague, Paddy Cooney, he was unusually reticent on the subject. I suspected it was a sensitive issue with the Fine Gael members of the government.

The Policing committee met again between 9.00pm and 10.00pm, but still no progress. The British had produced a further draft document, but it was no advance; there was nothing new to report to the Plenary Session. At the party meeting that followed, the mood was sombre. Gerry said it looked as if we were at the end of the road. He had been speaking to 'wee Brian' and he was adamant that without some movement by Heath on policing devolution, he could not agree to strengthening the police link with the Council of Ireland. Faulkner had told Heath that if he ended the talks now, the Unionist delegation could return to Northern Ireland as heroes. However, this he did not wish to do unless there was absolutely no alternative.

There was an additional worry. We were now approaching the Sabbath and there was some doubt as to whether the Unionists, especially those of the Presbyterian tradition, such as Faulkner, would be willing to work, or be seen to be working on a Sunday. Later, when the fears turned out to be groundless, a rumour circulated that the clock in the Unionists' conference room had been stopped at 11.59pm. Meanwhile, at our party meeting there was no diminution in our determination to have the strongest possible link between policing and the Council of Ireland. All of us had our own experiences at constituency level of trying to operate politically in a society where even our strongest supporters, people committed to non-violence, had deep reservations about being associated with the RUC. Even strong policing links with the Council of Ireland would encounter difficulty in providing the necessary identification. It would be the symbolism of the all-Ireland institution that would be the most potent. But of course, it was precisely this symbolism which worried the Unionists. On the level of policing devolution, we all agreed that if we were to share power, then the maximum power the better.

At the conclusion of our meeting, Gerry and John went to see Heath to bring him up-to-date on our thinking and to stress our determination that everything possible must be done to break the impasse. They reminded him of the agreement entered into at the beginning of the Stormont Castle talks that nothing would be agreed until everything had been agreed. If the deadlock on policing could not be broken, then all our historic progress would be lost. The Leader and Deputy Leader returned after about an hour. They reported that Heath was in a determined mood, that he was taking the initiative and going to meet Faulkner to press him to give ground on the Council of Ireland. Shortly after that, it was reported to us that the Prime Minister and Sir Frank Cooper had been seen entering the Unionist room.

At 4.35am most of the SDLP delegation was in the party room when, unannounced, Heath and Cooper walked in. Heath confirmed that he had been to see Faulkner, but little progress had been made. 'Brian,' he said, 'is still hankering after what he lost in 1972 and he is not getting it back.' He said he had warned him that if negotiations broke down now, Faulkner himself would be blamed. The inference was that the British government would ensure this. It was a remarkably candid exposition of his views and his commitment. We didn't escape either, although we were treated less harshly. We were standing on the cusp of government and it was unacceptable that the SDLP should have any reservations about fully supporting the forces of law and order. John responded that the unacceptability of the security forces had largely resulted from fifty years of one-party rule and the sovereign government's neglect of its responsibilities. After that things calmed down, and when Heath left us at 5.04am we understood he had agreed to fully support nominations to the Police Authorities after consultation with the Council of Ireland, that the Council should also have a role in human rights protection through an all-island Ombudsman and that he would continue to lean on Faulkner.

Shortly after this, someone in our delegation, I think it was Paddy Devlin, reported that there had been a stormy session between Heath and the Unionists and the latter were now threatening to leave. John and I reported this to the Irish government in a mood of some pessimism. As it turned out, things were not as bad as we had feared.

John and I had another meeting with Heath, which started at 6.25am and ended at 7.20am. We were both 'night men' and so, it appeared, was Heath. At this stage he hadn't slept for more than twenty-four hours. The Conference was supposed to have ended about sixteen hours earlier, and he had had to depart for a time to carry out an official engagement, which necessitated being helicoptered to London to meet the Italian Prime Minister. He certainly had staying power. This meeting was at Heath's request and he had had, or would be having, similar meetings with other delegations. He remained implacably opposed to the return of security functions to Stormont, but as it had been indicated to him that all three Northern parties had agreed that they would like, in certain circumstances, to see some form of policing function residing in the Executive, Her Majesty's government was prepared to agree to something along the lines suggested, to be implemented at a time when security conditions allowed it. My first reaction was that Faulkner had won, my second that this was Heath's last determined effort to achieve a considerable political and personal victory. John and I reserved our position until we had consulted with our colleagues, but when I eventually got to bed around 8.30am I had great difficulty in getting to sleep because of my feeling of elation.

There were further meetings on Sunday afternoon, but effectively the Heath decision was the clincher. Faulkner was of the opinion that the most he could get was a commitment from the British that when the security position had improved and the new institutions were seen to be working effectively, they would enter into discussions on the devolution of normal policing to the Assembly and the Executive. The Unionists had to accept this, or carry the odium of collapsing the whole painfully-pieced-together package of agreement. For our part, the SDLP had to accept that the policing link to the Council of Ireland, unsatisfactory as it was, was the maximum we were going to get in the circumstances as there was simply no room left for manoeuvre for Heath or the Unionists.

The final wording on policing was agreed in Heath's room at 7.35pm on Sunday evening, and the final Plenary Session commenced at 8.23pm. The short speeches were made in an emotional atmosphere. Taoiseach Liam Cosgrave said he was confident we had laid the foundations of a new and better Ireland. Brian Faulkner thanked the Taoiseach and his Ministers, paid a particular tribute to Frank Cooper, and finished by saying 'on this Sunday evening we should all thank God'. Gerry, quoting Gladstone, who had said his mission was to pacify Ireland, said to Heath, 'He didn't succeed, but I hope you have.' Oliver Napier said the conference had been the finest example of 'fellow Ulstermen working together for the good of Northern Ireland'. Prime Minister Heath thanked everyone for their help, said the outcome justified the hard and exhausting work and acknowledged that there would be difficulties ahead, but had no doubt they would be overcome if the same commitment prevailed. The conference officially ended at 8.36pm and the initialling ceremony by the five Leaders took place six minutes later.

I phoned Annita as soon as I was sure no hiccups would occur. It was a tearful discussion, a mixture of relief and joy. So much had happened in our lives in such a short time; maybe the future would now be better.

In the light of subsequent events, it has become almost a universally accepted truth that the SDLP and the Irish government were too successful at Sunningdale, that they imposed on Brian Faulkner, through the Council of Ireland, a task he was incapable of fulfilling. I did not accept that then and I do not accept it now. Part of the reason for my conviction is because Faulkner himself told me so. On that final Sunday afternoon at Sunningdale, after about four hours' sleep, I took a walk in the gardens to clear my head. I met Faulkner with one of his colleagues, on a similar mission. By this time we both knew of Heath's final position on policing devolution, and we both agreed on our attitude to it. He said that the British commitment did not go as far as he would have liked, but it was a start, and it would make it much easier for him to sell the agreement to his colleagues. He talked in optimistic terms of the future and said that neither Craig nor Brookeborough had achieved the guarantee for the future of Northern Ireland which had been obtained by him at this conference. He did not give the slightest indication during the ten minutes or so we conversed that he had been given an impossible task to deliver.

As we flew back to Aldergrove the following day we were all in fine form, cracking jokes, confident in the new closeness to each other forged by the common endeavour at Stormont Castle and at Sunningdale, and looking forward to working together in government. Perhaps we should have paid more attention to the weather forecast for Aldergrove, circulated by the RAF captain, and translated the climatic information into political terms: 'Weather at Aldergrove – cloudy, windy, showery and cold.'

20: POWER-SHARING EXECUTIVE

O n the last day of 1973, in advance of taking up office on 1 January, the members of the Northern Ireland Power-Sharing Executive were sworn in by the Lord Chief Justice, Sir Robert Lowry, at a ceremony in Stormont Castle. The form of oath taken underlined the changes that had taken place since the Stormont government and Parliament had been suspended less than two years previously. Back then, new ministers had to take the Privy Councillors' oath, which included the pledge 'to bear faith and allegiance to the Crown and to defend its jurisdiction and powers against all foreign princes, persons, prelates, states or potentates'.

The Constitution Act 1973 had abolished the Northern Ireland Privy Council and the oath we took on the eve of the first day of the New Year merely committed us to 'uphold the laws of Northern Ireland and conscientiously fulfill, as a member of the Northern Ireland Executive, my duties under the Northern Ireland Constitution Act 1973 in the interest of Northern Ireland and its people.' It was as well – to have had to defend the British Crown against potentates such as Liam Cosgrave, or prelates such as Cardinal Conway, really would have been too much!

We all took the oath, except for Paddy Devlin, who affirmed and received our letters of appointment from the Secretary of State, Francis Pym, in the following order:

Brian Faulkner, Chief Executive
Gerry Fitt, Deputy Chief Executive
Oliver Napier, Legal member and Head of the Office of Law Reform
John Baxter, Head of the Office of Information Services
Roy Bradford, Head of the Department of the Environment
Austin Currie, Head of the Department of Housing, Local Government and Planning
Paddy Devlin, Head of the Department of Health and Social Services
John Hume, Head of the Department of Commerce
Herbie Kirk, Head of the Department of Finance
Basil McIvor, Head of the Department of Education

Leslie Morell, Head of the Department of Agriculture

Ivan Cooper, Head of the Department of Community Relations

Bob Cooper, Head of the Department of Manpower Services

Eddie McGrady, Head of the Office of Executive Planning and Coordination

The last three, as members of the Administration outside the Executive, had to be re-sworn when it was discovered there was a separate wording appropriate to their positions.

The following morning I was driven in my new official car to Parliament Buildings at Stormont, where my Ministerial office was located. In through the impressive front gate, up the mile-long avenue, past Carson's statue, until finally the car stopped outside the magnificent building under a depiction of 'Ulster bearing the golden flame of loyalty to the Crown'. No change there then, just as it had been before. A uniformed attendant emerged to open the car door and as I entered the building a group of people, some of whom I recognised as civil servants, welcomed me to my Department and addressed me as 'Mr Minister'. As we ascended the marble staircase past the statue of Lord Craigavon, he of 'a Protestant Parliament for a Protestant people', I refrained, with effort, from giving him the two-fingered salute.

I had met my Permanent Secretary, John Oliver, on two or three occasions since being nominated as Minister. He had been in charge of the unified Department, of which the new Department of Housing, Local Government and Planning was part, and having built this empire he now had to dismantle it. There had been whisperings about him, which had been brought to my attention. He was so well-connected with the ancient regime that in the aftermath of Bloody Sunday he had been sent to the Washington Congressional Hearings to hold a watching brief. He may have been there, but he had not come to my attention when I was there. On the other hand, I was told he had been a Fabian and might even have secret socialist beliefs. I determined to treat him as I found him and to make up my own mind. There was another factor. Neither I nor any of my SDLP colleagues had experience of government at any level, whereas four of the Unionists had served as full Ministers. Our lack of experience seemed more of a disadvantage then – a time long before Tony Blair and most of his team took over the responsibilities of a national government without any previous experience. In 1974, however, it seemed to be important to offset our apparent disadvantage by taking on board experienced administrators, and John Oliver was the most experienced there was. Moreover, he was of an age, indeed just three years younger than my father, where he was coming close to retirement, so if the relationship did not work out it would soon be ended anyway. In the meantime, I would try to learn from the most experienced person in the entire service, who had specialised in the very sectors of government for which I now had responsibility.

It was a decision I have never regretted. He was a wise and wily old owl, and we got on extremely well on a personal level; some people commented that his attitude to me was almost paternalistic. As I had hoped, he gave me an insight and an understanding of matters outside my experience. On my third day in the Department he dropped in to see me (there was an interconnecting door between my office and his), greeting me with his favourite phrase, 'Minister, I would like to take your mind on a matter.' The New Year's Honours List had just been published, and a number of people in the Department and others connected with it had been honoured by Her Majesty. In the past, the Minister had written to the recipients to congratulate them; he wished to know my attitude. I explained that I was a republican and therefore not in favour of such honours, but I was also a member of a government that represented the two traditions and I understood that those of the unionist and British tradition had a different attitude, which I respected. He looked at me and asked, 'Minister, could I describe your attitude as one of benevolent neutrality?', to which I responded, 'Precisely, John'. It then transpired that in the period of Direct Rule he had actually made recommendations for Honours, so I suggested it would be fitting that he write to congratulate them. He further enquired about the preparation of the Birthday Honours List, due in June, and it was agreed he would continue his role as in the past. I later found out he had been honoured by a Companion of the Bath a few years earlier – not on his own recommendation, I hasten to add. I don't know whether on retirement he received a further honour, but in keeping with 'benevolent neutrality', I think he deserved one.

I had expected to find that fifty years of one-party rule would have had an effect on the civil service in terms of conditioning, and I was right. There were two civil servants in the Department, with whom I had relatively close contact, who I felt had difficulty accepting me. But there were two factors working in my favour: two years of Direct Rule had prepared them, to some extent, for a Minister who was not a Unionist; and some of the younger civil servants were known to me from student days at Queen's. John Oliver ran a regime that was not pyramidal, in that each and every issue did not come to me through the Permanent Secretary alone. In fact, he encouraged me to ask for the opinions of officials down the line and for those officials to come directly to me. It meant I had alternatives, rather than a single Departmental view.

In appointing my Private Secretary, I was again biased towards experience rather than political or religious background. I gave the job to Alan McArthur, who had previous experience as a Private Secretary and who had been helpful to me as an opposition MP. Time enough to promote new talent when I myself knew what I was doing.

On our first day as Ministers, Gerry and I stepped out from the dining-room at lunchtime and onto the balcony. Looking out over the beautiful grounds, towards the Castlereagh hills, Gerry turned to me and asked, 'If I pinch you, will you do the same to me?' The progress we had made in such a short time, since the beginning of the civil rights campaign, was almost unbelievable. The Caledon squatter was now in charge of housing; the former unemployed seaman was now second-in-command of the government of Northern Ireland!

Brian Faulkner's efficiency and impartiality in summing up the different points of view at the end of a discussion did not surprise me. He always aimed for consensus and indeed always achieved it, except at the very end of the Executive's life. He even managed to conceal his annoyance better than I did at the unpunctuality of some of our SDLP colleagues. (Throughout my lifetime in politics, North and South, I have never ceased to be surprised at the unpunctuality of so many politicians. It betrays an arrogant attitude I find inexcusable. It is saying, 'my time is much more important than yours'. And yet I have never known any of these same politicians to be late for a live TV interview.) In other ways, Brian Faulkner did surprise me. The lifelong teetotaller adapted to the new situation. The first time I noticed it was shortly after we came into office, when I had arranged to meet him to inform him of potentially controversial appointments I was making to the Housing Executive. Heading for his drinks cabinet, he enquired what I would like to drink. When I pointed out it was only 11.30am, he said, 'That doesn't stop Gerry.' The point was that in his previous ministries he would not have had a drinks cabinet, let alone offered a drink to anyone. On another occasion, this time an evening appointment, he reminded me of a Pioneer in terms of the amount he poured into my glass – Pioneers invariably fill the glass to the brim!

The Executive met in the former Prime Minister's office in Parliament Buildings. Here we experienced a certain lack of sensitivity towards the nationalist tradition, an insensitivity apparent throughout Stormont. Hanging on one wall was a portrait of Queen Victoria and on another that of Field Marshal Henry Wilson, who was shot on the orders of Michael Collins for his alleged anti-Catholic activities. On occasion, my attention would drift from the discussion at hand to a consideration of a replacement portrait to redress the balance. Would it be Wolfe Tone? Henry Joy McCracken? Perhaps one of the O'Neills, Hugh or Owen Roe, from my own county? Cahir Healy?

There were other insensitivities. The maiden city was invariably described as 'Londonderry' even though in private discussions with civil servants it was usually 'Derry'. On the first occasion I visited that city as a Minister, covered by a BBC 'Panorama' camera crew, I noted that the script, the basic construction of which I had agreed earlier, referred solely to 'Londonderry'. The 'Panorama' commentator saw it as the highlight of my speech that when I used 'Londonderry' I followed it immediately with 'Derry', thus emphasising the two traditions and the nature of the government I represented. Words such as 'Province' and 'Ulster' and 'the mainland', which jarred with the nationalist audience, often appeared in official scripts. And I did not use the official briefcase supplied, which was marked, in bold type EIIR (Elizabeth the Second Regina) – my constituents in Coalisland would not have been impressed.

Within a week I had to deal with an example of discrimination. A Fermanagh businessman and supporter rang me to complain about an advertisement run by my Department for the supply of JCBs. I did not see anything wrong with it until he drew my attention to the fact that there were other makes of diggers equal, if not better, for use in the construction industry and that the sale of JCBs was controlled by one agency in County Derry. On investigation, I found that the owners of this agency were related to Dame Dehra Parker, who was Minister for Local Government in the 1950s, and that ever since then 'JCB' had been specified by the Department. The advertisement was amended without any difficulty.

I enjoyed the work in the Department and the challenges it presented. I relished the opportunity of dealing with problems which had frustrated me in opposition. And I am glad to say I retained much of the idealism that had motivated me into politics in the first place.

My first priority was to try to ensure adequate housing accommodation for everyone in the North. From the beginning, and despite the reluctance of some of my officials who had presided over the problem, I insisted on stating it as I saw it: there was a housing crisis. Of the 450,000 dwelling houses in Northern Ireland, around 100,000 were unfit for human habitation. According to the 1971 census, 27% of households had no bath, 21% no hot water, 27% had no inside flush toilet, while 10% were not connected to a public water supply and 15% were not connected to a sewer. In 1974, in

Belfast's inner city, four houses in ten had no inside toilet. In Fermanagh, 47% of houses had no inside toilet and 41% did not even have an outside flush toilet. The Housing Programme had simply not been meeting the challenge. At the end of 1973, 14,000 houses were under construction, and I estimated that 20,000 new homes were necessary each year to solve the housing problem, alongside the modernisation and upgrading of existing houses. To achieve such a target would require output by the construction industry far in excess of its building record to date, therefore the industry would need assistance to meet the new demands. On top of all this, it had to be achieved in a period of continuing civil disturbance, bombs, intimidation and unpredictable population movements due to violence and intimidation. I knew I faced a difficult, possibly an insurmountable problem, but I was determined to succeed and the British government promised the necessary resources. At least the formation of the Housing Executive and the removal of the housing function from the Councils meant I did not have to deal with the injustice that had first focussed my attention on housing, ie, discrimination in allocation.

There were other problems which were going to test my mettle, not least because of a previous involvement I would not be allowed to forget. As part of the agreements at Stormont Castle and Sunningdale, the SDLP had committed to the ending of the rent and rate strike. It was now my obligation to implement this pledge. A more immediate problem provided the first challenge: intimidation had forced large numbers of families and individuals out of their houses in Belfast and elsewhere, and a considerable number of these displaced people were engaged in squatting. Many of these families had no alternative, but some were opportunists using the excuse of other people's misfortune to jump the housing queue. Ever since Caledon I had, of course, been identified with squatting and there was great interest, some of it morbid, in seeing how I dealt with the problem. I was careful to differentiate between 'squatting', which was the action of unfortunates with no alternative and 'queue-jumpers', who were opportunists. My activity in Caledon had been a protest against the latter.

I was soon tested by squatting at Farrington Gardens in North Belfast, where Protestants had burned down the houses as they left them in 1969. The houses had been rebuilt, but a group of Catholics had jumped the gun, and the queue, and occupied them. The Housing Executive couldn't sort out the problem, a local Protestant organisation was threatening all sorts of illegality, the issue was attracting negative publicity and there was a real danger of community strife. So the Housing Executive handed the poisoned chalice over to me. At a meeting, they demanded that I accompany them to meet the Secretary of State to ask him to make available the RUC and, if necessary, the Army to evict the squatters.

It was a major crisis for me and the Housing Executive knew it. Would I be prepared to tackle Catholic squatters? If not, my credibility as an impartial and effective minister would be completely undermined. But acceding to their request would also be a serious problem for me. At Sunningdale, I had made the point that the lack of a policing function for the Executive could be our Achilles heel. I had said an administration that could not enforce its own laws would be a eunuch. Now, the first challenge of that nature to the new government was to me and my responsibilities

I accepted the invitation of the Housing Executive to accompany them to the meeting with the Secretary of State and I listened as they put forward their case. The Executive had failed, despite their best efforts, to persuade the squatters to leave. They now had no alternative but to ask that force be used, otherwise squatting would spread like wildfire and the allocation of housing would be beyond their control. Francis Pym listened to them and then asked for my view, as the Minister responsible for housing. I sympathised with the Executive and agreed that this particular incident of queue-jumping had to be dealt with if the Executive was to have any credibility. However, I was not prepared to agree with their demand that the Secretary of State authorise RUC and, if necessary, military intervention. I thought this was an unnecessary escalation of the dispute, which in the present political climate, could have unforeseen consequences. Furthermore, I was not prepared to hand the problem to the British government, over whose actions I had no control, without exhausting other possibilities. I would deal with the problem myself. The Secretary of State was only too keen to say he agreed with the Minister. I was conscious of the disappointment of the Executive members, who had not had to concern themselves with a local Minister since Direct Rule, but now had to deal with one who was asserting himself and the powers of the Assembly. They had hoped to force a young, inexperienced Minister into a course of action where precedent would have been established.

My first move was to open lines of communication to influential Catholic individuals and organisations in the North Belfast area, emphasising that some of the squatters were queue-jumpers who were taking the houses from other Catholics and Protestants who were more needy and that, as Minister, and with my record, I could not tolerate houses going to people who were not most in need. I also told them what the alternative was – action by the RUC and the British Army. Could they use their influence to get the squatters to leave?

As luck would have it, I was presented with an opportunity to speak directly to representatives of some of the Protestant organisations, including the paramilitaries who were threatening action. I was invited to appear on the BBC's 'Spotlight' TV programme, chaired by Brian Walker, to discuss the Farrington Gardens controversy. Representatives of the Protestants were in the studio audience and when the programme ended, with no sign of agreement, I asked Brian if he could arrange for me to meet them, separately. Not only did he do so but, at my request, provided two bottles of whiskey. The people I met had probably never met a government Minister before and certainly not one from 'the other side'. They were flattered and impressed. I told them of my determination that the houses be occupied by those most in need, and of the efforts I was making to organise local opinion to talk to the queue-jumpers. I asked them to assist in this process by not making demands and by exercising some restraint on the more extreme of their supporters. By the time they left, the two bottles were empty. I had received the promises I had asked for and I had their telephone numbers, just in case. I had also proven I was a better whiskey drinker than most of them.

It worked well. Within a short period of time the queue-jumpers had left, those most in need were installed and a potentially serious community confrontation was avoided. I was praised widely in the Assembly, particularly by the Faulkner Unionists. However, I made a point of saying to Faulkner that the incident confirmed our shared fears of the dangers of not having a policing function.

Planning had been taken away from the local councils and was now centralised at Stormont. This meant that every planning decision, large and small, was under my ultimate control. It was a potent weapon, one which could be used to improve the quality of life for all the people of Northern Ireland. It also gave me clout with my ministerial colleagues as nearly everything required planning approval, be it industries, or amenities, or infrastructure, or individual houses in the country.

At Queen's I had studied geography as a subsidiary subject and liked the planning aspects of it so much that I might, in different circumstances, have become a town and country planner. I therefore took a genuine interest in the planning function of my Department and began to think in terms not just of infrastructure but of the social and political changes proper planning could bring about. Like any realistic politician, I saw the possibilities for my own constituency, particularly Coalisland, which I considered to be one of the worst places in Ireland from a planning aspect, a town that had been neglected for generations. I hoped to give it the attention it deserved.

I had problems with my Local Government portfolio. Most of the councils were unionist controlled and where the loyalists dominated, members of the Executive were not welcome. Dungannon, for example, was still unionist controlled and a motion was passed opposing the attendance of any Minister at any of its functions. My name was not mentioned, but it was a fair bet I was the one they had most in mind. I visited Magherafelt, which had an SDLP chairman, Paddy Heron, and received a courteous welcome. However, the Vice-Chairman, Reverend William McCrea, organised a rowdy protest outside, which received TV coverage. When the film showed me telling McCrea that I could teach him how to organise an effective protest, John Oliver quietly advised me that I should remember the dignity of my Office at all times. There were other councils, like Antrim and Ballymena, which had a unionist majority and where I was given a courteous reception, and Belfast was in the same category.

I enjoyed my participation in the Assembly, particularly Question Time, where I discovered I was good at the Dispatch Box with a capacity for thinking on my feet. Unfortunately, the opportunity for anyone to shine was minimised by the conduct of the loyalist opposition. Even before Sunningdale there had been unruly scenes and the House had been adjourned on a number of occasions because of grave disorder. On the day we were leaving for Sunningdale, there had been physical attacks on Faulkner supporters inside and outside the chamber. When the Assembly met again after Sunningdale, on 21 January, we found that the frontbench seats reserved for members of the Executive were occupied by Loyalists. They eventually had to be removed by the police, and the disgraceful scenes on television that evening did nothing to improve the image of democracy at work in Northern Ireland. The bully-boy antics of Paisley and his supporters, first seen on the streets in places like Armagh, were now being employed inside Stormont itself.

Other events put the Executive on the defensive, just four days after it came into office. Faulkner had to face a motion of no confidence at a meeting of the Ulster Unionist Council. He didn't really stand a chance, particularly as the rules allowed members of the DUP and Vanguard parties, present as Orange Order representatives, to vote. He lost by 53 votes out of 600+. He felt he had no alternative but to resign as Leader of the party, and this led to the defection of two more members from his Assembly party.

Then there was the Boland challenge to the constitutionality of the Sunningdale Agreement taken through the law courts of the Republic. Kevin Boland had resigned from the Irish government in 1970 when Charles Haughey and Neal Blaney were sacked for alleged gun-running. His legal challenge was based on the alleged incompatibility of the Status Declaration at Sunningdale with Articles 2 and 3 of the Irish Constitution. In due course, his case was thrown out, but in the interim the restraints placed on the Irish government in spelling out the reality of the Sunningdale position, and the fact that a defence had to be entered denying that there had been a sell-out of the aspiration of unification of the national territory, removed most of the advantage Faulkner had hoped to gain from the recognition of Northern Ireland by the Southern government. Boland himself must have known he had little chance of success, but as a spoiler his court case was more effective than he could have hoped for. Recognition of the Status of Northern Ireland, something not achieved by Craigavon or Brookeborough, was the trump card Faulkner had hoped to win with, but as a result of the constitutional challenge his political opponents within unionism were able to deride his claim.

Then there was the hammer blow of the Westminster election, announced by Heath on 7 February, to take place on 28 February. There have been few better examples of party political considerations overriding the common interest. Whitelaw and Pym, Faulkner and Fitt, the Irish government – all warned Heath that an election at this stage was bound to harm the Power-Sharing Executive, but the prospect of capitalising on anger with the miners and a three-day week was too attractive and the man largely responsible for Sunningdale took the decision which would play a major part in its downfall.

Faulkner had no armour and no weapons. He had resigned as leader of the Unionist party less than a month earlier and had not had sufficient time to create a new organisation. The Executive, just over a month in office, had no successes to highlight. The Boland challenge meant the Status issue was confused. Faulkner's opponents within unionism, on the other hand, were able to unite around opposition to Sunningdale and, in particular, the Council of Ireland. 'Dublin is only a Sunningdale away' became an extremely effective slogan. Uniting under the title United Ulster Unionist Council (UUUC), the different Loyalist groupings put forward only one candidate in each of the twelve constituencies, the most effective action they could have taken in first-past-the-post elections.

The SDLP decided to fight all twelve constituencies, a decision motivated more by the necessity to fight Bernadette Devlin in Mid-Ulster and Frank McManus in Fermanagh–South Tyrone than any calculation of the likely consequences of the election for Brian Faulkner. Devlin and McManus had opposed Sunningdale, and although there were the usual 'don't split the vote' critics in both constituencies, I felt we had no alternative but to take them on. In an election where the central issue was Sunningdale, we would not gain any credibility by not opposing two individuals who were as anti-Sunningdale as the loyalists. Not to have fought would have been seen to be sectarian as well as cowardly. Ivan Cooper rather easily beat Bernadette into third place, while Denis Haughey finished just a few hundred votes behind McManus and, of course, the Unionists won both seats. Gerry was re-elected in West Belfast and overall the party, despite a stronger challenge from Republicans and disappointment that internment had not been ended, gained 22.2% of the vote as opposed to 22.1% in the Assembly election the previous year.

However, for the future of Sunningdale the result was a serious setback. Eleven of the twelve seats were won by the UUUC and they obtained 50.8% of the total poll. All we could do was to reiterate that Assembly elections were not due for another three years and press on doggedly. But the result, and especially the overall majority for the loyalists, strengthened the doubt of the waverers in Faulkner's ranks.

Although I regretted Heath's loss of office, I did not have great fears for the future of Sunningdale. Despite my reservations about the trustworthiness of Harold Wilson, I did not worry unduly. Moreover, I had met the new Secretary of State, Merlyn Rees, on a number of occasions and had found him strongly supportive of the SDLP position. When Stan Orme, one of the founder members of the Campaign for Democracy in Ulster in the 1960s, joined the British team as Minister of State, I was particularly pleased. Of more concern to me at the time, however, was my own poisoned chalice: the rent and rate strike. It has been initiated as a protest against internment and also to provide an alternative to violence for the enraged Catholic community. During the negotiations at Stormont Castle, the ending of the civil disobedience campaign had been one of Faulkner's preconditions and at Sunningdale it had been accepted that the SDLP would play its part in doing so. At a joint meeting of the Assembly party and the Executive in Dungannon three days before we entered the Power-Sharing Executive, on 28 December, the party decided to end its support for the rent and rates strike.

'The Annual Conference of the SDLP recently asked the Executive of the party to review its position on the rent and rates strike as a matter of urgency. The review has now taken place and in addition we have taken into account recent political developments. In the light of all this we now ask people to withdraw from participation in the rent and rates strike.

The party, as mandated by the people in the recent elections, has negotiated the setting up of new institutions of government which will provide the basis for a fair and just society. It would be inconsistent with our participation in these institutions if we did not ask the people to participate as well.'

It was now up to me to implement the party decision. I couldn't really complain because I was more responsible than most for the strike in the first place and had been enthusiastic in organising it. From the first days of the Executive I was continually reminded by the Unionists and, in particular, by Herbie Kirk, the Minister of Finance, of the party commitment in this regard.

On 5 February the Executive decided *inter alia* that:

'(d) a further effort to persuade people to abandon the rent and rates strike should precede the introduction of tougher measures;

(e) accordingly the Minister of Finance should discuss further with the Minister of Housing, Local Government and Planning the general lines of the statement to be made;

(f) thereafter, the Minister of Finance should call a meeting of the inter-departmental committee (of civil servants)

(i) to establish the latest figures on the progress of the counter measures which should be incorporated in the proposed statement on an area basis

(ii) to decide upon the effective date for the introduction of further counter measures against those who did not respond to the appeal. These were to include an increase in the rates of allocation from security benefits (possibly applied only to those who had not already agreed to end the strike) and the introduction of collection charges, but from a later effective date than 1st March in both instances and

(iii) to draft the detailed statement to be made by the Minister of Housing, Local Government and Planning, which should re-emphasise that there would be no amnesty, give the detailed figures, make a public appeal for co-operation and state that the agreed tougher measures would be enforced from a stated date against outstanding defaulters.'

In advance of my meeting with Herbie Kirk – whose approval, as Minister of Finance, was required for any decision with financial implications – I became aware that Kirk was putting pressure on the interdepartmental committee to bring the new arrangements into force on 1 April. When we met, on 18 February, he immediately laid out his position on the matter. He told me that at every Unionist meeting the question was asked, 'when will the rent and rates strike end?' It was fast becoming an emotive and symbolic issue to a large number of Unionists. I understood his difficulty, and I wished to be helpful. I felt strongly that we were in a partnership government whose success depended on trust between the two sides. The SDLP had entered into a commitment to end the rent and rates strike and it was my job, more than anyone else's, to see it was honoured. It was clearly a nonsense for the Minister of Housing to be presiding over a situation where he was acquiescing in a strike against himself. And there was another factor, which I did not spell out publicly at the time but which was causing me growing concern. The Loyalist Association of Workers (LAW) had threatened civil disobedience against the Executive and there were fears that should electricity be brought under the jurisdiction of the Council of Ireland, loyalists would refuse to pay their electricity bills. My position would be intolerable if the loyalists launched such a campaign, especially if they used me as a precedent.

On the other hand, the civil disobedience campaign was a protest specifically against internment, we had pledged that it would continue until the last detainee had been released, and the British government had not yet delivered on its commitment to phase it out. There were some chancers and opportunists exploiting the rent strike, but there was also a good number of people who sincerely disagreed with the SDLP and maintained a principled stand. There were others, supporters of the Provisional IRA and Official IRA, who were politically motivated and enjoyed any embarrassment for the SDLP. There was also a further category of people, particularly the elderly, who found it convenient to have their rent deducted from their benefits at source, and who would therefore require some incentive to recommence paying their bills directly to the Housing Executive.

I had hoped that the SDLP statement would have resulted in a substantial number of people coming off the strike voluntarily. I could certainly have used such a development as evidence that no further action was necessary. Unfortunately, while there was a reduction – from 12,012 to 11,649 between the end of December and the end of January – it was not sufficiently great for my purpose, though I pointed out that in the aftermath of Christmas and the New Year, tenants had other matters on their minds.

Therefore, when I met with Herbie Kirk in February, I was not in a strong position. At this stage we were halfway through the election campaign and Kirk was determined to force a decision that would be helpful to Faulkner's candidates, while I, of course, was sensitive to the SDLP's election campaign. Helpful I might wish to be, but my party would not thank me for an unpopular announcement with polling day just ten days away.

Eventually, I made the required announcement on 3 April, at a time when the Executive was coming under increasing pressure as a result of the disastrous Westminster election. I did so in the best circumstances I could arrange in the Assembly: I made two statements that day, the first announced my decision to prohibit the proposed increase in Housing Executive rents, which was widely welcomed, particularly by SDLP backbenchers, and I followed immediately with my second statement, on civil disobedience. I made as strong a case as I could to explain clearly and fully what I knew was a controversial decision. I referred to the decision of the SDLP Assembly party and Executive of 28 December to end the rent and rates strike; the inconsistency of being in government and, at the same time, maintaining support for civil disobedience; the reaffirmation of the British government at Sunningdale to end internment; my belief, and that of my colleagues, that this commitment would be honoured; the fact that support for civil disobedience had lessened to a considerable extent – of the 26,000 involved in August 1971, just over 11,000 tenants remained on strike; my understanding that there were those who would sincerely disagree with me on principle, but others who were opportunists; and my pledge that no hardship would be caused to anyone (I promised to give personal attention to each individual case where hardship might apply). Then, I came to the new reality:

'Payment in full will be required. There cannot be an amnesty. Arrears must be paid ... a small number of people will not heed my advice and for reasons of their own, some political, some personal, will continue to refuse to pay. I must bluntly warn these people and those who would seek to use them for their own ends that new measures are being introduced to ensure that all arrears are paid. Let no one be in any doubt about the determination of my colleagues and myself in this matter.'

I then went on to announce that, as of 20 May, there would be an increase in the amount that could be deducted from benefits, in line with increased social welfare benefits, and that there would be a new collection charge of 25p per week to cover the administration costs of deductions from benefits. Lastly, anyone who made arrangements with the Housing Executive, before 20 May, to come off the strike would not be affected.

I had taken the precaution of explaining my intentions to SDLP backbenchers beforehand, and had of course received some criticism. It had been arranged that Michael Canavan would speak on behalf of the backbenchers in the debate to allow their position and the necessary assurances to be put on the record. In his straightforward, honest way, Michael honed in on the backbenchers' 'grave concerns': the SDLP had honoured its commitment, but the British government had not yet honoured theirs. 'We would like the Minister to assure us that before the operative date of 20th of May he will satisfy himself that the commitments of the British government, particularly in regard to the promised phasing out of internment, are being honoured.'

My courage and fairness were praised by Peter McLachlan (Faulkner Unionist), Bertie McConnell (Alliance) and David Bleakley (NI Labour), but it was my response to Canavan that was the political imperative. I answered him head-on. We had honoured our commitments and expected others to do likewise. 'I am confident that other parties involved in Sunningdale will honour their commitments too. This includes the British government on the issue of internment. It goes without saying that if a party to an agreement does not honour that agreement, the agreement will fail, the package will fall apart ... if I am wrong and commitments are not honoured then the situation will be reviewed in the circumstances prevailing.' I sat down, confident that Merlyn Rees could not ignore my challenge.

That speech and the decisions it contained was the most difficult I had had to make in my ten years in politics. In so doing, I was coming to terms with the harsh realities of political life. It was necessary, inevitable and unavoidable. Nonetheless, I knew that the contrast would be highlighted – to my disadvantage – between what I had just announced and my declaration on a public platform in Coalisland, just two-and-a-half years earlier, that rent should not be paid and should never be paid. Yet that statement too, in the context and time it was made, while not inevitable, was, to me, equally necessary and unavoidable. To some that did not matter, and for the rest of my political career a certain section – who would not have supported me under any circumstances – vilified me as '25p Currie'.

It was not only the obvious suspects, the traditional political opponents and enemies in the Nationalist–Republican camp, who caused me difficulties on this issue. Some of my own colleagues attempted to distance themselves from me. In his autobiography *Straight Left*, Paddy Devlin, wrote, in relation to the introduction of the 25p levy, 'there were clear divisions in SDLP circles on the issue. When the matter was raised in the Executive, Hume and I voted against it and I was appalled when Currie announced in the Assembly that he was going ahead with it, especially since I was the Minister who was to make the collection by deducting it from benefit payments. I was totally out of sympathy with this policy.'

Paddy and John did not vote against it. It was one of the proud boasts of the members of the Executive that the only vote which took place during the five months of its existence was that on the final decision to support arbitration with the loyalist strikers. No effort was made by anyone to force a vote on the issue of the rent and rates strike. Nor should Paddy have been appalled when I announced it in the Assembly because, as I have already quoted, the matter had been discussed as early as 5 February. At that time it was decided that action would be taken 'for the introduction of the further counter-measures against those who did not respond to the appeal.' These were to include an increase in the rates of allocation from social security benefits (possibly applied only to those who had not already agreed to end the strike) and the introduction of collection charges, but from a later effective date than 1 March in both instances. This decision was circulated (Ex Memo 10/74) to the relevant Ministers – Finance and Housing, Local Government and Planning, Health and Social Services and Commerce – on 17 February. John was circulated because, as Minister of Commerce, he had responsibility for electricity and gas. Furthermore, the interdepartmental committee that gave detailed consideration to the Executive decisions included senior civil servants from all the Departments involved. Also, on 2 April, the day before I made my announcement in the Assembly, my proposed statement, including the details of the collection charge and the responsibility of the Department of Health and Social Services for collecting it, was considered by the Executive. Again, there was no vote and no indication of principled opposition.

As Paddy admits, he was the Minister who had the responsibility to collect the 25p levy by deducting it from benefit payments. At no stage was there any doubt about that, nor was there any question about it. If Paddy had objected, the scheme could not have gone through. Paddy Devlin was an intelligent, hard-working Minister who prided himself for being 'hands-on'. There was no way he could have misinterpreted the position, or have been unaware of what his civil servants were implementing on his behalf.

On 17 May, at a meeting with Merlyn Rees, Gerry sent me a note across the table: 'What is Paddy up to?' He was sitting at the end of the table, not apparently listening to the serious discussion, but giving his whole attention to what he was writing. When finished, he folded his paper and sent it up the table to the Secretary of State. Rees read it, looked at Paddy and put the missive in his pocket. We later learned that Paddy had offered his resignation due to the failure of the British to provide 'hard evidence that internment or detention was being seriously phased out'. He wrote: 'In the circumstances, I could not participate in the imposition of penalties on householders suffering from the same misgivings about the ending of detention that I myself share.' He later asked that his resignation be 'frozen', but I have often wondered whether this action might have gone some way, in conjunction with other developments, to persuade Rees that the Executive was in terminal trouble and he should not go out on a limb to save it.

By this stage the Executive was in serious trouble. Two events, in particular, occasioned this development: first, the move by the Unionist members of the Executive to weaken the Council of Ireland by 'phasing it in', and secondly, a loyalist strike, better described as a *putsch*. These two developments plunged the Executive into deep crisis, exacerbated by the fact that they were contemporaneous.

The Westminster election result, with its emphatic rejection of the Faulknerite candidates and the almost 51% vote for the UUUC, had the Faulknerites running for cover, especially when, on 19 March, a motion calling for the renegotiation of Sunningdale was proposed by John Laird, an unpledged Unionist, and debated in the Assembly. This extremely acrimonious debate continued on a weekly basis until mid-May thanks to a mixture of Loyalist determination and Paisley's browbeating of the Speaker, Nat Minford. There were sufficient pro-Sunningdale votes to defeat the motion, but Unionist members of the Executive began to look for some way to draw the Loyalist fangs. On 4 March, the Faulkner group in the Assembly decided that there should be no ratification of Sunningdale and no Council of Ireland unless Articles 2 and 3 of the Irish Constitution were repealed. The pressure started to build on Faulkner for at least some delay in the implementation of the Council of Ireland. Meanwhile Roy Bradford, frustrated by his failure to ease Faulkner out of the Chief Minister's job and by his failure to get elected to Westminster, was considering his political options, particularly the possibility of strengthening his position with mainstream unionism.

On 13 March following the Supreme Court judgement in the Boland appeal, it was at long last possible for the Taoiseach, Liam Cosgrave, to spell out the Republic's factual position on the Status of Northern Ireland: 'I now therefore solemnly reaffirm that the factual position of Northern Ireland within the United Kingdom cannot be changed except by a decision of the majority of the people of Northern Ireland. This declaration, I believe, is in accordance with and follows from the resolve of all the democratic parties in the Republic that the unity of Ireland is to be achieved only by peaceful means and by consent.' It was a good statement, as strong as the Irish government could make it, but the delay had diminished its credibility and effectiveness.

Nor was the long overdue report of the Anglo-Irish law enforcement officers, set up at Sunningdale, of much help. It ruled out the idea of a joint, or common court and, as expected, rejected extradition because of the constitutional implications, instead coming down in favour of extra-territorial jurisdiction, where crimes committed in one jurisdiction could be tried in the other. Sam Silkin, the British Attorney-General, who had proven himself favourable to nationalist causes in the past, had no reservation about showing his displeasure. Again, the delay had not helped. In the Assembly on 26 March, Oliver Napier said, 'if effective means are not found to deal with fugitive offenders, I shall not sign [ratify] the Sunningdale Agreement.'

The Executive amendment to the Loyalist Assembly motion, moved by Faulkner, placed the ball firmly in the court of the two sovereign governments. The Assembly 'welcomes the declaration by the Executive that the successful implementation of its policy depends upon the delivery, in the letter and spirit, of commitments entered into by the British and Irish governments ...' The amendment represented the view of the three parties in the Executive that the two governments were letting us down.

Unfortunately, the security situation was also deteriorating as the extremists on both sides continued, and in some areas escalated, their campaigns of violence. Stan Orme stated in the House of Commons that between 1 January, when we took office, and 30 April, seventy-four people had been killed. So much for Faulkner's hopes for the ultimate justification of Sunningdale: that it would help to bring about peace.

In and adjacent to my own constituency, in what was becoming notorious as the 'Murder Triangle', some dreadful atrocities were perpetrated. On 17 January, Daniel Hughes, a seventy-four-year-old retired farmer, was shot dead by the UVF in an attack on Boyle's bar in Cappagh, a strong nationalist and republican area where loyalist murderers had not previously ventured. On 19 February, Pat Molloy and a Protestant, Jack Wylie, were killed when the UVF bombed Traynor's pub outside the Moy. On 11 March, Billy Fox, a Fine Gael member of the Irish Senate, was killed by republicans just over the border near Clones, in County Monaghan. On 15 March, Kevin Murray and Patrick McDonald, two members of the IRA, blew themselves up with their own bomb on the Ballygawley–Aughnacloy road. On 11 April, UDR man Harold Sinnamon was killed by an IRA booby trap in Dungannon. On 2 May the first female member of the security forces to be killed, UDR officer Eva Martin, died when the IRA attacked her barracks at Clogher. On 13 May, two IRA men, Eugene Martin and Sean McKearney, blew themselves up with their own bomb while attempting to destroy a petrol-filling station between Moy and Dungannon.

In the wake of these atrocities, which proved both sides were involved in murder campaigns, Faulkner and members of his Assembly party were not the only ones to feel the backlash. More and more I was asked, by Catholic and Protestant alike, what good Sunningdale was doing. Part of my response, to the effect that the activities of the IRA and UVF illustrated the necessity of Sunningdale because it could bring together both sections of the community and the two governments in a combined effort to reduce and ultimately eliminate terrorism, was of diminishing effect.

The murders which affected me most, on a personal level, occurred on 7 May, about a mile from my own home. I had been in Derry on SDLP business and had returned home around midnight. I was in the habit of entering the house via the sandbagged garage so I could say goodnight to the two policemen on duty and find out if anything was happening in the area. This evening, they informed me that news was just coming in, via the radio, of a shooting near Newmills, a Protestant village less than two miles away. I told them I would not be going to bed for a while and if they received additional information to let me know.

Annita was already in bed; she was nearing the end of a difficult pregnancy. I told her I was staying up to hear the news from the police. It soon came. Jim and Gertie Devlin, both good personal and political friends, had been shot dead at their home at Congo. Jim was one of the renowned Devlin brothers who had brought Tyrone their first Ulster football championship title in 1956, while Gertie had been a founding member of the Coalisland branch of the SDLP and rarely missed a meeting.

I decided to visit the Devlin home, but first I had to break the news to Annita. Gertie had known that my wife was having a difficult pregnancy and had paid her a visit just two days previously and they had spent a couple of hours chatting. Annita took the news badly, and I had to call the family doctor and arrange for a neighbour to stay with her before I could leave the house.

I found the Devlins' car in the laneway leading to their home. Jim was the manager of the family bar in Coalisland, and it was customary for Gertie to collect him and drive him home. Usually they would buy fish and chips on the way. On this occasion, Gertie had brought her seventeen-year-old daughter, Patricia, with her. Patricia had sat in the front passenger seat, with Jim in the rear. As they drove into the laneway, a uniformed man signalled them to stop and then opened fire. Jim and Gertie were killed, but Patricia somehow managed to get out of the car and, despite being wounded in the arm, shoulder and knee, crawled more than half-a-mile to raise the alarm. When I arrived on the scene, Gertie was slumped over the steering wheel and Jim lay across the back seat. I have witnessed a number of atrocities, but none had the impact on me that this one had. It wasn't only that they were friends; it was the smell. The smell of blood and chips. I can still smell it to this day.

I have another reason to remember this crime so vividly. Within days of my appointment to the Executive, a scramble phone was installed at my home for confidentiality. As it was a Saturday morning when the workman arrived to install it, I was at home. The young man who did the work was so pleasant that I gave him a tip. In 1975 that young man received a life sentence for driving the get-away car used by the murderers of Jim and Gertie.

It was clear that the security forces were not getting on top of the republican and loyalist killers, and despite the fact that the Executive had no security function, we suffered as well. Therefore, when the Unionist members of the Executive, supported by Oliver Napier, began to insist on a postponement of the implementation of the Council of Ireland, they had a certain credibility.

On 1 May, Faulkner gave his view of the situation to the Executive:

'My own view of what is realistic in present circumstances is as follows. If the Council of Ireland, as envisaged at Sunningdale, is not to be merely another casualty of the general constitutional upheaval which would result from the failure of this Executive, we must appreciate that progress can only be made in stages and that there is a limit to what can be accomplished as a first stage against the present adverse background of public opinion.'

Any notion of weakening the Council of Ireland in any way was, of course, anathema to the SDLP. The Council was central to what we had agreed at Sunningdale. It was our answer to those who alleged that we had accepted an 'internal' Northern Ireland settlement. It symbolised our attachment to the concept of a united Ireland, albeit down the road and subject to unionist consent. And this weakening of the Council was being demanded in the face of loyalist threats: to agree to diminution would be to surrender, once again, to a loyalist veto on progress.

Additionally, we were being asked to do so in circumstances where the British government had not delivered on its commitment to end internment. Indeed, Rees had started to re-intern. At the end of March the IRA had carried out a bombing blitz in Belfast, Lisburn and Bangor. A 500lb bomb planted outside Army HQ at the Grand Central Hotel was particularly effective in arousing Protestant anger. On 2 May, six Catholics were killed when the UVF threw a canister bomb into the Rose and Crown pub on the Ormeau Road in Belfast. Clearly, the SDLP was fighting an uphill battle in our efforts to have internment ended in these circumstances. Yet the very fact that this was so made it so much more difficult for us to compromise on a core principle.

As the Faulknerite pressure for a 'phasing in' of the Council of Ireland continued, the Executive set up a subcommittee, comprising Bradford, Morell, Napier, Bob Cooper, Hume and Devlin, to consider the matter. The proposal to the SDLP, in essence, was that the full Council of Ireland, as agreed at Sunningdale, would remain the ultimate objective, but there would be a two-stage implementation of it. In the first stage, the Council would have a consultative function only; in the second stage, the transfer of Executive functions and the appointment of a permanent Secretariat would occur after 'a test of opinion', effectively after the next Assembly election, due in 1977. The possibility of agreement on the subcommittee was not helped by the antagonism between Bradford and Devlin. In the initial stages of the Executive we had been able to joke about their mutual dislike, but it had now become so personal and so angry that one worried on occasions that it would degenerate into fisticuffs. At a time when the Executive was being buffeted on a number of fronts, a breakdown in personal relationships was a dangerous development.

As the month of May progressed a number of developments began to converge, none of them helpful to the Executive. The Assembly debate on the renegotiation of Sunningdale continued, growing more rancorous week by week, and the weakness of the Speaker, Nat Minford, in allowing himself to be bullied by Paisley into extending the length of the debate was a source of considerable anger to the supporters of the Executive, and a continuous reminder to the electorate of the insecurity of the Executive. There was a litany of problems: a rapidly deteriorating security situation where the IRA and loyalist paramilitaries were apparently murdering and bombing at will, and for which the Executive was being blamed despite the fact that it had no control over security; a British government clearly not in control of the situation, neither providing security nor moving to end internment; a Secretary of State for Defence, Roy Mason, creating doubts over the British government's long-term intentions when he said, in a speech in England, 'pressure is mounting on the mainland to pull out the troops; equally demands are being made to set a date for withdrawal'; the secret negotiations in the Executive on the future of the Council of Ireland which, if not successfully concluded, would mean the break-up of the Executive. Could things get any worse? Unfortunately they could, and did.

On 15 May I made my personal contribution to the problems confronting the Executive when I proposed a two-month postponement of the commencement of the collection of the 25p levy from those who were still on rent strike and were having rent payments deducted from their social security benefits. I gave some of my reasons to my colleagues. Since my announcement, on 3 April, that collection charges would be imposed on 20 May, there had been a very positive response to my appeal to tenants to come off the strike. In the first six weeks 3,079 had done so, and in the last fortnight the numbers coming off the strike had averaged more than 1,000 a week, leaving a total of 7,638 still on strike. A surprising feature of this reduction had been the number of those (from 2,950 down to 2,100) who had come off the strike even though they were not receiving any benefits and therefore would not have been affected by the collection charge. This clearly showed that it wasn't just the threat of the new collection charge which was having an effect, but rather that the appeal to come off the strike because of the new political arrangement was also working. I said:

'I have therefore come to the conclusion that the more mature political approach, in the interests of the whole Executive, is to adopt a bigger attitude, to commend those who have been settling (as I myself have been doing), to urge all to follow this example and to say openly that we do not wish to impose collection charges unless compelled to do so by a determined residual number of deliberate withholders and that the collection charge might have to be much more than 25p in view of the costs of overheads in relation to a smaller number of cases.'

I proposed to make an Order, with the approval of the Minister of Finance, postponing the date of collection from 20 May until 22 July. This latter date had been arrived at because of the increase in social welfare benefits due to take place then, which led the Department of Health and Social Services to conclude 'that there would be practical as well as presentational advantages in fixing the date at 22nd July to coincide exactly with the pension etc. improvements'.

There was another reason for my new proposal which I did not spell out to the Executive, but of which my SDLP colleagues were well aware. In replying to Michael Canavan in the Assembly on 3 April, I had agreed with him that all commitments entered into should be honoured, ie, the SDLP should honour its commitment to end the rent and rates strike and the British government should honour its commitment to end internment. In light of the failure of the British Government to honour its commitment, it was appropriate to review the situation, as I was now doing.

What I had not anticipated was the changes occurring in another context. The prolonged debate on 'phasing in' the Council of Ireland had hardened attitudes among some members of the Executive, and my proposal became a victim. Herbie Kirk, whose approval was necessary for the postponement Order to be made, dug his heels in. It soon became clear that I was not his target, but rather that he had the Council of Ireland in his sights. I did not push the issue. There had never been a vote on the Executive and I was certainly not going to press for one in these circumstances, when the result would inevitably go against me. I felt that by working behind the scenes, with the Chief Executive, or on a one-to-one level with Kirk, or through officials, I could, in time, bring the matter back to the Executive in a better atmosphere. However, events dictated that I was not to get that opportunity.

On 14 May, at 5.50pm, the Assembly at last had the opportunity to vote on the Loyalist motion in favour of renegotiating Sunningdale, and it was defeated by 44 votes to 28. The predictable outcome of the vote was underlined by the fact that four members of the Assembly did not vote, including Glen Barr, Public Relations Officer of the Ulster Workers Council and chairman of the coordinating committee that had announced its intention of organising a strike if the motion were defeated. So, we celebrated the comfortable majority and I looked forward to settling the two outstanding problems as far as I was concerned: the Executive debate on the Council of

Ireland, and the 25p collection charge. Those of us in the Stormont bar that evening, and indeed those opposed to Sunningdale who were not present, had no great concern that the strike, scheduled to begin at 6.00pm, posed any major threat to the Executive.

It was day three of the strike when I started to feel concerned. Since becoming a Minister, my transport arrangements had been to travel in the official car with my civilian driver and a policeman in the front passenger seat, with two policemen in an escort car following behind. On this morning the escort car, for the first time, drove off first and instead of taking our usual route down the M1 and up the Newtownards Road to Stormont, we cut off at Lisburn and travelled to Stormont via Knock. The escort car was following radio instructions to avoid roadblocks set up by the strikers, but we were still stopped on three occasions. The procedure was for ID papers to be produced by the plain-clothes police, whereupon my car would follow on through, hopefully without being stopped or me being recognised. It worked that first morning, and most of the time after that, but there were occasions when the official car became separated from the escort car and I was recognised. The thumping on bonnet and windows indicated my lack of popularity in certain quarters, but thankfully did not escalate to anything more serious.

It soon became clear that intimidation was to play a major role in the strike action. Men wearing masks and carrying cudgels were everywhere in Protestant areas. Not only did they set up roadblocks on exit roads from housing estates to prevent people from going to work but they blocked main roads as well. More direct action took place at major centres of employment, such as Harland and Wolff, where workers were ordered home with the threat that their cars would be burned out if found to be still in the car park. Whatever about the brains and the political direction of the strike, the paramilitaries were providing the muscle.

From the beginning the most effective weapon held by the strike coordinating committee was control of electricity. Many who wished to go to work, even some who were prepared to defy the intimidators in order to do so, couldn't see the point if the electricity at their workplace had been cut off.

I was not surprised at the effectiveness of this particular weapon. My brother, Vincent, who shared a strong family resemblance, had started working at the Belfast headquarters of the Northern Ireland Electricity Board (NIEB) the previous year. It was a job for which he was over-qualified, which is probably why he got it. He was the only Catholic in his office, among a staff of thirty. On his second day there, he was in the canteen at lunchtime when he noticed a very good-looking young girl. The following day he manoeuvered himself into a position behind her in the lunch queue and attempted to initiate a conversation. She turned, looked at him as if he were dirt and said, 'Fuck off, you Fenian bastard.' Clearly a relationship was out of the question! The following day, on inter-office notepaper, he received a death threat from the Young Citizens Volunteers. On my strong advice, one day soon after that he left the building never to return, even though the RUC had recommended, and he had actually obtained, a handgun. It seemed to me the money he was being paid did not justify the work atmosphere, the threat to his life and the fears of the family for his safety. I recount his experience here to illustrate what it was like for a young Catholic to work for the Electricity Board at that time. The NIEB had long been recognised as a sector of employment where anti-Catholic discrimination was at its greatest, a fact which had been widely publicised by the McCluskeys in the early days of the civil rights movement. So it was no surprise now that this Protestant, even loyalist, Bastille should be such an effective weapon in the hands of the strike organisers.

It would, however, be a mistake, and contrary to the factual position, to give the impression that the effectiveness of the strike (or *putsch*, as we preferred to call it) was based solely on intimidation and the control of the electricity supply. As it developed, it received strong support across the spectrum of Protestant opinion, including the social spectrum. The size of the agricultural vehicles used to block the roads and reduce traffic to snail's pace indicated that it was not only the working class in Belfast and the towns which supported the strike. The Protestant middle class, always a centre of power in the Unionist party and on whom Faulkner relied for support, was turning against its leaders. As the strike escalated, and without effective action against it, this new element in the story of Protestant resistance became more and more obvious.

There was another factor, which I recognised only later: for a significant section of the Protestant population, it was 'payback time'. Some of them felt that it had been one-way traffic since 1968, with the erosion of the Protestant and Unionist position and one defeat after another for them and one victory after another for 'the other side'. Over the years a number of unionists have told me that the appointment of the original squatter as Minister of Housing, the man they blamed for starting the Troubles, epitomised for them the extent of their loss of power. For some of these people, the appointment of Catholics to positions of authority was sufficient reason for opposition, never mind whether or not we were 'republicans'. That is not to say all who supported the strike were bigots, but for some, certainly, opposition to the Council of Ireland was a convenient cover for that more basic and primitive motivation. The Council was seen as being a bridge too far and claims of it being 'a vehicle to trundle us into a united Ireland' didn't help. Some Protestants were also genuinely angry that the 'verdict' on Sunningdale in the February general election was apparently being ignored by the Executive and by the government.

Nevertheless, I believe that had there been effective action, in the early days of the strike, to stop intimidation and to keep roads open, it would have fizzled out. We learned later that some leaders, including Glen Barr, were of that opinion, too. So why wasn't such action taken? I understand, and understood at the time, why action wasn't taken in the first couple of days. There was fear of overreaction – a fear that was shared by the SDLP members of the Executive – given how blunt an instrument the Army had proved to be in comparable situations in the past. However, from day three onwards it was clear to everyone that we were dealing with a ruthless threat not only to the Executive but to the British government, and that the law of the land was being flouted time and time again. And yet for the entire duration of the strike, a period of over fourteen days, there was not one effective action to assert the authority of the government.

A number of reasons have been suggested for this. First, the attitude of the Wilson government. Sunningdale was Heath's achievement; Wilson and his Ministers did not have the sense of ownership of the Agreement shared by those of us who had laboured at Sunningdale. And, of course, as in all political communities, the achievements of a predecessor, particularly one of a different political complexion, are not as strenuously defended as one's own accomplishments.

Secondly, there were the personalities of the two British politicians most involved: Wilson and Rees. As I have explained elsewhere, I never trusted Harold Wilson. In relation to Ireland, he was a populist. Every time I met him, and I believe this was the experience of many, he told me that he understood the Irish problem because in his Huyton constituency in Liverpool he represented more Irish people than any Irish politician. He would never have put pressure on the Unionist government except that the civil rights movement forced him to do so. The extent to which he could be depended on was a continual worry.

Merlyn Rees I had more time for. He had been opposition spokesman for three years before becoming Secretary of State, and he had been assiduous in visiting the North and consulting politicians of all shades of opinion. I have never doubted his sincerity or his commitment to the people of Northern Ireland. He had, however, one serious flaw, described succinctly by Paddy Devlin: 'Merlyn is always struggling with his fucking conscience. The trouble is it always ends in a fucking draw.' Unfortunately, decisiveness was the quality most needed in dealing with the loyalist strike. Rees had a habit of saying 'Yes sir, no sir, three bags full sir' in circumstances where the relevancy was not always obvious. However, what the Secretary of State lacked in decisiveness was usually made up for by his Permanent Secretary, Frank Cooper, who had on occasion, under Whitelaw, Pym and Rees, displayed a ruthless attitude. For some reason, this attitude was not apparent in his government's dealings during the loyalist strike, a factor which in itself raised certain questions in my mind about intentions and motivations.

What was the agenda of the British government during this crucial period? On coming into office on 5 March, Wilson and Rees promised to support Sunningdale and the Power-Sharing Executive. Yet just over one month later, on 10 April, Rees was, according to his own account, warning the Cabinet that 'it was unwise to make confident predictions about developments in Northern Ireland where the political climate can change unexpectedly but I felt bound to warn colleagues that there was a danger of political collapse' and that the British government should make contingency arrangements. His warning was based on the fear that differences in the Executive on the question of the Council of Ireland would lead to the breaking of the Executive, yet this was at a time when our discussions on the 'phasing in' of the Council were at an early stage and the loyalist strike was more than a month away. It hardly displayed the resolve and commitment that the promise of support for Sunningdale and the Executive had suggested.

I believe that the future of the Power-Sharing Executive was determined more in Lisburn, at the Headquarters of the British Army, than at Downing Street, or Stormont Castle. The Army top brass were determined not to have to fight a war on two fronts, against the resurgent IRA on one side, once again bombing in England as well as in Northern Ireland, and against loyalist paramilitaries operating in an environment of sullen and resentful Protestantism. Sir Frank Cooper, with his military background and destined shortly to become Permanent Secretary to the Ministry of Defence, would have been a conduit for those reservations. And I do not that think Merlyn Rees, given his own doubts on the future of the Executive, had the strength of character to stand against these formidable pressures.

On a general level I have to say also that, in my experience of Labour and Conservative governments, the Tories gave the impression that they were in control of the Army whereas there was sometimes a questionmark over Labour. The exception was Secretary of State for Northern Ireland Roy Mason, but then he came to that position from being Secretary of State for Defence. Maybe it had something to do with the English class system, or being at the same public schools.

To add to the growing despondency there came the dreadful news of the bombings in Dublin and Monaghan, which eventually resulted in the loss of thirty-three lives, the greatest toll in one day in the whole of the Troubles. Both the UDA and the UVF denied responsibility, though the available evidence from car registration numbers called their denial into question. Sammy Wilson, the Press Officer of the UDA, deserves to be remembered forever for his heartless statement: 'I am very happy about the bombings in Dublin. There is a war with the Free State and now we are laughing at them.' Every single one of the thirty-three who died was an entirely innocent victim.

As the overall situation began to deteriorate, the Executive continued to grapple with differences over the Council of Ireland. Reports from Ken Bloomfield, Permanent Secretary of the Office of the Executive, on 14, 15 and 16 May on behalf of the subcommittee that had been set up on 7 May indicated that little progress was being made. Events on the streets contributed to a growing sense of crisis. The Unionists were keen to get agreement in the hope of defusing support for the strike, but the SDLP was still opposed to any weakening of the Council, particularly if this could be attributed to Loyalist pressure. I knew that a calm discussion of my proposal to postpone the 25p collection charge would be impossible in the prevailing atmosphere. Roy Bradford, the only member of the Executive in favour of opening discussions with strikers, was later to say in relation to my proposal for postponement of the charge, 'on the one hand we were being asked to treat one form of civil disobedience – the UWC strike – as a rebellion, while on the other we were being asked to condone it in another form.' Not much sense of proportion there, but it was an indication of what feelings were like.

Events were now coming to a head on a number of fronts. On 19 May, Rees announced a State of Emergency. On the same day, without informing Faulkner and the Executive, Roy Bradford went public on his proposal for negotiations with the UWC. He was already under suspicion of leaking information to the strikers, and this action only served to intensify the suspicion. On 21 May a 'back to work' march led by the General Secretary of the Trade Union Congress, Len Murray, attracted derisory support. Despite strong words in the House of Commons from Stan Orme – 'we will not negotiate with the Ulster Workers Council. We have listened to what it had to say at a meeting. What it is asking for is not negotiable' – the situation on the ground was becoming desperate.

East of the Bann, Northern Ireland was coming to a standstill. In nationalist areas west of the Bann the main effect was the reduced electricity supply and the difficulty in getting petrol, but in mixed areas loyalists manned roadblocks, disrupted traffic with agricultural vehicles and cut down trees to block roads. On 24 May two of my constituents, Pat McGirr and Eileen McCrory, died on the Ballygawley Road when their car ran into a tree deliberately felled as a barricade.

I became aware of increasing anxiety among SDLP backbenchers, which was hardly surprising. Paddy Duffy was threatening to resign from the party because of internment. Seamus Mallon, the Chairman of the Assembly party, had a letter, signed by a large number of local branch officials, district councillors and prominent party supporters from South Down, Armagh and Tyrone, who wanted the SDLP to pull out of the Executive if Sunningdale were not fully implemented by July; Seamus himself did not disagree with their views.

A joint SDLP Executive/Assembly party meeting was held at Cushendun, County Antrim, on 19 and 20 May at which there was a lot of straight talking. Paddy and John reported on the subcommittee's discussions, insofar as they could – leaks would have been particularly unhelpful at this time – and I reported my frustration over the collection charges. The 'strictly confidential' minutes of the meeting outlined the party's priorities: 'The formal signing and the full implementation of the Sunningdale communiqué remains party policy and its main short-term objective.' 'The only point for negotiations is the phasing of the procedures to implement the communiqué.' There then followed a suggested timetable, which indicated the difference between the SDLP's interpretation of 'phasing' and that of the Faulkner Unionists.

As a wish list, it would have been more appropriate in the week before Christmas rather than in the reality of a situation where Northern Ireland was being brought to the verge of anarchy. The strength of feeling, and the positions taken, illustrated how difficult it might be to pass through the Assembly party anything that could be described as a 'weakening' of Sunningdale.

Over that same weekend of the SDLP meeting, the UUUC decided to give full support to the UWC. This was a significant development as it meant that

West, Craig and Paisley had decided that the UWC was going to win, and they wanted to be on the bandwagon. In the Executive, our hope that the strike would implode was further diminished.

On Monday, 20 May, despite the failure of the subcommittee to agree recommendations – partially due to the now profound antagonism between Bradford and Devlin – elements of an agreement began to come together. The central and controversial section consisted of a two-phase implementation, the second phase to be entered on only after a test of the opinion of the electorate, effectively the election due in three years' time. After this test of opinion, with the consent of the Assembly, there would be the full implementation of Sunningdale, including the transfer of functions from the Departments to the Council, the appointment of a Secretary-General and staff, nominations of members of the Assembly and Dáil to the consultative Assembly and location to permanent headquarters.

Considerable consideration was given to 'presentation' so that an accusation of weakening or watering-down would be more difficult to sustain, and also to highlight the fact that these matters had been under discussion long before the loyalist strike and were therefore not the product of loyalist pressure. As it eventually emerged, it was a model of draftsmanship, pointing up support for Sunningdale and its full implementation, but there was no disguising the major differences between the draft and what the joint SDLP Assembly party–Executive meeting had approved just two days previously.

On Wednesday morning, 22 May, there were two meetings, one of the SDLP Assembly party and, later, one of the Executive. I went to the Assembly party meeting in a mood of depression. I expected opposition to the 'phasing in' of the Council of Ireland, but thought it would be approved – despite a surprising development. In the early hours of the morning, Gerry had telephoned me to tell me that Paddy Devlin was going to vote 'No'. He had apparently said so at a party meeting in Belfast the previous night, based not on the terms of the phasing, which would have been difficult since he had agreed to it in the Executive, but on the timing of the announcement, which he said would be seen as a victory for the UWC. This news was bad enough, but my depression was for another reason. Would our sacrifice be in vain?

The meeting was worse than I had anticipated. There were a number of emotional and angry contributions, mostly aimed at the British government for welshing on its commitments and for its failure to deal with the loyalist strike. There was no direct criticism of the leadership, but it was implied in a number of the contributions. Gerry, John and I warned that Faulkner and his colleagues were not bluffing. Unless we stood by the new phasing agreement, which required endorsement by the Assembly party, the Unionists on the Executive would resign, supported by Alliance, and we would bear the responsibility for the collapse of the Executive. Some Assembly members were still of the opinion that the Faulknerites were bluffing and that their bluff should be called, despite the public position of Bradford, which would ensure Faulkner had no alternative. When the vote was taken, the leaders' recommendation to endorse the new arrangements was defeated by 11 votes to 8.

The rest of the Executive was still in session when we returned with the bad news. Gerry emotionally told them what had happened, but then unexpectedly, before Faulkner could bring matters to the only conclusion possible, he asked for more time to discuss the matter with the Assembly party. Always resourceful, committed more to power-sharing than to the Council of Ireland and determined to do everything he humanly could to preserve the Executive, he had one more card to play. He knew that SDLP members had great respect for Stan Orme, the Minister of State. Orme had been a supporter of the Campaign for Social Justice even before the civil rights marches began. Along with Paul Rose and Kevin McNamara, he founded the Campaign for Democracy in Ulster in the dark days when, by convention, civil rights abuses in Northern Ireland could not even be raised in the House of Commons. He was an old friend of Gerry's, and one of the Labour MPs who had visited Coalisland and other parts of the North at his invitation in 1967. While we may have had our reservations about Rees, no one in the Assembly party doubted Stan Orme's commitment to the SDLP and to the Power-Sharing Executive.

Members of the Assembly party were summoned back to the party room by Paddy O'Hanlon, the Chief Whip, and found, to their shock, that the Deputy Secretary of State was waiting for them there. Gerry introduced him and then left, saying he just wanted us to hear what Orme had to say. I suspected the tension was too great for him and he was heading for the bar! Orme said Gerry had told him of the result of our previous meeting and, while it was our decision, he thought there were a few matters we might not have fully considered. On our decision rested the future of the Executive, as Faulkner had already informed Rees that he would tender his resignation if the SDLP Ministers withdrew their agreement to the phasing arrangement. As a result, the SDLP would be blamed for the fall of the Executive, the UWC would be victorious and Northern Ireland would be in a situation similar to the collapse of the Weimar Republic. The paramilitaries on both sides would be the only gainers. He recognised the SDLP's disillusionment with the British government over internment and lack of effective action against the loyalists, but part of the reason for the unwillingness to commit was the doubt over the future of the Executive. Once agreement was reached on the Council of Ireland, effective action could be taken.

It was an excellent performance, hitting the chords that mattered. It was also, of course, an intervention in the internal business of the party, and only someone with Orme's record could have got away with it. A vote was quickly taken and the previous decision was reversed by 14 votes to 5, this time with Paddy Devlin in favour.

We returned to the Executive room to much rejoicing and Faulkner decided to announce agreement in the House as quickly as possible. The word had spread that the Executive had fallen and loyalists were already taunting Executive supporters. Oliver Napier made arrangements to intervene in the debate that was taking place, on Paddy Devlin's Departmental estimates; Paddy had had to leave the party meeting early to attend this debate and had communicated his vote to the meeting via Ivan Cooper. Contrary to the rules of the House, but with the cooperation of the Assistant Speaker, Lord Dunleath, of Alliance, who was in the Chair, and Derrick Crothers, also Alliance, Faulkner was allowed to make an urgent statement on the Sunningdale Agreement, which he described as 'perhaps the most important that has ever been made in this Assembly or in the Parliament that was here before that'. Important it was, but that did not prevent the Speaker, Nat Minford, who had hurriedly returned to the House, from voicing his displeasure that proper procedure had not been followed.

For all the blood and sweat, the phasing-in of the Council of Ireland did not make the slightest impact on the loyalists, or their strike. Had it been done earlier, maybe it would have had an effect. But I doubt it. In the event, the UWC announced that 'the strike must now continue until negotiations are opened up with Her Majesty's government concerning the Constitution Act, the Sunningdale Agreement and new elections for the Assembly.'

In the Assembly the following day, 23 May, members from all three pro-Executive parties expressed their anger at the worsening situation. Bertie McConnell (Alliance) said, 'The Executive must go to Mr Merlyn Rees, who is in charge of law and order, and tell him in no uncertain manner that we want to see law and order and basic civil rights restored before they break down completely and irreparable damage is done to the whole community.' Seamus Mallon, describing how difficult it was to travel because of the roadblocks and how members of paramilitary organisations were deciding who got petrol, said, 'when we have this type of situation and when we have the massive force of the British Army, the RUC, the RUC reserve and the UDR [and they] are not in a position to take any action, I think we can safely say we have arrived at a state of anarchy.'

The SDLP was not alone in calling for action by the security forces. Lord Dunleath, describing how the law was being blatantly ignored, commented, 'there are 16,500 regular soldiers, 7,000-odd UDR men and, what is it, 5,500 RUC in this country and yet this can happen and those gentlemen who are doing it can go unmolested. Have there been any arrests? Have any charges being prepared against them? ... this week has brought law and order into more contempt than ever before.' Mrs Anne Dickson (Unionist) added, 'it seems to be a chosen people, a master race who can get fuel; no one else is considered worthy ... I do not want to see my country brought down. I do not want to see it bankrupt. I do not want to see queues of people on the dole. That is the prospect unless something is done urgently.'

John Hume, as Minister responsible for electricity and oil supplies, replied to the debate. He said all speakers had underlined the threat the strike posed not only to the livelihood but to the very life of the Northern Ireland community. As a result of the near-paralysis of the electricity system, factories had had to close down, the agricultural industry was distressed and severe personal hardship and inconvenience had been brought to every house in the North. Now those responsible were interfering with the supply of oil, upon which the whole life of the community depended. The Minister finished by saying, 'I want to make one thing very clear, that I am very well aware of my statutory responsibilities for these services. I am also aware of the steps which are necessary to enable me to see that they are provided and I have informed the Secretary of State of the steps which he must take if I am to do so.'

Naturally, John had not spelled it out in public, but the provision of oil supplies and the assistance of the Secretary of State as the person responsible for the security forces was to be the crunch issue – the test of the commitment of the Executive and the will of the British government. The 'oil plan' was for the Department of Commerce to take over, control and distribute petroleum products and liquid petroleum gas to essential users. The Harbour Estate in East Belfast, where the refinery and the LPG plant were located, would be requisitioned and guarded by the Army, and the oil distributed by tanker to essential users, such as hospitals and food processing plants and to twenty-one garages throughout the North, which recipients would also be guarded by the Army. Essential users, estimated at 6,500, would be identified and provided with special coupons.

It was becoming clear that the Army did not have the expertise to run the electricity power stations and would require the help of civilian technicians, and that any effort to take over the stations could lead to sabotage. In the circumstances, if the government and the Executive were to be seen to be taking effective action, it would be by successfully implementing the oil plan. Unfortunately, despite some initial indications of Army cooperation, the Army authorities began to have second thoughts and then to actively oppose the proposal. It took sustained pressure from Hume and a meeting of the three party leaders with Wilson at Chequers on Friday, 24 May, for the necessary commitment of troops to be promised. Amazingly, despite the authorisation of the Prime Minister, the Army continued to raise objections, unwilling to take action when they could not be sure of the end result. In particular, the GOC feared that implementation of the oil plan would lead to a confrontation with the UWC, and he then would have his war on two fronts.

As the debate continued and Rees wavered, Wilson spoke to the nation on TV and radio. The nation he spoke to was more the British nation than the Irish, unionist or nationalist. Instead of a commitment to firm action to restore law and order, his references to 'spongers' only succeeded in provoking Protestant anger and solidifying support for the strikers.

By Sunday, there had still been no action to implement John's plan, and the SDLP Ministers, frustrated and angry, met at Gerry's house on the Antrim Road and decided enough was enough. Unless the British government took effective action to enable the Executive to implement the oil plan, we would resign with effect from 6.00am the following morning, Monday. All six of us signed a letter to Rees, effectively an ultimatum. Cooper and Devlin were sent to Dublin to brief the government and Opposition, and the rest of us went to Stormont Castle to deliver the letter. Rees wasn't there. Despite receiving the PM's authorisation for the use of troops just two days earlier at Chequers, Rees had felt it necessary to again consult with Wilson and had flown to Cornwall, where Wilson was holidaying close to the Scilly Isles, to meet with him. That morning, before he left, Gerry had told him that the oil plan was a resignation issue for the SDLP, so there was no longer any doubt, or room for prevarication. Wilson faced the inevitable and again authorised Army action. At Stormont Castle, Stan Orme accepted our letter on behalf of Rees. It did not need words to tell us he agreed with us.

The following morning at 5.00am, one hour before our resignation became effective, the British Army moved into the refinery at Sydenham, in Belfast, the oil storage installation in Derry, and began to take up positions at the twenty-one selected filling stations. The operation was no surprise to the UWC; they had been tipped off the day after the plan was proposed.

It was too little, too late. That Monday morning Faulkner had met with the top civil servants and had been given a 'Doomsday' report. When the Executive met in the afternoon, it was evident that the fight had gone out of the Unionists. Faulkner reported on his meeting with the civil servants and told us that messages had been received from a large number of individuals and organisations which had been supportive of the Executive, pleading for some move to break the impasse. The Chief Executive said it was his view that some way would have to be found to communicate with the strike leadership, preferably through some individual who would establish the facts and see if a way could be found to end this intolerable situation. I wondered why it was necessary to have someone to establish the facts. Surely we already knew them? Clearly it was an intermediary he was proposing. The SDLP Ministers reiterated that they had not changed their minds on negotiations with the strikers, and it was agreed to meet again the following morning.

We met again at 11.20am, Tuesday, 28 May 1974, a date I will never forget. The Chief Executive gave us his most recent update on the situation: a minimal petrol and oil supply was being operated by the Army; the power stations were near to total shutdown and the Army was not capable of operating them; the water and sewage services were at grave risk, with the possibility of raw sewerage polluting the streets and threatening the health of the population; the UWC had stopped supplies of foodstuffs to farmers and food distribution was in danger. We had, he said, only two options. We could sit tight and hope to break the strike eventually, which would mean great hardship and almost inevitably deaths, or we could seek to negotiate, either directly or through an intermediary. He and his Unionist colleagues were not prepared to inflict such hardship on the Ulster people and, accordingly, he proposed that we approach the Secretary of State to ask him to support us in seeking to end the strike by discussions through intermediaries. If Rees did not agree, we should hand in our resignations.

Gerry, John and I (Paddy had not yet returned from Dublin) strongly opposed this proposal and had partial support from Oliver Napier, who was in favour of an intermediary but against resignation. I said that what was being proposed was a capitulation to the loyalists. As a result of our commitment to the Executive we had swallowed a bitter pill the previous week in the Sunningdale phasing debate, but now our sacrifice was to be made meaningless. Only two days ago, at our insistence, the British government had at last committed its troops in support of the oil plan. We were now proposing to capitulate without knowing the full effects of that initiative. It was a Weimar Republic situation, and the only benefactors would be the extremists on both sides. The IRA would gain because the fearful Catholic community were looking for protection. If we really believed in Sunningdale, if we believed we had done the right thing, we should proceed to the formal ratification of Sunningdale and then see about intermediaries if we still needed them. All to no avail. Faulkner left at 12.16pm to talk to Rees.

When we reconvened at 1.40pm (Basil McIvor was missing), Faulkner gave a report on his meeting with Rees. The Secretary of State was not prepared to negotiate with the UWC, nor to do so indirectly through an intermediary. Faulkner had then offered the resignation of the Unionist members of the Executive. The SDLP Ministers refused to resign, on principle; we would make it clear we were being forced out of office by a Fascist *putsch*.

As we continued to debate the issue, a secretary from the outer office approached me to say there was a phone call for me. It was the South Tyrone Hospital in Dungannon. Annita had been in the hospital for the previous week with complications, and she had gone into the labour ward. When I returned to the Executive room I must have looked strained as wee Brian asked me if anything was wrong. I told him, adding that there was a history of my children being born on important occasions and cited Estelle's birth on the day of the first civil rights march. He looked at me and said, 'Austin, promise me, after this one, no more.'

It was, of course, an emotional occasion. Despite the heated discussions over the Council of Ireland and the differences at the end, when we had our only vote, over the issue of negotiation, external pressure had cemented personal relationships. When the end came, I was able to say to Faulkner, with absolute sincerity, 'Brian, whatever the future holds, I now know from working with you that I can trust you.'

The Assembly was scheduled to meet at 2.30pm and I was due to answer questions. Faulkner had to make a statement on his position at some early stage and the SDLP had to see Rees to state our position. It was decided among us that I would carry on as normally as possible in the Assembly. After all, I had not resigned and was still Minister.

I had another bit of business to transact before I went to see Rees. I had in my pocket a document headed, 'Payment for Debt. Costs of Collection (Revocation Order)', which stated, 'The Payment of Debt (Costs of Collection) Order

(Northern Ireland) 1974(c) is hereby revoked.' Internment had not ended, the Executive was falling, my power to influence internment was gone – there was no good reason why I should continue to carry the odium of the 25p collection charge. Herbie Kirk had now resigned, so I asked Gerry, as Acting Chief Executive, to sign it as Acting Minister of Finance, and he did so.

When we met Rees, I gave him the document and asked him to see it was implemented. I have never been able to verify the legality of the Order, but it was made by two Ministers; it was the following day that Rees signed an Order dismissing us. The fact that we were still Ministers at the time we signed the document was confirmed by a letter, dated 29 May, which I received from Rees:

> Dear Austin,
> Now that Mr Faulkner, the Chief Executive member, and his supporters in the Executive have resigned, it is clearly inappropriate for the remaining members of the Executive to remain in office. In order that the appropriate constitutional steps can now be taken in accordance with the Northern Ireland constitution act 1973 I am writing to confirm that, on her Majesty's behalf, I have signed a warrant terminating your appointment as a member of the Executive with effect from 29 May 1974.
> Sincerely,
> Merlyn

But whether my Order was valid or not, or whether Rees made a separate Revocation Order under his own name, not a single 25p was ever collected. That, of course, did not prevent my political opponents from saddling me with the epithet '25p Currie' for many years.

On my return from Rees, I went straight into the Assembly to answer Questions. There was a reply I was particularly keen to give. A scheme known as SPED (special purchase of evacuated dwellings) had been introduced in 1971 to enable the Housing Executive to purchase houses from owners who had been intimidated, but who could not sell their houses because of trouble in their area. Representations had been made to me that the conditions imposed were unduly restrictive and hardship was being caused. I announced that I was abolishing the restrictions. It was the last Ministerial announcement in the Assembly. I was not to know that, fifteen years later, I myself would take advantage of that widening of the definition of special hardship.

In the course of his response to my reply, David Bleakley (NILP) referred to speculation that the Power-Sharing Executive was coming to an end. He gave me the opportunity to put the following on the record: 'Irrespective of what happens and how this community may go in the future, somebody at the end of the day is going to have to come in and pick up the pieces, no matter how shattered those pieces are. When he does that, someone will remember – and I would like to think a lot of people will remember – and say there was an idea about once; the idea was partnership in the North between Catholic and Protestant and partnership on the island between Irishmen.'

I knew it would take time, but not as long as twenty-four years, until the Good Friday Agreement!

As I left Stormont in my official car for the last time, word was circulating that the Executive had fallen and the long avenue was beginning to fill with exultant loyalists, many with very expensive-looking tractors and balers and sewage tanks. We managed to get away through the side gates and I instructed my driver to get to the South Tyrone Hospital as quickly as possible. It took twice as long as usual because some of the barricades were still in place and we had to make detours. I had plenty of time to think. The last few weeks had been awful for me and my family. The number of threats had increased over the course of the loyalist strike. The Provisional IRA decision, taken in January in the aftermath of Sunningdale, that Executive Ministers were to be considered the enemy had increased the security threat. My house – with its sandbags and bullet-proof glass and searchlights and security devices and a concrete block wall over 2 metres high along the back and armed policemen twenty-four hours a day – was more a fortress than a home. Apart from the possibility of attack on me, or on my guards, it also put the lives of Annita and the children at risk. These were pretty intolerable conditions to ask a woman and three young children to live in.

To make matters worse, Annita's current pregnancy had been a difficult one and the murder of Gertie Devlin had hit her badly. My work as a Minister had given me tremendous satisfaction, but it meant I was away from home even more than before, and the increased stress of recent weeks had affected Annita as well as me. She was brought into hospital a few days after the start of the loyalist strike. The children were farmed out to kind neighbours, the Killens, Hamills and McCullaghs, and to my cousin, Pat, and his wife, Margaret. Estelle, only five-and-a-half, insisted she was staying with me, to look after me, with the result that she spent most of her time with Gemma and Pat Killen, across the road, and I spent some of my nights there too. How wonderful, and how lucky we were, to have good neighbours in an emergency. I had felt guilty about this situation and thought that the one beneficial effect

– the only one – of the loss of my ministerial position would be that I would be able to spend more time with my family. That is, if we managed to survive the next few weeks of loyalist triumphalism.

When I arrived at the South Tyrone Hospital, I found that the message about Annita's condition wasn't the whole truth. She had been rushed to the labour ward because she was haemorrhaging badly. I was only able to see her briefly; in those days fathers were not expected to be present at the birth, nor did this one wish to be present. The nurses were keen to get rid of me, and I wasn't objecting. On my way to the hospital exit I was stopped by a number of constituents who sympathised with me on the fall of the Executive, delaying me for maybe twenty minutes. I heard a commotion at the front door and saw a man whom I recognised as John Watson, the esteemed gynaecologist, rushing down the corridor. A few minutes later one of the nurses came to tell me that Mr Watson had been summoned to an emergency – my wife. The same nurse reappeared a few minutes later to congratulate me on the birth of my son, but there had been complications and my wife wished to see me. With great foreboding I ran down the corridor to Annita and she told me that the new baby was in danger of dying and that a priest had been summoned to christen him. The priest who promptly arrived was a Fr Larkin, brother of my SDLP colleague in the Assembly, Aidan. Michael Austin was christened in the incubator and immediately transferred to Craigavon Hospital, where there were better facilities. Later that night, as the telephone rang continually with people offering their sympathy on the fall of the Executive, I was able to surprise them by saying I was celebrating. Thankfully, my son soon responded to the marvellous care of the doctors and nurses in Craigavon Hospital. The last task of my driver in the official ministerial car was to transport Annita home from the South Tyrone.

2 1 : T H E N A D I R

The period following the downfall of the Power-Sharing Executive was one of depression and frustration, personally and politically, a time when light at the end of the tunnel was more likely to be an approaching speeding truck than an indication of hope. The *post-mortem* lasted a long time.

On the positive side, we in the SDLP had much to congratulate ourselves on. The power-sharing experiment, short-lived as it had been, had been a success. We had proved it was possible for Catholics and Protestants, Nationalists and Unionists to work together for the good of the community in extremely difficult circumstances. Brian Faulkner had once described such an arrangement as a recipe for 'a Bedlam Cabinet'. He had been proved wrong, and indeed had been a major contributor to proving himself wrong. It could never again be said that it could not work. The SDLP Ministers had proven our capacity to do the job. Indeed, in terms of individual performance, we had been praised even by those who were opposed to our involvement in government. If there was a serious criticism of our role, it was not incapacity, or lack of commitment, or generosity, or compassion, but as Ken Bloomfield put it in his memoirs, a lack of ruthlessness. Bloomfield referred specifically to Paddy Devlin's determination to avoid hardship by paying benefits to strikers, and to John Hume's decision not to take action against Hugo Patterson, spokesperson for the Electricity Service, a public utility under the control of John's Department, whose reporting helped to create a sense of crisis. As Bloomfield commented, 'we were all too humane for a savage situation'.

On the negative side, whatever might be said about how successful the Power-Sharing Executive had been, the harsh reality was that it took two to tango, and there was now no group on the unionist side willing, or able, to share power with the SDLP. Nor was there likely to be for the foreseeable future. To make matters worse, there was considerable doubt about the intentions of the British government. In the aftermath of the downfall of the Executive, Merlyn Rees convinced himself that 'Ulster nationalism' was the new political force, and that what was required was a Constitutional Convention so that Ulstermen themselves could work out their own future, without outside interference. Speaking in a debate at the Oxford Union on

31 October, I predicted what the future would be for the Convention:

'Everyone in Northern Ireland who knows anything about politics could tell you right now exactly what the position will be when that Convention takes place. They will tell you there will be a loyalist majority and that the SDLP will be the largest party in the minority. But it must be clear even to the British Government, that it will not solve anything, that no solution will come out of the Convention and one wonders what the British Government intends to do in a situation like that. Will they accept majority rule and approve the creation of what effectively will be the return of the old Stormont; will they be prepared to do that? Will they decide on a continuation of Direct Rule, knowing that that must mean a continuation of violence? Will they withdraw from Northern Ireland in circumstances where there would almost inevitably be a civil war in which the South would almost inevitably become involved? Or will they stick by the pledges which have been given consistently that they will support a power-sharing situation in Northern Ireland and a new institution between North and South to cover the Irish dimension.'

I went on to point out that, in the most recent Westminster election, the loyalist vote accounted for 1.18% of the total UK vote:

'... these are the people who say to the British Government, we will not accept power-sharing, we will not accept an Irish dimension and at the same time these are the people who say they are loyal to Britain, they are loyal to the British Parliament and they wish to remain in that loyal position.'

Would this 1.18% be allowed to dictate British government policy?

I had made the same points face-to-face with the Prime Minister, Harold Wilson, as a member of the SDLP delegation that had met him in Downing Street the previous month. But in the privacy of the Downing Street meeting, and at a meeting with the Irish government at around the same time, I and other delegates had warned the government, in the strongest terms, about our increasing fear of a 'Doomsday' situation. We warned that in the prevailing situation of political instability, where the intentions of the British government were unclear and where the loyalist paramilitaries, flushed with their success in bringing down the Executive, were increasing their attacks on innocent Catholics, the whole Catholic community, but particularly those living in isolated and sensitive areas, could come under threat. We asked the two governments to give urgent attention to political and security measures to ensure the necessary protection. In our representations we also expressed concern at what we described as the predictable growth in support for the IRA, which, as I told Wilson, was a reaction against the 'spineless' behaviour of his government. The IRA was attempting to make a comeback as the 'defenders' of the Catholic community and was also intensifying its campaign in Britain.

It was a bad time to be a constitutional politician and, unfortunately, it was to get worse. Indeed, the period between the fall of the Executive in 1974 and the end of the decade were my worst years in personal and political terms.

I made a point of condemning all violent deaths in my constituency and attended as many appropriate funerals as I could. I say 'appropriate' because I did not think it appropriate to attend IRA-organised funerals, or funerals where I thought my presence would be unwelcome. Sometimes I would visit the house privately, or write or ask someone to express my personal condolences. And sometimes I attended funerals after much agonising and, in the case of funerals of some members of the security forces, it required considerable courage, both personal and political, to do so. However, I felt I had to be seen to be opposed to violence, irrespective of the victim, or the perpetrator.

I was kept busy attending funerals in those years. I don't remember them all, but some of them, because of the circumstances or because the victim was personally known to me, I have never forgotten.

On 24 July 1974, Patsy Kelly, a community councillor from Trillick, in my constituency, disappeared while on his way home from the pub he managed. His body was found nearly three weeks later in Lough Erne, with two 56lb weights attached to it. No one has ever been convicted for this crime. Controversy surrounds Patsy's death to this day, but there was no doubt that he was murdered by Protestant paramilitaries, almost certainly with connivance and assistance from members of the UDR. His brave wife, Teresa, gave birth to a son eight months later and took over her husband's council seat. In September, I attended the funerals of two judges shot by the IRA in their homes, Rory Conaghan and Martin McBirney. I knew both of them personally, as I have previously recounted.

In November I attended the funerals of Hugh Coney and Patrick Falls. Hugh Coney was an internee from Annaghmore, Coalisland, whom I had met at Long Kesh and whose family was known to me. He was shot dead while attempting to tunnel out of Long Kesh with a number of others. Patrick Falls was shot by the UVF while working in his brother's pub at Aughamullan,

Coalisland. He was entirely innocent of any paramilitary involvement, having just returned from England, and some members of his family were strong SDLP supporters.

At the end of January 1975, George Coulter, a RUC sergeant, was murdered by the IRA at a T-junction within half-a-mile of my home in Donaghmore. He had just left my house, where he had called with the two policemen on guard duty there. His death was to lead to controversy, which I will recount later.

On 10 February 1975 two men, Eugene Doyle and Arthur Mulholland, were killed when UVF gunmen shot up Hayden's bar near Rock. Members of the Hayden family had been intimidated out of the same premises in the 1920s. The following day a relief milkman, Christopher Mein, was shot by the IRA at Glenbeg cottages, Galbally. The murder was probably a reprisal for the previous night's killings, but the IRA did not get the person they were after and it was a most cowardly act. In April, the 'Murder Triangle' lived up to its name with sectarian assassinations near Castlecaulfield and Ballygawley.

Marion Bowen, eight months' pregnant, and her two brothers were blown to bits by a UVF booby-trap bomb planted at the house the brothers were renovating for her and her husband. Owen Boyle, a father of eight, was shot by the UVF through the window of his new home as he and his wife were washing dishes. My statement of condemnation said that his was the nineteenth Catholic death in the Murder Triangle for which no one had been brought to justice. I also referred to the fact that there had been no public condemnation of these murders by loyalist politicians, or even by local Protestant churchmen, despite the fact that the victims were innocent civilians, not affiliated to any paramilitary organisations.

At the beginning of August I attended the funeral, in Caledon, of Brian McCoy, the trumpet player in the Miami Showband, who was killed by members of the UVF (some of whom were also members of the UDR), along with two band members. One of the UVF men blew himself up while planting the bomb in the band's van. He was named as Wesley Somerville from Moygashel, Dungannon, who was suspected of involvement in attacks on my home. Towards the end of August, John Farmer from Moy was one of two men returning from the All-Ireland football semi-final when they were stopped at a UVF roadblock outside Newtownhamilton and shot in the head. I knew John and his wife well, and there was certainly no involvement with, or even sympathy for, the IRA. He was shot because he was a Catholic, easily identifiable as such because he was coming from the Gaelic football match.

On 2 August, George McCall, a young former member of the UDR, was brutally murdered in the Moy by the IRA as he was returning from the pub with his wife. Less than a month later, and possibly in retaliation, Dinny Mullan was murdered by the UVF at his home outside Moy. He and his wife Olive were members of the SDLP, and they were personal friends of mine. Dinny had served as chairman of the Moy SDLP branch, and he had recently been promoted to the position of ambulance controller at the South Tyrone Hospital, the first Catholic to hold the position. I was in Dublin, at Garret FitzGerald's home, when I heard the news of his murder. I broke down and cried. The entire leadership of the SDLP attended the funeral at Collegeland church, presided over by Cardinal Conway.

In October, again near Moy, Peter and Jane McKearney were murdered by the UVF, apparently in the mistaken belief that they were related to a girl with the same surname who had been described in the media as 'the most wanted woman in Britain'.

On Hallowe'en night, a seventeen-year-old boy from my village left his rented flat in Dublin, telling his girlfriend he was just popping out for a packet of cigarettes. He was Columba McVeigh. Columba never returned and became a member of a group of people who became known as 'the Disappeared'. Columba, his father and mother, brothers and sister were personal friends of Annita and mine, and indeed his mother had looked after two of our children. It was only in 1999 that the IRA finally admitted responsibility, claiming that Columba had been an informer. Even if this allegation were true, what sort of so-called disciplined organisation would entrust to a seventeen-year-old boy information so valuable as to justify his death and the secret burial of his body? Paddy McVeigh, Columba's father, went to an early grave in 1997 not knowing of the fate of his son and still hoping against hope that he would turn up. The obituary notice of Paddy's death in the local Press referred to Columba as if he were still alive. When asked if she ever went on holiday, his mother, Vera, responded, 'Sure, what if Columba called and we weren't here?'

Of all of the atrocities committed by the IRA during the Troubles, the treatment of the Disappeared and their relatives ranks among the worst. For an organisation that goes to such lengths to commemorate and honour its own dead, the behaviour of the IRA in dishonouring the bodies of the Disappeared is particularly inhumane and hypocritical. The evidence that such treatment was centrally organised, and involved some people still in leadership positions today, adds to the barbarism of their activity. One can only hope that the heroism and commitment of parents and relatives, such as

Vera McVeigh, will be rewarded by the recovery of the bodies of their loved ones before they themselves die.

On 25 November a phone call was received at Dungannon RUC station saying that a man had been killed in a road accident in County Monaghan and would the RUC inform his sister, who lived at Clonavaddy, Dungannon. Sergeant Paddy Maxwell and Reserve Constable Sammy Clarke were sent, with another officer, on the errand of mercy after an attempt had been made to check the authenticity of the message. On the laneway to the house, the waiting IRA men opened up on the car and Maxwell and Clarke died in a hail of bullets; the other policeman was injured. Paddy Maxwell was a Catholic and I attended his funeral at St Patrick's church, Dungannon. The only other politician in attendance was John Taylor. That afternoon I also attended Sammy Clarke's funeral in the Presbyterian church in Castlecaulfield. All of the leading loyalist politicians were in attendance, including the Reverend Ian Paisley, Harry West, leader of the official Unionists, Ernest Baird, the deputy leader of Vanguard, as well as John Taylor. Two members of the police force had been murdered at the same time, in the same barbaric incident, both family men with wives and children. Why did one merit a full turnout of politicians while the other did not? Why did more attend the funeral of the Reserve Constable than the Sergeant? It illustrated the bigotry and hypocrisy of those who said they unreservedly supported the RUC and did not differentiate between its members.

It was not an easy decision for me to attend Sammy Clarke's funeral. I suspected there would be those in attendance who would not welcome my presence. Only one man objected, saying, 'you have a fucking nerve coming here', but I received a warm welcome from some, although there was an atmosphere I found chilly. There was another reason I might have absented myself. Sammy Clarke was the Sergeant instructor of the Castlecaulfield platoon that had shot up my house in August 1969 and had fired shots on the Donaghmore Road in Dungannon on the night when three young people were injured, lucky to escape with their lives. Bigotry and intolerance is not all on the one side, though. One of Sergeant Maxwell's sons developed into a fine Gaelic footballer, playing for my club, Edendork St Malachy's. On one occasion I was present when he was playing a stormer against a neighbouring club. Every time he caught the ball, a small section of the rival supporters, mostly women, began to chant, 'SS RUC'.

There were other horrific murders of people known to me, some of them personal friends. I will refer only to two. Rory T O'Kelly was my opponent for nomination when I was first selected for East Tyrone, and he later served as my election agent in two elections. He was a good personal friend. Rory was from Coalisland and of an impeccable republican background. His father, the local headmaster in Coalisland, had organised the IRA locally during the War of Independence and afterwards. As a local solicitor, Rory had identified with the civil rights campaign and had defended civil rights supporters in the courts. One of the *Hunt* reforms was to take prosecutions out of the hands of the RUC and give the responsibility to the Director of Public Prosecutions. Rory was offered, and accepted, the position of Assistant Public Prosecutor for County Down, based in Bangor. He moved there, where he was not involved in any controversial political cases. Rory liked a drink and when he visited his hometown he enjoyed the *craic* in the local bars. That is where he was on 4 March when an IRA man walked in and shot him in the head. That was the reward for a member of a distinguished family who had given generous service to the local community. He was murdered as 'part of our continuing attacks against British imperialism's judiciary and administration'.

Seamus McAvoy and I were born within months of each other in houses one hundred yards apart. His father owned the house in which I was born. We attended the same school. He was not academically inclined, but was a successful businessman, employing almost one hundred people in one of the North's worst unemployment blackspots, Coalisland. His was the only Catholic firm out of seven capable of doing the work his company did, which included providing mobile buildings to the security forces. I know that he was threatened on a number of occasions because he told me so. Demands were made for 'protection money' and on one occasion the IRA demanded £50,000. Seamus was shot in the back and chest by the IRA in Dublin. He died, leaving a wife and five children. At the funeral, Cardinal Ó Fiaich described his killing as 'an attack on the very fabric of the Irish Catholic people and on society as a whole'. I described it as being 'more to do with Al Caponism than patriotism'.

I have described these murders in an attempt to illustrate how wretched life was for my constituents in the years following the downfall of the Power-Sharing Executive, particularly in the Murder Triangle. People did not feel safe anywhere – in their homes, on the streets, in bars and restaurants, at their place of employment, even at their place of worship. The paramilitaries fed and fattened on each other. Politicians like myself felt frustrated and useless. The only relatively safe place was deep in the ghetto, surrounded by your own – that is, if you were prepared to acquiesce in the rule of the godfathers and the 'protectors' – or, if you had the money, among the barristers and other professionals in areas such as the 'Gold Coast' of North Down. Elsewhere, you lived in constant fear of a further deterioration to civil war, or re-Partition, or a 'Doomsday situation'.

The Currie family was, of course, affected by these developments, living, as we did, in the Murder Triangle. My position as a politician, sometimes a controversial one, created an extra dimension of insecurity and danger. I have already described the conditions in which we were living, protected by the RUC around the clock. During this period in the 1970s, twelve members of the RUC were killed in the Dungannon police district. All of them were known to me, either through my official duties, or, in the case of reserve policemen, because they were local constituents, or because they had been part of protection at my home. Those in the latter category were, of course, known to my wife and children, too. Indeed, since they spent far more time at home than I did, Annita and the children were closer to these men than I was. It was understandable, in the confined space of a 1,050 sq. ft bungalow, that they should be on first-name terms. On occasions, Annita found herself in the role of counsellor to young men under stress and naturally it was impossible to keep our young children away from the company in the garage.

Inevitably, we were all affected by the death or injury of these policemen. It was impossible to explain to the children why the men in uniform, who were there to protect us, were being shot at by those who said they were the protectors of the Catholic community. The grief of police relatives was shared in my household. There was one young man who was particularly popular with my children. John McCambridge came from Ballycastle in County Antrim and had the distinctive accent of that area, and his outgoing personality and generosity with sweets meant he was a favourite. He was murdered by the IRA, shot down from behind a hedge, and he was mourned in our home. It did not help that I suspected, rightly as it turned out, that his killer was also well-known to me personally.

I had not asked for police protection. The RUC authorities had insisted on it after the brutal attack on Annita in November 1972, and I had had no alternative but to accept the offer. The safety of my family had to be the first consideration and the presence of the RUC seemed to be the lesser of two evils in an impossible, no-win situation. My difficulty was further complicated by the SDLP policy on policing, with which I fully concurred. The SDLP position was that full support could not be given to the RUC in the absence of agreed political institutions. While we welcomed the changes which had occurred since the *Hunt Report* and gave unequivocal support to the RUC in impartially upholding the law, we also faced the reality that the RUC was not acceptable to a large number of Catholics. The recent evidence of partiality during the UWC strike had increased that confidence gap. There was, therefore, a high degree of sensitivity in a situation where the RUC was guarding me and my family, and yet I was not giving 100% support to my protectors. I was only too aware of the contradictions inherent in my position and, of course, my political opponents took every opportunity to attack me on it, while members of the RUC, including, and maybe particularly, those on guard duty, were highly conscious of it.

The murder of George Coulter by the IRA on 31 January 1975 focussed attention on my anomalous position. The Police Federation issued a statement that tied the murder of Sergeant Coulter to his duties on the guard at my home, and suggested that he had been an easy, soft target because of those duties, as the location of my home made it easy for the IRA to plan the murder. The statement inferred that his death was too high a price to pay for protecting one who refused to give full support to the RUC. This statement, which to me was shockingly irresponsible, inevitably led to attacks on me by loyalist politicians and to an increase in my hate mail. I responded by pointing out that 'when the late Sergeant Coulter called at my home that evening his visit was purely coincidental, was not pre-arranged, did not conform to any previously established pattern and had nothing to do with guard duties at my home'. I also pointed out that upon leaving my house the Sergeant had gone to the crossroads, from where he could have gone in four different directions. He was unlucky to have taken the road where the IRA lay in wait for a police or Army vehicle. It didn't matter what I said. A large section of the Protestant community believed that I shared responsibility for Sergeant Coulter's death and that his life had been wasted on me, a person who expected the police to protect me while refusing to give them political support.

Unfortunately, these events encouraged the IRA to greater activity, since any action at my home was guaranteed publicity and was also a political embarrassment for me and for the SDLP. Shots were regularly fired at the house and bombs and booby traps placed on the approach roads.

On 22 June 1977 the local unionist paper, the *Tyrone Courier*, carried a front-page story headed, in large black type: 'Unbelievable, 20 police on guard every day'. It reported:

'The police guard at the home of Mr Austin Currie, Tullydraw, Donaghmore, has been trebled from two to six constables, in three eight-hour shifts, making a total of 18 policemen employed every 24 hours. To add to that a further two of a bodyguard, who are always on call whenever and wherever Mr Currie wants to travel, makes a total of twenty … As far as we can ascertain there is no one else living in this island or in any other country that requires such a high degree of protection. The SDLP, of whom Mr Currie is Chief Whip, claims to have reservations concerning the police. Many people will ask, "Is it not time this hypocrisy and sham of the SDLP was brought to an end?" Just consider the fact that if this guard continues it will cost the taxpayer around £100,000 per year. With all due respect to Mr Currie the question must be asked, is he at any greater risk than other people in the community (many of whom have been threatened, wounded and murdered)?'

It was an unfair and irresponsible piece of journalism. It was also untrue. There had been no increase in numbers of guards at my home. The same complement remained: two on duty at my home, working eight-hour shifts, and two on my personal guard. In addition, the report made no mention of the circumstances in which the guard was first provided, the fact that it was provided on the insistence of the RUC, and that the same arrangements were in force for a number of politicians, including John Taylor. The immediate effect of the *Courier* 'revelations' was a substantial increase in the hate mail and the abusive phone messages.

The following week's issue (29 June) had a headline, 'Guard off politicians'. The story had now been extended to other politicians as well as me. 'The police guards at the houses of two local politicians, Mr Austin Currie and Mr John Taylor, have been removed at the weekend. It is understood that all political figures in the province will have their guards removed.' The *Courier* either didn't know or preferred not to print the full story. There had been a mutiny in the local police station in Dungannon!

Following his retirement from the RUC in 1988, Chief Inspector Ivan Duncan (the same Ivan Duncan who had been Sergeant in Caledon) wrote his memoir, *From Insult to Injury*. As the officer responsible for supervising the policemen on protection duty at my home, he had this to say about the circumstances in which the guard was eventually removed:

'Gradually over the years things improved but constables still had to approach the house from either side, leaving them very vulnerable. The police then found a way through a farmer's laneway and field that allowed them to approach the house without driving on the Main Road for any great distance. This was fine for some time until the IRA sawed down a tree and planted a bomb. Thankfully it was discovered by a farmer before the police approached and the constables were stopped in time. It proved to be the last straw.

The constables refused to perform any more duty at the Curries' home. It was a mutiny in the true sense of the word. They disobeyed my orders and refused to go out to relieve the men who had been on duty during the day at the house. I consulted higher authorities and was told to approach each man and warn him of the consequences of his actions. I did so, and each individual I approached refused point-blank. I then had to see as many men as possible on the morning detail and order them out on duty. All refused. It looked like a conspiracy but I believe it wasn't.

The Divisional Commander was called in and then Mr Jack Herman, assistant chief constable, was alerted to the situation at headquarters in Belfast. By this time the men who were covering Curries' were long overdue their relief, so myself and another Inspector had to go out and replace the men. We were there all day – a long, boring time with interludes of activity. Austin Currie was in residence at the time and knew of the difficulties. Chief Constable Herman and Chief Supt Harris were back and forth all day discussing the situation with him. I am now aware of what went on in these discussions.

The authorities wanted Mr Currie to get them out of a hole by asking for the guard to be withdrawn. He refused by saying, "I did not ask for it to be put on and I am not going to ask for it to be taken off. If I ask for its removal and I am attacked you will say I demanded the guard be taken away." After long negotiation back and forth we were relieved of duty and the Army took over for the night. A gang of workmen arrived the next day and installed armoured glass, floodlighting and direct radio link with the station …'

There was, of course, a conspiracy, and it was mutiny. Despite the danger, it was a great relief to have the house to ourselves after almost five years of constant surveillance. I was able to have a row with Annita and give off to my kids without being overheard by strangers. However, the attacks on my home, mostly by Provo supporters, didn't stop. Leaving aside isolated incidents of the odd shot being fired from passing cars and stones and bottles being thrown, there were more than thirty quite serious attacks on my home during those years, and the departure of the police guard meant the responsibility for protecting my family and home became mine. The bullet-proof windows were particular targets, usually on Saturday night or Sunday morning. The attackers came prepared, carrying sledgehammers and/or concrete blocks to throw at the windows. I would often sit up, waiting for them, the lights off and the double-barrel shotgun at my side. On one occasion I heard them coming, slipped out the back door and had three of them in my sights as a sledgehammer was raised. I had often wondered what I would do if such an opportunity presented itself. I was tempted, but shot over their heads and watched them run away like the cowards they were.

We continued to live in these conditions until we left the house, which meant that for a period of twenty years our home was regularly attacked and my wife and children suffered for my political activities. And it wasn't only at home that they came under pressure. It was only in later years that I learned of the intimidation at school, on the school bus, at sport and recreation. They hid it from me at the time. Nor was it confined to my immediate family. Some of my brothers and sisters and their families also suffered from attempted intimidation. Many Catholic families were split politically. It was not unknown in a large family for some to support the SDLP while others supported the Provos, the Officials, or Alliance. I was lucky in that all of my family supported me politically, and indeed I was doubly lucky to have the support of a large number of in-laws as well. As the competition between the SDLP and the Provos intensified, particularly during and after the hunger strikes, many of my relatives experienced the consequences of Provo wrath.

Despite SDLP warnings, in public and private, Merlyn Rees pressed ahead with his plan for a Constitutional Convention, which was held on 1 May 1975. Less than a year after the fall of the Executive, and despite our deep and bitter disappointment and anger over the manner in which it had been brought down, our serious doubts on future British intentions and our scepticism regarding the possibility of agreement, the SDLP nonetheless fought the election on a strong theme of partnership between North and South. Tom Daly and I were again candidates in Fermanagh–South Tyrone, a five-seat constituency, and we were joined on the ticket by Tom Murray from South Fermanagh.

The republican movement decided to boycott 'this British-imposed election' and it turned out to be a bitter and acrimonious contest. I said at the time it was almost as if a candidate called 'Boycott' was running. Throughout the campaign I was a major target, particularly in relation to the 25p collection charge. Intimidation was rife. Postal voting had been extended at the time of the Border Poll in an effort to reduce intimidation. Now, so-called 'republicans' were pressurising elderly and sick people to hand over their postal ballots for public burnings. Postmen were held up and postal votes (and in some cases all the mail) stolen from them. On the morning of polling, bombs were planted in a number of nationalist areas and trees were cut down on approach roads to polling stations. At Galbally, three miles from my home, I witnessed the names of voters being noted down by known republicans, with the implied threat that action would follow; this happened in a number of areas. Cars with PA systems toured the housing estates advocating boycott, while SDLP cars transporting voters to the polls were attacked and windows in the tally rooms were smashed. In Coalisland, the roadway leading to the main polling station was blocked off three hours before the polls closed. SDLP posters did not have a long lifespan!

Father Denis Faul, rather surprisingly and, I thought, naively, advocated boycott as a protest against the continuation of internment. He had not foreseen how Provos would use his call and when I, rather angrily I admit, pointed out that his statement was being distributed with the Provo boycott literature, he issued a statement deploring the attempts being made to link his action with that of the Provisionals. He stated his only intention had been to make internment an issue in the election. I think Fr Faul learned a valuable lesson, one which stood him in good stead in his extremely valuable and courageous work in the future: the Provos would use anyone and anything to their advantage.

Most of the boycott activity was confined to my end of the constituency and in Catholic areas, so I was the one most affected. I still managed to be elected on the first count, 1,141 votes above the quota, but my vote was down 1,032 from the Assembly election in 1973 and Harry West topped the poll. Republican abstentionism prevented the SDLP from taking three seats out of five. The vicious nature of that campaign prepared me for what was to come when the Provos entered the political arena fully, with 'a ballot paper in one hand and an armalite in the other'.

The purpose of the Constitutional Convention was 'to consider what provision for the government of Northern Ireland is likely to command the most widespread acceptance throughout the whole community'. As I had predicted in my Oxford Union speech, there was no hope of agreement in the Convention. The United Ulster Unionist Council (UUUC), comprising the official Unionist party, the Democratic Unionist party and the Ulster Vanguard party, had forty-seven members, the SDLP seventeen, Alliance eight, Faulkner's Unionist party of Northern Ireland five and the NILP one. In other words, it was forty-seven to thirty-one.

I participated fully in Convention business, indeed was one of its leading lights, but like most in the minority I was only going through the motions.

There were some interesting aspects. I had, for example, wondered about the wisdom of appointing the Right Hon. Sir Robert Lowry, Lord Chief Justice of Northern Ireland, as Chairman; I thought that someone more fitted to negotiate, to wheel-and-deal, might be more appropriate. As it turned out, in view of the make-up of the Convention and the impossibility of the job the Chairman had to do, whoever was in the Chair didn't really matter. Indeed, in the limited role open to him, Lowry performed well, with integrity, fairness, common sense and good humour, not always the attributes I had identified with judicial figures in the North. Additionally, he had two able advisors, John Oliver, my former Permanent Secretary, and Maurice Hayes, who had helped to mastermind Down's All-Ireland victory in 1961 (the first time a team had brought the Sam Maguire cup across the border), was former Chairman of the Community Relations Commission and a man with sensitive political antennae. They helped to keep the Lord Chief Justice in the land of political reality.

Along with Paddy Devlin and Seamus Mallon, I was asked to serve on the Rules Committee, among whose members were Paisley and Taylor and the newly elected David Trimble. Not that it really mattered who represented the SDLP on a committee chaired by Paisley and a majority UUUC membership determined to do whatever was necessary to ensure a report that would recommend a majority-rule government and Parliament. Since I expected little, there was only one real disappointment. In an attempt to open our minds to possible constitutional models in the wider world, someone had suggested we should visit a number of countries, namely Holland, Belgium, Switzerland ... and Fiji. The UUUC were having no part of it. Maybe Paisley feared the effect of grass skirts on his delegation!

There was, however, one surprising development. Hume, Devlin and I were involved in bilaterals with the other parties, something that appeared to be a pretty useless exercise, when all of a sudden Bill Craig, who was Chairman of the particular UUUC committee, put forward a proposal for voluntary coalition. I was surprised, but not shocked. I had known Craig well when he was Minister of Development, before civil rights. Indeed, I had been his 'shadow' when the Nationalist party became the official opposition. Furthermore, it was not unusual, after hours of committee discussion on the New Towns Bill, for us to have a drink, or two, together afterwards. After 5 October in Derry, Craig had become stubborn and arrogant, easy for us to demonise and, on occasions, I wondered about his mental stability. But in those relatively stress-free early days he was innovative. Now here he was, while professing his undying hostility to what he called 'imposed' power-sharing à la Sunningdale, proposing a voluntary coalition for the duration of Northern Ireland's emergency similar to the coalition in Britain during the two world wars. To add to our interest, he was prepared to be liberal in his definition of what would constitute an emergency, extending it beyond law and order and security matters to the necessity for a period of stability for economic regeneration.

Naturally, the SDLP delegation was interested. It was the only positive proposal on the horizon. An indication of support for SDLP Ministers in government in any circumstances, from any section of the loyalist coalition, was in itself a major advance. Could we handle it in such a way that it could be negotiated and advanced to an arrangement we would find acceptable? Or, failing that, could we bring about a split in the apparently rock-solid unity of the UUUC? And if we could reach agreement, could we sell it to our party and supporters, particularly if Craig was to be Prime Minister, as he clearly wished to be? After all, it was Craig who had said only three years earlier, 'if and when the politicians fail us, it may be our job to liquidate the enemy'. Faulkner had been hard enough to sell; would Craig be tolerated? We could also see the advantage of a period in government long enough to allow the concept of power- or responsibility-sharing to become accepted.

Clearly we had to know who Craig was speaking for and if he was speaking for a majority in the UUUC. Could we negotiate sufficiently water-tight guarantees to be sure we were not being sold a pig in a poke and find ourselves in a position where we had been seduced from power-sharing 'as of right', only to have the new arrangements collapse around as?

The genesis of the Craig approach to the SDLP was based on Paragraph 8 of the UUUC policy document, relating to the possibility of coalition government, and particularly subsection (iii), which stated, 'where an emergency or crisis situation exists and parties by agreement come together in the national interest for the duration of the crisis'. The proposition was that an emergency did exist because of the security and economic situations. To deal with that emergency, political parties would join together in government for a limited period of time, on the basis of an agreed programme. The questions which had to be answered included the length of the period, the programme of social, economic, security and other policies on which the government would be based, the powers to be devolved to it and the guarantees and safeguards required by the participants.

From an SDLP viewpoint, there were obvious dangers. The voluntary coalition proposal was based on the British wartime model, which existed for the definite period of the duration of the war and, at the end the war, would revert to the normal British majority-rule system. Throughout the emergency period the Prime Minister retained the right to select the Cabinet, to allocate and change portfolios, to dismiss Ministers and to seek a dissolution of Parliament. Clearly, we would have been total idiots to have entered into any such an arrangement without the most water-tight and binding guarantees.

There was also the question of security, the lack of which had helped create the conditions the voluntary coalition was designed to remedy. What security policies would we have to support, or even implement? A government that would have a majority of UUUC members and would contain Craig, and possibly Paisley, would almost inevitably wish to introduce the most extreme measures to put down the IRA, but it might not be so keen to use similar methods against Protestant paramilitaries.

Then there was the question of 'the Irish dimension' in a situation where the UUUC was insisting 'that good neighbourly relations should be welcomed but that imposed institutionalised associations with the Republic of Ireland should be rejected'. Is it any wonder we entered into discussions with extreme caution?

The principals on the UUUC side were Bill Craig (Vanguard), Austin Ardill (Official Unionist) and the Reverend William Beattie (DUP), and for the SDLP, Devlin, Hume and myself. The back-up to the UUUC included a young barrister and member of Vanguard, David Trimble.

The SDLP delegation presented a Draft Constitution when the parties met on 26 August 1975. The Constitution would operate for a period of ten years and a Constitutional Convention would, before the expiry of the term, review its operations and make recommendations for the future. The Draft Constitution was largely the work of Donal Barrington, a prominent Senior Counsel and later a distinguished Judge in the European Court and the Irish Supreme Court, and it skilfully sought to maintain the basic SDLP policy positions while marrying them to the voluntary coalition concept. The following day, in a public statement on the UUUC policy document, the party expressed interest in voluntary coalition and guardedly said it would welcome more information as to the UUUC thinking on the proposal. 'The SDLP is very conscious of the emergency and crisis which exists in Northern Ireland at the present time and is open to all suggestions as to how this might be surmounted in the interest of the people of Northern Ireland.'

The discussions between the SDLP delegates and the UUUC

representatives were more positive and constructive than I had anticipated. We realistically examined our problems, the reasons for our differences and the great difficulties involved in bridging the divide. We talked about the guarantees, the 'copper-fastened guarantees', each side would require. We discussed social and economic policies and, just as in the discussions at Stormont Castle, prior to Sunningdale, the more radical proposals of the SDLP gained acceptance, and we felt that progress could be made on this front. Even in relation to security policy we found convergence of ideas. The SDLP view on the necessity for Executive control over the security forces had hardened since Sunningdale, and the UUUC proposal for a locally recruited security force to replace the British Army in addition to the police was of interest to us if a way could be found to guarantee its impartiality. This was, of course, a big 'if' and the spectre of the B Specials loomed large, but the very fact that such a discussion was considered useful was an indication of how wide-ranging the debates were and the realistic terms in which they were conducted. Beattie and Ardill seemed as enthusiastic as Craig.

What happened next later became a matter of controversy, so I will quote from the Chairman, Lord Lowry, speaking in the Convention on 3 October:

'On Thursday 28th August at four o'clock the six negotiators came to see me. They said they had reached an impasse. American committees were very briefly discussed. They said that nobody was particularly interested in that. I said, "In what way can I help if you have reached an impasse?" All six said, "We are by no means committed but Paragraph 8 (iii) has been discussed. We would like you to see the two groups separately in order to see whether there is any possibility of any progress being made on Paragraph 8 (iii)." I agreed to do so. I would make it quite clear that none of the six gentlemen present expressed any commitment or any definite support or even any definite interest in Paragraph 8 (iii). That I must stay in fairness to everybody, including myself. Later on, on Wednesday the 3rd September, the three UUUC negotiators came to see me. They requested me to prepare a paper on a voluntary coalition solution. I said I would do so provided the SDLP also wished it. An hour later I confirmed with the SDLP that its representatives would also like such a paper. That paper was issued on the 4th September.'

Bill Craig said in the same debate, 'I should like to confirm that the document you, Mr Chairman, prepared on the voluntary coalition was prepared at the request of the three negotiators representing the United Unionist Council and, furthermore, that the three of us made that request with the approval of our policy committee.'

Five days after the request for a paper on a voluntary coalition solution, on 8 September, the UUUC rejected power-sharing with the SDLP in any circumstances. The motion was proposed by Paisley and only Craig voted against it. There were two abstentions, but both Beattie and Ardill voted for the motion. In the Convention also on 3 October, Beattie attempted to justify his position by saying that the suggestion for the paper came from the Chairman, but Lord Lowry quickly intervened, as I have already quoted. John Hume commented on Beattie's performance: 'Rarely have I had the experience of hearing a public representative coming to the Dispatch Box to twist facts in such a manner in order to preserve his political skin.' Devlin and I were even more scathing. Beattie was deputy leader of the DUP, and in the private discussions we had held he had been fully in support of Craig, even more so than Ardill. Craig's isolation in the UUUC on voluntary coalition with the SDLP effectively meant the end of his political career. He announced his resignation from the leadership of Vanguard at a press conference a few days later, flanked by Glen Barr and David Trimble. I'm glad to say that this disreputable episode also marked the beginning of the end of influence within the DUP for William Beattie.

It was Paisley who had pulled the plug. Paisley's career has been motivated more by religion than by politics. On the occasions he has had to make a choice between looking after the interests of the Free Presbyterian Church and his political career, the Church has always won. The future of his Church has also determined his attitude to holding political office. The Church is anti-Establishment, and for Paisley to become an Establishment political figure would be incompatible with his religious philosophy. Thirty years later, I believe this still to be the case. In this instance, leading figures in the Church expressed their total opposition to any form of participation in government with the SDLP, and Paisley responded accordingly.

In the aftermath of the UUUC decision on voluntary coalition, it was suggested by some of his former colleagues that Bill Craig had been less than honest in his dealings with the SDLP. Jean Coulter, the official Unionist from West Belfast, told the Convention that Craig had told UUUC members 'that in return for allowing these people [the SDLP] into government, the enemies of Northern Ireland as our electorate considered them, they would allow us the re-establishment of Stormont and the return of the Governor, the Queen's representative in Northern Ireland. They would give their full support to the RUC. They would allow draconian measures to be used against the IRA to wipe them out and they would support the re-establishment of the B Specials.'

Ivan Cooper responded, 'The only thing I can say to that is that I feel certain that if the Hon. Lady member had been offered a package like that she should have snapped it up straight away.' On another occasion, Thomas Edward Burns, DUP member for South Belfast, said to Craig's face, 'I would like to remind Mr Craig that in Room 17 at about 4.30pm on 8th September he suggested that we should lead the SDLP up the garden path by giving it a seat in the Cabinet and then sack that person when Stormont was established.' Craig responded, 'my colleagues tell me that I was not there at 4.30pm on that day.' He had the opportunity to elaborate, but chose not to do so.

Whatever the truth in these allegations, which were repeated in private by other UUUC members, I have always tried to deal with people as I find them. In my discussions with Bill Craig I found him direct and sincere and apparently honourable.

Similar questions might be asked about the motives and intentions of the SDLP. Were we as white as the driven snow? At the beginning of the inter-party talks we were sceptical, cynical even. The UUUC was using the bulldozer of a majority to push their report through the Convention. There was a good possibility that Craig was trying to con us in the knowledge that a majority report would not be acceptable to the British government, and that any measure of agreement with the SDLP would improve its chances of being acceptable. An agreed report, whatever its contents, would have been seized on with joy by the government. But there was no way the SDLP was going to pay such a price. We knew that and, presumably, so did Craig. To a large extent the operation was an exercise in reasonableness, to prove it was the other side that was intransigent, and on this level the SDLP won. The loss of nerve by the UUUC in bringing an end to the talks meant that we were never seriously challenged as to how far we were prepared to go in relation to extremely sensitive and controversial matters, such as compromising on the Irish dimension and supporting a locally recruited defence force under the control of a Stormont majority Parliament. I, for one, would not for one moment have agreed to such a deal, and I am confident none of my colleagues would have done so either.

The ending of the Convention meant I was out of job after almost twelve years as a full-time politician. The pay ended in May 1976, and there was no severance or redundancy. Nor was I entitled to unemployment benefit since a politician was categorised as self-employed, therefore the only entitlement was to sickness benefit. I had a dependent wife, four children under the age of seven and no savings.

Reluctantly, I was forced to the conclusion that I would have to give up politics. A political career, particularly a controversial one like mine, was not considered to be an asset by employers. Even those prepared to consider the possibility of hiring me inevitably asked the question, 'what guarantee do I have that at the first opportunity of getting back into politics you will not desert me?' I would explain that the possibility of such political developments were remote and that the political landscape would be barren for a long time, but none really believed me. Teaching was the obvious suggestion, but I had only taught for a few months in London and I did not have a H. Dip. Anyhow, as one principal said to me, 'who would want controversial people like you or Hume on the staff?' I concluded that only an unequivocal public statement to the effect that I was finished with politics for good would enable me to get a job.

I confided my intention to John Hume, and within twenty-four hours I received a call from Garret FitzGerald, asking me to meet him. We met at Paddy Donegan's house at Monasterboice, outside Drogheda, where Garret pleaded with me not to leave politics. He recognised my personal situation and the fact that my family and I had lived in intolerable conditions for a long time, but my leaving, particularly at this juncture when morale in the SDLP was so low and the Provos were on the ascendant, would send out a message of despair and hopelessness. I argued with him, but I recognised the force of what he was saying. He couldn't make any promises as he had no jobs at his disposal, but he would talk to some of his friends to see if they had any suggestions. Annita and I had agonised over my decision to leave politics, and now I had to tell her I had changed my mind, or, more accurately, had my mind changed. As always, she rose to the occasion, and though she was deeply disappointed that the pressure of politics was not to be removed from the family (the police guard still remained at this stage), she decided she had no alternative but to return to teaching.

If I were to remain in politics, I would have to continue to do constituency work. In strictly legal terms, this should have ended with the Assembly, since the Convention was established for the sole purpose of determining a future government for Northern Ireland, but my constituents did not recognise the distinction and now, in 1976, although the Convention was gone and I did not hold public office, they still came to me with their problems. My SDLP former Assembly and Convention colleagues had a similar problem, and eventually the Secretary of State had to come to terms with it. He agreed that former Ministers, me included, would have right of access for constituency problems.

My difficulty was that no funds or expenses were provided for the service, and I was in a position where, without any means of income, I had to provide a constituency service out of my own pocket without any assistance from the state, not even for telephone bills, or postage stamps. Therefore, when Annita returned to teaching, she still had the burden of being my unpaid secretary, typing my letters and speeches, answering the phone, interviewing constituents who came to the house when I was absent, etc.

In the academic year 1977–1978 I was appointed to a research fellowship in the Faculty of Economic and Social Studies at Trinity College, Dublin, the remuneration for which came from an educational trust. I was never told who was responsible for this extremely welcome development, but I know Garret FitzGerald had spoken to the Provost of Trinity, FS Lyons, about the matter. Recently, I have again had reason to thank Trinity and those responsible for raising the funds, as the research done at that time has been valuable in the writing of this book.

I am also grateful to former Irish Commissioners Richard Burke and Peter Sutherland for giving me the opportunity to work for them in Brussels in the early 1980s as a part-time advisor on the EU anti-poverty programme; I was able to contribute practical personal experience! The contract was for only twenty days per year, but the opportunity it gave me, operating from the centre of power in the Commission on the thirteenth floor of the Commission Headquarters, the privilege extended to me of attending Cabinet meetings, and the unique chance it gave me to work with some of the brightest officials in the Commission, such as Richard O'Toole, Liam Hourican, David O'Sullivan and Catherine Day, all enabled me to widen my vision and, momentarily at least, to escape from the frustrations of 'the dreary steeples of Fermanagh and Tyrone'.

22 : MORE WESTMINSTER ELECTIONS

ollowing the Convention election, in accordance with the standing orders of the SDLP Assembly party, elections had to take place for Leader, Deputy Leader, Chief Whip and Chairperson. Gerry and John were re-elected, but at the prompting of a number of members I stood against Paddy Devlin as Chief Whip and won. Paddy was then elected as Chairman, the fourth position in terms of seniority. The following year John and I were put in charge of all dealings with the government and opposition in the South.

SDLP thinking continued to be influenced by uncertainty about the future intentions of the British government, and action focussed on efforts to have its position clarified. The intransigence of the Unionists in relation to power-sharing, as exemplified by the Convention report, led some members of the SDLP to explore possible alternatives to the policy of power-sharing with an Irish dimension. The policy alternatives we examined included a British Declaration of Intent to withdraw, a nine-county Ulster, as suggested by Sinn Féin, and negotiated independence, a position advocated by some loyalists. I favoured examination of all possible options and I was fond of saying that if a problem appeared insoluble in the current context, then we should seek to change the context, but it seemed to me that some of the suggestions being made derived more from frustration than from any realistic assessment of the situation.

Around this time, in late 1975, an opinion poll in the *Daily Telegraph* raised hope amongst some, and fear among others, regarding possible British future policy: 64% of British people favoured a withdrawal of troops from Northern Ireland, compared to 55% in 1974 and 34% in 1972.

South of the border, in October 1975, Michael O'Kennedy, the Fianna Fáil spokesman on the North, threatened the bipartisan policy by advocating a 'British withdrawal' line. Jack Lynch invited John and me to dinner at his home to discuss Northern policy with him and O'Kennedy. It did not take us long to realise that the purpose of the get-together was to talk sense to O'Kennedy. But it was also clear to us that O'Kennedy was voicing a view that was becoming increasingly common within Fianna Fáil, and one which Lynch would find it difficult to stem. When O'Kennedy left the dinner party early, probably not convinced by our argument, but in no doubt about the views of his leader and the SDLP, Lynch produced a bottle of Paddy whiskey, only to discover that John and I were as partial to his favourite tipple as he was.

I welcomed James Callaghan taking over from Harold Wilson in April 1976. Callaghan had first-hand knowledge of Northern Ireland, and the SDLP had a good personal and political relationship with him. His appointment of Roy Mason as Secretary of State was a disappointment, however. Mason struck me as arrogant and bumptious and, as is so often the case with small men, particularly those in a position of power and influence, he seemed to feel that he had to dominate every discussion. The former miner designed his own ties and loved to be dined and wined by the Unionist bigwigs at their country homes. In his favour, on the other hand, when Paisley attempted to re-run the loyalist strike, he nipped it in the bud very decisively, in a way Merlyn Rees had failed to do.

Continuing doubts about British intentions, fuelled by the pressure for change within Fianna Fáil, were having their effect on the SDLP. At the 1976 annual conference, Composite Motion No. Thirteen was debated, calling for the British Government 'to declare its intention of withdrawing to give the divided people of Northern Ireland the opportunity to negotiate a final political solution and a lasting peace in Northern Ireland.' The motion was proposed by Paddy Duffy and seconded by Seamus Mallon, but was strongly opposed by myself, Gerry and John. It was a tremendous debate, passionately argued by both sides, and it resulted in a victory for the opposition, but only by 153 votes to 111. However, it was noted in the media that of those Convention party members who had voted, there was a majority of 10 to 4 in favour of British withdrawal. In addition to the proposer and seconder, the supporters of the motion included Paddy Devlin, Ivan Cooper, Eddie McGrady and Joe Hendron. Also, a motion in favour of a study of negotiated independence, also proposed by Duffy and Mallon, was passed by 147 to 51. It was a chastening experience for the Leadership. We had won the day, but the fact that so many of the leading lights in the party supported a radical change in direction could not be ignored. The fact that a majority of the Assembly party, which had elected the leadership, had opposed Gerry, John and myself on the crucial policy position could clearly have repercussions for us.

The following year the agonising continued and finally came to a head in August over a policy document written by John Hume, which became known as *Facing Reality*. John argued that Unionist intransigence was a clear rejection of policies passed overwhelmingly by the British Parliament, and that the apparent acceptance of that fact raised pressing questions about British policy, which the SDLP had to consider seriously. We had come to the conclusion that the British government 'should state clearly and unequivocally that its long-term intentions while remaining in Northern Ireland are to promote reconciliation and an end to divisions among all Irish people, leading to the establishment of structures of government which allow both traditions in Ireland to flourish freely and to live together in unity and agreement.' All the resources of the British government should be used to consistently promote that policy. In the immediate future, and as part of the long-term strategy, the two governments should set up talks involving all of the Northern political parties. At the same time, the British government should enter into discussions with the Irish government on how best to progress a whole range of socio-economic matters to mutual advantage, North and South. 'The reality of the Irish dimension should be clearly visible,' the document concluded.

Nothing very dramatic there, in view of the debates within the party over British withdrawal and an independent Ulster. It was John's attempt at finding a policy to unite the party by updating the traditional policy and asking the British for a Declaration of Intent different from the Declaration being demanded by the 'greener' elements in the party and in Fianna Fáil. Opposition to the document should have come from the more extreme of the 'Brits out' advocates; instead, there was an onslaught from Paddy Devlin.

Paddy issued a statement that went well beyond criticism of the Hume document and which announced his resignation as Chairman of the Constituency Representatives Group (CRG), as the former Assembly party was now known. There had, he alleged, been an obvious drift of policies and attitudes away from that of a social democratic party; the document did not encompass the large-scale review of policy – involving, amongst other concepts, a look at ideas of negotiated independence – to which the party had committed itself at the last annual conference; the party was turning its back on its earlier policies and spurning the fruits of its own efforts to attract Unionists; the decision to 'push the Irish government into the front line of talks at this stage is an invitation to the Unionist party to apply a veto on any movement forward. Hence, we have collision politics on a grand scale – the ingredients of which total warfare is made.'

It was a curious statement. The document about which he complained was only a draft. Paddy could have sought to amend it at Constituency

Representative and Executive level as he was a member of both bodies, indeed Chairman of one. His opposition to a strengthening of the Irish dimension on the grounds of its likely effect on Unionists came from one who, at the previous annual conference, had voted for British withdrawal. At the time, I thought Paddy's criticisms were directed more at the author of the document than anything else. References to a statement by President Carter and SDLP support for membership of the EEC indicated quite clearly that John Hume was the main target of his wrath. I believed then, and I have no reason to think otherwise now, that Paddy's personal antagonism towards John increased substantially when John made it clear that he would be opposed to having a running mate in the coming European election.

As Chief Whip, it fell to me to handle the distasteful task of disciplining a founder member of the party. The public way in which the criticisms had been made, followed by the widespread public comment, including editorials, resulted in a strong demand within the party for action. Paddy had resigned as Chairman of the Constituency Representatives, but had not resigned from that body, and he was still also a member of the Executive. He had said he wished to continue as a member of the party, but there were calls for his expulsion. The only person who publicly supported him was Ivan Cooper, and that more for personal than for political reasons.

I was determined that no more action than was necessary would be taken. Politically, there was no point in creating a martyr, and personally, we had come through too much together since 1969 for it to end in bitterness and rancour.

At a meeting of the Constituency Representatives on 31 August, it was unanimously decided to repudiate all of Paddy's allegations, to view his conduct in making them to be damaging to the party, to accept his resignation as Chairman, to relieve him of membership of the party Executive, to suspend him from all party spokesman roles and to initiate procedures for withdrawal of the Whip. Seamus Mallon was elected to replace Paddy as Chairman, the party Executive unanimously endorsed the decisions of the Constituency Representatives, and it was left to me to have the decision in relation to withdrawal of the Whip implemented.

I wrote to Paddy the following day in 'Dear Paddy' and 'Yours fraternally' terms, informing him of the decisions and giving him notice that the Constituency Representatives would meet in ten days' time to decide on withdrawal of the Whip, a meeting he had the right to attend and to speak at. Paddy did not reply, nor did he attend the meeting, held on 10 September, and so the Minutes report: 'Motion re Whip: The motion (activated under Standing Orders) to remove the Whip from P. Devlin was unanimously approved on the proposal of G. Fitt seconded by J. Hume.' It was a sad end for one of the founding fathers, but in the circumstances it was inevitable. As one of the leading political commentators said at the time, 'The trouble with Paddy Devlin is that for such a sensitive man he does such insensitive things. His humanity and big-heartedness are celebrated, his kindness and social concern almost a legend – and yet he can be fierce and even brutal with others. That applies not just to those outside the SDLP but to party colleagues – as Austin Currie, Frank Feely and others can testify.' He contributed enormously to the development and growth of the SDLP and never let us forget our obligations to the less well-off in society. Behind the effing and blinding and the fiery temper was a shrewd political brain. And he was honest. Later, in his autobiography, he wrote of the events leading to his expulsion from the Constituency Representatives: 'On reflection, I regret the way events ended. It was a most unworthy squabble in which I was not an innocent party. I had nothing to be proud of in the exchanges.'

At the 1977 party conference, held less than two months after the events just described, *Facing Reality* was approved as party policy, with only seven votes cast against it. This decision meant that motions on British withdrawal were not debated, and it appeared that the campaign for a British Declaration of Intent to Withdraw was running out of steam. However, at the beginning of the New Year, Taoiseach Jack Lynch gave a TV interview in which he called for a British Declaration of Intent to Withdraw, and a week later, in a newspaper interview, the new Archbishop of Armagh, Tomás Ó Fiaich, said, 'I believe the British should withdraw from Ireland. I think it is the only thing that will get things moving.' These statements greatly encouraged those in the SDLP who shared those sentiments, members like Paddy Duffy and Eddie McGrady and, in particular, Seamus Mallon, who, since Devlin's resignation, was now number four in the party. Gerry confided to me, 'If the party goes down that road, it will do so without me.'

Other events in 1978 continued to push the SDLP in a more radical direction. Airey Neave, Conservative party spokesman under Margaret Thatcher – the party that looked likely to be the next government – declared that power-sharing was no longer 'practical politics'. Prime Minister Callaghan, now effectively in a minority government situation, announced an increase in Northern Ireland's representation in the House of Commons contrary to a pledge given to the SDLP and in return for Unionist support. In

August the *Daily Mirror* announced its support for British withdrawal. As part of their protest against the removal of special category status in the prisons, more than three hundred republican prisoners were now on 'dirty protest', wearing only blankets and smearing their cells with their own excreta.

Travelling around the constituencies as Chief Whip, I became aware that opinion in favour of a British Declaration of Intent to Withdraw was growing among our members and supporters, and that some members of the Constituency Representatives were organising to reverse the Conference decision of two years previously. It will be remembered that ten out of fourteen of the then Convention party had voted for British withdrawal, and they were now confident that with the public support of the Taoiseach and the Archbishop of Armagh they would be successful this time round. My opposition was based on my fear that the loyalists' response to such a Declaration by the British would be to jump the gun and make an attempt to seize control in advance of actual withdrawal. This could lead to effective re-Partition with enforced 'repatriation' of minority populations and widespread loss of life. Those who were pro-withdrawal argued that a British Declaration of Intent to Withdraw at a stated time in the future would bring loyalists face to face with reality, forcing them to negotiate with fellow Ulstermen of the nationalist persuasion and with the Southern government, and they might have been right. But they might have been wrong, and it was too much of a potentially catastrophic risk to take. Additionally, there was no way I wanted my party to be associated with the simplistic 'Brits Out' demand of an organisation that was killing and maiming on an almost daily basis.

I decided to take the initiative and persuaded the Coalisland branch to sponsor a motion, at the annual conference, which I would propose. The motion read: 'Conference believes that British disengagement from Ireland is inevitable and desirable; that it ought to take place as part of an overall political solution which would provide guarantees for both traditions in the North and minimise the possible dangers in the political, security, economic and financial fields and that the British government, immediately after the Westminster election, should call a quadripartite conference of the two Sovereign governments in London and Dublin and representatives of the two traditions in the North with a view to finding a permanent solution to the Irish problem.'

In the course of my remarks, I said:

'The SDLP view can be bluntly put. The British Government and Parliament are the sovereign authority. They have the resources, the authority, the power. They have the responsibility for governing Northern Ireland. They must be prepared to accept that the major responsibility for the resolution of the problem here rests with them. Either they accept that responsibility even at this late stage or they continue to abdicate it. And if they continue to abdicate their responsibility then their continuing presence in Northern Ireland becomes an impediment to a political solution.

The British created our problem, they are part of that problem and ideally should be part of the solution. I hope they will be. The only real role which remains for Britain in Ireland is to contribute to a lasting solution to the Irish problem.'

The motion provided the main debate at the 1978 conference and due to the number of delegates wishing to participate, Standing Orders had to be extended. I summed up to a standing ovation and the motion was passed with only two votes against and one abstention. The decision effectively ended the issue of British withdrawal as a divisive one within the SDLP, and the role proposed for the British government was eventually adopted by that nation. It took twenty years, from 1978 to 1998, wasted years in terms of death and destruction, frustration and despair, but the Good Friday Agreement was the culmination of the long-desired change of policy by the British government.

The next year, 1979, was a year of personal tragedy for the Currie family. We lost our father, aged sixty-eight, in a traffic accident. Given that our family was so large, we were lucky that this was our first experience of death in the immediate family circle, but it hit us hard. My mother never really recovered and died four years later, aged sixty-four. Like so many families of that generation, parents and children did not get to know each other well until the children were grown up, so it was only in the last ten years or so of his life that my father and I had an easy, close relationship, though it had always been good. My father had lived his life for his wife and children, always putting them first. Like most children, I only appreciated his role in my life as I grew older. He had wanted the best for all of us, encouraging us to stay at school at a time when extra wages would have been very useful for the family. He had great patience with us and with our children, who called him GaaGaa, and they too have happy memories of times spent with him on the farm. He had always been there for me, encouraging, praising, but also ready to be critical if he thought it necessary. His death left a void in my life and for years afterwards there were times when I wished he was there to consult, to share with, and to love.

At the height of the mourning process I was forced to take political decisions. Just five days after the funeral, nominations closed in a by-election to fill two seats on Dungannon District Council. The vacancies had been caused by the death of Joe Higgins, an SDLP councillor, and the resignation of Major Hamilton Stubber, an official Unionist. I felt it was imperative that the SDLP run a candidate, otherwise an extra Unionist or Provo-backed Independent would take the seats. Prior to my father's death, I had been trying to persuade the late councillor's son to run. Now, two days before nominations closed, he gave me a final negative answer and another alternative candidate also declined. I was left with no option but to consider running myself. I consulted the family in case it might have been thought disrespectful, but my mother said my father would have approved and besides, it would take my mind off the bereavement.

The interest caused by my intervention can be gauged by the unprecedented 82% turnout in the by-election. The Unionist candidate and I were returned, with an increase in the SDLP vote of 7.4%. It was a considerable achievement, but had taken a lot out of me, and before I could recover, physically or psychologically, I found myself in the midst of a Westminster election.

There had been two Westminster elections in 1974. In the first one, in February, which did so much harm to the Power-Sharing Executive, Denis Haughey had been the SDLP candidate in Fermanagh–South Tyrone. We had decided to fight the seat against Frank McManus because he was as bitter an opponent of the SDLP and the Power-Sharing Executive as was the Unionist candidate, Harry West. Inevitably, West won, but unfortunately Denis finished third, only 800 votes behind McManus. Finishing third meant the accusation of 'vote splitter' and that put the SDLP in a weak position when another Westminster election followed just eight months later. Added to this was the fact that West, now Leader of the Unionist party, was deeply unpopular with nationalist voters and his scalp a much-desired victory, all of which led to the nomination of Frank Maguire as the agreed non-Unionist candidate. Maguire won the seat.

Now, in April 1979, the dreary steeples emerged again and this time I was sucked into the flood. I had better explain that reference. It is taken from Winston Churchill, speaking in the House of Commons in 1922 in a speech where he recounted the history of the relationship between Britain and Ireland:

'Then came the Great War. Every institution, almost, in the world was strained. Great Empires had been overturned. The whole map of Europe had been changed.

The position of countries has been violently altered. The modes of thought of men, the whole outlook of men, the whole outlook on affairs, the grouping of parties, all have encountered violent and tremendous change in the deluge of the world but as the deluge subsides and the waters fall short we see the dreary steeples of Fermanagh and Tyrone emerging once again. The integrity of their quarrel is one of the few institutions that has been unaltered in the cataclysm which has swept the world.'

Almost sixty years later 'the integrity of their quarrel' was again graphically illustrated by three elections in the constituency in 1979 and 1981, which confirmed how little things had changed, how deep still ran the political and religious differences, how strongly the underlying currents exposed the raw reality of Northern Ireland politics.

Frank Maguire had a republican record, which was why he was acceptable to Sinn Féin in the first place in spite of his intention to take his seat at Westminster. He had been OC in Crumlin Road jail during the IRA campaign of the 1950s. He had rarely attended at the House of Commons, and in the four-and-a-half years he had been a MP, he had not made his maiden speech. In the vote of confidence that had recently brought down the Callaghan government, he had travelled to Westminster 'to abstain in person'. But what really angered me and made me determined that he would be opposed was his refusal to condemn even the worst atrocities of the Provisional IRA. His silence was the payment for Sinn Féin political support.

Once again the question of contesting Fermanagh–South Tyrone and Mid-Ulster became a matter of serious division within the SDLP, although less so in the latter constituency because in the previous election the SDLP candidate had finished second to the Unionist and Paddy Duffy was insisting that this gave him the right to be the sole nationalist candidate this time round. There were other complicating factors, particularly the imminence of the European election on 7 June and the possible effects of a split vote in Fermanagh–South Tyrone on John Hume's chances of winning a seat in Europe. But there was a factor in our favour: unusually, there was dissension in the Unionist ranks. The UUUC leadership had fallen out and Ernest Baird, the Vanguard member in the Assembly and in the Convention for Fermanagh–South Tyrone, was determined that his rival, Harry West, would not get a clear run.

On 7 April, four days after my victory in the by-election and just after my father's Month's Mind the SDLP Executive discussed Fermanagh–South

Tyrone, where a Selection Convention had been called for 17 April. Seamus Mallon proposed that we not contest the seat, but that proposal was defeated by 10 votes to 6. It was decided to leave the matter to the Selection Convention, and to hold a special meeting of the Executive on 21 April to consider ratification of the Selection Convention decision.

Unusually, therefore, when the Selection Convention was opened by party Vice-Chairman Alban McGuinness in Mahon's Hotel, Irvinestown, there was no recommendation from the Executive as to whether the seat should be fought. After a long and sometimes heated debate, the deciding factor to emerge was the possibility of a split vote on the Unionist side, whether Baird would indeed nominate against West. If this happened, then a split non-unionist vote could still result in a Nationalist victory.

I took the strong line that it was our duty to contest the seat irrespective of how many Unionists were in the field. If the SDLP did not contest, we would be seen as supporting Maguire, who had refused to condemn IRA atrocities, and we would be tarred with the same brush, and rightly so. But since I recognised the strength of feeling in relation to the split Nationalist vote and the disbelief of so many delegates that the Unionist vote would be split, I pointed out that there was a period after nominations closed when nominations could be withdrawn and that we could avail of this if the second Unionist didn't nominate, or, having done so, subsequently withdrew. It was not a principled position, but it seemed to be the only one that could swing the Convention in favour of contesting. If we did not contest the seat, we would be attacked as sectarian and equivocal on violence. But if we did not nominate in circumstances where two Unionists were in the field, we would be doubly condemned for throwing away possibly our only chance in the foreseeable future of taking the seat.

Eventually, this line of argument won the day, but only just, by 50 votes to 47, and I was selected unanimously to fight the seat, but with the proviso that two Unionists must also be standing. At the special meeting of the Executive on 21 April in the Europa Hotel, in Belfast, I was present as Chief Whip, but I did not have a vote. Gerry Fitt was not present, but Deputy Leader John Hume was in attendance. I quote from the Minutes:

'The Chairman, (Bríd Rodgers), explained that the meeting had been called to take final decisions regarding the contesting of the Fermanagh–South Tyrone, East Belfast and North Down constituencies.

Fermanagh–South Tyrone. B. Gillen and J. McGarvey reported on the Selection

Convention held on 17th April at which, by a 50–47 vote, it had decided to nominate A. Currie to contest the seat if two Unionists were in the field. A. Currie indicated that preparations were already under way to fight the seat.

The Chairman invited comments from interested members. These showed a clear majority against fighting the seat. S. Mallon was critical of Executive over the delay taken in reaching a decision on this issue.

A. Currie made a strong plea that the seat should be fought and said that a contrary decision could have serious implications.

S. Mallon proposed that Executive should not ratify the decision to fight Fermanagh–South Tyrone and that the decision should be made public immediately. D. McMullan seconded. The proposal was carried by 12 votes to 3 with two members abstaining.'

The decision made me extremely angry and frustrated. I could have understood it if the proposal had been to fight the constituency, fullstop, but to refuse to fight even in a situation where the Unionist vote was split was inexcusable. It was cowardly and short-sighted. It was clear to me that the resistance to contesting the constituency, in any circumstances, was largely motivated by fear of repercussions for the candidatures of Seamus Mallon and Paddy Duffy in the adjoining constituencies of Armagh and Mid-Ulster and that of John Hume in the forthcoming European election.

The decision not to fight was to have far-reaching consequences, some immediate and some further down the road. Two years later it was extremely difficult to argue that the SDLP should 'split' the vote when there was only one Unionist in the ring, given that we had refused to do so when there were two.

My warning of 'serious implications' had not been spelled out, but it soon became clear what I had meant. I consulted no one but my immediate family. I already had a nomination paper, which required a proposer, a seconder and eight assentors in the constituency. My mother proposed me, Annita seconded and my assentors were my brothers and sisters. This was done to reduce any possible 'collateral damage' to Paddy Duffy, John and Seamus. I then had to make absolutely sure that the terms of my candidature, laid down by the Constituency Council, were implemented. Had I nominated in circumstances where only one Unionist was in the field, my political career would have been at an end. Not only would I have split the vote but I would have been conned by the Unionists and have become a figure of derision.

Accordingly, I planned it carefully. The Chairman of the SDLP Dungannon branch, John Fox, lived two doors down from the Returning Officer's office, and his house afforded a clear view of everyone who entered and left the premises. When I lodged my papers, two minutes before nominations closed, there were two Unionists in the field, an Alliance candidate and the incumbent MP, Frank Maguire. In an attempt to unify the Unionist camp, Harry West had stood down and his nephew, Raymond Ferguson, was standing in his stead. Baird, as I had predicted, stood firm. I took no chances. For most of the hour during which nominations could be withdrawn my eyes did not stray from the door of the office, and for the last ten minutes I actually sat opposite the Returning Officer in his office in case of a last-minute withdrawal. It was only when I had his final confirmation that no withdrawals had taken place that I rang Dan McAreavey, the party General Secretary, told him what I had done and resigned as Chief Whip. Clearly my 'Independent SDLP' candidature and my responsibility for party discipline were incompatible.

Bríd Rodgers, party Chairman, and Seamus Mallon, Chairman of the Constituency Representatives, issued a statement: 'There is no such thing as an Independent SDLP candidate – a candidate is either ratified by the party Executive or he is an Independent. We are confident that the party organisation in Fermanagh–South Tyrone will abide by the decision made by the party Executive.' However, the front-page headline in the *Irish News* the following morning was, 'I back Currie in go it alone bid – Fitt', and another party founder, Paddy O'Hanlon, also publicly supported me and offered to canvass for me. The Chairman of the constituency offered his full support and Anton Rodgers, husband of the party Chairperson, came to my home with a sizeable donation for my campaign.

I was strongly motivated, and I had to be for it was a bruising campaign. I believed I was doing the right thing, that I was providing a voice for those nationalists in the constituency who abhorred sectarian violence and were alienated from Maguire due to his refusal to condemn its perpetrators. In my election manifesto I made it clear that I did not seek the votes of those who perpetrated or condoned violence. There was also, of course, an element of personal ambition. I had come to the conclusion that Republican diehards would make sure that I never had a straight run for Westminster, and the circumstances of this contest, with both traditional camps split, represented my best and probably only chance.

I had predicted I would beat Maguire two to one. Well, at least I got the proportions right. In an 88.9% poll the result was: Maguire F. (Ind.), 22,398; Ferguson R. (Off. U.), 17,411; Currie A. (Ind. SDLP), 10,785; Baird E. (UUUP), 10,607; Acheson P. (All.), 1,070. I was more accurate in my prediction that the 'split vote' would not throw the seat to the Unionists. While obviously disappointed at not winning the seat, I was proud of having been the standard-bearer for almost 11,000 people who were not prepared to be in any way associated with violence. I felt sure that as the bulk of my vote had come from the South Tyrone end of the constituency, I had a secure base for any future Assembly-type election. On a personal level, and continuing the Currie tradition of births being associated with political developments, Emer was born two days before polling day. Thankfully, this birth was without complications.

There was a price to pay, of course, for my rupture of party discipline. If I had won the seat it would have been different, but I hadn't, and having previously resigned as Chief Whip I now held no party office. I was still in this no-man's-land six months later when Gerry resigned as Leader and John was elected to succeed him. Had it not been for my adventure in Fermanagh–South Tyrone, I would probably have run for Deputy Leadership, with some prospect of success. As it was, Seamus Mallon took over without a contest.

Gerry's resignation came out of the blue. I did, of course, know he was unhappy with what he saw as the 'greening' of the party, as illustrated by the Conference motions in favour of British withdrawal. But this had been happening for some time – the big debates had occurred in 1976 and 1978. Paddy Devlin's resignation had been a challenge for Gerry, but that had been two years earlier, and in the recent election he had had his largest majority ever. At the party Conference at the beginning of November there had been two motions from the Mid-Ulster constituency that were mildly critical of him, and a motion from the same constituency suggesting talks with the republican movement had angered him, but there had been no indication of an imminent crisis. He and I had socialised at the Conference and in his wickedly humorous way he had left me in no doubt about his attitude to those he considered 'sneaking regarders' of the Provos, singling out Paddy Duffy and Seamus Mallon in particular, but there was nothing very unusual about that. His main concern was the increasing vulnerability of his family and home to attack by Provo sympathisers. Three years earlier he had been forced to defend himself with his legally held gun, and now he was fearful of the effect the tension was having on his wife, Ann, who suffered severe asthma.

The actual occasion for his resignation was the publication of a consultative paper by the new Tory Secretary of State, Humphrey Atkins, which proposed a conference where the Irish dimension could not even be discussed. Gerry had made it clear on a number of occasions that, for him, the Irish dimension was secondary to power-sharing. Indeed, one of the motions critical of him at the recent party conference was quite blunt on the subject: 'Conference asks the party leader to concern himself more with projecting the Irish dimension and leave others to project the British dimension.' Gerry welcomed the Atkins document 'with reservations', but said, 'I see some hope in it so far as it says in each of its six options that there has to be guarantees and security for the minority.' Unfortunately, for a document that specifically excluded the discussion of an Irish dimension, no welcome, not even one with reservations, was acceptable to the great majority of his party members. Gerry compounded his misjudgement by breaking an agreement with my successor as Chief Whip, Eddie McGrady, that no statement would be made until the party had had an opportunity to study the paper. When the Constituency Representatives met, followed by a joint meeting with the Executive, the Atkins *White Paper* was rejected unanimously.

There was strong criticism of Gerry and the statement issued after the meeting said that it had been unanimously decided that the Atkins proposals were 'absolutely inadequate' as the basis for a conference. It was clearly an embarrassing situation for Gerry, but his position was not irretrievable. There was no demand for his resignation and the spin could have been that the reservations he had expressed were supported by his party in even stronger terms than anticipated. I, for one, would have supported that line, and I believe John, recently triumphantly elected to the European Parliament with the highest SDLP vote ever, would have done so too. There was great affection for Gerry throughout the party, and only a few would have favoured humiliation.

However, Gerry saw it differently. He flew to Westminster the next day and that night announced his resignation at a press conference. As is often the case in these circumstances, differences tend to be drawn in black and white. The reasons Gerry gave for his resignation were quite definitive and concentrated on his opposition to and inability to be part of a party that had departed from its socialist origins and become too nationalist. These were precisely the criticisms Paddy Devlin had voiced when he left the SDLP, just over two years earlier. On that occasion, Gerry had proposed the motion to remove the Whip from him. In his criticisms of nationalism, Gerry seemed to have forgotten that at the time he joined the SDLP he was a member of the Republican Labour party. I was disappointed with him, and told him so. I suspected that he had given to the British government the impression that he could deliver the SDLP to the Atkins Conference, and was seriously embarrassed that he had failed to do so.

It was an uncharacteristic error of judgement for a man whose political antennae had always been finely tuned to the sensitivities of his constituency. His split with the SDLP was a major reason for his defeat in the next election. There were other factors too, particularly his courageous refusal to be intimidated by the hunger strike campaign, but his resignation from the SDLP and his criticisms of it left the party with no option but to run a candidate against him, and it was this that ensured his defeat.

When the Pope visited Ireland, two months before Gerry's resignation, Annita and I had sat beside him and Ann at Drogheda as we listened to the Pope's appeal to the IRA: 'On my knees I beg you to turn away from the Paths of violence and to return to the ways of peace.' It was a very emotional occasion, and Gerry was deeply affected. He was incensed when the IRA subsequently threw the Pope's plea back in his face. I believe that this experience strengthened Gerry's determination to confront violent Republicanism, and created within him such a strong abhorrence of it that it led him to detest even the constitutional republicanism he found in the SDLP. He paid a political price for it, but it was a price he was willing to pay.

Gerry's departure left me feeling even more isolated within the SDLP. John and I got on well on a personal and political level, but my relationship with Gerry had been special, going back more than fifteen years. John was a more remote and introspective man, and he didn't confide in me as Gerry had done, nor did he, I believe, confide in anyone in the party. When he did discuss things with me, I sometimes wondered about an unspoken agenda.

I had had an honourable defeat against Frank Maguire in Fermanagh–South Tyrone, but it was still a defeat, and my chances of ever getting to Westminster seemed very remote. Almost equally remote was the possibility of sufficient agreement with the Unionists to bring back a devolved Assembly at Stormont. Indeed, a future based on politics seemed decidedly bleak. I did not need the deluge that now descended on me.

On 1 March 1981, Bobby Sands, the IRA commander in Long Kesh (or the Maze prison as it was now officially called), who was serving a fourteen-year sentence for firearms offences, went on hunger strike for political status. Four days later, Frank Maguire MP died. These two events and the repercussions stemming from them were to change the nature of nationalist politics.

In 1972 William Whitelaw had conceded 'special category status' to republican hunger strikers. This resulted in a prison system where the prisoners effectively controlled their own compounds, responding to orders from their own officers commanding, were allowed to wear their own clothes, were not forced to work and enjoyed additional visits and food parcels. In November 1975, Merlyn Rees announced that this 'political status' was to be phased out, starting with those convicted of terrorist crimes committed after 1 March 1976. The response from republican prisoners was a collective refusal to wear prison clothing, which they described as an effort to criminalise them. Instead, they initiated the 'blanket protest', covering their bodies only with blankets. As a result, remission was lost, which added to their sentences, and there were no more family visits.

Outside the prisons, the republican movement and likeminded organisations began protests in support of the prisoners, which unfortunately were accompanied by the murder of prison officers by the IRA. The failure of these protests to activate sufficient support, or to put the desired pressure on the authorities, led to an escalation of the campaign, involving a 'no wash' and then a 'dirty' protest. This novel tactic gave them the publicity they wanted. Cardinal Tomás Ó Fiaich visited Long Kesh and described conditions there as being similar 'to the plight of people living in sewer pipes in the slums of Calcutta'. But there was still no widespread support outside the prisons. Indeed, the election of Maggie Thatcher in 1979 meant an even harder line by the British government. She warned: 'I want this to be utterly clear. There can be no political justification for murder or any other crime. The government will never concede political status to the hunger strikers or to any others convicted of criminal offences in the province.'

The hunger strike began in October when seven prisoners, including one member of the INLA, made five demands: the right to wear their own clothes, no work, free association, weekly visits and the restoration of remission lost as a result of the 'dirty' and 'blanket' protests. After fifty-three days the prisoners called off their hunger strike, with one of their number critically ill, claiming they had received a document from the government that effectively had conceded their demands – a claim denied by the Secretary of State. The circumstances in which the strike ended created a negative climate, which ultimately led to the second and more determined strike.

The strategy this time was to exert maximum pressure on the authorities by a phased operation. The OC of the prisoners, Bobby Sands, was the first to go on strike, on 1 March 1981. A second hunger striker joined Sands after two weeks, and others joined at weekly intervals. The IRA leadership opposed the strike, believing it would be unsuccessful and that its failure would harm the cause. They hadn't reckoned on the support generated by the intransigence of Thatcher and the commitment of their own men. Ironically, the victory achieved by the republican movement came not from their campaign of violence, which was supported by the hunger strikers, but by non-violence and self-sacrifice. Terence MacSwiney, who died on hunger strike in 1920, had said it was not those who inflicted the most who eventually won, but those who endured the most. I had often quoted MacSwiney during the civil rights campaign. I did not know his sentiments would be fulfilled in these paradoxical circumstances.

In the midst of this deliberately orchestrated heightening of communal tension, the by-election to fill the vacancy in Fermanagh–South Tyrone was declared for 9 April. The SDLP, as always in relation to this particular constituency, was in disarray and divided. The media speculation was that the party would fight the seat and that I would be the candidate. I did not contribute to the speculation. The memory of my treatment in 1979 still rankled. Then, my candidature had been opposed when there had been a split Unionist vote and I had a chance of being elected. Now, some of those same people who opposed me in 1979 were supporting my candidature, in a situation where there would be only one Unionist candidate and, almost inevitably, the nationalist vote would be split, meaning I would have to fight a rancorous campaign in the highly charged emotional atmosphere of the hunger strikes. On the other hand, I believed the seat ought to be fought by the SDLP, regardless of the circumstances. The Fermanagh–South Tyrone circus would end only in circumstances where it was taken as given that the SDLP would fight all elections there. Other parties or individuals would have to decide their attitude in the light of that fact.

So when I left home to attend the Selection Convention in Mahon's Hotel, Irvinestown, my hope was that someone else could be found to accept the poisoned chalice, but to take it myself if there were no alternative. I also had my long-suffering wife's advice ringing in my ears. She had put up with election campaigns that left us in debt for years, she had supported me the last time, even though she was heavily pregnant, she had campaigned for John Hume in the European election, had fed election workers, addressed envelopes, answered phones, typed letters and speeches, and now I was asking her to support me again in a campaign she knew would bring attacks on the house, attacks on canvassers and great physical danger. Worst of all, Annita felt this was being asked of us by some of those who had betrayed me in 1979. Her advice, delivered amid tears, was not to come back as the candidate. For once, she couldn't face the Convention, and Estelle accompanied me instead.

The Convention was chaired by the party Chairman, Sean Farren, and the Leader and Deputy Leader were in attendance. The Convention proceeded according to the usual, and by now traditional, Fermanagh–South Tyrone pattern, pretty evenly balanced between those who wished to fight and those who didn't.

Gradually, the smoke began to clear and a number of guidelines emerged. Under no circumstances would the candidature of Bernadette Devlin McAliskey as a 'H-Blocks' candidate, or indeed under any guise, be acceptable. Nor would Frank McManus or a Sinn Féin candidate be acceptable. However, if Noel Maguire, who was not thought to be as republican as his deceased brother, were prepared to run, as he had already announced, he should be supported. There were other suggestions. If the party Leader and Deputy Leader were so keen on the seat being contested, why didn't one of them stand? John and Seamus expressed their thanks, but declined. The name of Bobby Sands was mentioned only in passing; he had not emerged as a contender at that stage. We did not know it, but elsewhere that very night his nomination was being seriously promoted.

Without committing myself, I spoke strongly in favour of an SDLP candidate – with one proviso. This was a by-election and we should fight it as by-elections in the South were fought, which meant all party resources in terms of personnel and funding should be concentrated in the constituency for the duration of the campaign. Indeed, our friends in Fianna Fáil, Fine Gael and Labour should be asked to help us in saturating the constituency. Only on this basis could a SDLP candidate hope to be successful.

The Convention adjourned for ten minutes to allow delegates to discuss the options among themselves and when we resumed, forty minutes later, there was a discernible change of atmosphere. Noel Maguire had been contacted and he had given 'water-tight' assurances of his determination to fight the seat. Those from Fermanagh who knew him personally said his word could be trusted. When the vote was eventually taken, at nearly 2.00am, there were 59 votes in favour of contesting, 42 against and 27 abstentions. It was then unanimously decided that I should be the candidate. I took the precaution of asking Estelle to ring Annita to break the news to her. By the time I got home, my brave and loyal wife had come to terms with the situation.

I was pleased that the Convention had voted in favour of contesting, but in other respects it was unsatisfactory. It was clear to me that the commitment from Noel Maguire had had a strong influence on delegates. The high rate of abstention on an issue on which delegates traditionally held strong views told its own tale; the hope was that I would not be endorsed against Maguire by the Executive. I was therefore not too shocked at what transpired.

The following morning the newspapers announced that Provisional Sinn Féin was putting forward Bobby Sands, now on the twenty-sixth day of his hunger strike, and that commitments had been received from Noel Maguire and Bernadette Devlin McAliskey to stand down in his favour. Any 'commitment' from Noel Maguire would, of course, have been contrary to what he had told the SDLP at the same time as he was supposed to be giving the opposite assurances to the Provos. The media reported that Noel Maguire had not confirmed the Sinn Féin claim.

The SDLP Executive met the night before nominations closed. In their reports of the Selection Convention, John and Seamus both stressed the extent of division, especially in Fermanagh. The great majority of those who spoke, as I had anticipated, were against contesting in order to leave the field clear for Noel Maguire. Eventually it was agreed to issue a statement declaring that the party would not contest and was instead reserving its resources for the local elections in six weeks' time. No mention was made of Maguire, and the statement said that I had agreed with the decision. I had actually spoken against the decision not to contest, but I knew it was a gesture.

My only public comment on the Executive decision was, 'I am unhappy and that is the only comment I am prepared to make.'

Nominations closed at three o'clock, allowing one hour for withdrawals. I was in my office at Irish Street, Dungannon, with a nomination paper, signed by a proposer, a seconder and eight assentors, in the drawer of my desk. I had considered what I would do if Maguire withdrew, and had decided that I could not repeat my action of 1979. That would have meant lodging my nomination paper minutes before three o'clock and then, if Maguire remained in the field, withdrawing it at a minute to four. But then, maybe Maguire would use such intervention as an excuse to withdraw and the whole thing would degenerate into a farce. I had no alternative but to sit it out, and hope Maguire would hold his nerve and not be intimidated, or bluffed, or both. I was convinced that if he did so, Sands' name would be withdrawn and Maguire would have a straight fight against West, a contest he was bound to win. The republican leadership would not risk Sands finishing third, which would happen in a contest with West and Maguire. As was disclosed afterwards, Gerry Adams had two statements ready – one if Sands had a clear run, the other in the event of his name being withdrawn as a consequence of Maguire staying in the field.

Above: The Curries with President Eamon de Valera, 1973.

Above: Newly elected SDLP Assembly party, 1973, with Paul O'Dwyer from New York and John C Duffy, General Secretary.

Below: Founding members of the SDLP at press conference to launch the party.

Right: Founding document of the SDLP, typed by Annita Currie on her portable and annotated by John Hume and Austin Currie. 'In the' was added to make absolutely clear that the party was committed to the consent of the majority in Northern Ireland for any change in the constitutional position, and 'anti'-sectarian was substituted for 'non'-sectarian at the suggestion of Gerry Fitt.

1. The name of the organisation shall be "The Social xmx Democratic And Labour Party".

2. The policies of the Party will be based on radical left of centre principles.

These policies will be worked out democratically and in detail at the Annual Party Conference and will include the following aims ---

) To secure a just and adequate distribution of wealth.

) To uphold and support the democratic rights and principles of organisedv labour.

) To, promote the spread of financial, consumer, industrial and agricultural co-operatives.

) To work for the provision of a minimum living wage for all workersand to support the principle of equal pay for equal work.

To secure civil rights for all citizens irrespective of race, creed or political outlook.

To support the reintroduction of P.R. as the fairest and most equitable means of presentation and the one most suited to the needs of the people of this area.

To promote and encourage the development of all aspects of our culture.

To ensure public ownership of fishing rights of all inland waters.

To formulate radical policies for the agricultural, social and economic development for rural areas.

To work for the establishment of state industries PARTICULARLY in areas of high unemployment.

To promote the fullest co-operation in all fields between North and South of this island.

To promote co-operation, friendship and understanding between North and South with the view to the eventual re-unification of Ireland through the consent of the majority of the people in the North and IN THE South.

The Party shall be democratically organised at every level and will be open to all who accept its principles and rules and who are not members of any other political party or organisation. The Party will be ANTI— non-sectarian and will have no connection with any secraet, or sectarian organisation.

Above: Annita with Estelle and Caitríona after assault by loyalists, 1972.

Left: With son Dualta following shooting at home, 1973.

Opposite, top: Members of the Executive with Secretary of State Francis Pym and officials.

Opposite, bottom: At home in Donaghmore with Annita, Estelle, Caitríona, Dualta and Austin Óg, 1975.

Above: Addressing The Friendly Sons of St Patrick, Philadelphia, 17 March 1986.

Below: Victory in the 1989 Dáil elections. In the picture are Gerry Leahy, John Lynch and Tom Kavanagh, with Caitríona and Annita in foreground, and Dualta behind.

Above: With Commissioner Peter Sutherland in Brussels, 1986.

Below: Meeting the Pope in Rome after the Presidential election, November 1990.

Left: Inspecting Guard of Honour as Minister of State, Department of Justice, 1996.

Below: Wedding of Austin Óg and Hiroko, June 2003. Back row (*left to right*): Dualta, Sean and Estelle, Austin, Emer, Caitríona and Cynan. Front row (*left to right*): Annita, Hiroko and Austin Óg.

At one minute past three o'clock, I rang the electoral office where nominations took place and spoke to Allister Patterson, the Deputy Returning Officer. He confirmed there were three candidates in the field. At one minute past four o'clock I rang him again. 'Two in the field,' he said, 'Mr Sands and Mr West. Mr Maguire has withdrawn.' He might as well have put a stick of gelignite under me. My first angry reaction was, 'The Provos have won.' My second reaction was, 'The SDLP has lost.'

It didn't take me long to get the details. Noel Maguire had arrived with just ten minutes to go and withdrawn his nomination. He told the assembled media that his decision was a matter of conscience: his decision to step down could save Sands' life. Pointedly, he refused to endorse Bobby Sands' candidature, or to ask for support for him. 'For the people who would have voted for me, it will also be for them a matter of conscience.'

I have no doubt that Noel Maguire was intimidated, physically and morally. I have heard rumours that a gun was produced at the meeting between him and the Provos who were supporting Sands. That allegation didn't surprise me, but I do not know if there is any truth in it because Noel Maguire, as far as I am aware, has never told the full story of that encounter.

On election morning, 9 April, Annita and I visited at the polling station at Donaghmore. I was interviewed by RTÉ on the way out and I tore up the ballot paper that I had, illegally, taken with me. My action, and the interview I gave in which I advocated spoiling the vote, received wide coverage. When the ballots were counted, Sands had won by 30,492 to 29,046 in an 86.9% poll. There were 3,280 spoiled votes. At least I knew what had happened to some of the votes that had gone to me in 1979. There was also widespread personation. Just to give one example: a Catholic curate suspected of less than 100% loyalty to the Sands cause turned up to vote three-quarters of an hour after the polls opened, only to find he had, apparently, already cast his vote.

Sands' win was a huge victory for the republican movement. It gave it a major boost and was of immense propaganda value around the world, both politically and militarily. It was difficult for me to see a positive side to it at the time. Later, I was able to evaluate it more objectively and see that the Sands result turned the minds of leading republicans towards political activity and the possibility of an alternative to war. Although a welcome development when it eventually came, that was, unfortunately, a long way down the blood-splashed road. At the time, as a practising politician, I had to deal with the consequences of Sinn Féin's victory and the SDLP's demoralisation.

Unfortunately, the nadir had not yet been reached. Bobby Sands, or, as a gable wall in Coalisland described him, The Rt. Hon. R Sands MP, died on the sixty-sixth day of his hunger strike, on 5 May, less than a month after becoming MP. The writ for a by-election is normally moved by a Parliamentary colleague of the deceased MP, but as Sands did not have a colleague, the writ for an election on 20 August was moved by a Plaid Cymru MP, at the request of republican elements who wished to maintain the momentum of the Sands' victory. Gerry Fitt objected strongly. There was no need for an election during the summer recess and, he added, 'Have you taken into account the effect that a dead or dying body of a hunger striker may have? An emaciated body is a more lethal weapon in the arms of the men of violence than an armalite rifle?' His advice was ignored.

The following day *The Irish Times* had a headline which read, 'SDLP decision to fight'. Sean Farren, the party Chairman, was reported as saying that there was no indication as yet who the SDLP candidate would be, but the newspaper speculated on Seamus Mallon. On 2 August Kieran Doherty, who was serving twenty-two years for firearms and explosives offences and who had been elected to the Dáil in the June election, became the eighth hunger striker to die; on 8 August, Thomas McElwee, who was serving twenty-two years for the manslaughter of a woman, died; and on 20 August, Michael Devine, who was serving twelve years for firearms offences, became the tenth hunger striker to die. These deaths, and the possibility of many more as additional prisoners joined the strike, provided the background and created the climate in which the SDLP had to take its decision.

We already knew it was the intention of Sinn Féin to nominate Owen Carron, Sands' election agent, as a 'anti-H Block proxy political prisoner'. The 'proxy' referred to the quick, even precipitate, action of the government in barring prisoners from running. For the SDLP the important factor about Carron was that he was a member of Sinn Féin. The SDLP Selection Convention met in the Dunowen Inn, Dungannon, on 4 August. The Chairman of the Selection Convention was Alban McGuinness, party Vice-Chairman, and the attendance included John Hume, Seamus Mallon, former Chairman Bríd Rodgers, Chairman of the Constituency Representatives Joe Hendron and Executive member Hugh Logue. Again, the old arguments were trotted out, until John O'Kane, a Fermanagh delegate, introduced a new dimension:

'The British Government has driven all the moderates to support the H-Block protests with Thatcher's hardline attitudes and to call a by-election during the summer recess has never been done before. It shows the contempt by the British for this constituency. In my personal view we should not field a candidate because if we did a Unionist would be elected and Maggie Thatcher would be able to claim that the nationalist people no longer supported the hunger strikers.'

Eamon Flanagan from Enniskillen reminded delegates that while we had the greatest sympathy for the deceased hunger strikers, the fact remained that the organisations to which they belonged, the IRA and the INLA, were continuing to murder and maim, and Owen Carron supported their campaign. From among the visitors who spoke, Joe Hendron made the strongest speech in favour of fighting: 'If we do not fight, the Provos win, if we do fight, the UDR win [a reference to Ken Maginnis' membership of the much hated UDR]. But if Carron wins, he will go to the USA and help to raise thousands of dollars which will be used to murder our fellow countrymen.' John and Seamus also spoke in favour of fighting the seat, but not in terms of a ringing endorsement of the Executive decision nor in words or tones to galvanise the troops. I repeated my call of the previous Convention for the mobilisation of all our resources in the constituency, backed by an appeal for the Southern parties to involve themselves on our behalf. A motion not to contest was passed by 48 votes to 44, and the Executive later ratified the decision.

The decision was strongly criticised by other parties and by sections of the media, particularly in the South, largely on the basis that the party had left nationalist voters with no alternative but to vote for a member of Sinn Féin who supported murder and mayhem. But the truth was that the party was in a no-win situation, partly because of previous decisions, but principally because of the revulsion, shared by all of nationalist Ireland, of the callous and intransigent policy implemented by Thatcher. The ordinary nationalist deplored the activities of the IRA, but in the confrontation that had now been arrived at, Thatcher was English, the hunger strikers were Irish, and whatever they had done in the past they were now showing courage and commitment and were dying for their principles. Thatcher had forced people to choose, and the mixture of patriotism and religious symbolism won the day. In these circumstances, those of us who urged consideration of the broader picture – that a victory for Carron would be used in America and elsewhere as a mandate for the Provo campaign – were on a hiding to nothing.

The result, in a poll of 88.29%, was: Carron, 31,278; Magennis, 29,048; Close (Alliance), 1,930; Moore (Workers party), 1,132; Green (General Amnesty), 249; and Hall Raleigh (Peace), 90. The spoiled votes were reduced to 804 because of the alternatives for strongly committed SDLP voters. Three days later, Sinn Féin announced that in future it would contest all elections in Northern Ireland.

With the end of the hunger strikes in October, efforts began to retrieve the political initiative from the Provos amid growing fears for the future of the SDLP. Jim Prior had become Secretary of State in September. His undoubted ability was undermined by lack of support from Thatcher, and he described Northern Ireland as 'the dustbin of British politics'. The proposal he came up with was known as 'rolling devolution' – an elected assembly to which power would be devolved when the parties reached agreement. Prior was later to claim, and Thatcher to admit, that a chapter in his *White Paper* dealing with the Irish dimension had been deleted by the PM. Prior had no chance of SDLP support. His proposals were viewed as an exclusively internal initiative which excluded the Irish government and which, if implemented, would be a settlement that could lead to the return of majority unionist rule. We considered the proposals to be dangerous and unworkable.

I spelled out my views in a number of speeches in 1981, particularly in a debate at the Oxford Union on 27 February where I had said, *inter alia*:

'So where do we go from here? What lessons are to be learned from the failure of forms of government based firstly on Protestant/unionist domination and then on power-sharing? The first lesson is that Northern Ireland has failed as a political entity. The 1920 settlement had been a failure. The artificial state created had within it the seeds of its own destruction. It provided neither political stability, nor economic prosperity, nor justice for all its citizens, nor, above all, has it provided peace and security for its citizens. And a terrible price had been paid in human lives and human misery. Its failure underlines what has been true for centuries but has been disguised by the Partition experiment. The problem is not one of minority–majority relationships in Northern Ireland but that of a minority unionist tradition on the island of Ireland. And the question for the present and the future is to find constitutional or institutional methods of reconciling the two. The "Northern Ireland problem" and the "Irish Problem" is in fact "The unionist problem".'

I said the problem would have to be tackled in a new context and added,

'The new context is the unique relationships which exist between North and South in Ireland itself, between Britain and the North and Britain and the South, and between our two islands and the EEC. In their unique relationships and in this new context solutions can be found to our three "relationship problems" – one, inside Northern Ireland, two, between North and South and three, between Ireland and Britain.'

Clearly there was a very substantial difference between SDLP aspirations and what Prior was proposing in his *White Paper*, and this was reflected in our discussions. The issue was not whether we found his proposals acceptable, but whether to participate at all in the election he had called for 20 October 1982. There was strong support within the party for boycott. I argued strongly in favour of fighting the election, entering the Assembly, proposing a motion supporting power-sharing on the first day and then withdrawing when the Unionist majority voted it down. The strength of my advocacy was boosted by my belief that the SDLP was in existence to fight elections, that boycotting would be a return to the barren policies of old nationalism, and that we should have learned the lesson of our recent non-participation in the Fermanagh–South Tyrone by-elections.

There was another factor worthy of consideration. Participation in the Assembly, even for only one day, would entitle us to salaries and expenses and we could once again operate as full-time politicians. Only two SDLP members held paid political office: John had been in the European Parliament since 1979; Seamus had been appointed to the Irish Senate by Charlie Haughey a few months previously. There was no doubt that the party's performance had suffered because so many of us had to devote time to earning a living.

The decision finally reached was the worst of both worlds. We decided to fight the election, but not to take our seats. Had we boycotted, we would have forced Sinn Féin and the Irish Independence party to do likewise and Prior might not have gone ahead. A decision to take our seats, even for a day, would have had the financial advantage I have mentioned. The decision we took was a compromise. I eventually voted for it because of my abhorrence of boycott politics and the vote was 25 in favour of contesting and 14 for a boycott. Even with the compromise, Paddy Duffy and Michael Canavan, in favour of boycott, declared they would not be candidates.

I was wrong to have voted for the compromise. It would have been better to have boycotted for we found ourselves involved in a campaign where the electorate, naturally enough, saw little difference between ourselves and Sinn Féin, and we suffered as a result. I waged a vigorous campaign, but it was my worst election result ever. I came third on first preferences in the five-seat constituency, behind Carron and Maginnis. Between us the three SDLP candidates received 12,000 votes and the two Sinn Féin candidates received 16,725 votes, in a poll of 82.98%. I suppose I should not have been disappointed in view of the emotions roused by the hunger strike and the negative message we were giving to the electorate. There was some consolation, too, in the fact that I had a relatively safe seat. However, it was obvious that something radical was required if the SDLP were to keep ahead of Sinn Féin. Overall, the SDLP had 18.8% of the poll and Sinn Féin 10.0%; 14 seats to 5. Among the five were Gerry Adams and Martin McGuinness.

The decision of the republican movement to fight all elections provided a challenge not only for the SDLP but for all the political parties, and indeed for the electoral process itself. All political parties depend, to a large extent, on voluntary workers. The definition of 'volunteer' changes when the worker is a member of the IRA or the political organisation inextricably linked with it. Indeed, in politics, as in all spheres of life, there is a big difference between 'request' and 'order', and when the possible consequences of a failure to obey are taken into consideration, there is a much better chance of the allotted task being performed. And often without much regard for legalities.

Not that legalities have always been observed in Northern Ireland politics, or indeed in Ireland as a whole. Very high polls, in excess of 85%, for example, are not brought about by voter enthusiasm alone. A high degree of organisation is required and the voters require assistance in a number of ways not always envisaged by those responsible for drawing up electoral regulations. A lot also depends on the time of year, not just in the climatic sense but in the fact that the new register comes into operation in February and there is a better chance of a high poll immediately after that date, before many people have died or moved away. Later on in the year the register can be reduced by as much as 10%, leaving an effective voting percentage of 90%. Most political commentators, certainly those in democracies outside Northern Ireland, would consider an 85% poll phenomenal in these circumstances, and 90% impossible. Nevertheless, I was first elected in 1964 on an 89.99% poll and in 1969 it was 89.9%. I was disappointed at the reduction!

Under the old Stormont, voter registration was the responsibility of the rate collectors and since in my area these were all unionists, there would never have been the possibility of winning an election if nationalists had not looked after the electoral register. Each January, revision sessions were held at which claims and objections to the draft register were contested. These were sectarian occasions: nationalists claimed for Catholics and objected to

Protestants, and the unionists vice versa. Indeed, in some areas the agents involved were called 'Catholic Registration Agents', and on the unionist side the work was done by Orangemen. In those days, when only two parties were involved, it was crude and effective.

In East Tyrone I had inherited a registration organisation that was largely based on the AOH, an organisation of which my predecessor, Joe Stewart, had been a leader for many years. It had carried out the essential business of registration, even at times when abstention was in vogue, and in my area it was its main interest. I added my own people for reasons of efficiency and also, of course, of loyalty and within five years I could boast that I had an organisation that looked after the electoral needs of nationalist voters from the cradle to the grave – and beyond! It was no idle boast. I had a registration agent in my local electoral area, Tommy McGuigan, who was typical of the older agents. He was a member of the AOH, as his father had been before him, and he inherited his registration duties from his father. Tommy had left school early and was employed as a road worker with the Council. For him, registration was a year-round process. He kept a copy of the electoral register at his home and updated his information on a weekly basis. Weddings and deaths in the local papers were noted. Often a wedding report would say, 'On return from honeymoon the happy couple will be residing at …' The cutting from the local unionist paper the *Tyrone Courier* would be triumphantly produced by Tommy at the Revision Sessions to back up his objection to the bride's place of residence at the qualifying date. He would cycle around Catholic houses in each townland – in later years my father would be enlisted to drive him – getting details of the birthdates of children and other data, which would then be laboriously written into his register for use maybe five years later. The contest between Tommy and his unionist counterpart, Tommy Kempton, was one of the highlights of the Revision Sessions, sometimes very humorous.

The humour began to disappear as the Provo campaign developed. Unionist agents became reluctant to disclose any information on the whereabouts of certain individuals, particularly those with connections to the security forces, fearing that the information might get into the wrong hands. It was understandable, but it was an insult to people like Tommy McGuigan.

The local information gleaned by the registration agents was extremely valuable at election time. The agents would know who might not be able to travel to the polling booth because of illness, or advanced pregnancy, or absence from home, or work, holidays, or whatever. Such information provided the basis for personation. The tales told by Gerry Fitt of caravans containing a variety of coats and even dresses, used to disguise the fact that it was not the voter's first visit to the polling station, were not all apocryphal. It was not so easy to do this in rural areas where people were better known to each other, and the party agent would intervene with the possibility of arrest and a fine, and so the postal vote became the preferred way of subverting the democratic system.

There were two types of postal votes. The first, the Sickness vote, was available for those who claimed to be incapable of travelling to the polling booth because of illness, the second, the Absence vote, for those who, because of their occupation, were away from their home area on the day of the election, including students, but not people on holiday. The difficulty about the postal vote was that application had to be made within a short period after nomination day and shortcuts were often taken. The well-organised party centralised the process and often the local doctor would be presented with dozens of applications for signature at short notice. Some doctors would sign without really looking at the names, but others took their duty seriously and would refuse if the alleged patient was not on his panel, or was perfectly healthy, or, occasionally, was deceased. Some of these latter doctors would have been surprised to see some of the applications they had refused to sign being submitted to the Returning Officer with a very good imitation of the doctor's signature. I had in my organisation an individual who was superb at forging doctors' signatures. He worked in a pharmacy and handled dozens of doctors' prescriptions daily. Those who could not be accommodated by a Sickness application often ended up as an Absence application. Commercial travellers, long-distance lorry drivers and students qualified, but holidaymakers did not and since elections often coincided with holiday periods, that was a problem. So a registered voter going on holiday to Spain might be applied for as attending a trade conference in Barcelona, or a pensioner overlooked for a Sickness vote might turn out to be a student. The Returning Officer could do nothing about it if, on the surface, the application was properly filled in and witnessed. On occasion, I would attempt to introduce some levity – an eighty-nine-year-old applied for an Absence vote as a student of Ancient History.

It was an abuse of the democratic system. It was fiddling, it was illegal, it was dishonest. But both sides were doing it, we only voted 'our own' and each side did it to balance what the other was doing. The entry of Sinn Féin into the electoral process changed that. In the old days, during their sporadic interventions into electoral politics on an abstentionist basis at a time when republicans did not recognise the State, or the 'Partitionist Parliaments', or the courts, Sinn Féin took pride in abusing the electoral process and even defended their action on the level of principle. I was elected in a by-election caused by the death of my predecessor, Joe Stewart. Three months later, Sinn Féin fought the Westminster election. Joe Stewart was postal-voted care of a public house in County Monaghan. Well, he had been a publican, after all!

Now, in the early 1980s, Sinn Féin entered electoral politics with determination and the old rules among the parties, whether legal or conventional, meant nothing to them. I had insisted that whatever 'aid' my workers might give in making an application for a postal vote, the voter should in no circumstances be deprived of marking the ballot paper as he or she wished. In circumstances where a voter was away on holiday, a relative would be given the opportunity to mark the vote. The Provos dispensed with these formalities. On occasion, the vote didn't even reach the house; the postman was held up and relieved of the post. In other cases, the postman would be followed on his round and the house visited as soon as he had delivered the ballot paper. Elderly people were intimidated, and there were instances where the voting paper had been completed and the envelope sealed, only to be steamed open and the vote changed.

Some of my agents had arrangements with elderly people, who were rarely out of the house, to collect their postal vote and deliver it to the Returning Officer. Now some of these agents were being threatened and forced to hand over the envelopes. One SDLP agent in the Dungannon area, as far back as the Convention Election in 1975 when the Provos were collecting ballot papers to publicly burn as part of the boycott campaign, had a gun put to his head with the demand that he hand over postal votes which had been given to him. He had concealed the voting papers under the carpet on which his 'visitors' were standing and they ransacked the house before leaving empty-handed.

It took considerable courage to work for the SDLP in these elections. Many of the Sinn Féin workers saw the election as an extension of their war campaign, which of course it was ('a ballot paper in one hand and an armalite in the other'), where both intimidation and persuasion were acceptable. There were housing estates where it was advisable, when canvassing, to drive to the far end and face out to minimise the possibility of being trapped. Gangs would follow canvassers from estate to estate, under the guidance of Sinn Féin activists. Posters were systematically pulled down. On one occasion I travelled part of the way with a team that erected posters every 200 yards or so on the road from Ballygawley to Enniskillen, over a distance of some fifteen miles – a job which took hours. Returning home after attending a meeting in Enniskillen, we found nearly every poster had been removed; we actually saw the 'patriots' at their work. On another occasion an attempt was made to force the car I was in off the road. I had the satisfaction of seeing the Sinn Féin supporter responsible convicted of the offence.

It was not just during elections that intimidation occurred. Known SDLP members and supporters suffered in various ways. Windows in houses and business premises would be broken and buildings sometimes blown up, or burned down. A stretch of road outside Coalisland was a favourite spot for hijacking cars for use in IRA activities. It was no coincidence that the vehicle hijacked was invariably SDLP-owned. Children of SDLP parents were more likely to be beaten up at discos and other social functions.

There was one polling station not far from where I lived that became notorious for personation. It had a large Catholic vote and I neglected it at my peril. The unionists postal-voted most of their supporters and didn't provide agents to stop personation, or just maintained a token presence. Because of intimidation, or the fear of it, I had difficulty in getting people to man the booths. Eventually I decided it was not fair to ask anyone from the area to do so. My brothers, Vincent and Brendan, volunteered. They did not have the necessary local knowledge, but supporters in the area marked the register for them: such a person was dead, so and so was 'on the run', someone else was refusing to vote, Mrs So and So had just gone into hospital ahead of time to have her baby. It proved so effective that in the first two hours of voting five attempted personators were challenged and arrested. When the word spread, the attempts stopped.

That night, just before the polling station closed, I received word from the police that a mob was gathering outside, angry at the arrests, and that the RUC intended to airlift my brothers out by Army helicopter. I did not want it to be said that Curries had to be assisted in this way, in my own constituency, by the British Army. Ivan Doherty, a Fine Gael official, later to be General Secretary of that party, had travelled from his home in Sligo to assist me in the campaign. He had a southern-registered car, which I thought might confuse some people, and having collected a burly member of the Coalisland branch we travelled to the polling station. It was only when we were near to it that I told Ivan the purpose of our mission and instructed him that under no circumstances should he allow the car to be stopped. I knew the location well and had arranged by telephone to approach it from the top end, away from the main entrance where the mob had gathered, where there was another entrance. We managed to get into the playground of the school safely, but with much heart-thumping. We had been seen, however, and members of the crowd rushed to the upper gate to block the exit. Again, my brothers and I declined the offer of a helicopter escape. We had hoped that the mob would get fed up waiting and disperse, but the opposite was happening. Eventually, it was decided, in consultation with the police, that it would be better to attempt a breakout sooner rather than later and preparations were made. The police made a sudden exit and, with batons drawn, forced the crowd back sufficiently to enable Ivan to drive through with minimal damage to the car and thankfully none to his passengers. It was not over yet. A number of cars pursued us along the road. Ivan didn't notice three flashes from the leading car, and I didn't draw his attention to them. It had been a scary enough evening without him knowing he was being shot at.

I recount these experiences to remind readers of the reality of political life in those days. History is being rewritten and those who now talk about their mandate and the sacredness of the ballot paper would prefer us to forget some of the methods used to attain their present position. But chiefly, I have told of these experiences to pay tribute to the commitment of the men and women in the SDLP – and indeed in other constitutional parties – who stood up to those with a Fascist mindset and refused to be intimidated or cowed. They formed a thin line that prevented the paramilitaries from being able to claim majority support for their barbaric campaign.

The circumstances under which the SDLP operated should be borne in mind when making a judgement on our handling of the hunger strike elections. Few constitutional political parties have had to operate in a situation of such raw emotion, amid the thud of bombs and guns, and have survived.

23: NEW IRELAND FORUM

It was the survival of the SDLP that was now a major issue. In October 1982, the SDLP manifesto for the Prior Assembly election had proposed a Council for a New Ireland to be established by the Irish government. It was a John Hume initiative, which he was to elaborate on in his annual conference speech the following January, and it had my full support:

'I am proposing the setting up of a Council for a New Ireland where all constitutional politicians committed to a New Ireland would together define what we really want this New Ireland to be. The SDLP is doing no more than asking the democratic parties in the Republic to join with us in challenging the underlying assumptions of British and Unionist unwillingness to change and in unlocking the key to meaningful dialogue with both. I am convinced that the difficult process in examining the obstacles in the way of a New Ireland will force those parties and ourselves to take many hard and painful decisions about the definition of Irishness, about the economic implications of unity by consent, about State–Church relations, decisions which they would ordinarily want to avoid and which public opinion in the South ordinarily does not consider.'

John added that the Council should draw up a definition of Irishness that would include everything it meant to be a Northern Protestant, including the sense of British identity, and 'following the preparation of an option or a number of options for agreed unity, those of the Protestant tradition should be invited to say how the proposals could be improved.'

His proposal was unanimously supported by conference. *The Irish Times* reports me as receiving loud applause when I said, 'What we are effectively saying to politicians in the South is to put your money where your mouths have been over the years.' I was also applauded for saying that the SDLP should continue to assert its independence of all the Southern political parties.

We had put it up to them, the government in particular, in a way that couldn't be dodged. Ruairi Quinn spoke at the conference, representing the Socialist International, of which Irish Labour and the SDLP were members, and pledged support for the proposal, but the following day there was some question that he might have been precipitate. There were bound to be members of all political parties in the South, including members of the government, who would fear a can of worms would be opened that would distract from the bread-and-butter issues. But all of these politicians were members of political parties, and indeed some of them had personally contributed to lip service to a united Ireland for generations and deserved no sympathy or support. We later found out that when Garret FitzGerald brought his proposal to the government to implement the SDLP proposal, though not of course in those words, twelve members of the government opposed him and only two were in favour and he had to be a bit devious to get his way. It took until mid-March before agreement was reached within the government, between the government and the SDLP, and between both and Fianna Fáil. By this time the 'Council for a New Ireland' had become a 'Forum' and all constitutional parties, including the Unionists, would be invited instead of just the constitutional nationalist parties. There was, unfortunately, no chance of the invitation being accepted, and so the original Hume proposal, as enunciated at the party conference, was effectively agreed.

Sinn Féin and others described the Forum as 'an exercise in saving the SDLP'. In part it was, as all the constitutional parties involved were concerned at the inroads Sinn Féin had been making into the nationalist vote, as evidenced by the Prior Assembly election. Additionally, it provided the SDLP with an alternative to sterile abstentionism, as the Assembly of the Northern Irish People had been designed to do when we boycotted Stormont in 1971. While Unionists and Alliance were performing in the Assembly, we were to be seen involved in creative and positive politics, preparing the way for a future constitutional settlement. It was also helpful for those of us who had been ploughing the barren Northern political landscape without pay. It was decided not to pay us a salary, but the *per diem* allowance and expenses were very welcome.

However, the concept of the Forum was much more imaginative, and indeed revolutionary, than merely assisting the SDLP. The idea was for the constitutional parties to, at long last, get their act together, to put forward proposals for ending the violence, reconciling the two traditions on the island and securing peace and stability – proposals which would form the basis of and a negotiating mandate for an overall agreement between Ireland and Britain.

The New Ireland Forum had its first formal meeting in Dublin Castle on 30 May 1983. It was a historic occasion, but doubly so for Northern nationalists who, for over sixty years, had been cut off from the mainstream of Irish political life and now found ourselves in these splendid and symbolic surroundings, helping to draw up a blueprint for our country's future. In some respects the setting was even more alien than Stormont.

The symbols of British rule were everywhere: St Patrick's Hall, where we held our Plenary meetings, with its ceiling paintings including a panel showing King Henry II receiving the submission of the Irish chieftains in 1171; the gallery busts of the Duke of Wellington, who is reputed to have said, in response to a reminder of his Dublin birth, 'Just because you are born in a stable doesn't mean you are a horse'; the portraits along the walls of Lord Lieutenants and dignitaries who had ruled Ireland in the British interest; the King's bedroom; the Queen's bedroom; the gunpowder room; and, most symbolic of all, the Throne room, with the throne presented to the Castle by King William of Orange himself.

In another respect, however, it was also more symbolic than Stormont, where there was not the slightest indication that there was another, non-British tradition on the island. Dublin Castle now represented the victory of that other tradition. What had been the centre of British rule in Ireland, what Michael Collins had described as 'that dread Bastille of Ireland' was also where, in 1922, Collins, on behalf of the Provisional Government, had received the surrender of the Castle from the last Lord Lieutenant, where James Connolly had been brought as a wounded prisoner before being taken to Kilmainham jail and executed, tied to his chair, and also now the place where the President of Ireland was inaugurated and great State occasions were held. Looking at its history from the two perspectives, it occurred to me that it was a fitting location for the great enterprise on which we now embarked: the reconciliation of the two great traditions on the island.

The four party Leaders – Garret FitzGerald, Dick Spring (Taoiseach and Tánaiste), Charles J Haughey and John Hume – met twice to plan for the opening meeting and to agree on the seating arrangements, numbers in delegations, etc. This body was to become the Steering Group of the Forum, where major decisions would be taken, some with great difficulty, as the Forum progressed. One of their first decisions was to appoint an independent Chairman, Dr Colm Ó hEocha, President of University College Galway, a choice that was to contribute substantially to the success of the Forum.

The party Leaders also decided that there should be twenty-seven members and fourteen alternate members, comprising nine full members, four alternates from Fianna Fáil, eight members and three alternates from Fine Gael, five members and two alternates from Labour and five members and five alternates from the SDLP. The Fianna Fáil delegation included several prominent members from their frontbench and former ministers, such as Brian Lenihan, Gerry Collins, Ray MacSharry, John Wilson and Rory

O'Hanlon. Their Secretary was Veronica Guerin, who went on to became a journalist and whose murder a dozen years later shocked the nation as one of the worst examples of the growth of gangsterism in Irish society. The Fine Gael delegation included Peter Barry, the Minister for Foreign Affairs, John Kelly, Nora Owen, Paddy Harte, Maurice Manning and future Fine Gael leader, Enda Kenny. The Labour party had in its ranks Frank Cluskey, a former leader, Mervyn Taylor, a future Cabinet Minister and, as an alternative, the future President, Senator Mary Robinson. The SDLP delegation appointed by the Leader was Seamus Mallon, Austin Currie, Joe Hendron and Eddie McGrady, and as alternates, Sean Farren, Frank Feely, Hugh Logue, Paddy O'Donoghue and Pascal O'Hare. Denis Haughey was our Secretary.

I was probably the only member of the Forum who already knew all the other members personally. In 1980, as an indication of my 'rehabilitation' after my intervention in Fermanagh–South Tyrone the previous year, I had been appointed as Spokesman on North–South Affairs at the same time as Seamus Mallon had been appointed Spokesman on Westminster matters. I had enjoyed the job and, if I may say so, I was good at it, representing the SDLP viewpoint to the Southern politicians and theirs to the SDLP. Access to the Members' bar in the Dáil was of great assistance in enabling me to do my job. Only members and former members of the Oireachtas and visiting Parliamentarians from other jurisdictions were allowed entry, and it provided the best possible location for me to have discussions with Ministers, Deputies and Senators.

It had its exciting times, particularly in relation to Fianna Fáil and the different leadership heaves within the party. My North–South role also coincided with important developments in British–Irish relations and gave me an insight that was to prove most useful to me in helping to prepare a position, through the Forum, for future negotiation between the two governments.

The first session of the Forum was opened by Colm Ó hEocha before an invited audience of members of the Diplomatic Corps, the Judiciary, politicians and media. The speeches of the party Leaders indicated their interpretation of what the Forum was about, and the differing emphases suggested, to the sensitive ear, that these, for now *sotto voce* differences might cause difficulty further down the road.

The Taoiseach, Garret FitzGerald, said:

'We often talk of the need to secure the consent of the Northern unionists. Perhaps we need first to secure the real consent and commitment of the South, a consent based on a true awareness of the political and economic realities and not on a myth or on bravura or on chauvinism. I believe we, in this part of Ireland, will achieve this true awareness through the Forum ... Moreover, given that there will be a newly elected government in Britain, the early completion of our work is clearly desirable in order to facilitate the process of seeking jointly with the government a review of policies with respect to Northern Ireland which should not be delayed.'

Charles Haughey told us:

'For the first time in sixty years political parties North and South that support the restoration of Irish unity by peaceful means have come together to determine what new political structures are needed to achieve peace and stability on this island. Our purpose is to construct a basic position which can then be put to the all round constitutional conference, convened by the Irish and British Governments as a prelude to British withdrawal ... it is the British military and political presence which distorts the situation in Northern Ireland and inhibits the normal process by which peace and stability emerge elsewhere. The process can only develop and peace and security be secured under new all-Ireland structures in the context of which an orderly British withdrawal can take place.'

A new constitution would be required for a new Ireland, he said, and:

'we may have to consider some degree of autonomy for Northern Ireland, be it on the basis of the same area or a smaller one. We have the example in the State of Great Britain, for instance, of Scotland, with its own legal system and its own education system, an administration in Edinburgh, a Cabinet Minister and a Grand Committee of Scottish MPs at Westminster who legislate on Scottish affairs.'

He reminded us that Eamon de Valera had put forward such a proposal, in 1938, involving a transfer of sovereignty from London to Dublin.

The Tánaiste and Leader of the Labour party, Dick Spring, put the emphasis on the economic and social changes required: 'The Forum affords us the opportunity to analyse and discuss the nature of society that we wish to see evolve on this island and challenges us in the Republic to face up to the reality that our society just as much as Northern Ireland will have to change if we are serious in our aspiration of Irish unity.'

John started with a pledge committing 'myself and my party that we shall not place the short-term or the long-term political interest of the SDLP above the common good', and asked the other parties to do likewise.

'The common good of which I speak is – and has to be – reconciliation. The reconciliation of the seemingly irreconcileable problem of this island. Let reconciliation start today in this room, between us ... There are two particular audiences to which we must address ourselves – the Unionists in the North and the British people and government. They must fully understand both the seriousness of our commitment and the effort.' *It was not a nationalist conspiracy or a nationalist rescue mission.* 'It is nothing less than a major effort to understand the encounter between our own ethos and the ethos of those who live with us on this island and who refuse to share it with us.' *There was a belief by the Protestant tradition on the island that their ethos couldn't survive in Irish political structures.* 'This should become the focal point of our deliberations and the central target of those who wish to join with us in that important task.'

As I sat there and listened to the Leaders of constitutional nationalism, representing the great majority of the Irish people – 90% of the nationalist population and almost 75% of the population of the island – a number of thoughts passed through my mind. The importance of the work we were engaged in and the major challenge it represented; pride that my party had initiated it and that our Leader had made the most relevant contribution; the potential for difficulty evidenced by the contribution of the party Leaders. The recognition that the differences of approach, particularly the emphasis of Charles Haughey on British withdrawal, mirrored differences within my own party. The unity of the SDLP, as well as the unity of the country, would require considerable attention.

I found Charlie's speech interesting for another reason. I was reminded of a meeting the previous September when John, Seamus and I were invited to his home, Abbeville, at Kinsealy in north Dublin. It was only when I saw the house and grounds and the splendour in which he lived that I understood properly why he was called 'the Squire'.

The then Taoiseach was accompanied by Brian Lenihan, the Minister for Foreign Affairs, and from eleven o'clock in the morning until about four o'clock, with a break for lunch, we had a most amicable and fruitful discussion covering all the important aspects of the current Northern situation. We had a pre-lunch drink in the private bar downstairs, a well-stocked bar serving draught as well as bottles and spirits, as good a bar as you would get in the best small hotel in the country, with the drinks poured by the Boss himself, the Taoiseach. Afterwards we had a splendid lunch, served by what appeared to be the butler. In the afternoon's discussions we had the only disagreement of the day, and it centered on me. I suggested that power-sharing in the North would be necessary, even in the context of a united Ireland. Charlie intervened to say that since there would be power-sharing between the nationalist majority and the unionist minority at national level in Dublin, power-sharing locally in the North would not be necessary. I responded that power-sharing in the North would still be necessary for both nationalists and unionists. For nationalists because the political parties in the South, even though they would have to adapt to the changed political realities of a united Ireland, would continue to seek power, and that a coalition with Northern Unionists would be the most likely vehicle to achieve it and that, in these circumstances, as had happened with power residing in Westminster, unionist local councils in the North would continue to exercise power and possibly abuse it. If Westminster had not been able to stop them, what chance would Dublin have? I might be wrong, but it was a risk we would be irresponsible to ignore. On the other hand, unionists would seek guarantees that in a united Ireland they would not be discriminated against. The sensible thing would be to build in the type of power-sharing the SDLP was currently demanding into a new Assembly in the North. Charlie was quite dismissive of my argument and, to my astonishment, since we had discussed this matter on a number of occasions within the party, I got no support from my colleagues.

There was another difference of opinion that caused me some amusement. In passing, I referred to a coming meeting of the British–Irish Association in Oxford. It was held each year, alternating between Oxford and Cambridge, and was attended by politicians from Ireland and Britain, academics, higher civil servants and opinion-formers generally and I had in the past found it valuable for making contacts, particularly as the SDLP no longer had representation at Westminster and we were not attending the Assembly. The Taoiseach responded strongly, saying no one should attend as the Association was 'a front for MI5'. I enquired if Brian would be attending and, having been assured he would not be, I suggested that the Association be informed since in the programme I had received the Minister for Foreign Affairs was hosting a reception at the conference. Brian, rather shamefacedly, said he would do so. Afterwards, as Charlie took us on a tour of inspection of the grounds and with great pride showed us the horses in his stables, Brian muttered to me with a half-smile, 'Damn you!'

I was amazed at the way Charlie Haughey treated his Ministers, and even more amazed that they tolerated the treatment. Grown men, some of them with years of Cabinet experience, allowed themselves to be treated like little boys. There had been two or three occasions in my dealings with Charlie when

I felt he was trying to treat me in a similar fashion. I had always responded negatively, and it was a disappointment to me that some of my colleagues tolerated his behaviour. I had always taken the line that in the SDLP we were our own people. We were beholden to no one. We were the people on the ground in the North, we were in the front line and our views were worthy of complete respect. I did not believe in kissing the ass of Southern politicians, irrespective of party.

It was, therefore, of some satisfaction to me to note that in his Forum speech, Charlie spoke about 'some degree of autonomy for Northern Ireland' and referred, approvingly, as might be expected, to de Valera's proposal, which would have meant the retention of a Stormont Parliament. Such an arrangement without inbuilt power-sharing was unthinkable.

Despite the initial expectation that its work would be concluded within a few months, the Forum took a year to produce a report. There were a total of twenty-eight private sessions, thirteen public sessions and fifty-six meetings of the Steering Group. In addition, sub-groups examined economic issues and different constitutional models. Written submissions were requested through advertisements and a total of 317 submissions were received, not only from Ireland, North and South, but from America, Britain, Belgium, France and Canada. Some were of great interest and quality, some verged on the idiotic. From the written submissions, thirty-one individuals and groups were invited to make oral presentations, which they did at public hearings. There was competition among members of delegations to cross-examine in front of the TV cameras and Press, particularly when the Catholic Church appeared. I had to be content with the Protestant Churches! In addition to the main report, and with the assistance of consultants, other reports were prepared analysing different aspects of the problem, such as 'The cost of violence arising from the Northern Ireland crisis since 1969', 'The economic consequences of the Division of Ireland since 1920' and 'A comparative description of the Economic Structure and situation, North and South'. Additionally, studies were commissioned on economic policy, the legal systems, North and South, and the implications of integration in the agriculture, energy and transport sectors.

These reports were valuable and necessary, but the main focus was on the political dimension of the Northern Ireland problem, on how lasting peace and stability could be achieved in a new Ireland and the new structures which would be required to achieve that objective. And, unfortunately, but perhaps predictably, as discussion moved to a stage where conclusions had to be reached on the central issues involved, it became more and more a matter of Fianna Fáil versus the rest, with a minority of the SDLP siding with Fianna Fáil. This is what I had feared from the beginning and why, at the party conference, I had sought to underpin SDLP independence of all Southern political parties. From the formation of the party up to the time I left it, I had always taken a very strong line on this, and I still believe that such an independent stance has been in the best interest of the SDLP and, indeed, of the national cause generally.

I enjoyed the Forum. I felt I was making a positive contribution, along with my peers, jointly involved in an enterprise that could make a major contribution to solving the Northern Ireland problem. After nine years of frustration since the fall of the Power-Sharing Executive, it was good to be involved in something that was hopeful, encouraging and optimistic. It wasn't just the actual work in the Forum, contributing towards the production of the agreed report. In a year when so-called republicans burst into a Pentecostal church in Darkley, South Armagh, and gunned down members of the congregation during Sunday service, killing three elders and wounding seven others; when a unionist member of the Assembly, Edgar Graham, was murdered by the IRA at Queen's University; and when Catholics in the Murder Triangle were departing from a lifetime practice of congregating near the back of the church in fear of loyalist retaliation, it was good to be able to travel regularly to Dublin. I valued being able to sit in a pub without a gun in my pocket, though, as was pointed out to me on more than one occasion, I was still inclined to sit at the corner of the bar with my back to the wall and a view of the door. Southern members of the Forum noticed other things too. Nearly all of the SDLP delegation smoked, while it was the opposite in the other delegations.

Surprisingly, the most obvious example of stress came not from a member of the SDLP but from the person I least expected. Just before Christmas strong views were expressed at a private meeting of the full Forum on a particularly damaging leak to the Press. It was the culmination of a number of such leaks and it was condemned by all of the Leaders present and by others. Dick Spring, who had been delayed at the Dáil, raised the matter when he arrived and blamed the Fianna Fáil delegation. Responsibility was denied by Charlie Haughey and a heated argument ensued, with charge and counter-charge across the floor and the Fianna Fáil Leader demanding a retraction or else he would lead his delegation out of the Forum. Sitting opposite, I had a good view of what happened next. Charlie had just said that he, more than anyone else, had suffered from journalists' stories. Then his voice faltered and he began to sob. Ray MacSharry, sitting beside him, tried to comfort him, but after a minute or two he had to be led from the room, his shoulders shaking.

I could hardly believe what had happened. This was the former Taoiseach, the most experienced politician in the country, a man who had had ups and downs in his career but had fought his way to the top and probably would be there again. Who would have thought he was so thin-skinned? It was later speculated that his breakdown came not from anything Dick Spring had said but from the publication of a book about him, *The Boss*, released the previous day, which had seriously upset members of his family. It gave me a new perspective on Charlie Haughey, and made me more sympathetically disposed towards him.

I suppose it was inevitable, in view of the nature of the subject at issue, that the SDLP delegation would find itself pulled in two directions. British withdrawal and the circumstances in which it should occur had been a divisive issue in the party only a short time earlier, as I have previously related, and still evoked strong feelings despite the unifying motion I was responsible for at the 1979 annual conference. Now, in the Forum, Fianna Fáil was insisting on making withdrawal central to any solution. In addition, another divisive issue began to surface – the importance to be given to the Unitary State as the only structure of government in a new Ireland, or as one of a number of options. This question became the most serious matter of contention as the Forum moved towards finality.

The SDLP members of the Forum had had the advantage of a pretty thorough preparation for the work of the Forum. We had a particularly useful weekend get-together in Gweedore at which a number of papers, prepared by Denis Haughey, Sean Farren and Hugh Logue and outlining all of the options, were discussed: a Unitary State, Federalism, Confederalism and Joint Sovereignty. The latter, of course, was not a new concept to the SDLP, as it had been central to our *Towards a New Ireland* document more than ten years earlier.

I was surprised to find it was a constitutional arrangement that apparently had not been given much consideration by the other delegations, particularly Fianna Fáil. When confronted with it at the Forum, some of the delegates found it difficult to accept, particularly those who saw British withdrawal as the central demand, without which there could be no solution. One leading member of the Fianna Fáil team was particularly scathing when I discussed

Joint Sovereignty with him privately, describing it as a 'Brits in' proposal. To him, it was not just a radical rethinking of traditional nationalism, it amounted to a sell-out.

My discussion with this leading member, a former minister, helped me better understand the somewhat surprising attitude of Charlie Haughey. I had expected him to support a more 'advanced' form of republicanism, in line with the image projected from the Arms Trial, and also because Fianna Fáil was 'the Republican party' and such a position would not be conceded to Sinn Féin. I also understood that he probably had his eye on the coming negotiations with Britain and was being careful in taking up a position in advance of anything his political opponents in government would be likely to deliver. But I thought these political requirements could be served by advocating unity in the context of a federal or confederal arrangement, as well as a Unitary State. I was therefore surprised to find that he was advocating a Unitary State as the only option – and disappointed to find he had support for this view within the SDLP delegation.

Seamus Mallon and Charlie were close. Charlie had appointed Seamus to the Seanad, and though he sat there as an Independent – and it was part of the agreement for such appointments (it was the same later when Bríd Rodgers was appointed by Garret) that the appointee was not expected to play a party political role – members of Fianna Fáil considered him 'one of ours'. Shortly after the Forum began, John told me of his fear that Seamus was becoming too strongly involved with the Fianna Fáil delegation, contrary to the now traditional non-alliance policy, and effectively asked me to 'mind his back' within the party. A complicating factor was the finding of a bugging device at the home of a family Seamus stayed with when in Dublin. The loyalty and commitment to the SDLP of the family involved could not be doubted. It had existed long before this incident and continued long after it, and the father and mother were not just party supporters but personal friends, particularly of Seamus, but also of other members of the party, myself included. I do not know the full circumstances, but Seamus was dissatisfied with the Garda investigation, apparently felt that his hosts were being impugned and blamed Garret. The whole episode did not help in fostering the good relationships necessary for the close harmony required at the Forum.

Eventually, the issue of the Unitary State as the only option came to a head at a meeting of the SDLP delegation. Seamus argued the one-option case strongly, largely on the grounds that if the Forum report was to be the basis for negotiation with the British, then it made negotiating sense to argue from the strongest position. It was an intense meeting, with Seamus receiving strong support from Pascal O'Hare, elected to the Assembly from north Belfast, a man who had always advocated a strong republican stance and who was later to resign from the party in protest with the Anglo-Irish Agreement. They were, however, the only advocates and the meeting went against them by eight votes to two. Seamus loyally accepted the decision and was later to play an important role in helping to end the impasse when he and Wally Kirwan, an Assistant Secretary in the Department of the Taoiseach and main coordinator of the Forum, came up with a formula that brought about agreement.

The formula was a compromise that described the Unitary State as 'the particular structure of political unity which the Forum would wish to see established'. The unitary state to this extent was prioritised over the other two models – Federal/Confederal and Joint Authority. This, along with the insertion of a statement that the Forum remained open to other views that might contribute to political development other than the models described, meant agreement was reached among the parties.

It had been touch-and-go, but at the end the consequences of a failure to agree exerted enormous pressure on the delegations; it would have been disastrous. How could we have hoped to convince the unionists and the British if the nationalists themselves could not agree on the type of unified Ireland they wanted? It would have set back the possibility of political progress for years, and the debacle of constitutional nationalists failing to agree among themselves would have given a major boost to those who believed that a solution would only come from the barrel of a gun.

Despite unfortunate differences of presentation, both at and after the Press conference, when Charlie Haughey felt it necessary to say that the Unitary State was 'not an option but a conclusion' and that unionist consent applied only 'to the particular structures of unity, not to the principle itself', we now had a blueprint for negotiations with the British government.

It had been necessary, in my opinion, to keep our options open as much as possible, and this had been achieved. But in another respect the *Forum Report* was an extremely useful document. Chapter Five, entitled 'Framework for a New Ireland: Present realities and future requirements', contained an analysis of the Northern Ireland problem and made proposals in relation to necessary elements of a framework within which a solution would be found. These proposals raised and transformed the case for a New Ireland to a higher plane, suited not only to the particular conditions of 1983 but long into the future.

While the Forum was sitting, and too early for the SDLP to gain electoral advantage from it, there was another Westminster election in June 1983, just ten days after the Forum had met for the first time. Those who feared for the future of the SDLP had their fears confirmed when Sinn Féin received 102,701 votes and 13.4% of the total poll, compared to the SDLP's 137,012 and 17.9%. John was elected for Foyle, but Seamus lost in Newry and Armagh by 1,554, and Eddie McGrady lost to Enoch Powell in South Down by 548. Gerry Adams won West Belfast from Gerry Fitt, who finished third as an Independent to Joe Hendron. Sinn Féin nearly picked up a second seat when Danny Morrison lost in Mid-Ulster by just 78 votes.

This time there had been no messing about in Fermanagh–South Tyrone. The SDLP annual conference had decided that all seats would be fought and the Selection Convention and the party Executive, for once, were in agreement. This time, to my delight – and to the joy of Annita – the poisoned chalice passed me by. Rosemary Flanagan, a mother of three from Enniskillen, bravely took up the challenge. She and her husband, Eamon, had consistently supported the SDLP, fighting the seat in all circumstances, and she had my full support. In an 88.6% poll the new Unionist candidate, Ken Maginnis, got 28,630, Carron 20,594, Rosemary got 9,923 and a Workers party candidate received 649 votes. Again, it had been a campaign where the viciousness and vindictiveness of the Provos was hurled against the SDLP candidate and her workers.

The *Forum Report* was published on 2 May 1984. Among its other effects, it gave a new focus to the direction of SDLP policy. We had fully committed ourselves to the successful attempt to draw up a negotiating position for Irish nationalism and now had to face the fact that in doing so we had reduced our significance in relation to the role of the Irish government. The responsibility was now on the shoulders of the government to carry forward the negotiations with the British, and we had to rely on its commitment, judgement and ability to do so. We couldn't very well complain. This was part of the plan, what we had aimed for and, of course, it was the responsibility of the national government to do so and the government had the resources to do the job effectively. However, we were the people on the ground, doubts about our viability had contributed to the setting up of the Forum in the first instance and we had to be seen to continue to make a contribution to the solution of the problem. It was essential that there be the closest cooperation between the government and ourselves, and that the government be sensitive to our wishes and problems.

Luckily, in Garret and Peter Barry we had two people in whom we could have confidence. I had first met Peter Barry in 1977 or 1978, and from the beginning I formed the impression that he had a real interest in Northern Ireland and a strong sympathy and identification with Northern nationalists. During the Forum, my colleagues in the SDLP and I always felt we could rely on Peter's strong constitutional nationalist instincts and we were not let down, then or later.

The SDLP also had confidence in the Irish officials who were involved in the negotiations. Ireland has been particularly lucky in the calibre of its public officials, particularly those in the Department of the Taoiseach and in Foreign Affairs, which had responsibility for Northern Ireland. Members of the SDLP came to know some of them very well. Since 1969, when Dublin was forced to recognise that a solution to the Northern problem had to be the number one national priority, many of the officials who worked towards this end were men of exceptional ability and they served well above and beyond what duty required. This was particularly true of those whose job it was to report on conditions on the ground in the North, making contacts, assessing opinion in both Northern communities, explaining Dublin to the North and the North to Dublin. It was a difficult job and sometimes a dangerous one. A southern accent, southern car registration, being agents of a 'Foreign State' in the wrong place at the wrong time could have led to a bullet in the head. Men like Eamon Gallagher, Sean Donlon, Daithí Ó Ceallaigh, Brendan Scannell and Dermot Gallagher were officials of exceptional ability who were later to distinguish themselves in high positions in the Foreign Service.

At this time, in the aftermath of the *Forum Report*, Daithí Ó Ceallaigh, who had served with me on the buses in Bournemouth, was the man on the ground and it was from him that I, and others in the SDLP, got regular reports on what was happening in the negotiations between the sovereign governments. His powers of reassurance were severely tested in the aftermath of the Brighton bombing, when the Prime Minister his government had been seeking to win over to support nationalist Ireland was almost killed by an IRA bomb and again, soon afterwards, when that same Prime Minister threw us into deep depression with her 'Out, out, out' verdict on the three models of the *Report*.

It was a very substantial political and diplomatic achievement for the Irish government to keep the show on the road after these two shattering blows. The 'Out, out, out' rejection dismayed and angered nationalist Ireland, including, of course, the SDLP. It was a serious embarrassment and humiliation to the Irish government. It could have destroyed the SDLP. The woman who insensitively had contributed to the death of ten hunger strikers was again displaying her unionist credentials. 'What was the point of talking to her? What had been the point of the *Forum Report*? Brighton was the only thing she understood.' These were the sentiments being expressed to me around Coalisland and Dungannon, and not all of those who expressed them were Provos. In the immediate aftermath our faith in the non-violent approach as the only way forward was tested. Many took their cue from Charles Haughey:

'To the Taoiseach I say, You have led this country into the greatest humiliation in recent history. You have failed ignominiously in an area of vital national interest. Because of your incompetence, misjudgement and ineffectiveness, you have done grievous damage to our national political interest and our pride. History will record that it would have been better if your visit to Chequers had never taken place.'

Fortunately, Garret, Dick Spring and Peter Barry were not blown off course by such comments and by the strong anti-Thatcher feelings in the South and managed to retrieve the situation. What Thatcher had done was inexcusable – in the words of *The Irish Times*, 'she is as offhand and patronising as she is callous and imperious' – but it was the three models of Unitary State, Federalism and Joint Authority that she had rejected, not the essence of the *Report*. The section headed 'Present realities and future requirements' concluded with the words, 'The parties in the Forum also remain open to discuss other views which may contribute to political development'. As John Hume was to say, 'There were four proposals in the *Forum Report*, not three. The fourth one was there because some of us foresaw she might say "out, out, out".' The negotiations continued on this basis, with and in the context of British hopes of involving the South in security cooperation to defeat the IRA, the apparently weakening position of the SDLP and increasing American and European pressure for a settlement.

Towards the end of July I received a phone call from an official in the Department of the Taoiseach. Garret was anxious that I be fully briefed on developments. Since it was now almost the August holiday period, would I care to join the Taoiseach in West Cork – and would I like to bring Annita and the children with me? Accommodation would be provided. The invitation to mix business and pleasure was accepted immediately. We had no other holiday plans. Garret and Joan were staying with their friends Gay and Jacinta Hogan near Schull, while Annita and I stayed in a bungalow at Bantry. For the week or so we were there, the Taoiseach and I met almost every day and we discussed the current position in relation to Northern Ireland in all its aspects. He was most forthcoming on the problems ahead and how he hoped they would be resolved. I gave him my view of the situation and how I felt the SDLP would respond to different scenarios. We discussed these matters around the table, walking in the fields, around the secluded and isolated house, in a small boat out in the bay, playing croquet on the lawn – I could not have had a more intensive briefing on the state of the negotiations, and I hoped I was helpful to him in assessing likely SDLP reaction in circumstances where a favourable response was essential. I even found a solution to a problem I had had with Garret from the beginning. He tended to speak nineteen-to-the-dozen, and I sometimes had difficulty in understanding him. My solution was to interrupt and say, 'Slow down, Garret'!

It was also a most happy holiday. The Hogans were extremely hospitable, the bungalow at Bantry comfortable, the people of Bantry extremely welcoming and the weather fine. Annita and Joan FitzGerald got on well together and my five children, then aged six to seventeen, were treated almost as grandchildren. Visitors would have been surprised to see how tenaciously the Taoiseach fought every shot of table tennis against my very competitive fourteen-year-old, Dualta. Estelle and Caitríona still remember him taking them out in the boat and giving the Gardaí protecting him the slip. All the children were able to enjoy the freedom and safety: the boys fished for mackerel in the harbour; they all went to the cinema, a rare treat; and Annita and I managed to have a quiet meal out together while they were there. On one occasion Austin Óg left his hard-earned holiday money on the wall where he had been fishing, and was overjoyed to find it still there when he went back. For Emer, our youngest daughter, the Cork accent proved a constant challenge, and she spent the entire holiday imitating the lilt and pronunciation to the point of extreme annoyance for the rest of us!

The Anglo-Irish Agreement was not concluded until shortly before its signing on 15 November 1985, and between my meetings with Garret and November, a number of important points had to be agreed at Ministerial and official level. But the intense briefing I had had in August, supplemented by updates from Daithí Ó Ceallaigh, made me confident that I knew what was going on and I would be able to transmit this to some of my more doubting colleagues in the party, which was probably part of what Garret intended!

The Agreement was signed by the Prime Minister and the Taoiseach at Hillsborough Castle, the residence of the former Governors of Northern

Ireland and thus highly symbolic for both traditions in the North. The aims, as outlined in the Joint Communiqué, were to promote 'peace and stability in Northern Ireland; helping to reconcile the two major traditions in Northern Ireland; creating a new climate of friendship and co-operation between the people of the two countries; and improving co-operation in combating terrorism.'

For the Irish government and the SDLP, the Agreement was a remarkable feat of negotiation in view of Thatcher's background and inclinations and her experience at the hands of Irish extremists at Brighton. The unionists considered it a disaster of almost unbelievable proportions. The constitutional status of Northern Ireland was affirmed as long as a majority in Northern Ireland did not wish to change it, but in the future, if a majority declared for a united Ireland, the two governments would 'introduce and support, in the respective Parliaments, legislation to give effect to that wish'.

An Intergovernmental Conference was established within the framework of the Anglo-Irish Intergovernmental Council, which had been set up in 1981, to deal on a regular basis with political matters, security and related matters, legal matters (including the administration of justice) and the promotion of cross-border cooperation. It was agreed that the Irish government could put forward views and proposals on matters relating to Northern Ireland that were not the responsibility of a devolved administration in Northern Ireland and 'in the interest of promoting peace and stability determined efforts will be made through the conference to resolve any differences'. The conference would be mainly concerned with Northern Ireland, but some of the matters under consideration would involve cooperative action in both parts of Ireland and possibly also in Great Britain.

The Conference would meet at ministerial and official level as required ,and when at ministerial level an Irish Minister and the Secretary of State would be joint Chairmen. A Secretariat would be established by the two governments to service the Conference.

The conference would be a framework within which the two governments would work together for the accommodation of the rights and identities of the two traditions in Northern Ireland and 'for peace, stability and prosperity throughout the island of Ireland by providing reconciliation, respect for human rights, co-operation against terrorism and the development of economic, social and cultural co-operation.'

The UK government committed itself to a devolved administration in Northern Ireland 'on a basis which would secure widespread acceptance throughout the community' and it was agreed that the Conference would be a framework within which the Irish government could put forward views and proposals for bringing about devolution insofar as they related to the interests of the minority community.

Under Article 5, the conference would concern itself with measures to recognise and accommodate the rights and identities of the two traditions, to protect human rights and to prevent discrimination.

'If it should prove impossible to achieve and sustain devolution on a basis which secures widespread acceptance in Northern Ireland, the conference shall be a framework within which the Irish government may, where the interests of the minority community are significantly or especially affected, put forward views on proposals for major legislation and on major policy issues which are within the purview of the Northern Ireland Departments and which remain the responsibility of the Secretary of State for Northern Ireland.'

The conference would consider security policy, relations between the security forces and the community, particularly the nationalist section of it and prisons policy. On legal matters, including the administration of Justice, the conference would consider measures which would increase confidence in the administration of justice and policy aspects of extradition and extra-territorial jurisdiction between North and South.

Under Article 9, a programme of work would be undertaken by the conference to enhance cross-border security cooperation involving the Gardaí and the RUC, which would continue to have operational responsibilities.

Article 10 dealt with the economic and social development of those areas, in both parts of the island, which had suffered most from the Troubles. In the event devolution would not occur, the conference would be the framework for the promotion of cross-border economic, social and cultural cooperation. Article 12 pledged the support of both governments for the establishment of an Anglo-Irish Parliamentary Body, if that were the wish of both Parliaments.

While this historic document was being launched at Hillsborough, I was on my way to Dublin to participate in an RTÉ television programme on the Agreement. It had been arranged that I would first be briefed by officials in the Department of Foreign Affairs so that I would be completely up-to-date. Dick Spring was also at the Department and he kindly gave me a lift to the RTÉ studio. RTÉ put on a programme worthy of the historic nature of the occasion and all viewpoints were represented (except for Sinn Féin – banned from the airwaves). Again, I was surprised at the negativity of Charlie Haughey. My experience of him at the New Ireland Forum, and particularly at the Press conference when the *Report* was launched, had prepared me for the possibility that he would nit-pick and seek for the opportunity of party political advantage. But I thought he would do so in a way that would enable him to claim credit for those aspects of the Agreement which were clearly advantageous to the Irish national interest. He could have done so with credibility, as it was his summit with Thatcher in December 1981 that had agreed to the establishment of joint studies on the 'unique relationships' between the two islands and 'the totality of relationships within these islands'. He could have claimed to have initiated the process that had now led to the Agreement, which, had he still been in power, would have been a better agreement. But no, he went for the jugular: 'for the first time the legitimacy of Partition has been recognised by the Republic'.

On my discussion panel I put forward the view that the Agreement was not a solution but a framework within which a solution could be found; that the unionist veto over political progress had gone; that the British-Irish context had been necessitated by the intransigence of the unionists, who had only themselves to blame for the isolated position in which they now found themselves; that while the Agreement did not underwrite any of the three models in the *Forum Report*, it was in conformity with 'present realities and future requirements'; that while it did not give the South a direct executive say in the government of Northern Ireland, the role was much more than a mere consultative role, and that the Secretariat, to be based in Belfast, would be effective in giving teeth to the conference and would provide a channel through which we in the SDLP could push for change and an end to alienation.

Gerry Collins, the Fianna Fáil Spokesperson on Foreign Affairs, took the Haughey line and asserted, 'This Agreement is the end of constitutional nationalism on this island'. I considered this an outrageous remark and said so. John Healy, monitoring the airwaves for *The Irish Times*, commented the following day, 'Currie came back again [on Collins] – If British civil servants returned again to Dublin Castle; if they had the right to discuss law and order, to sit in on the making of appointments of senior Garda officers and the Commissioner himself, how long would we go before we had an outcry that our sovereign constitutional position was undermined?'

What angered me most about the Fianna Fáil attitude was that it showed no consideration for the position of the SDLP. Everything was based on building a party political base from which to attack the FitzGerald government. What Haughey and Collins were saying was providing ammunition to those who opposed the SDLP, the most serious and numerous of which were those in Sinn Féin and the IRA. The threat to constitutional nationalism on the island came not from the Agreement but from those elements Fianna Fáil was now assisting to undermine the constitutional nationalists of the SDLP. My anger was intensified when I learned that Haughey had sent Brian Lenihan to the United States to speak to Tip O'Neill and other Irish-American leaders to prevent them from supporting the Agreement and, in effect, to sabotage the support of Irish-Americans – so patiently and successfully built up by John Hume and Sean Donlon – for constitutional nationalists as against the Provos. The Fianna Fáil response to the Anglo-Irish Agreement permanently soured my attitude towards Charlie Haughey and towards those in the party who supported him, and would have later consequences.

The other big surprise to me was the resignation of Senator Mary Robinson from the Irish Labour party on the grounds that the Anglo-Irish Agreement was 'unacceptable to all sections of unionist opinion': 'I do not believe it can achieve its objective of securing peace and stability within Northern Ireland or on the island as a whole.' I could not help wondering to myself, perhaps cynically, the extent to which her attitude was determined, as a Trinity College Senator, by the number of Northerners of the unionist tradition who were on the electoral roll.

At the end of the month I was in the Visitors' Gallery of the House of Commons, listening to the debate on the Agreement. The most memorable speech came from Harold McCusker, as he described his feelings as he stood outside Hillsborough Castle waiting to receive a copy of the Agreement:

'I went to Hillsborough on the Friday morning ... I stood outside Hillsborough, not waving a Union flag – I doubt whether I will ever wave one again – not singing hymns, saying prayers or protesting, but like a dog, and asked the government to put in my hand the document that sold my birthright. They told me they would give it to me as soon as possible. Having never consulted me, never sought my opinion or asked my advice, they told the rest of the world what was in store for me ... I felt desolate because as I stood in the cold outside Hillsborough Castle, everything that I held dear turned to ashes in my mouth ... Even in my most pessimistic moments, reading the precise detail in the Irish press on the Wednesday before, I never believed the Agreement would deliver me, in the context that it has, into the hands of those who for 15 years have murdered personal friends, political associates and hundreds of my constituents.'

As I listened to him, I remembered a discussion I had with him the previous year when we had both been in the United States for St Patrick's Day. Harold was on the left of the Unionist party and freely admitted that had he lived in Britain he would have been in the Labour party. He was emotional in his politics, but not an extremist, and was a staunch Orangeman who loved to beat the Lambeg drum. He was also sociable – one of the few Unionists you could enjoy a drink with. So here we were, late into the night of St Patrick's Day, in a hotel in New York City, discussing our attitudes to what we had witnessed during the day. He said to me, 'Austin, you are a nationalist and at home in Northern Ireland you are in a minority. But you are in a majority on the island of Ireland. As we saw here today in New York and on TV in so many cities throughout the United States, your nationalist tradition is celebrated by millions. You are also part of a worldwide Church with which you can identify wherever you go. I, on the other hand, am in a majority in Northern Ireland and I identify and give my loyalty to Britain and to Protestantism. But I don't fool myself that my loyalty is reciprocated. We Protestant Ulstermen are anathema to many on the mainland and they would like to get rid of us. While you, Austin, could join in the celebrations and identify with them, I feel isolated. You may feel alienated at home, I am alienated here.' It occurred to me that, to a large extent, Harold personified that crisis of identity that was at the core of unionism. As I listened to him in the House of Commons, I did so with sympathy, but also in the belief that when he came to terms with the new political reality and the sense of betrayal diminished, he was one with whom I could do business. Unfortunately, within five years Harold was dead, after a courageous battle with cancer.

That debate at Westminster was the occasion on which I first met Margaret Thatcher. Gerry Fitt had brought me down to Annie's bar and we had walked out to the terrace overlooking the River Thames. I was surprised to see her there with her husband, Dennis, as it was the end of November, but apparently Dennis had persuaded her to say hello to friends he was entertaining. Gerry introduced me as 'the one who started all the trouble', and we had a few moments' conversation in which I thanked her for the Agreement. She was smaller that I had imagined, even smaller than she looked when viewed from the Visitors' Gallery in the House, but what struck me most was her skin. It was like a doll's, almost luminous, Dresden-like. Later, back in the bar, Gerry said it was reported that half of the Cabinet fancied her. We agreed there was no accounting for tastes.

I was surprised at the strength of the unionist rejection of the Agreement.

To a considerable extent it wasn't so much what was in it, but the fact that it was Maggie Thatcher who had concluded a deal that gave the Republic a say in the affairs of Northern Ireland. She was the Prime Minister who was reported to have said that Northern Ireland was as British as Finchley and who had said 'Out, out, out' to any form of Irish unity. The sense of betrayal was widespread and sincerely felt. There was also a feeling among many ordinary Protestants that their Unionist leadership had let them down, that they had been out-manoeuvered by the Irish government and by the SDLP. Many wondered why Enoch Powell, who was supposed to have influence with Thatcher and whose position in unionism was largely based on his supposed ability to read the British Establishment, had been caught offside. Okay, the Unionists might not have been briefed by the British government to the same extent as the Irish government had advised and consulted the SDLP, but the leaks from both the British and Irish sides had been sufficient to mark the cards. At the very least, it was political incompetence on the part of the Unionist leadership. Perhaps this knowledge contributed to the militancy and bitterness of their reaction.

As part of their protest, the Unionists resigned their seats to force by-elections so that the strength of their opposition could be measured, as in a referendum. As part of the strategy to ensure a contest and to maximise the vote where the SDLP did not provide a contest, a 'Peter Barry' was nominated in four constituencies by unionist supporters. The SDLP, to minimise the effect of the unionist campaign, nominated in only four marginal seats – Newry and Armagh, South Down, Mid-Ulster and Fermanagh–South Tyrone.

I had no alternative but to be the candidate. The election was about the Agreement, and as a frontbench member of the New Ireland Forum I had played my part in preparing the negotiating position on which the Agreement had been based, and I had enthusiastically endorsed the outcome. My advertising was to the point: 'Austin Currie is the only candidate in this constituency in favour of the Anglo-Irish Agreement. Another step forward – Give the Agreement a chance.'

Owen Carron was again the Sinn Féin candidate, released from prison, where he was on remand on a charge of firearms possession, to fight the election. The Provos, recognising the popularity of the Agreement among the nationalist electorate, did their best to avoid the central issue, which, of course, put them in the same camp as the unionists, and concentrated instead on attacking me personally. I was forced to issue a challenge: 'If anyone either inside or outside the constituency can prove that I was responsible for the collection of the 25p levy or was responsible for the seizing of cattle or goods, then I will personally pay that person £1,000.' The money, which I did not have, was safe!

The election, fought in the depths of winter (24 January), had a turnout in the constituency of 80.9%. The organisation put into it can be gauged from the fact that 8,087 were postal-voted! The result was: Maginnis (Official Unionist), 27,857; Carron (Sinn Féin), 15,278; Currie (SDLP), 12,081; and Kettlys (Workers party), 864. I was able to claim at the count, 'The SDLP vote has gone up by 2,000. Ken Maginnis' vote has gone down. The Provo vote has dropped by 5,000. The SDLP has been continually under pressure from the fall of the Power-Sharing Executive in 1974, but this is where we stand – we are on the way back.' I was particularly pleased that the area in South Tyrone I had represented since 1964 still stood by me and guaranteed a safe seat for any Assembly election in the future. I was not to know it was the last election I would fight in Northern Ireland.

Owen Carron didn't turn up for the count; he had skipped bail and fled over the border. The following week I applied to the Northern Ireland Office for the release from prison of a constituent to attend his mother's funeral, and was told that because Carron had absconded, release on compassionate grounds had been temporarily suspended.

Overall, in the four constituencies we fought, the SDLP vote was up by 6% and Sinn Féin down by 5.4%. The Unionist strategy came unstuck when they lost Newry and Armagh to Seamus Mallon. Eddie McGrady narrowly lost to Enoch Powell in South Down and was to win in the general election the following year. Nevertheless, the Unionists managed to obtain 418,230 votes against the Agreement and there could be no argument that the majority of the unionist electorate was against what the two sovereign governments had negotiated. The 'Ulster says No' campaign escalated throughout 1986. There were mass rallies, Days of Action when industries were forced to close down, unionist-controlled councils refused to carry out all but the most essential business and eighteen of them refused to strike a rate. Extra troops had to be brought in to support the RUC, many of whom were intimidated out of their homes. In August, Peter Robinson was arrested when he led up to five hundred loyalists over the border and took over the village of Clontibret as a protest against the Agreement. He was fined IR£5,000 and when he paid it, rather than go to jail, he became known as 'Peter Punt'. In September, Harold McCusker said that as a result of the Anglo-Irish Agreement, the union with Britain was not worth fighting for, much less dying for. On 15 November, on the first anniversary of Hillsborough, 250,000 protested at City Hall in Belfast.

All to no avail. Despite reports that shortly after she signed the Agreement her unionist predilections led her to regret it, the 'Iron Lady' stood firm. John Hume had commented, 'Mrs Thatcher is the right person in the right place at the right time and they [the unionists] are recognising that she will not be broken.'

Ironically, the first sign of movement from the unionist *laager* came from the loyalists. In January 1987 the Ulster Defence Association (UDA), through its think-tank, the New Ulster Political Research Group, published a document, *Common Sense*, that advocated a United States-type constitution and power-sharing. The document was mostly the work of John McMichael, the political Spokesman for the UDA and also one of its military commanders. I was one of those nationalists who publicly welcomed *Common Sense* and shortly afterwards I received an invitation to meet McMichael to discuss the document. This presented me with a problem. I felt that any movement within unionism should be built upon and that the Protestant paramilitaries should be encouraged to give up their killing and concentrate on politics. However, I had my suspicions about McMichael. My enquiries about him suggested he wanted to have it both ways, rather like the Provos – ballot paper in one hand and an armalite in the other. So I took precautions. Fearing a set-up at his suggested venue, I met him at the home of Eamon Hanna, the General Secretary of the SDLP, in South Belfast. That decision would cause me worry later when I was informed that while he was meeting me, McMichael's men were involved in sectarian murders of Catholics in Belfast and that he was personally involved in intimidation in Lisburn. I worried that by identifying the home of Eamon and Carmel Hanna, I had put them and their young family under threat. They showed courage and commitment by complying with my request. I found McMichael most conciliatory and over three or four meetings we found a considerable common ground. Rightly or wrongly, I felt I was making progress in deepening his commitment to the peaceful way forward, but the IRA put an end to my speculation when they killed him a few weeks later.

The New Ireland Forum, the Anglo-Irish Agreement, the increased vote for the SDLP and the growing recognition among unionists that the old days were not coming back created a situation of possible political mobility there hadn't been since the fall of the Power-Sharing Executive. I felt all political options should be explored.

24: DUISBURG

I first met Eberhard Spiecker in early 1987 when he visited Northern Ireland. He described himself as a lawyer and notary by profession, resident in Duisburg, West Germany, a leading member of the Lutheran Church, active in honorary positions in the churches, chiefly involving various ecumenical aspects of their work. In 1978 he had been asked by the then General Secretary of the Irish Council of Churches, Reverend William Arlow, 'to help in working towards a cessation of the Irish conflict and for this purpose to establish contact with the paramilitaries on both sides'. This would have been consistent for the Reverend Arlow was one of the Protestant clergy who had organised a meeting with leading Provisionals at Feakle, County Clare, in 1974. Herr Spiecker had been active during the hunger strike period and had met Gerry Adams, among others, in an attempt to find a resolution. He had also had discussions at that time with Cardinal Ó Fiaich and Archbishop Runcie of Canterbury. When he met me in 1987 his concern was to help bring about peace, but also, as an immediate objective, to end the impasse in the aftermath of the Anglo-Irish Agreement and to find some way of getting the various parties to the conference table.

He had organised a get-together at Essen in May 1987, apparently after consultation with Cardinal Ó Fiaich and David Bleakley, the new General Secretary of the ICC. Sean Farren and I attended at Essen on behalf of the SDLP, and Reverend Martin Smyth MP was there on behalf of the unionists. It was too close to the Hillsborough Agreement for any progress to be possible, so Eberhard tried again and eventually organised a meeting at Duisburg on 14/15 October 1988.

Martin Smyth could not attend, but he received permission from his party Leader, Jim Molyneaux, for Jack Allen, Chairman of the party, to substitute for him. Sean Farren had been invited to attend along with me but had other commitments, so I attended with the approval of my party Leader. Peter Robinson MP, Deputy Leader, represented the DUP, and Gordon Mawhinney, the Deputy Leader, represented Alliance. A Redemptorist priest, Fr Alec Reid, based at Clonard monastery, who would later become well-known as a 'go-between' with the republican movement, was also in attendance.

It was a considerable achievement for Eberhard Spiecker that such a meeting was held at all, never mind some of the personalities in attendance.

Unionists were refusing to enter into talks while the Anglo-Irish 'dicktat', as they described the Agreement, remained in place. In a way, there was a comparison with the position of the SDLP after internment. Duisburg was the first significant effort by the OUP and the DUP to get to grips with their problem.

The personalities in attendance were also significant. Jack Allen was Chairman of the OUP. He was no lightweight and his position guaranteed that his party was officially involved. But the attendance of Peter Robinson was even more important. As Deputy Leader of the DUP he could not have attended without the permission of Paisley, but he must have had to work hard to obtain that imprimatur. A Unionist Task Force, of which Robinson had been a member, had reported the previous July and recommended a compromise that could have led to discussions with the government, but it had not found favour with Paisley and Molyneaux. I had, the previous June, welcomed comments of Robinson in the *Sunday Tribune* that unionists 'may have to accept things that in the past they were not able to. The ideal solution is not always attainable; we have to make the choice between strength and force or consensus and compromise.' I looked forward to seeing whether he really meant it.

When we met in the Hotel Angerhof, in Duisburg, Eberhard Spiecker introduced us to Helmut and Ella Becker, friends of his, and Ella, from Northern Ireland, acted as Secretary. Eberhard emphasised the confidential nature of our discussions and said he understood the sensitivities of our meeting in view of the current polarisation of opinion in Northern Ireland. There was consensus between the British and Irish governments: would it be possible to have consensus within Northern Ireland between the parties? Fr Reid made just one brief contribution. He said that an important element of opinion was missing: there had to be dialogue with republicans. Their public representatives had to be involved in discussion. The republican movement must be dealt with. After that, he just sat and listened. The role he had undertaken as a 'go-between' was not then well-known. Had it been, I am sure the others would have objected, particularly Peter Robinson. Had they suspected, they probably would not have been there. Attending the conference was risky enough, considering the state of unionist opinion, but to do so in the company of a close associate of Gerry Adams, and a priest to boot, would have been a risk too far. Looking back, I find it strange that in the controversy that later developed and in all the public comment about the Duisburg meeting, the presence of Fr Alec Reid was never mentioned. A mixture of unionist fear of such a disclosure and his reticence, perhaps?

I was mindful of protecting my back, as I am sure the others were too, so the first thing I did was to present each of the participants with a copy of the *New Ireland Forum Report* and draw their attention to the chapter entitled, 'Framework for a New Ireland: Present realities and future requirements'. Having established the SDLP negotiating position, I then felt free to engage with whatever the others wished to discuss. Allen and Robinson likewise stressed their bottom-line: devolution within the United Kingdom and the necessity for the removal of the Anglo-Irish Agreement. The necessary pre-conditions out of the way, we got down to business, a wide-ranging discussion on how each of the participants saw the current situation, the difficulties that had to be faced and possible ways forward. I said if we were again to have devolved government, I wanted the maximum power possible, including police powers. I suggested one way in which all the parties could get off all hooks was to negotiate on the basis that any agreement entered into would be subject to a referendum on the final package. The other three agreed there were possibilities in the suggestion. Peter Robinson said, 'I might want the return of policing, but the British government does not want us to have that power.' He attacked the SDLP for 'always running to Dublin' and said this really antagonised DUP supporters. He had come into politics because of the murder of a friend of his, and this explained why he was so determined to see the end of terrorism. He understood the necessity of the two traditions identifying with the institutions, but this was impossible for Unionists with the current position, under the '*diktat*' of the Anglo-Irish Agreement.

Jack Allen made the official unionist case in a reasonable manner. To my surprise, it was Gordon Mawhinney who rippled the waters. He was the least experienced politician there, but he started to preach to the rest of us. There were 'irreconcileable' differences between the two traditions, between unionism and nationalism; the SDLP was lacking in morality by not giving full support to the RUC; there could only be one police force for two or more would be Catholic and Protestant police forces. Some of his language was most 'un-alliance' and I believe the others resented his preachiness as much as I did.

Eventually, late in the afternoon and after dinner, we got down to the central issue: was there any way in which inter-party talks could be facilitated in view of the unionist commitment not to enter discussions while the Anglo-Irish Agreement remained in being? I was aware of a suggestion going the rounds that some sort of an interval could be arranged between meetings of the Intergovernmental Conference so as to create a window of opportunity when Unionists could enter into discussions. The Unionists were pushing for a suspension of the Conference and for Maryfield, the Secretariat, to be shut down. There was no way, I said, that I could, on behalf of the SDLP, agree to these demands, but maybe we could consider what we meant by 'suspension' and 'shut down'. What we were in fact discussing, though no one said it, was how to arrange and describe a break in the meetings of the Conference and the work being carried out by Maryfield that could be described by the Unionists as 'suspension', but that the SDLP and the two governments could say was not. It was finally agreed that I would try to draft something overnight for discussion in the morning.

The following morning we met after breakfast and I presented my draft. It didn't take long to read out. I was to inform the Leader of the SDLP of the following: 'I have heard a suggestion which, in my opinion, is worthy of further consideration – The meetings of the Conference will not be held for a period (specified) to facilitate dialogue involving the major constitutional parties in Northern Ireland.' That was it. Hardly Earth-shattering and certainly not worth the controversy that it attracted at a later stage. There was some further discussion involving suggestions of the length of the specified time, six weeks, three months, six months, but I did not budge and the draft was agreed. I took the precaution of reading the sentence over to Ella Becker so that it could be accurately entered in the record of the meeting. The OUP and DUP representatives had to leave Duisburg after lunch for a meeting in Belfast that night. Eberhard and I viewed wild boar in a wood nearby and later that evening enjoyed roast boar and German beer. I told him that I came from a place that once must have been similar, Edendork, its name in Irish meaning 'the wood of the wild boar'.

I returned home on Saturday and the following Monday I informed John Hume, by telephone, of what had happened. After asking a few questions, he said he would consider the suggestion, but 'I am very chary of it'. Eight days later, at a meeting in the Nuremore Hotel in County Monaghan, I informed Dermot Gallagher of Foreign Affairs, for the information of the Irish government. I had fed my information and my assessment of the situation into the system and I felt it was up to others, who might be aware of a broader picture, to take the position forward.

It soon came to my attention that someone was leaking. On 3 November, David Hurst of *The Guardian* rang me to enquire, 'Were you speaking to Ian Paisley in Germany two weeks ago?' I had no difficulty in telling him, 'No, it is years since I spoke to Paisley.' When Michael Nesbitt of the BBC rang the following day, I am sorry to say I lied. Peter Robinson and Jack Allen were the vulnerable people and if the confidential meeting was to be disclosed, it was up to them to do it.

On 9 November, John Hume telephoned me from the Irish Embassy in London, saying he was concerned by a document that had come into his possession (he did not say from Embassy sources) and which he was faxing to me for my comments. When I saw it, I recognised the reason for his concern. It purported to be a record of what had been agreed at Duisburg. The two governments would make a statement that the next meeting of the Conference was to be fixed for a future date (to be stated in the announcement), sufficiently far in advance to facilitate discussion involving the major constitutional parties in Northern Ireland; the Secretary of State would then invite the parties to enter into discussions and he would be in a position to confirm to the Unionist Leaders that, on that day, the two senior civil servants in Maryfield were not in their posts; 'it was further agreed' that if they had to return to their posts for any reason during the discussions, their return would be handled sensitively; 'it was agreed' that the four politicians would try to sell these proposals to their respective parties; 'Austin Currie agreed' that if the proposition found favour in his party, the SDLP would propose it to the Irish government; 'it was agreed' that private talks could be taking place during the period of the review of the Anglo-Irish Agreement; and 'it was agreed' that the parties would not say or do anything which would make the situation more difficult for others.

Obviously this was a considerable embellishment of what had occurred at Duisburg, going well beyond what I had reported to my party Leader and the Irish government. It put a questionmark over my credibility. I was thankful I had been careful to have my draft written into the record and I was able to respond to John on the following day saying, 'The only agreement entered into by me at the meeting in Duisburg was to inform you of the following – I have heard a suggestion which in my opinion is worthy of further consideration – the meetings of the Conference will not be held for a period (specified) to facilitate dialogue involving the major constitutional parties in Northern Ireland.' I added, 'I repeat there was no agreement on any matters other than the one matter I have mentioned which was drafted and put to the meeting by me.' John had not told me where he had got the document, or who had given it to him. However, from internal evidence linked to things he had said at Duisburg, I strongly suspected Gordon Mawhinney.

About the beginning of December, Sean Farren spoke to me about a document, *Possible Scenarios*, which had emanated from the two Unionist parties following discussions between Hume, Robinson and Allen, probably at Westminster. Sean had been asked by John to review the document and I suggested some alterations to it. The document contained quite detailed suggestions as to how the talks could be set up during a gap in meetings of the Conference, including what might be said to the media.

Then, on 9 December, I received another document from John, unheaded, which was the SDLP's response. The Unionist document was described as 'a serious effort by those parties to break down the barriers that stand in the way of dialogue' and went on to say, 'the SDLP had no objection to using the period between meetings of the Anglo-Irish Conference in order to have talks between the parties but we would not wish to give any impression whatever that the Anglo-Irish Agreement and its workings had been suspended. In the SDLP view the other proposals in the Unionist document are designed to give that impression and lack credibility insofar that they imply that the full facts should be kept from the public. We believe that such an approach is neither possible nor desirable.'

The document went on to say that the parties should openly declare that they were going to engage in talks completely outside the framework of the Anglo-Irish Agreement: 'We should declare that our objective in these talks would be to achieve an agreement that will transcend in importance any previous agreement ever made and that the agenda of the talks will address all the relationships that can contribute to the realisation of peace and stability.' The SDLP document finished by suggesting, as I had proposed at Duisburg, that before the talks between the parties began, they should agree on 'the mechanisms whereby any agreements reached should be endorsed by the people'.

I was very disappointed by this document. The whole purpose of Duisburg, as far as I was concerned, was an attempt to find a formula that would enable the Unionists to get off their hook of not talking while the Anglo-Irish Agreement remained in existence. To get them off their hook and to restore dialogue seemed to me to be in everyone's interest. Devolution was part of the Anglo-Irish Agreement, supported by the two governments, and, as recently as the 1987 annual conference, a central plank of SDLP policy. For the two Unionist parties to accept the SDLP proposal for talks 'outside the framework of the Anglo-Irish Agreement' was a political impossibility for them. Why couldn't we have provided them with their fig leaf, which would enable them to enter talks, and then, in actual discussions, put proposals to them for the transcending agreement? The protection of the Agreement was largely in our hands. If we felt the Unionists were deliberately stringing out the talks to threaten the Agreement, we could end the discussions. The SDLP response to the Unionists, which was effectively John Hume's response, did not cover the exigencies of the political situation. I began to fear another agenda was at work.

On 1 February 1989 a SDLP delegation met the Secretary of State, Tom King, in London and I stayed overnight and met up with Gerry Fitt the following day. Gerry took me on a tour of a few of the many bars in the Lords and Commons and we then returned to his office in the Lords. The *craic* was good. Gerry was telling his yarns and we were reminiscing about years gone by, when the phone rang. It was Gerry's daughter, Eileen, who worked with the BBC. There would be a major news story on the six o'clock news about a breakthrough in the Northern Ireland impasse – something had happened in Germany.

Gerry did not have a TV in his office, but we found one and I watched with disbelief as the BBC's Ireland correspondent, Dennis Murray, told us that as a result of a meeting in Duisburg we were 'at the gateway of what could become the most important breakthrough since the start of the Troubles'. Gerry was suitably impressed, but wondered why I hadn't told him about it. The report was so exaggerated in terms of what it alleged had been agreed that it bore little relation to the meeting I had attended. Someone had sold Denis Murray a pup, and the most likely salesman was Gordon Mawhinney.

I tried to phone Annita after the programme ended, but the line was always engaged. When I eventually got through she told me that nearly every media outlet was looking for me. I decided to stay offside until I had worked out what had happened, and how I should respond to it; I postponed my flight home until the last plane. The following day I gave a press conference at SDLP Headquarters where I presented the documentation I had to prove there had only been the one agreement at Duisburg. Jack Allen, Peter Robinson and I backed each other up (without consultation between us) and the finger was pointed at Gordon Mawhinney for leaking to the BBC. An exercise that had great potential, which could have broken the log-jam, unfortunately ended in controversy and recrimination. What I did not recognise at the time, because I was not party to everything that was happening, was that the end of Duisburg was a watershed and that devolution had been moved down the list of SDLP priorities.

25: MEETING SINN FÉIN

O
n 28 January 1988, John Hume telephoned me and asked me to meet him. We met at the Knocknamoe Hotel in Omagh. He told me he had been in discussion with Gerry Adams, that they had established a basis for further discussion that would involve teams from both sides, and would I join the SDLP team with him, Seamus Mallon and Sean Farren. I told him I would have to think about it.

I had not envisaged the political future in terms of agreement with the republican movement. As far back as 11 November 1981, speaking to Junior Chamber in Tullamore, County Offaly, I had said:

'There is no possibility of real political progress until the two Ps of Provisionalism and Paisleyism have been isolated from the great majority of the population. This isolation ought to be a deliberate aim of policy ... The demarcation line is violence, those in favour and those against. A new majority, a new coalition consisting of people from both traditions can be built in opposition to the men of violence ...'

On 12 December 1985, speaking to Belfast members of the SDLP, I was still on the same theme, 'This isolation [of the two Ps] ought to be a deliberate aim of policy and in the aftermath of the Anglo-Irish Agreement circumstances now pertain in which it can be achieved.'

In an interview in *Fortnight* magazine in June 1987, I was still isolating the two Ps in the run-up to the Westminster election of that year and in the aftermath of the Loughgall ambush, when virtually all of the IRA's East Tyrone unit was wiped out by the SAS, I said: 'Loughgall underlines once again that there cannot be a military solution. The Provos can't beat the British militarily and the Brits can't beat the Provos without using methods which would be counter-productive. There can only be a political solution and politically the IRA is dead. Sinn Féin is dead if only they had the wit to stiffen. They have so clearly failed in their political efforts in the South, only getting 1.9% of the vote [in the election the previous February]. I believe they have failed politically in the North and the election results will confirm that.'

The *Fortnight* interview showed my commitment to devolution and power-sharing: 'The existence of the Anglo-Irish Agreement and the guarantee that gives to nationalists should encourage us to go into a power-sharing operation rather than the reverse – simply because, if any arrangements we entered into were to fail, for any reason, then the position would revert to the Anglo-Irish situation rather than to the position prior to the Agreement. So I would argue that the Agreement is an incentive to the SDLP to get involved in a devolved power-sharing situation.'

Against this background of my long-held views and public commitment to them, John had to argue strongly to get my agreement for entering into talks with Sinn Féin and for my involvement in the team. He was at his persuasive best. The clincher was that if we were successful in convincing Sinn Féin that our policies were right and a political alternative to violence could be built for the republican movement, then that could lead to the ending of violence. It was on this basis that I agreed to join the talks, in the hope that it would help save lives. I suspected that part of John's motivation in inviting me to join was along the lines of Lyndon Johnson's aphorism: that it was better to have me inside the tent peeing out than outside it, peeing in.

On the morning of 23 March 1988 I found myself at St Clement's Retreat House, attached to the Redemptorist Church of St Gerard's, in North Belfast, with Cavehill in the background. I stood for a minute or two admiring the view and thinking to myself that it was an appropriate setting for republicans to meet since it was close to the spot where the United Irishmen had been founded in 1791. I was on time and as I stood there I saw a black taxi making its way up the steep driveway. The occupants went in a different door from me, not the front entrance, which suggested to me that they, or at least some of them, had been here before.

Father Alec Reid introduced us to the Sinn Féin team: Gerry Adams, Danny Morrison, Tom Hartley and Mitchell McLaughlin. The first two I believed to be members of the IRA, the other two I didn't know. I had reservations about being in their presence at all. The IRA men belonged to, were in fact leaders of, an organisation that had been responsible for hundreds of deaths, including the murder of a number of people I had known personally. Only a few days earlier I had witnessed, on television, two British Army corporals being shot by the IRA in the most harrowing and brutal of circumstances. It was only four months since the organisation these men represented had been responsible for the Poppy Day bombing in Enniskillen, when eleven of my constituents were killed.

Members of their organisation had shot at my home, terrorised my wife and family and intimidated, and continued to intimidate, my friends and political supporters. Even the members of the delegation who might not be in the IRA were committed to supporting 'the armed struggle', and if they, personally, had not murdered anyone, they supported or at least condoned murders. I wondered why Martin McGuinness was absent. Did this signify a difference in the IRA and Sinn Féin? I gritted my teeth and shook hands. In politics, one prefers to deal with political opponents than with political enemies. But as the old saying goes, 'That which cannot be cured must be endured' for a higher objective.

I was later to describe that first meeting to Eamonn Maillie for his book with David McKittrick, *The Fight for Peace*:

'There was a certain amount of tension at the beginning. It was a very sparse room, and there was nobody in the chair; we sat opposite each other at the table. Father Reid was present and just before the meeting started he sat down at the table and invited us to join him in a prayer. He prayed to the effect that he wished God's blessing on our deliberations, and he himself added that he thought it important that there should be a degree of unity between the parties of the nationalist tradition. He then withdrew.

I hadn't met any of the others apart from Adams, once during the hunger strike, and I had a certain amount of apprehension. We had coffee before we started, and there was no intrusion from the outside between that and lunch-time. The thrust of our dialogue was essentially building on the argument, which we had been making publicly since the Anglo-Irish Agreement, that the British were now neutral on the question of remaining in Ireland. Sinn Féin challenged that, of course.

We went on from that basic point to point to the futility of violence. We said violence was demonstrably futile – the British were no nearer to leaving Ireland than on the first day shots had been fired at them, and in fact it was reinforcing division. These were what you might call the classic SDLP arguments.

Sinn Féin had, as I understood it, two immediate objectives. One was to identify a number of practical local objectives on which the two parties could co-operate. Fair employment was one they suggested, but we made it clear that even on those more immediate social and economic issues there could not be any co-operation as long as the IRA campaign continued and as long as Sinn Féin was condoning or endorsing it. Their second, more important objective, which I suppose had been implied by Father Reid's opening reference, was the creation of a broad agreement, a broad front, across the nationalist family, the nationalist parties in

Ireland. Again, we in the SDLP would not go along with that, or even consider it, as long as the campaign of violence continued. So, in a sense, you could say that for the rest of the meeting, we were almost logjammed from the start.

The main point on which we felt we could begin to make any real contact with them was on one phrase that we had identified in their document "Scenario for Peace". It referred to the wishes of people indigenous to, or domiciled in, the island of Ireland. And that in a sense was the embryo from which the thinking on self-determination would evolve in the future. We picked that out of their document as something on which we might be able to build some kind of common understanding.

We were saying the British were disengaging – it was no longer in the British interest to stay. They didn't accept that because there wasn't sufficient movement, and it was clear something from the British side was necessary. We sought to persuade them that there was a political way ahead, that the continuation of their campaign was self-defeating, that the British wanted to go anyhow – that the job we had to do was to persuade the Unionist people that their future lay in an agreed Ireland.

The proposition the SDLP was putting forward was what Sinn Féin later agreed to – that the IRA should give up their violent campaign, that they should embrace the constitutional way forward. I had no doubt that Adams wanted an alternative strategy: I got the impression from both him and McLaughlin that they wanted an alternative.'

Initially we had two documents before us. John had written a 'Dear Gerry' letter that summarised the views he had put to Adams at their previous meeting in January, and he expanded on this. He delivered what I considered a damning indictment of the Provo campaign and questioned whether their methods were now more sacred than their cause. There was effectively no difference between a British Declaration of Intent to Withdraw over a given period and an actual departure. The political vacuum would be filled immediately by violence as each section of the community moved to secure its own position. This was the route of maximum risk in terms of communal violence and it was a risk no one had the right to take. Thousands would die and the possibility of a united and peaceful Ireland would be delayed for generations. John honed in on sovereignty and the right to self-determination and he posed five questions to the Provisional Republican movement:

1. Do you accept the right of the Irish people to self-determination?
2. Do you accept that the Irish people are at present deeply divided on the

question of how to exercise self-determination?

3. Do you accept that in practice agreement on exercising the right means agreement of both the unionist and nationalist traditions in Ireland?

4. If you accept 1, 2, and 3 would you then agree that the best way forward would be to attempt to create a conference table, convened by an Irish government, at which all parties in the North with an electoral mandate would attend? The purpose of such a conference would be to try to reach agreement on the exercise of self-determination in Ireland and on how the people of our diverse traditions can live together in peace, harmony and agreement. It would be understood that if this conference were to happen that the IRA would have ceased its campaign. It would also be understood in advance that if such a conference was to reach agreement, it would be endorsed by the British government.

5. In the event of representatives of the unionist people refusing to participate in such a conference, would you join with an Irish government and other nationalist participants in preparing a peaceful and comprehensive approach to achieving agreement on self-determination in Ireland? Would we, in fact and in practice, take up the challenge laid down by Tone?

John finished by expressing the hope – and the objective that had brought me to these talks – that we could bring an end to all military and violent activity on the island of Ireland. John's document was five pages long. The Sinn Féin case, outlined by Gerry Adams, was in a document entitled *Towards a Strategy for Peace*, and was twenty-one pages long. As I write I have a copy of it before me, which has my own comments in the margins, written as Adams spoke. He argued that the British presence, always malign, always in British self-interest, was the problem; that unionists had been given a veto and upon that veto rested the pretext for British rule in Ireland; that Britain's actions totally contradicted SDLP claims that Britain was now neutral on the constitutional issue; that only the people of Ireland could decide the future of Ireland; that faced with a British withdrawal a considerable body of loyalist opinion would accept the wisdom of negotiating their own future; that in these circumstances sectarianism would shrink and a left–right alignment would occur; that the armed struggle to force an irrevocable Declaration of Intent was a political option made necessary because Britain had no intention of withdrawing its political, military and economic interests from the Six Counties and other forms of struggle had been ineffectual; and that the SDLP, by supporting the Anglo-Irish Agreement was the lynch-pin in the British government strategy, that we had accepted Partition and the British State in Ireland and were prolonging the struggle.

Adams finished his elaboration of *Towards a Strategy for Peace* by making seven proposals upon which the SDLP and Sinn Féin might agree:

'–to endorse the right of the Irish people to national self-determination;

–to agree that Britain had no legitimate right to be in Ireland;

–to agree that the IRA were politically motivated in its actions and its volunteers were not criminals;

–that we agree that the British government and its forces in Ireland were not in a peacekeeping role;

–that failure to rule out nationalist participation in a devolved arrangement would protract the conflict;

–that we agree on a common solution and the SDLP and Sinn Féin would join forces to impress on the Dublin government the need to launch an international and diplomatic offensive to secure national self-determination.'

My annotations on the margins of the Sinn Féin document indicated my attitude to a number of the arguments and proposals. Opposite the statement that 'only the domiciled people of Ireland, those who live in this island can decide the future of Ireland and the government of the island', I wrote 'Exactly - ALL who are domiciled on this island', meaning that a unionist was entitled to his say in equality with a nationalist. This was my follow-up to a paragraph that had objected to the unionists having 'the continuing powers to veto Irish Unity and upon that veto rests the pretext for unionist rule in Ireland'. I had written, 'Are unionists part of the Irish people and, if so, is the veto not in fact that of one section of the Irish people over the rest? Is it in fact any different than the veto which the Provo movement, as part of the Irish people and representing only —% of it, seeks to exercise over the great majority of the Irish people?'

In the margin beside the contention that 'a considerable body of loyalist opinion' would, in the aftermath of British withdrawal, enter into negotiations, I wrote, 'What percentage is "a considerable body" and what do you do with the rest of them?' To the statement that British withdrawal would lead to a situation where we would 'see sectarianism shrivel and with the emergence of class politics a realignment of political forces along left and right lines', I wrote, 'Will it? What indication is there, what precedent?'

To the contention that 'an irreversible Declaration of Intent would minimise any loyalist backlash', I noted, 'Minimise? By how much? How many thousands would be involved? Who would defeat and disarm them? And who will suffer?'

To 'armed struggle is seen as a political option', I responded, 'Ending of armed struggle should also therefore be a political option'. To the contention that the IRA had consistently pointed out that its actions were aimed at the six-county State and not at the twenty-six counties and that 'there is no campaign or armed conspiracy against the institutions of the twenty-six-county State nor will there be', I noted, and later said it straight across the table to Danny Morrison, quoting him at the Sinn Féin Árd Fheis, 'Will anyone here object, if with a ballot paper in one hand and an armalite in the other, we take power in Ireland?'

To the argument that strategic interests 'are now the most important consideration in British interference in Ireland' and that even the prospect of a neutral Ireland was regarded as a serious threat to British and NATO's strategic interests, I observed, 'Outdated Second World War theory. An unstable Ireland is what Britain really fears – if the price of a stable Ireland is British withdrawal, then Britain will pay that price.'

I had a number of other observations in the margin, but I think I have quoted enough to indicate my scepticism of the Sinn Féin position and the gulf that I felt separated the two parties. There were five more meetings, in March, May, June, July and September, all in the same location and all with the same teams. I soon realised there was no chance of a ceasefire. Martin McGuinness went out of his way to emphasise that at the Easter Commemorations. At our first meeting, Adams had stated the delegation represented Sinn Féin and not the IRA, though, when pressed, he added, 'People here might have an individual relationship with the IRA' and they had influence with the IRA. The phrase 'ending all military and violent activity' kept cropping up, but in the context of an overall political solution, not in terms of a ceasefire.

Indeed, in the course of our meetings, between March and September, the IRA intensified its campaign not only in the North but in Britain and on the Continent. In May, in The Netherlands, the IRA killed three off-duty British soldiers. In June, six soldiers taking part in a 'fun run' were blown up. In July a 1,000lb bomb near the border, intended for a judge, instead killed a couple and their six-year-old son. In August, the IRA exploded their first bomb in Britain since Brighton, killing one soldier and injuring nine. In August, too, eight soldiers were killed near Ballygawley, in my constituency, by a culvert bomb.

In these circumstances it was impossible for us to argue that our involvement with Sinn Féin in talks was having an effect in terms of a reduction, never mind the ending of violence. The most hopeful and optimistic of us, trying to find a bright side to what was happening, could speculate that the escalation was a preparation for a cessation so that the Provos could argue they were calling off their campaign from a position of strength. But I, for one, could not convince myself of it. I had to admit the possibility that we were being used to give credibility to Sinn Féin and that there was no intention on their part of bringing an end to 'all military and violent activity', particularly if the SDLP were to get credit for it. There was also the possibility that the discussions were being strung out deliberately to prevent talks with the unionists, who were, not surprisingly, dismissing any possibility of talks between the SDLP and them while the SDLP–Sinn Féin dialogue continued.

It was with a great sense of relief on my part that the Sinn Féin talks came to an end in September. The statement we issued, on 3 September, attempted to gloss over the fact that the talks had been a failure. The introduction stated, 'The talks between the SDLP and Sinn Féin have ended without at this time reaching agreement on the objective of the talks', and 'at this time' was repeated, suggesting that they might bear fruit in the future. But the IRA was still murdering, with no indication they were thinking of stopping.

There were, I thought, some points on which we had scored so heavily that they had impacted on the people across the table from us and might have an effect in the future. We had agreed that the Irish people, as a whole, had the right to self-determination and that included the unionists as part of the Irish people. It was the division among the Irish people on how that right to self-determination was to be exercised that was the central problem, and clearly the agreement of the unionists could not be obtained by force. The veto the unionists had was nothing to do with the British presence. It was the presence of the unionist people, domiciled on the island of Ireland, their numbers and their geographical location, which required, of necessity, their agreement with the rest of us on how we shared the island.

My experience of the Sinn Féin talks convinced me more than ever of the necessity of finding a way of opening talks with the unionists. An IRA cessation would have made it easier, but that had not happened and time had been lost. The statement announcing the end of the SDLP–Sinn Féin talks was made public at the beginning of September. On 14 October, I was in Duisburg.

At this point, the police guard had been taken off my home, but the attacks had continued. At the beginning of 1986 there were three attacks within three months. That meant three occasions when my wife and children were awakened by the sound of hammer blows and breaking glass. On the first occasion, two cement blocks were thrown, and on the other occasions the police said sledgehammers had been used in an attempt to penetrate the bullet-proof glass. Further attacks, including the firing of shots, occurred between the attack on Loughgall RUC station in May 1987 and the Westminster general election the following month, even though I was not a candidate.

We had always tried to keep life as normal as possible for the children, but it was difficult. Attacks occurred the night before examinations or other big occasions in their lives. In September 1987 our eldest daughter, Estelle, had just finished school and was heading off to Queen's to study for the same degree as I had completed. She persuaded Annita and me to go on holiday, on our own, for the first time since 1969. We were away three days when she telephoned to tell us the house had been attacked again, but they were all fine, in fact, the other four children had slept through it. No one was ever made amenable for any of these cowardly attacks, but I strongly suspected Provo supporters.

Their wrath was directed not only at me. My brother, Sean, and a brother-in-law, Shane Corr, were hospitalised as a result of an election-night attack on the SDLP Headquarters in Coalisland. Anyone connected to me had to take precautions, even when not directly involved in political activity. For some of us, this circumscribed social life. We had to be very careful where and with whom our children socialised. At school the girls, who attended a girls' Grammar School in the village of Donaghmore, were taunted and insults were written on their books, but, unfortunately, the boys had to travel to Dungannon, where the school had an intake from a much larger catchment area. There were many incidents I never found out about until years later, but with unexplained bruises, black eyes, torn jumpers and not very logical explanations, we finally got the truth.

They coped very well and did extremely well at school, all going on to university, two of them to do the same degree as myself. One of the worst incidents that I know of happened after I had moved to Dublin, during the Presidential election campaign. Austin Óg went to a disco in a local hotel in Dungannon, ordered a taxi to go home and when he was told it had arrived went outside to be met by a hostile crowd who attacked him in a most vicious manner. Only for the bravery of some local people, who intervened and took him to hospital, it might have had a tragic end. We all had to be careful where we went, particularly in relation to licensed premises.

They were difficult years for all of us. Talking to the children years later, their memories on the negative side are of 'safe places' in the house during attacks, learning what not to say when answering the phone, how to answer the door safely, checking the car for bombs every morning before leaving for school, police guards in the garage, searchlights, laser beams and alarms, Daddy missing from school concerts or parent-teacher meetings. There were funny incidents, too, however, like the day the metal ironing board fell down in the garage and everyone dived behind the door thinking the house was being attacked, or the occasion when, during an election campaign, an irate loyalist thought it a good idea to moon at a teenage girl canvassing for her father.

But if life was tense and difficult at home, we made up for it on holidays. In the early 1980s we went camping in France, where anonymity was heaven for us as a family and I was able to spend what would now be called 'quality time' with Annita and the children. There were also wonderful holidays spent in Ireland, thanks to the generosity of friends who saw the need for us to 'escape' and invited us to use their homes while they were away, or invited us for weekends. The highlight of these holidays for the children was the compilation of a 'family tape'. For weeks before departure an A4 sheet was fixed to the fridge and everyone chose three pieces of music, which Estelle then compiled on a tape. Once on the road the cries would start, 'Can we play the tape now?' I used to delay as long as possible, for once started I knew extreme embarrassment was in store. Songs like 'Patricia the Stripper' (Chris de Burgh), 'DIVORCE' (Billy Connolly) and 'She's so beautiful' (Cliff Richard) were invariably included, and no matter how hard I tried to avoid it, they were always played at full volume, with all the windows down, and the children belting them out as we drove through towns, enjoying every minute of my discomfort!

The generosity of friends and strangers constantly surprised me. One couple in Dún Laoghaire lent us their home in the summer quite a few times while they were on holiday. Two outings in particular on these holidays were great thrills for the children: to travel into Dublin on the top deck of the bus and home on the Dart; and the visit to the amusements at Bray, where an elderly gentleman in charge of the rides recognised me and let them go on every ride free of charge. There were also holidays in Connemara, Stillorgan and West Cork where we made true lifelong friends. Our particular thanks are due to Kathy and Peter Newman, who gave Austin Óg a home for a year while he finished his secondary education in the North.

I attended an SDLP fundraiser, a poker classic organised by Denis Haughey in Cookstown for the Mid-Ulster constituency. I have always enjoyed a game of poker, but on this occasion my luck was out and I left early while the others were still playing. About ten minutes after my departure, armed men burst in, announced they were from the IRA, ordered everyone to lie on the floor and proceeded to collect all the money, including personal money from wallets, etc. It was not just a robbery, it was a political act directed at the SDLP. It could have been worse. I was armed and, had I been present, I would probably have resisted my gun falling into Provo hands!

In 1980 I opened an estate agency business in Dungannon – just in time for the business slump in provincial towns which accompanied the hunger strike. Dungannon soon became known as the most bombed town in Northern Ireland and almost weekly shops and businesses closed, either on a voluntary basis or as a result of intimidation, in one form of protest or another. It did not help matters that almost every weekend my windows were smashed and the window display of properties for sale strewn over the footpath. On two occasions petrol was poured through the letter-box and attempts made to burn down the building. The home of my secretary was attacked and her family terrorised, but she very bravely refused to give up her job until, eventually, I was forced to close down and to transfer my business to my home, where once again Annita took over duties as secretary. I now began to expand the business by utilising my experience of government Departments and of Brussels bureaucracy to set up a consultancy service offering advice on grants available to business people, and how to claim them. It was a service that could be availed of by both sections of the community, where there was no competition at that time and which was non-'boycottable'. Thankfully, I began to make some money.

Annita was progressing well in her career. When I had ceased to be a full-time politician, she had, of necessity, returned to teaching, despite our young family. While pregnant with Emer, our youngest child, she applied for a position as Centre Organiser for the Music Service of the Southern Education and Library Board, covering the area of South Tyrone, and was successful. She then decided to do a part-time degree course with the Open University, specialising in Education, studying into the night after coping with a nine-to-five job, the needs of five children and a less than domestically competent husband. Years later, the older children told us how much they had enjoyed doing their homework while Mammy did hers! It was a very proud day for all of us when she graduated in the Whitla Hall at Queen's. When the Council for Catholic Maintained Schools was created in 1988, she applied for and obtained the position of Education Officer. This position was even more demanding of her time and covered all of Fermanagh and parts of counties Tyrone, Derry and Armagh, with many night-time meetings of Boards of Governors and weekend conferences. She had an office at home and managed to keep job and home running.

I was still maintaining a constituency service, looking after the needs of my constituents, maintaining links with government and local authority departments, issuing statements, doing media interviews (which, in the case of TV and radio, had the great advantage of being paid), participating in party delegations to Belfast, Dublin and London and generally performing the functions which, in normal societies, were the responsibility of an MP or TD. In 1986, through the intervention of John Hume, I received a grant from the Joseph Rountree Social Service Trust, which helped considerably with the financial burden of maintaining a political career.

Despite the opposition of the SDLP, the British government had increased the number of Northern Ireland seats at Westminster – ironically to the advantage of the party – enabling John Hume to be elected for the new seat of Foyle, Seamus Mallon for the new seat of Newry–Armagh and Eddie McGrady for the revised seat of South Down. No such advantage accrued to me in Fermanagh–South Tyrone. As long as Sinn Féin was identified with violence, I would do my best to ensure their candidates would be opposed by the SDLP and Sinn Féin would not tolerate giving me a clear run against the Unionists. The only winner in this situation was Ken Maginnis, but frankly I preferred to be misrepresented by the traditional enemy rather than someone who would use his election as a mandate for murder.

My uncle, Jimmy O'Donnell, a long-time Labour councillor in Birmingham, had suggested to me on a number of occasions that I should consider taking up a job in Birmingham as a teacher or lecturer and get involved in Birmingham politics, possibly succeeding him as a councillor and then seeking a nomination as MP or MEP. Annita and I considered it and came to the conclusion that at that stage of the development of our family, my being away during the week and, if it developed into a political career, at weekends as well, would place an intolerable strain on family life. Nor did we find acceptable the suggestion that we should move to England as a family. The strain such uprooting would cause for the children and for us would have been too great. Things worked out well in the end, but looking back to the dark days from the mid-1970s to the mid-1980s, I have often thought a move at that stage would have been easier on my wife and children.

There was another proposal, which I found easier to make up my mind on. On two occasions, two years apart, I was asked by credible sources, 'would you like to be in the House of Lords?' The idea of Lord Currie of Edendork chairing the AGM of Edendork St Malachy's Gaelic Football Club amused me, but, no, as I explained in a earlier chapter, in terms of family history the Curries were always closer to coal than ermine!

I worked for my constituents, for the SDLP and for the people of Northern Ireland up to the end, until literally the last minute. My diary for the beginning of 1989 illustrates how busy I was just a few weeks before taking the decision that was to change the rest of my life. On 11 January I met Congressman Brian Donnelly from Boston, a man with a practical interest in bettering the lives of Irish and Irish-Americans, and had the pleasure of showing him around Castlecaulfield in County Tyrone, originally Baile Donghaile, the home of his ancestors. On 21 January, I participated in the 'Kenny Live' programme on RTE and received a marvellous response from the studio audience and the viewing public. On 28 January, I met again with Eberhard Spiecker to see if we could build on the talks at Duisburg. On 1 February, I was a member of the SDLP delegation that discussed the political future with Tom King, the Northern Ireland Secretary, in London. The following day, and for some days afterwards, I was involved in the fallout from the BBC 'exposé' of the Duisburg discussions. On 23 February, I met with the Prime Minister, Margaret Thatcher, as part of a delegation of politicians and trade unionists to discuss the future of Harland and Wolff, the Belfast ship-building firm.

Once again I was the organiser for the SDLP in the local elections in Dungannon, which resulted in a tie between the Unionists and non-unionists and the election of my brother, Vincent, to the Town Ward in Dungannon at his first attempt. I was delighted to have helped the SDLP maintain its lead over Sinn Féin by five councillors to three. I was also pleased that the election result consolidated a historic milestone for Dungannon Council. The previous year the Council had agreed to revolve the Chairmanship and Vice-Chairmanship between Unionist and non-unionist on a six-monthly basis. The council, whose predecessors Dungannon Urban and Rural had been symbols of discrimination and sectarianism had now become the model for the 'New Ulster' of power- and responsibility-sharing. It was a tribute to those on the Unionist side, like Ken Maginnis, Ralph Brown and Derek Irwin, and to those in the SDLP and former SDLP members, like Michael McLoughlin, Jim

Cavanagh, Owen Nugent, Patsy Daly, Anthony McGonnell, Pat McGlinchey, Joe Higgins and Jim Canning, who had been prepared to stand up to the violence and intimidation. I took a little credit myself: the two Ps had been isolated in Dungannon, at least.

I had one major disappointment during those weeks. In March the Campaign for a Devolved Parliament (CDP), a largely unionist organisation which included Harry West, the former Unionist Leader, and one of its sponsors invited me to speak at a rally in the Ulster Hall, in Belfast, on 3 May. I accepted immediately and looked forward to the rally with great anticipation. It was not just the opportunity to help forward devolution – an objective to which I had long been committed and which was SDLP policy and had been included in the Anglo-Irish Agreement – it was also the venue.

In 1886 Lord Randolph Churchill had spoken at a mass rally in the Ulster Hall against Home Rule. He received what he later remembered as the best reception of his political life as he reminded the cheering unionists that 'for nearly two hundred years your motto, your password, your watchword and your cry has been "No Surrender" and that in the coming crisis, "Ulster will fight and Ulster will be right".' In 1912 his son, Winston, First Lord of the Admiralty and a Minister in the Liberal government that was pushing a Home Rule Bill through Parliament, accepted an invitation from the Ulster Liberal Association to speak in favour of Home Rule in the same Ulster Hall. The Orangemen weren't having the Ulster Hall desecrated, no matter who his father was, and Churchill, protected by an enhanced garrison of the First Cheshire Regiment and the King's Own Scottish Borderers, was lucky to escape with his life as he travelled through the streets to the alternative venue, Celtic Park, in the Catholic end of the city, where he spoke in the company of John Redmond. When the meeting ended, he was smuggled to the railway station where he boarded a special train for Larne, with its blinds down. At Larne, as he and his wife scurried up the gangplank, dockers hurled rotten fish at them.

So I looked forward with anticipation to speaking in the Ulster Hall, to speak where Churchill wasn't allowed to and on the same subject, Home Rule – albeit in the different context of a devolved Parliament at Stormont with inbuilt power-sharing and an Irish dimension. I put a lot of work into preparing my speech for I was conscious of the sensitivities of the other speakers, principally Ken Maginnis and Sammy Wilson of the DUP. I was conscious of the sensitivities for another reason – on the night, the Ulster Hall might be a volcano waiting to explode. So my prepared speech was big on the potential for economic, social and political progress, if representatives of our two traditions could come together in government to tackle our joint problems. I also emphasised that if we were to share power, it had to be real power and that included control of policing.

On 13 April, Chris McGimpsey, on behalf of the CDP, wrote to me outlining the arrangements and adding 'we are of the opinion that the proceedings on 3 May will be the most significant public meeting to have been held in Belfast for many years'. He and I should not have wasted our time. Winston had not been allowed to speak in the Ulster Hall, and neither would Austin. Sammy Wilson withdrew first, claiming that 'certain politicians' (not me) were portraying the meeting as 'Duisburg Mark II'. Ken Maginnis followed suit the weekend before the rally was due to take place, after a meeting of the Ulster Unionist Executive at which he alleged that party Leader James Molyneaux had ordered that the rally be cancelled. One of the organisers later told me that it was the symbolic nature of the venue that was the major problem and, he added, 'your presence there to some would have been similar to a priest saying Mass in an Orange Hall'. Had I been allowed to speak, I believe my contribution and the opportunity it would have provided due to the inevitable publicity would have pushed the case for devolution up the list of political priorities.

It was another wasted opportunity. And, as it happened, it was my last chance to make a major contribution as a practitioner in the political life of Northern Ireland.

26: CROSSING THE RUBICON

O n 10 May 1989, after a meeting of the Coalisland branch of the SDLP, I arrived home after midnight to find Annita and Estelle waiting for me with the news that Garret FitzGerald had telephoned and wished me to contact him when I came home, no matter how late it was. He would be flying to Eastern Europe the next day and he wished to speak to me on a matter of some urgency.

His first words were, 'How would you like to stand for a safe seat in the Dáil?' I recovered sufficiently to say that there was no such thing as a safe seat in a multi-member constituency under PR. He then explained that an election declaration was imminent, that John Kelly, the former Attorney-General, had informed Fine Gael he would not be running and that as a result there would be a vacancy in one of the safest Fine Gael constituencies in the State. It had been decided at the highest level in Fine Gael to ask me to stand. He knew I would need time to think about such a momentous decision, but when I had done so would I telephone Alan Dukes, who had succeeded him as Leader of Fine Gael. In view of the near certainty of an election declaration, I should give the invitation the most urgent consideration.

For the next three hours, until almost 4.00am, Annita, Estelle and I discussed the situation. They were of the opinion that, if possible, I should accept the offer. It would, of course, require a move to Dublin and this would present problems, especially for the children. However, my wife and daughter encouraged me to think in terms of a future where I, and my family, might live a relatively normal life away from the pressures and frustrations of the past twenty years.

I knew it would be a big gamble, an irrevocable act, a crossing of the Rubicon as far as a future in Northern Ireland politics was concerned. On the other hand, the opportunity might not come again. I was coming up to my fiftieth birthday and the emphasis in politics was increasingly on youth. In the short, or even medium term I could not see a future for a devolved Assembly and government, and there was no chance of representing Fermanagh–South Tyrone at Westminster. The Anglo-Irish Agreement, Garret had pointed out to me, with its increased involvement in Northern affairs for the Irish government would mean the Dáil would benefit from the unique experience I had to offer. With the encouragement of my family, I decided to go for it.

The following day I rang Alan Dukes and we met on Sunday, 14 May at Walker's Hotel in Drogheda. I had met him only briefly when he was a Minister and had formed the impression that he was a bit of a cold fish, an economist more concerned with facts and figures than with people. On this occasion, I got an entirely different impression. I liked his commitment to the disadvantaged in Irish society and also to the ideal of a united Ireland. We got on well and I had agreed, in principle, to seek a nomination from Fine Gael when he made a proposal that made me draw back. Garret had suggested 'the safe seat' in Dublin South, but would I consider running in Dublin West where, with Jim Mitchell TD, I could secure a second seat for the party? As far as I was aware, I had never been in any part of Dublin West. At least I knew where Dublin South was: both UCD and RTÉ were in that constituency and I had been in both places many times. Annita's sister, Norrie, and her husband, Jack, lived in Dundrum, and Donal and Mary Daly, whom Annita and I had met on holiday in Italy in 1969 and who had become close friends, lived in Kilmacud. Hardly the required knowledge of a constituency one hoped to win, but at least a start! About Dublin West I knew nothing and, as far as I was aware, no one. Alan said he knew he was asking a lot and that the offer of Dublin South still remained, but I could do more for the party and for myself by fighting Dublin West. He did not elaborate on the latter and I did not enquire. Without requiring any guarantees about the future, or seeking to impose any conditions, I agreed to meet Jim Mitchell to further discuss nomination for Dublin West.

The meeting was delayed until I had completed my task as Director of Elections for the SDLP in the local elections and celebrated the success of my brother, Vincent, in Dungannon. But I met Jim within a week and, as it turned out, just two days before Charlie Haughey called the general election. We met at the home of a friend of his, a chemist, in Ardee, County Louth. I had met Jim on a couple of occasions previously, but did not know him well. I was aware of his reputation as an able and successful politician, the youngest ever Lord Mayor of Dublin and a Minister in Garret's administration. But chiefly he was talked of as a politician who knew his grass roots, was able to calculate the odds and had masterminded a *coup* in Dublin West, which had resulted in Fine Gael thwarting the plans of Charlie Haughey to appoint one of the Fine Gael TDs for the constituency (Dick Burke, my benefactor in Brussels) as a European Commissioner and thereby create a vacancy he hoped would be filled by a

Fianna Fáil TD. No one had greater knowledge of my proposed constituency, or a better track record in assessing it, and when he told me he was confident I would win the second seat for Fine Gael, I put my faith in his judgement.

Two days later the election was declared. The following morning, Friday, 26 May, I carried out my last political act as a member of the SDLP in Northern Ireland when, as John Hume's agent in Fermanagh–South Tyrone, I delivered to the Electoral Officer for the European election a batch of application forms for postal votes. Among them was one for myself on the grounds that 'I will be outside Northern Ireland on business on polling day'. The Electoral Officer, Allister Patterson, remarked that it must be important business to keep me away on election day. I did not tell him it would also be election day in the South. At a few minutes past twelve I left the Electoral Office. By four o'clock I was at Fine Gael Headquarters in Dublin, declaring my candidacy. At a hastily arranged press conference on the steps of Headquarters, one of my questioners was Vincent Browne, a former Northern Editor of the *Irish Press* and well-known to me for asking awkward questions. On this occasion he asked, 'Austin, can you name three streets in Dublin West?' I waffled, but it was obvious I couldn't.

A Fine Gael nomination was not inevitable. An able and popular councillor, Marian Sheehan, was also a candidate and rightly had expectations that her claims would be recognised. Not surprisingly, a section of the membership resented the attempted imposition of a 'parachute' candidate who had joined the party only two days before the Selection Convention and was attempting to displace Marian, who had a proven commitment to Fine Gael and a record of electoral success in the constituency. I heard I was being described as the 'cuckoo' candidate. It seemed appropriate, and I hoped not too many of the delegates knew the rhyme my father used to recite:

> The cuckoo comes in April, it sings its song in May,
> By the middle of June it has finished its tune,
> And in July it flies away.

I first appeared in the constituency on 26 May and the election was on 15 June!

Within hours of the announcement of my decision to seek one of the two nominations for the constituency, I attended a meeting of the Lucan branch where I was proposed as a member and obtained the branch's support. The visit to Lucan reminded me that I had been there before. In

August 1969, Annita and Estelle had, as I have already recounted, been refugees to Gormanston Military Camp following an attack on our home. While there, they had been visited by two journalists, Michael and Ethna Viney, who had kindly invited my wife and daughter to stay with them at their home in Lucan. The following weekend I journeyed South to visit them, not knowing their specific location but with the Vineys' telephone number. On arriving in Lucan, I was reminded of the association with Patrick Sarsfield by the first public house I saw and decided to stop there to phone Vineys' for detailed directions. I ordered a pint of Smithwicks from the middle-aged gentleman behind the bar, enquired as to the location of the pay-phone and left a ten shilling note on the counter to pay for the drink. On my return the pint was there, and so was my ten shillings. When the barman, who turned out to be the owner, returned, I proffered the money. His first words to me were, 'Mr Currie, your money is no good in this house.' Such was my introduction to a local legend, Bob Carroll, and my first free drink in Lucan! It was to this village, twenty years later, that I was returning to ask them to elect me as their TD.

With the support of Jim Mitchell and party Headquarters, and under the guidance and management of the constituency organiser, Brian Brady, I made contact with as many of the delegates as was possible in the two days available for canvassing them. Since I did not know where I was, I had to be ferried everywhere and I was extremely lucky to have for that purpose Tom Kavanagh, a bus driver and also a TV personality for fundraising causes, who knew every inch of the constituency.

From my point of view it was a most successful convention. I had enough experience of such occasions, albeit North of the border, to know that it is seldom the speeches that decide the issue, since most delegates already have their minds made up. Considering the exceptional nature of this convention, however, and the short time given to delegates to make up their minds, my speech on this occasion may have been more influential than usual. Marian Sheehan made a most dignified and constructive contribution, rising above what must have rankled as an unfair and unjust imposition. The result was Currie 54, Mitchell 48 and Sheehan 38. Jim Mitchell had more than delivered on his commitment to me.

Despite not knowing my way about and being ignorant of the local issues, I found canvassing an enjoyable experience, certainly in comparison to Fermanagh and South Tyrone. My name and face were well-known from innumerable appearances in the media over the years, and this name- and face-recognition gave me an advantage over most of the other candidates, although not over my party colleague, Jim Mitchell, born and reared in the constituency and a former Minister. Nor over Brian Lenihan, whom I had first met when I had invited him, as President of the New Ireland Society, to speak at Queen's nearly thirty years earlier. Brian was Tánaiste in the outgoing government and shortly before the election was called he underwent a life-saving liver transplant operation. He was now recovering in an American hospital and the re-election campaign was being run on his behalf to a background of considerable personal sympathy.

The stress that accompanied Northern canvasses was completely missing – no Provos or Protestant extremists to worry about. I did encounter a few republican diehards who accused me of betraying the freedom fighters, or of deserting the Northern struggle, but these encounters tended to be amusing rather than frightening and mostly came from people with northern accents. On one occasion, a burly individual came to the door and in response to my request for his number one vote told me, in a strong South Derry accent, 'Not if you were the last fucking man in Ireland'. Thankfully, the great majority of those with northern accents were welcoming.

Shortly after I began canvassing, I became aware of widespread cynicism about politicians and the political process. I made a speech, which was widely reported, where I said that this cynicism was more damaging to political institutions than the Provo use of the gun and the bomb. There were also serious allegations of corruption, particularly in relation to the planning process, and the name of Liam Lawlor, a Fianna Fáil TD and candidate in the constituency, was often mentioned. It was to take a number of years for some of these allegations to be substantiated before the Flood Tribunal. But at the time it was very evident from the posters, the newspaper advertising, the four-wheel-drive vehicles and the number of canvassers, most of them reportedly paid, that very substantial amounts of money were being spent. Some relatively small incidents gave me cause for thought. Canvassing a working-class estate, I was asked by an elderly lady if I had a bag of coal with me. I wondered, but did not pay much attention until the same question was asked at four or five houses. When I enquired further I was told, 'Oh, Mr Lawlor always gives me a bag of coal during the election.'

On election day, touring the polling stations, as I entered one I met a group of about a dozen men coming out, identifiable as what used to be described as 'members of the travelling class'. I watched as they piled into a Hiace van. About an hour later as I emerged from another polling station, I met the same group. Obviously not recognising me one asked, 'Is this where you vote for Mr Lawlor?' For a moment I thought I was back in the North, but I soon put a stop to that operation.

Jim Mitchell was a strong believer in 'constructive tension' among party candidates in order to maximise the vote. It was undoubtedly effective, but sometimes the tension was more obvious than the constructive, not only between the candidates but invariably between their supporters. I was lucky, seeing as I had not met any of the individuals concerned before, to have around me as advisors and organisers a group of men (surprisingly, no women) who knew Jim's electioneering methods and were sufficiently experienced not only to respond but, on occasion, to initiate. In addition to Brian Brady and Tom Kavanagh, whom I have already mentioned, the inner group consisted of Jim Fay, a member of Dublin County Council, Gerry Leahy, an estate agent, and John Lynch, a school principal. Not only did they successfully steer me to a seat in Dáil Éireann but, at a later stage, were central to what was probably the major decision of my political career in the Republic.

The 'Currie Mafia' – Annita and the children, a number of my brothers and sisters and their spouses – came South to help out. I was advised not to use them for canvassing, but instead for jobs such as postering, driving, addressing envelopes and making tea, where their Northern origins would not be obvious. It was a practical consideration in circumstances where I had already detected signs of partitionism. I do not wish to exaggerate, it was not widespread, but I was asked sufficiently often, in a negative way, about my nationality that I found it useful to carry my Irish passport with me. What I found surprising was the number of those who made negative remarks about my origins and who professed to be supporters of 'Fianna Fáil – the Republican party'. To be fair, I also came across many committed Fianna Fáil supporters who warmly welcomed me to Southern politics, albeit with the reservation, 'Pity you joined the wrong party'. To those who pushed me on this issue my reply was, 'Two words, Charlie Haughey'. Or, when I wished to be more positive, 'One word, Garret'. I would then explain my disillusionment with the Fianna Fáil leader over the Anglo-Irish Agreement and the contribution Garret had made to the advancement of Northern nationalists through Sunningdale and the Anglo-Irish Agreement.

Occasionally, I was accused of deserting the SDLP. I would meet this head-on by reminding the critic of my twenty-five years' involvement in Northern politics and my belief that I could continue to contribute to a solution of the Northern problem through membership of the National

Parliament. However, I was not helped by what was being seen as a less-than-generous response from the SDLP to my move South. I understood the concern, but thought it unlikely that my involvement with one party in the South would have a negative influence on the SDLP's relationship with the other parties. I also understood that my departure from Northern politics might be seen as a statement of pessimism about the political future of the North, and I attempted to counter such a suggestion. Mary Holland in *The Irish Times* praised my contribution to Northern politics, but said my decision could be, 'The kiss of death for Devolution'. My former colleague, Paddy Devlin, said, 'It is our loss and Fine Gael's gain'. A number of Unionists, particularly Ken Maginnis, regretted my decision, in the words of *The Irish Times*, 'on the grounds of his reputation as a man who wanted to do business with them and was committed to creating circumstances which would allow political movement towards devolution to begin in the North.' The greatest praise came from the *Irish News* in an editorial headed, 'Currie flouts border limits'. Media speculation generally was that I was taking 'an awful risk', which, if unsuccessful, would be the end of my political career.

In a statement John Hume said, 'Austin Currie has informed me of his decision to accept a Fine Gael nomination in the forthcoming election in the South. The outstanding service he has given both to the party and the people of Northern Ireland is well known and I thank him for it. His decision is a purely personal decision. It has been long-standing SDLP policy, and will remain so, that we do not interfere in the internal politics of the South.' I would have appreciated some expression of best wishes for my future career, but I recognised his sensitivity to relationships with the other parties. I did not appreciate the further statement from party Headquarters, which interpreted the Hume statement as 'Thank you and goodbye'.

It was almost five months later that I received a letter from Joe Hendron, the Chairman of the SDLP Constituency Representatives, who had always been supportive of me, thanking me for my outstanding contribution to the SDLP.

It was not long before I found out, on the doorsteps, what the issues were which most concerned people: unemployment, health cuts, housing, emigration and taxation were what mattered, issues that would also have been the major concerns in Northern Ireland elections except for the almost exclusive emphasis on the constitutional question. I enjoyed being involved in a 'normal' election. Halfway through the campaign, I was confident of my ability to talk to anyone about the problems my future constituents were worried about and to suggest solutions more or less in line with Fine Gael policy. My campaign was attracting favourable publicity, I was getting a good reception on the doorsteps, yet I had doubts. It was too easy. If all the constituents who had promised to vote for me actually did so, where were the votes for such tried-and-tested poll-toppers as Brian Lenihan and Jim Mitchell? In the North, you knew where you stood, sometimes uncomfortably so. Here, were they too accommodating?

My doubts would surface in the middle of the night. What sort of eejit was I and how enormous an ego to think I could walk into a constituency where I knew no one and presume I could get elected after three weeks of canvassing? I was used to making my own judgements. Now, I had to rely on others. I was also lonely. Annita was working and looking after the children back in Donaghmore, and she and other members of my family could only join me at weekends. I was meeting hundreds of people every day, but from Sunday night to Friday night I was not in contact with anyone I had known for longer than two or three weeks.

The five-seat constituency embraced the social spectrum, from the leafy avenues of Castleknock to the working-class estates of Ballyfermot and north Clondalkin. It was explained to me that there were some estates where it would be a waste of time for me, or any Fine Gael candidate to canvass; an hour spent in a middle-class area would garner more votes than a week in a run-down estate. It wasn't that they wouldn't vote for Fine Gael, they wouldn't turn out in any numbers for anyone. As a matter of principle, I insisted on canvassing these areas. It was a vicious circle. If politicians ignored such areas because of the low turnout, the neglect would cause a further deterioration and the position would get worse until, almost inevitably, there would be an explosion. My Northern experience told me that.

The conditions I found in some of the estates in north Clondalkin appalled me. The houses weren't old, indeed the vast majority had been built in the last fifteen years, but the people were congregated in large estates with a minimum of amenities. Many of them had been settled from the inner city and a high percentage of those were unemployed at the time of transfer, and remained unemployed. The business and professional people who worked in the area, including teachers and police, invariably lived outside it. Most of the houses had been built by Dublin Corporation in the County Council's jurisdiction and many of the residents believed they had been dumped and forgotten about. Educational facilities were inadequate and truancy high. A relatively small minority had created a worryingly high crime rate and Garda resources were inadequate. A major drug problem had developed and

385

so-called joy-riding was a major source of danger. There were horses everywhere, ridden bareback and often by pre-teenage children. Guard dogs, usually alsatians, snarled at one's approach; man's best friend had become a symbol of his insecurity.

Conditions in these estates were a cultural shock for someone like me from a rural background. I couldn't help making comparisons with the North, particularly as a former Housing Minister, and wishing that the resources and expertise of the Housing Executive were available to my new constituents. I was not surprised when, two years later, serious rioting broke out in a part of north Clondalkin that forced the authorities to coordinate activities and focus resources. Later, as I got to know these areas better, I became a great admirer of the myriad of voluntary community organisations and the number of individuals who dedicated themselves to improving the conditions in which they lived. The number and the vibrancy of community organisations far exceeded what I had experienced in the North, where there was greater reliance on public resources, largely from the British Treasury.

The election result was a tremendous relief. I finished fourth on first-preference votes and was elected behind Brian Lenihan (FF), Tomás Mac Giolla (Workers party) and Jim Mitchell (FG), and ahead of Liam Lawlor (FF) – all incumbent TDs. But just over a week later, I nearly caused a by-election. I had travelled North for Cemetery Sunday at Edendork. It was an emotional occasion, gathered with my wife and children, brothers and sisters and other relatives around the grave of my parents, and afterwards being congratulated by neighbours and SDLP friends. The following morning I was travelling on the road between Coalisland and Dungannon when a car, coming in the opposite direction, pulled out from behind a lorry to overtake and smashed into me. I was lucky to survive. The car was a write-off and the police told me the safety-belt had saved my life. I was cut out of the car, with a twisted ankle and bruising to the chest and head, and brought to the South Tyrone Hospital. An enterprising young local journalist contacted the BBC and RTÉ, with the result that the first Annita knew of my accident was on her car radio as she travelled between schools, twenty miles away. The bulletin said I had been seriously injured and was in intensive care. Just when things were looking up, after years of frustration and insecurity, was this how it was going to end? Thankfully, reports of my near demise turned out to be greatly exaggerated. But for Estelle, who was working in America, it was a terrible shock when she rang to wish me luck on my first day in the Dáil.

The crutch and dark glasses did not diminish the joy of my arrival to take my seat in Dáil Éireann. I was acutely conscious of the honour and privilege it was for a Tyroneman, born and reared in the partitioned North, to be taking a seat in the National Parliament. The people of Dublin West had conferred this great honour on me and the only way it could have been bettered was if the people of Fermanagh and South Tyrone had had the opportunity. Some day perhaps...? As it was, I was the only person ever to have been elected to, and to have taken a seat in both Parliaments on the island. Pride is one of the seven deadly sins; I wallowed in sinfulness that day!

Shortly after taking my seat, Sean Shiels, the manager of the Dáil bar, showed me an entry in his Visitors' Book for 3 September 1971. Hume, Devlin and I had signed it, and I had written, 'Here, as of right'. I was now here 'as of right, as of right'. On 10 May Garret had phoned me about running for the Dáil. On 26 May I had declared for Fine Gael. On 28 May I had been selected as a candidate. On 16 June I was a member of Dáil Éireann. I was now practising as a politician in a different State, in a different Parliament, in a new constituency and in a new party. It took me some time to come to terms with my new position.

To move from Donegal, or Mayo, or Kerry, or indeed any rural area to Dublin presents challenges in terms of the pace of life and adapting to the new urban environment. The transition from an area that was different in certain respects in the first place, going back to the Plantation of Ulster in the seventeenth century, and where 'separate development' had occurred since Partition presented even greater challenges. I had told myself I knew the South well. I had travelled in every part of it, holidayed there, read the daily and Sunday newspapers and watched and listened to RTÉ on a daily basis, engaged with the politicians, identified with all-Ireland sport, shared the religion of the great majority and the national aspirations as enshrined in the Constitution. I was prepared to have to come to terms with certain differences. I looked forward to breaking loose from the straitjacket of Northern sectarianism, where the constitutional issue determined attitudes to almost everything and where one of the first thoughts on meeting someone new was, 'What foot does he/she kick with?' It took me some time, too, to get used to the fact that the person who had just bought me a pint was a policeman or a soldier. I had to continually remind myself when I was annoyed at some evidence of partitionism that it cut both ways, and that my own attitudes were coloured and conditioned by seventy years of separation.

In my first few months in the Dáil I was engaged on a steep learning curve. Over the summer I spent a lot of time in my new constituency, driving around, getting to know the geography and the location of housing estates, schools, administrative offices and such matters which a TD would be expected to know. Embarrassingly, I often got lost. Even more embarrassingly, I sometimes had a problem with the accent, particularly in the working-class areas. Later, when I joined with one of the local councillors, Therese Ridge, in an Advice Centre, it was sometimes remarked that she was with me for two-way translation purposes. It wasn't always a joke!

I had to gen up on such matters as social welfare, health, housing, employment, education and generally the regulations and criteria of matters of concern to my constituents, and where there were often considerable differences from the situation North of the border. Luckily, my experienced Dáil secretary, Marie Meegan, was an expert on these matters and she kept me right. I have already referred to the number and variety of voluntary organisations, many made necessary by the lack of funding from central government. As I got to know the voluntary sector better, especially in relation to education and residents' and tenants' associations, I became aware of the pervasive influence of party politics. I have no knowledge of a society where the tentacles of the political parties are so deeply entrenched in all matters affecting local communities, certainly not in Northern Ireland, or in Britain. Tip O'Neill memorably coined the phrase, 'All politics is local'. That was not news to his Irish fellow political practitioners at home or abroad.

At the beginning, I had to tread carefully through the minefield that is internal politics in a multi-member constituency. Churchill once said, in the House of Commons, that your opponents were across the House, your enemies behind you. He had reason to know, having gone from Tory to Liberal to Tory again, but he had never experienced the pressures of sharing a constituency with four others, including a member of one's own party.

Jim Mitchell had a well-deserved reputation for inviting candidates into his constituency in order to increase the party's number of TDs and therefore the chances of being in government. He was held up by the leadership as an example to the 'quota squatters', those TDs who looked after their own position, often to the detriment of the party. Jim was rewarded for his courage and leadership by high office in the party, and by successfully bringing me into Dublin West he again gained kudos. He was a full-time politician with a wife and family and he could not afford to take unnecessary risks. He knew his constituency, kept abreast of political opinion and trends by regular polling and his risks were calculated.

Inevitably, as always happens in a multi-member constituency where there is more than one TD of a party, we soon had Mitchell and Currie camps, which made things interesting, particularly at the Annual General Meetings of branches and constituency. Fortunately, Jim and I had a good personal relationship and we recognised that the tension between our supporters was in both our interests and, as long as it did not get out of hand, was a positive factor. One element of uncertainty was the rapid increase of our electorate due to major expansion in west Dublin. Constituency boundaries had to be reviewed after each census (five years), and Dublin West was continually being changed. On one occasion I complained to Brian Lenihan that I had only just managed, by dint of hard work, to get to know one part of the constituency and it was now being transferred elsewhere. Brian's reply was, 'Austin, you and I have something in common. People think they know us from the goggle-box in the corner. It's better to move on before they get to know us too well.'

Shortly after my election, Denis Haughey, one of my former colleagues in the SDLP, asked me how I was getting on with the 'hanging and flogging party'. I assumed such a knowledgeable person as Denis was joking, but I was aware that, despite the recent experience of Fine Gael being led by Garret and Alan Dukes, such an impression lingered in some minds. In fact, I found the ordinary membership to be not unlike the SDLP. There were hangers and floggers, but they were few. There was a big emphasis on law and order, which was not unexpected in a party that prided itself on the creation of the State, but in my constituency, and judging from the annual Árd Fheis, the majority was in the centre and left of it. On social policy the majority tended to be anti-abortion and pro-divorce, which represented my own view. Fine Gael was strongly pro-European, indeed the most pro-European party in the State, a position I strongly supported. My one reservation was that Fine Gael belonged to the Christian Democratic grouping in Europe, which to me suggested sectarianism, and I warmly welcomed the later change of title to the European People's party. To be honest, I would have preferred a link with the Socialist group, along with the Labour party and the SDLP.

The election had been held on 15 June but it was 1 July before a government was formed. Indeed, for a while it looked like another election would have to be called, and my relief that this was avoided was obvious in my comment on taking my seat that it was the first time I had celebrated on the Twelfth. It was a historic occasion, the first time in the history of the State that Fianna Fáil paid the price of coalition in order to gain power. We did not know at the time that Charlie Haughey's financial position meant he would have paid almost any price to continue in government. Fianna Fáil's 'core value' of non-coalition was jettisoned in favour of a deal with the Progressive Democrats, and the six Progressive Democrat TDs who had left Fianna Fáil largely in disgust at the leadership of Mr Haughey swallowed their pride and their principles to put him back in power. It was my first experience of the raw reality of power politics, south of the border.

It was fascinating to watch Charles J Haughey in action in the Dáil. I have already indicated reasons why I found him unacceptable, but it was impossible not to be impressed by his mastery of the Dáil, his hauteur, his supreme confidence, his knowledge of all aspects of government policy, the leadership capacity and indeed his sense of humour. I particularly enjoyed his sallies with the down-to-earth Fine Gael TD from Goleen in West Cork, Paddy Sheehan. Irrespective of who else contributed, Haughey always responded to PJ, and he did so in a way that was humorous but suggested he could relate to the problems of the plain people of Ireland. In stature he resembled Napoleon, and the gestures, the demeanour, the way he walked and indeed the nose suggested that he may not have been unaware of the possible comparison.

I had looked forward to participation in a sovereign Parliament instead of what I and other nationalists had derided as 'a glorified County Council' at Stormont. My main interest, naturally, was in Northern Ireland and the continuing conflict there. I was, however, aware that my constituents had other interests and that if I did not cater for them, I would not long remain TD for Dublin West. I was determined that my unique experience of the North would be used for the greater knowledge of the Dáil and the government and would not be partisan. So throughout my career in the Dáil, in contributing to debates and particularly at Taoiseach's Question Time, I sought to add to the knowledge of the House and to contribute to a bipartisan approach. I often remembered that this was what Frank Aiken had had in mind when he had tried to persuade me to run for the Dáil in the early 1970s. In my first Northern Ireland speech I started by saying, 'Throughout my political career I have been a strong believer and advocate of consensus on Northern policy among the major parties in the Republic. My presence in this House and on these benches has not changed that conviction.' I would often tee up a question to enable the Taoiseach of the day to respond in a positive manner. During my time in the Dáil I found taoisigh and ministers for Foreign Affairs very willing to talk to me in the corridors, as well as in their Departments, and on occasion they would ask to meet with me to consult on aspects of the Northern Ireland problem. On the other hand, I found that some civil servants, including one or two with whom I had had a valuable two-way relationship before I became a TD, tended to distance themselves. Their loyalty to their political masters was admirable, but I felt both they and I lost out from the distancing.

During the election I had had an experience that had a lasting impression on me. I knocked on a door in an underprivileged estate and eventually it was opened – as far as the security chain allowed – by a small, thin woman who started to tell me that she hadn't been out of the house for over two years. I was taking details of her case, including her telephone number, when a hand appeared and someone made an effort to pull open the door. I could see, standing behind the woman and towering over her, a male in his late teens who had Down's syndrome. He was making a very determined effort to get out and only with difficulty did his mother, as the woman turned out to be, succeed in slamming the door shut. Later that evening, I rang her. Her son was the reason she had not been out of the house for over two years, not even to go to the shop or to Mass. Her husband did the shopping, if somewhat erratically, spent most of his time in the pub and refused to have anything to do with his son. So there was no one except her to look after him. When I was elected, I determined to do what I could for this unfortunate woman. The first satisfaction I got as the TD for Dublin West was in successfully arranging respite care so that she was able to escape from the house occasionally.

My maiden speech of 25 October brought together two of my interests: a NESC report which concluded that the rich were getting richer and the poor, poorer; and the impact of the European Community on our problems at a time when Ireland was about to take up the Presidency of the Community. I had decided that there were enough TDs looking after the interests of the well-off. It was the less privileged, of whom there were too many, who needed our attention.

I have already said that I looked forward to involvement in a sovereign Parliament. However, in some respects the Dáil was just as parochial as Stormont. The great majority of TDs had come through the councils and most retained their membership of local authorities. The conversation at the dinner table and in the bar and contributions in the House reflected this interest. Ireland might have the Presidency of the EU, we might hold important positions in the United Nations and our officials in the Department of Foreign Affairs might do us proud with their grasp of international affairs, but these matters were secondary to Maggie Murphy's planning approval, or who held what position in the county council, particularly if the person was a potential rival in the next Dáil election. Having held no position in local government in the twenty-six counties, or indeed in Northern Ireland, except for a brief period, I had little interest in these discussions and regretted that they pre-empted what I considered to be more worthwhile contributions on national and international affairs. Additionally, the fact that the majority of the Senate was elected by councillors meant that Senators and TDs, fearful of a future where they might have to go on the Senate circuit, paid inordinate attention to visiting councillors. The person guaranteed free drink in the Visitors' bar was a councillor. Because of the electoral system in the Senate, parochialism was entrenched at the heart of the National Parliament.

I found most of my colleagues to be very hard-working. The multi-member constituency left us with no alternative. The constituent gained from the opportunity to pick and choose from the TDs in the constituency and sometimes gave his or her problem to all of them and the competition kept TDs on their toes. In another respect the life of a TD had changed. When I had visited the Members' bar in the 1960s and 1970s there had always been a fair number of hard drinkers there. Some of the older ones, representing constituencies outside Dublin, would tell me they were delighted when the Dáil was sitting as it gave them the perfect excuse to get away from the pressures in their constituency. Backbenchers and indeed some Ministers made full use of their freedom. However, the situation changed with the retirement of older members, the greater turnover (twelve deputies retired at the 1989 election and twenty-seven lost their seats), even greater competition among members in the same constituency and an increased tendency for the media to report transgressions.

After the initial teething period I began to enjoy political life south of the border. I was much in demand for speaking engagements and media interviews, even over the summer recess, traditionally a less busy time. In August I opened the O'Carolan Harp Festival at Keadue, County Roscommon, and, a great honour, gave the Oration at the annual Michael Collins Commemoration at Béal na mBláth, and had I accepted all of the invitations I would have seen little of my family, or my constituency. Fine Gael functions, post-election victory celebrations and party fundraisers were often enjoyable, but required a strong constitution. One in particular stands out in my memory, a function in County Cavan to mark the retirement of Tom Fitzpatrick, former Ceann Comhairle and Minister. Tom was an old friend so I agreed to attend and speak on the Friday night, despite having to be in Dublin to meet passengers on a 'Peace Train' from Belfast the following morning and accompany them back to Belfast. The Cavan people excelled themselves. The hotel was packed, the drink was flying, the *craic* good, the political gossip slanderous – all of this before the function actually commenced! About midnight the speeches began, and by one o'clock I realised that everyone on the crowded platform was intent on speaking. I managed to 'escape' some time around 4.00am, vastly relieved that I had brought a driver with me for I certainly was not fit to drive despite considerable rudeness on my part in refusing drinks bought for me. Disparaging stories are told about Cavan people, but in my experience, on this and other occasions, their hospitality and generosity could not have been bettered. But occasions like this one were tough on the head and the liver!

Over the next number of months it continued. Not just Fine Gael functions but debating societies and Chambers of Commerce and the like all over the country: debates at the L&H in UCD and the Hist. in Trinity, three days in Brussels in October, travelling to Cork, West Mayo, Leitrim, Donegal, Belfast, a television programme in Paris, meetings at the House of Commons as a member of the newly formed British-Irish Interparliamentary Body, as well as Dáil and constituency business. Then, at Easter, my first foreign 'junket' as part of an Oireachtas delegation to Taiwan at the invitation of the Taiwanese administration. Even there I was not able to escape totally from Northern Ireland. On Easter Sunday, a number of us, with some difficulty, found a church for Mass. At the Consecration there were a number of loud bangs. The woman in front of me, wife of a TD, threw herself to the floor exclaiming, 'It's Currie. They are shooting at him.' It turned out to be the Chinese way of celebrating the Risen Christ by letting off firecrackers.

The visit to Taiwan was made more enjoyable by the fact that Annita was able to accompany me. It helped to make up for so much enforced separation over the previous year. So, life was good and appeared to be improving. Then, one late June afternoon, after Taoiseach's Questions, Madeleine Taylor Quinn dropped into my Dáil office. Madeleine was a TD for Clare, a member of the frontbench and a strong supporter of the party Leader, Alan Dukes. I liked her, she was lively, humorous and good company and had a good political brain. I assumed initially she had just dropped in to 'shoot the breeze', but then I realised, with a shock, that she was actually there to propose that I should be a candidate for the highest office in the land – the Presidency of Ireland.

27: THE HIGHEST OFFICE

I had been present on the platform at the Fine Gael Árd Fheis in March 1990 when the party Leader, Alan Dukes, had spoken about the possibility of a party candidate in the Presidential election in November. I had listened as Alan had said that Fine Gael would 'produce a candidate of vigour and stature' and I had noted Garret's body language indicating a strong 'No'. I had assumed it was Peter Barry he was referring to, and hoped I was right. Peter, in my opinion, would have made a superb President. This was my first Árd Fheis, but I also noted, as an experienced public speaker, and wondered why it was, that the party Leader was finding it difficult to enthuse an audience conditioned to respond positively.

Now, three months later, here was Madeleine seeking to persuade me to run. I am sorry to say I laughed. Was she out of her mind? I was less than a year in Southern politics. I was still finding my way. I had to concentrate on my new constituency. I hadn't even thought about the role of the President. Hell, I was only fifty, it was too early to retire from active politics. As Madeleine left, she could have been in no doubt as to the strength of my negative response.

The next development was an invitation from Tom Enright TD, Chairman of the Parliamentary party, to have lunch with him. I wondered why we were eating at the St Stephen's Green Club and not the Dáil restaurant, but it turned out that Tom was a member there and I assumed he saw it as part of his function to have a good relationship with members of the Parliamentary party. To my dismay, after a short general discussion he came straight to the point and said, 'Austin, I think you would make a great President'. This time, I didn't laugh. It was clear to me now that I was being headhunted – and from the top. Again I responded in what I considered forceful terms. I was relieved when the Dáil recess came on 13 July as a number of my colleagues, not all from Fine Gael, and one or two journalists were enquiring about my intentions. Annita and I, Austin Óg and Emer had arranged to go on holiday to Yugoslavia on 20 July, and I was keenly looking forward to getting away from everyone for two weeks. The night before our departure, Alan Dukes rang. Could we meet? I was sorry, said I untruthfully, we were going on holiday the next day. There was, he said, a certain amount of urgency about what he wished to discuss with me, so would I contact him as soon as I returned?

Yugoslavia bored me. I would have found it more interesting had I known the Federation would fall apart within a year, but the police, uniformed and in plain clothes, were omnipresent and in control. So Annita and I had plenty of time to discuss what I was sure Dukes wanted to talk to me about and to consult with our two youngest children. Emer, aged eleven, loved the idea of living in the Phoenix Park next to the Zoo, which she had visited on a school trip from the North. We were at the time looking at houses in Dublin. Was this house in the Phoenix Park big enough so she could invite all of her friends from Donaghmore to visit? Austin, aged fifteen, was a bit more doubtful. Would there be police guarding us, just as there had been in Donaghmore?

Annita and I had no doubt. It was a great honour even to be considered for the Presidency of our country, particularly for someone from the North whose nationality had always been under attack. But no, certainly not now, maybe in seven years' time when I had properly found my feet in Southern politics and the children would be able to cope with the challenge. Halfway through the holiday, Alan Dukes rang. Marie always had my telephone number in case of an emergency, personal or political, and I assumed he had obtained it from her. He just wished to confirm when I would be home. Two days later he rang again: would Annita and I like to have dinner with him and his wife the evening after our return and maybe stay overnight?

The 'P' subject wasn't mentioned at dinner at the Dukes' home, a short distance outside Kildare town. Annita and Fionnuala Dukes got on well from the beginning, and after a pleasant dinner Alan and I left them in animated discussion while we moved to his study, and he got straight to the point. Fine Gael needed a Presidential candidate. Was I interested? I didn't avoid the question. No, I wasn't. I repeated the reasons I had already given to Madeleine Taylor Quinn and to Tom Enright (which I was pretty sure they had reported to him), but I added another one which, as the person who had first suggested I might run in Dublin West rather than Dublin South, I felt he would appreciate. My constituency had been messed around a lot in recent years. After a magnificent electoral achievement in returning three Fine Gael TDs, Dick Burke had gone to Brussels as Commissioner in a stroke by Charlie Haughey to consolidate his government. Against all the odds Fine Gael had won the ensuing by-election, but the successful candidate, Liam Skelly, had run into difficulties with the party and in the 1987 election Fine Gael had been reduced to one seat, that of Jim Mitchell. It was in these circumstances that I had been successfully parachuted into the constituency. Feelings were still raw among the membership and I had assured them I was there for the long haul. A Presidential bid by me would renew their distrust of the party leadership and would cause problems for me for the future (since I did not expect I would be elected), by leaving me open to the criticism that I was only using the constituency as a stepping stone to higher things. Additionally, I told him my experience in the North had conditioned me to give a high priority to personal loyalty and I felt I was attracting that in Dublin West, but loyalty was a two-way process and I would not let them down.

Alan said he understood my position, but the party interest required a candidate and he hoped I would reconsider. He did not say I was the only one in the frame, and I took the opportunity of expressing my strong support for Peter Barry who, because of his involvement with the Anglo-Irish Agreement and the confidence Northern nationalists had in him, would be a President of All the Nation. Alan again expressed the hope that I would think seriously about running and I reiterated that I had already thought it through and my mind was made up. We parted on good personal terms. On the way back to Dublin the following morning, I told Annita that I hoped this would be the end of it.

On return to my rented house in Lucan a few days later, I received a letter from John Lynch, one of the team that had helped to organise my election and who I continued to meet on a regular basis for advice and consultation. John wrote:

'I hope you will not think it impertinent of me, but I think the idea of running for the Presidency which is being floated in some sections of the "Gossip media" should be buried or laid to rest nice and quietly. There is a wider agenda which you should look at and then come to a decision. Anyway, whatever you decide, rest assured of my full support and loyalty.

Much to my regret Alan Dukes is in real trouble. This gives me no joy because I joined Fine Gael when he became leader, but he has failed to inspire or get the message across that there is an alternative to the "Cuteness" of Fianna Fáil. He just has not caught the imagination of the ordinary five-eighth out there. This brings us to the point of the Presidency. His survival and the Presidential campaign are intertwined.

Quite frankly, if you allow your name to go forward you will in effect be "bailing him out". You owe him nothing. More important, you have to realise you are a first division player and players of your calibre are not brought on in the last ten minutes when the side is being walloped. The whole thing was handled very badly from the start and I see no reason why they (Dukes + the shy men) should use you now when they have backed themselves into a "no win" situation.

THE HIGHEST OFFICE

It's been a good twelve months for you politically. You have "dug in" so to speak and have not put a foot wrong at local or national level. My instinct tells me "the best is yet to be", even with the constituency re-jigged. One other observation I will make. There is a certain "begrudgery" in the Irish mentality. The scenario goes something like this, "Who is the bloke who comes in and takes a seat and now wants to go for the Presidency? Who does he think he is?" I know it is a latent partitionist mentality in your case, but that Irish begrudgery is there all the time.'

I ought to have made copies of that letter and left it in places around the house where I would have been reminded of the advice it contained, possibly the most prescient of my political career.

It being August and, unlike the North, the traditional holiday month, I spent a few days in my constituency, then in Donaghmore and from there to West Cork, where I was when the Dáil was recalled to discuss developments in relation to the Goodman beef company. I should have ignored the whip and stayed in West Cork, or Tyrone, or anywhere except Dáil Éireann. The only question exercising the minds of Fine Gael TDs was the Presidency and the effect of a failure to find a candidate on the future of the party Leader. Clearly there was a crisis just around the corner. I couldn't escape the questions and my laugh and smile were becoming more than a little forced. However, I did give an interview to Richard Balls of the *Sunday Tribune* confirming that I had no intention of running for the Presidency.

The Dáil sat on Tuesday and Wednesday, 28 and 29 August. On both days Alan asked to see me. On both occasions I again said 'No'. On the second occasion he told me that the party had commissioned a public opinion poll that measured my support and that of Peter Barry and Avril Doyle against Brian Lenihan, Mary Robinson and John Wilson. I had not done as well as Peter, but was better than Avril. However, the main reason for my low standing, pre-eminent among the reasons given why respondents would not like me to be elected, was 'not here long' and my Northern origins. He said he was confident this apparent disadvantage could be transformed into an asset during the campaign. I told him of John Lynch's advice about begrudgery, said the opinion poll confirmed it and fled, not to Lucan but to my Northern fastness.

There I had time to study the details of the opinion poll, which he had given me at my request. It didn't take long. Nine pages in all, but I noted the first page was marked (5) and the last (51). Nevertheless the message was clear to me: 70% of those polled were not prepared to vote for me because of 'N.I./INT. IN NORTH/NOT HERE LONG' and on suitability rating I finished last of the six candidates, with a 39% rating for 'Reasonably unsuitable or very unsuitable'. Brian Lenihan rated 18% in these categories, as did Mary Robinson. Thirty-eight percent of Fine Gael voters deemed me in the unsuitable category. The egotist in me drew consolation from the fact that I was highly rated in every other quality seen to be important for holding the highest office in the land. The poll confirmed that if Fine Gael were to have a candidate, then Peter Barry was the right one, with a good chance of pulling it off. I assumed the remainder of the opinion-poll findings, which I had not been given, would bear that out.

To my dismay I was only home a few hours when Dukes rang. Could he see me as a matter of urgency? I told him I had no intention of returning to Dublin in present circumstances and that if he wished to discuss further the subject we had already discussed on a number of occasions, there was no point in meeting. He insisted, however, and when he said he was prepared to travel to Donaghmore, I felt I could not refuse to meet him.

We met at the Glengannon Hotel, on the outskirts of Dungannon, and I escorted him to my home in Donaghmore. I had had to ring Annita, who was at work, and tell her we had a guest for dinner. She was surprised, but went to some trouble. The first course was a local delicacy, Lough Neagh pollen; I couldn't help thinking that a slippery eel from the same source might have been more appropriate considering the fate I was determined to avoid. Dualta, Austin and Emer were at the table and the interaction between Alan and my children would have surprised those who thought of him as cold and remote.

After dinner he came straight to the point. Fine Gael needed a candidate and I was the only one who fit the bill. I should forget about Peter Barry, who was not willing to run. He was asking me, in the interests of the party, to allow my name to go forward. I responded as I had on the previous occasions, adding that I thought the MRBI poll findings were conclusive. No, he had had discussions with a number of people and he was confident my Northernness could be turned into an advantage. I reminded him of the partitionism I had encountered, including the occasion in the Dáil when a voice from the Fianna Fáil benches (too cowardly to identify himself, then or later) had told me to 'go back'. He responded that the reaction to that remark indicated the real view of the Irish people.

We got down to the nitty-gritty. The nomination of a Presidential candidate, I told him, could not be divorced from his future as party Leader. I, or any other candidate, could be the sacrificial lamb, with those opposed to him deviously using the campaign to undermine the candidate and his sponsor. He agreed there were people in the party who would like to get rid of him, but in the face of the common enemy they wouldn't dare not pull their weight. I said I would be particularly vulnerable as I had not been long enough in the party to build up my own base of support and therefore would be relying to a much greater extent on the efforts of others. Anyway, even in my own constituency I would not have the support of party activists, especially those closest to me, whose allegiance was essential for my future career. He asked who they were and when I told him, he said he was prepared to meet them. That threw me a bit, but I was so confident of their attitude that I provided him with their telephone numbers. I was fed up with what now was approaching harassment. The meeting with the team would provide finality.

Nevertheless, I took no chances. When Gerry Leahy rang me to say Dukes had telephoned him and he and the other four of my team were meeting him on Tuesday night, I decided to return to Dublin to meet them and did so on Monday night. I already had John Lynch's strong feelings on paper and Brian Brady, Jim Fay, Tom Kavanagh and Gerry Leahy joined with him in supporting my determination not to stand. I have in front of me as I write my typed 'riding instructions' to them. They could not have been in the slightest doubt about my wishes. I was in no doubt about the outcome of the meeting.

I was on my own in the house in Esker Lawns that evening, Tuesday, 4 September. Caitríona, who lived with me during term, was working in America for the summer. I expected a phone call from one of the team as soon as the meeting concluded. Around one o'clock in the morning, the phone call came, but not from my activists. It was Alan Dukes. He told me the meeting was over and that my friends had agreed to support me as the candidate. I was so shocked I could only mutter something to the effect that I would have to hear the news directly from them. He asked me to ring him in the morning. Those were the days before mobile phones and all of the team were married men with children, so I was reluctant to wake up the households by telephoning them at that hour of the morning. Anyway, they might not yet have returned home. They might have been thirsty after an intense meeting. If what Alan had said was correct, maybe they were reluctant to break the bad news? The phone didn't ring and I didn't get any sleep. It was after 9.00am when I phoned Gerry Leahy and had the shocking truth confirmed. To this day I have not received a detailed report of what happened that evening, only that the party Leader and the General Secretary, Joe Kenny, also a constituent, were at their most persuasive and convinced the team that it was in my interests, and the interests of the party, that I should run. I now had no alternative. In all honour, I had to accept the poisoned chalice. Shortly after ten o'clock, I was in Alan Dukes' office to tell him I would run. 'You have made me,' he said, 'a very happy man.'

It has been suggested that I extracted a price for agreeing to stand – a position on the frontbench, or some other political preferment. My diary note on the occasion of Dukes' visit to Donaghmore reads, 'Name your price'. This was a statement of my opinion of what I could have done in view of the obvious desperation to get a candidate. But to be fair to Alan Dukes, he did not try to bribe me, and I did not hold out for a reward. Had I been into such dealing, the time to have done it was a year earlier when he had asked me to run in Dublin West instead of Dublin South.

According to Dan Egan and Alice Cullen, who compiled a report, between the date of my selection as the Fine Gael candidate on 12 September and the election on 7 November, I travelled a total of 14,422 miles: 10,500 by car and coach, 347 by rail, 2,681 by plane and 894 by helicopter. I visited every county at least twice and most on a number of occasions. I also visited London to meet with representatives of agencies working with Irish emigrants in Britain. I do not have the time or space to comment in detail on the campaign. I will content myself with a number of observations.

My initial disadvantage of late entry became a permanent one. By the time I announced, the public had become used to the idea of a two-horse race. In particular, Mary Robinson had been campaigning since 1 May, more than four months before Fine Gael's candidate. My reluctance to accept the nomination had contributed to the delay, but even when I was first seriously approached it was already too late, not only for me but for any Fine Gael candidate, except Garret or Peter Barry. To have had a reasonable chance, and to get the electorate accustomed to someone of my background, required a much longer period.

The Lenihan controversy over the Duffy tape was the deciding issue. It wasn't just that it raised questions of his credibility and judgement, it created a very strong for and against Lenihan factor that polarised opinion between him and Robinson and squeezed me in between. I had, in my very first speech in the campaign proper, on 1 October, raised the question of Lenihan's capacity to be independent from Fianna Fáil, and from Charles Haughey in particular. I had cited his alleged phone calls to President Hillery as an example and said, 'The issue of the independence of the President will be a major issue in this campaign.' I had no idea how big an issue it would become. I did not, nor do I, believe that Fine Gael knew about the tape at that stage. Even when the issue was raised on RTÉ's 'Questions and Answers' programme we did not know of the tape. When controversy erupted, the established facts confirmed my judgement of the central issue in the campaign. Unfortunately, I did not get the credit. Part of the reason for that was the public perception that Fine Gael had set a trap for Lenihan, a perception added to by Jim Mitchell's unfortunate statement to that effect.

I have no doubt that the public opinion polls were self-fulfilling. They encouraged tactical voting and, particularly in the aftermath of the tape controversy, encouraged Fine Gael voters to vote Robinson in order to beat Lenihan. Some have argued, because of this factor, that polls should be banned, and indeed legislation was introduced for this purpose a few years ago. To me this is not a practical proposal as unofficial poll results will always be leaked, sometimes irresponsibly, but their capacity to at least tilt the democratic process must be recognised. Additionally, their effect on morale, for and against, can be an important factor. The most difficult part of my Presidential campaign was invariably on a Monday morning, in the aftermath of weekend polls, trying to raise my own morale and then transmitting this to my foot soldiers.

What annoyed, indeed angered me most was the suggestion that because I came from the North I was not a real Irishman. I had encountered this, what I called 'Partitionist mentality', when I fought Dublin West, but my decision to seek the highest office in the land, the very symbol of our nationality, brought out the worst in certain people. Some said it to my face, 'The President should be an Irishman', or alleged I had a British passport, or asserted that someone who had sworn an oath of allegiance to the British monarch (as I had been forced to do in order to hold a Parliamentary seat) could not represent the Irish nation. I could deal with these matters when they were raised directly with me. What was more annoying was the whispering and the inferences, some from the very top. Ray Burke, Minister for Justice, speaking at the Fianna Fáil rally in O'Connell Street, outside the GPO, the symbol of our freedom and independence, said, 'Alan Dukes had to go to Tyrone to find a candidate for the Presidency.' There were other comments designed to paint me as less than Irish, as an outsider, to build on the perception that I was a 'blow-in'. I tried to counter that Eamon de Valera had been born in New York, James Connolly in Glasgow, Erskine Childers born in London of British parentage on both sides, Thomas Clarke, the first signatory of the Proclamation, was a Dungannon man. Was I less Irish than them? Some of these people professed to support an Ireland where Catholic, Protestant and dissenter would be treated equally. What chance did a Protestant and unionist have if these same people treated me as an alien? The whispering continued on the doorsteps, given credence by the fact that, as John Lynch had so presciently pointed out to me, I had been involved in the public life of this State for just over a year.

It was hard to take, particularly from so-called republicans. After all I, like all nationalists in the Six Counties, had had to fight to establish my nationality. We had suffered for proudly wearing the badge of our Irish nationality, even for insisting, as my brothers and sisters had, on being called Seamus, Sean and Mairead. Was I not right to consider myself at least as good an Irishman as Ray Burke, or Charlie Haughey?

Even Emily O'Reilly, distinguished political journalist (and current Ombudsman) had this to say in her book, *Candidate – the truth behind the Presidential Campaign*: 'How could Currie, a resident in the South for little more than a year, speak with credibility and in detail about an office which few people imagined he really knew about? The President is perceived as someone with a wide knowledge and familiarity with every aspect of Irish life. On that score Currie, in the public mind, simply wasn't at the races.' A person might have a degree in political science and have specialised on the role of the Presidency in the United States, in France, in Ireland, even in the Soviet Union, but being born and reared and trained in the white heat of Northern politics was a disadvantage he apparently could not overcome.

I believe it was accepted by impartial reporters and critics that I won the TV discussion programmes on which the three candidates debated together, 'The Late Late Show' and 'Today Tonight'. Unfortunately, there were not enough such appearances and they came too late in the campaign to help me sufficiently. This was due in part to Fianna Fáil's strategy of limiting Lenihan's appearance on such three-way programmes in the belief that he had least to gain from them. Towards the end of the campaign, it was Mary Robinson who had most to lose.

Throughout the campaign a number of women journalists were extremely biased in favour of Mary Robinson, and I was not surprised to find out later that some of them had actually been involved in her campaign as advisors. One of those who interviewed me wrote an article that trivialised and damned with faint praise and concluded, 'Maybe it's just the contrast with the North, but I'll say one thing for Austin Currie, after half a cup of coffee with him, he thinks it's really great down here.' The writer of that article, in my opinion, had a duty to disclose that she had been involved in the Robinson campaign.

As I feared, the divisions within Fine Gael, especially over the leadership of Alan Dukes, were affecting the campaign. I had spoken to John Bruton, the obvious alternative, on the day I had accepted the nomination, had bluntly told him of my fears and asked him to use his influence with those who might be tempted to hold back. He committed himself to assisting me in every way he could and said he would try to influence others. I had no way of knowing what influence he used with others, but in terms of his personal contribution to my campaign he was as good as his word in canvassing with me, and separately with Annita, within and outside his constituency. He also took charge of my own constituency. There were others who promised full support to my face and then got offside, or more often put in a token appearance, or didn't organise a canvass properly and didn't pull their weight in all the ways a devious politician can find to cover his or her hidden agenda. I became quite good at sussing them out. And if I myself did not detect a lack of enthusiasm, there was always someone in the entourage to whisper in my ear.

Of particular concern were a number of my female colleagues in the Dáil. I understood the position they were in. They identified with Mary Robinson, had the same standards and aspirations, and believed that the election of a female President would strike a blow for the advancement of women. Indeed, because of the delay in selecting a Fine Gael candidate, some of them had already identified with the Robinson campaign. I sympathised with the dilemma of those TDs and other leading female members of the party. Again, it was the hypocrisy that angered me: promises, even written promises, of full support versus token delivery. The best example was the one who canvassed with me in Connemara, but got offside in her own constituency. Having said that, I have to add my admiration for the great majority of women in Fine Gael who, notwithstanding their common purpose with a female candidate, put their party and its candidate first and gave me their total commitment.

I had another difficulty, which related to Northern Ireland. Jim Mitchell, as Director of Elections, knew that a major initiative was required if there was to be any chance of me making a breakthrough, something that would grab the headlines and force the other two candidates to respond positively, or even negatively, and show them to be following my lead. Jim decided that the major initiative should be on Northern Ireland, but unfortunately the motivation, in my opinion, had more to do with the potential for a dramatic impact than as a serious contribution to the Northern problem. The proposal was for me to suggest a referendum to allow the people of the Republic to state, categorically, that there could not be unity without the consent of the majority in Northern Ireland. I had no problem about that, but I did have a problem with the proposition that talks on a Northern settlement should not take place until the referendum had been passed. Agreement on the principle and then the wording, followed by the referendum, would require considerable time, further delaying a talks process already too long delayed. But more importantly, as far as I was concerned, it was a cynical exercise to make an impact for electoral gain, and I believed it would be seen as such and probably portrayed as such north and south of the border. It would destroy the one quality I had over the other two candidates: my integrity in relation to the North. I was not prepared to sacrifice that integrity, built up over so many years, for the Presidency or anything else. I did not want the Presidency that much.

My refusal to endorse the proposal led to a major disagreement with Jim Mitchell and the advisors around him, and eventually a meeting was called at Headquarters in Mount Street to sort it out. It was that night that I realised, for the first time, how much of a shambles the Presidential campaign was in. When I arrived a meeting was just concluding and there had clearly been disagreement. Dukes and Mitchell were shouting at each other and others were joining in. It wasn't just my proposed speech on the North, for it wasn't mentioned in the few minutes I listened to them before I intervened to say I was going next door to finish the drafting of an alternative proposal. This I did, proposing a 'Peace Pledge' that all three candidates would sign, which would express the wish of the people that unity would only come about by agreement, specifically by the agreement of a majority of people in the North, and that we should also declare that the use of violence for political ends was contrary to the will of the people of the State. The Pledge would form the basis for a Referendum at the earliest possible opportunity. It was not what Jim Mitchell wanted, it did not lead to the 'positive controversy' which might have given a boost to the campaign, but neither did it lead to accusations that I was prepared, cynically, to use the North to boost my electoral ratings in the South. A clear conscience helped to minimise the despair and anger I felt at the evidence of how poor personal relationships were among some of those responsible for the organisation of my campaign, and the chaos this was causing at Headquarters. However, the experience was the nadir of my campaign in terms of my lingering hopes.

Fortunately, there were other experiences which made up for it, occasions when, despite the opinion polls and the realisation that I had an Everest to climb, I actually enjoyed myself. I will always remember the night in Cavan, the rally in Market Square that was reminiscent of earlier times and which appealed to the historian in me with the flowery oratory and the torch-lit procession. And the similar torch-lit procession in Listowel prior to a public meeting where the atmosphere brought out the best in me. (I remember also, on a high after the meeting, looking forward to *The Irish Times'* report, only to find that Deaglán de Bhreadún had missed my triumph, finding the company of John B Keane more hospitable and invigorating on a late October night. To this day when I meet Deaglán he calls me 'Mr President', and I remind him of that night.) I remember too the meeting in Bantry when my old friend, Paddy Sheehan, told the assembly that Austin Currie and he had much in common, including being born halfway up a mountain.

I remember travelling in an open-top Daimler, accompanied by Paul Connaughton TD and Senator Liam Naughton, through Ballinasloe to the Horse Fair; the *faux pas*, after being allowed by pilot Ulick McEvaddy to take the controls, of describing at a press conference how I had expertly held the Jockstick, instead of the Joystick; the experience of being interviewed on 98FM by Fr Michael Cleary on the moral dimension of politics (if only I had known!); the embarrassment of being thrown into the air by a large female stallholder in Moore Street who felt my 'credentials' as she did so, but fortunately pronounced that I would make a good President; the wonderful photograph of John B Keane and me at the premiere of *The Field* where he is pointing at my reflection in a mirror on the wall saying, 'Mirror, mirror on the wall, who'll be President in the Fall?'; the beauty of the Boyne Valley as we arrived by helicopter for a lunch hosted by Lord Henry Mountcharles at Slane Castle; the fun of making the TV Party Political Broadcasts and the retakes because one or more of the children, or indeed Annita, would collapse in giggles as we ran across the sands in Killiney, or gathered around the piano for a 'family sing song'; the thousands of ordinary Irish men and women who received me warmly and made me conscious of the honour of being considered as their President.

Once again I had good reason to be grateful for the support of my wife and children. Annita took two months' leave from her job and most of the time had a separate itinerary from me. She gave media interviews all over the country, which were all extremely positive. She delivered speeches, not only to women's groups and organisations catering for children but to a cross-section of the electorate. On 'The Late Late Show' that featured the three spouses, it was almost universally accepted that she was the winner. All my children did me proud, contributing what they could according to age and experience, from Estelle using the political skills she had acquired as a student politician at Queen's to Emer, canvassing with the question, 'Will you vote for my Daddy?'

Four days before the election, Mary Robinson and I announced our agreement on a voting pact, urging the electorate to vote Currie number one and Robinson number two, or Robinson number one and Currie number two. Throughout the election the opinion polls had shown me at between 14% and 19%, so it was obvious who had most to gain from our agreement. As we walked together from the Shelbourne Hotel, where we had agreed the pact, across to St Stephen's Green to deliver the statement to the media, it suddenly struck me that what I was about to do would almost certainly mean the election of Mary Robinson as President of Ireland. And I didn't even like her. I thought she was too cold, too impersonal, too artificial. On a personal level, I much preferred the man who now would almost certainly finish second.

As soon as it became clear that the opinion polls had been accurate, and that my transfers were electing her, I issued a statement congratulating the President-Elect: 'The electorate has given its verdict. The democratic process to which we all owe allegiance has taken place. We will now have a President who deserves the full support and respect of us all.' It was a responsible and dignified statement, but unfortunately it was issued from the Berkeley Court Hotel and not in the presence of the President-Elect at the count centre. That is something I have always regretted.

I had, of course, no previous experience of procedure or practice in relation to the declaration of the Presidential election result, so I relied on others and on my Director of Elections in particular. Jim assured me that he would look after whatever had to be done and that there was no need for me to attend at the count centre. There hadn't been a Presidential election in seventeen years, and others I enquired from couldn't add to my knowledge.

At a stage during the election campaign when morale had been particularly low, I had promised Annita that when the election was over we would get away from it all and go to Rome, our favourite holiday destination in the world. The arrangements had been made discreetly through Tony Brazil of Limerick Travel, a strong Fine Gael supporter; if the arrangement had leaked it would have been a strong indication that I did not believe I would be President after the election and that would have further diminished my vote. On the day of the count, Annita and I were advised to continue our preparations for the journey and we returned to Lucan to do so. It was in the house there, watching the TV, that I became aware that Brian Lenihan and the Taoiseach, Charles Haughey, were both at the count, but that no one from Fine Gael appeared to be present. I made frantic phone calls to try to contact Jim Mitchell, but without success. I watched with dismay, and a sense of shame, as Brian Lenihan made a dignified speech accepting defeat and congratulating the President-Elect. I felt strongly that many people, including a large number of Fine Gaelers, would wonder why I was not present, particularly as it was my transfers which had decided the outcome. I feared I would be thought of as a bad loser and bitterly regretted not heeding my own instinct that I should have been present.

The reality soon became clear to me. The *putsch* against Alan Dukes was already under way. The organisers didn't want me at the declaration of the result because I was sure to be questioned about Alan's future and the conspirators suspected that I would support the party Leader. Everyone knew that serious questions affecting his leadership would arise from the election result, that there was a certain inevitability that he would be ousted, but the speed and ruthlessness of the move against him took most commentators by surprise, including me. Indeed it shocked me, and the episode diminished my respect for my adopted party. It happened again ten years later when the victim was John Bruton.

Meanwhile, Annita and I were putting the election result behind us by enjoying the sights of Rome. I tell people that if you have an interest in history, then Rome is your city, if you have an interest in religion, or culture, or architecture, or food, or drink, or sex (so I'm told!), whatever your interest may be, Rome will cater for it. We went to Rome as private citizens, but someone tipped off the Ambassador, Paddy Power, to our presence there, and we had the privilege of a semi-private audience with the Pope and a private guided tour of the Sistine Chapel.

By the time Annita and I returned home, Fine Gael had a new leader: John Bruton. Alan Dukes had paid the price for me finishing third, but the skids had been under him for some time, certainly before the campaign had begun. It was inevitable, but unfair. He had shown considerable courage in supporting the minority Fianna Fáil government by propounding the Tallaght Strategy and had put the country before party. I regretted his rejection on personal grounds as well. The experience of shared adversity had thrown us closer together. The Leader had gone. What was to be my future?

The media was kind to me. Colm Boland in *The Irish Times*, in an article titled, 'Currie salvages honour from the wreckage of Fine Gael campaign', wrote, 'In spite of his poor third place in the Presidential election, there was a surprising degree of agreement that the Fine Gael candidate, Mr. Austin Currie had enhanced rather than damaged his stature in Irish politics. While there was much talk of *post mortems*, wakes and inquests within the Fine Gael Party there was little evidence of recriminations about the calibre of the candidate himself or of his performance during the campaign.'

I was pleased to find that this appeared to be the generally held view within Fine Gael and the political community. Indeed, some commentators were predicting a bright political future. I was less hopeful. I suspected that it wouldn't take long for the memory of my good personal campaign to recede and the actual first-count result would be there for the record:

Currie 267,902 – 17%
Lenihan 694,484 – 44.1%
Robinson 612,265 – 38.9%

Politics is ultimately about power, obtaining it and exercising it. Power comes to the winners. I was a loser and Fine Gael, through its treatment of Alan Dukes, had shown its attitude to losers. My morale was improved, however, by messages from people whose estimation I valued. The hundreds of written and verbal messages confirmed to me that I was right not to risk my integrity on the North for a boost in the opinion polls, or even for the Presidency itself. In this regard I was particularly grateful to Professor Enda McDonagh, Douglas and Dorothy Gageby, Peter Barry TD, Alf McCreary from Queen's and the *Belfast Telegraph*, Conn and Patricia McCluskey and one of my GAA heroes, Eamon Mongey. A particularly warm and intriguing letter came from an old political foe, Harry West, former leader of the Unionist party:

Dear Austin,
Although we were never on the same political wavelength I have always regarded you as a friend and it is in this spirit that I write to congratulate you most warmly on your performance during the Presidential election campaign. Your showing on all the TV programmes that I saw, if calculated on pure merit alone, should have earned you much greater electoral support and made you a serious rival to Mary Robinson, but I am afraid you were a

victim of your Ulster heritage.

However, I feel very sure that you have made a very favourable impact on the electorate of the country of your adoption and who knows where this might lead to in the future. I wish you well. In the showing of the spouses Annita made an outstanding contribution on your behalf. Please offer her my congratulations.

Sincerely,

Harry West

The letter from Douglas Gageby, former Editor of *The Irish Times* and a republican in the 1798 tradition, was co-signed by his wife Dorothy and read:

Dear Austin,

This is one family that, in the immortal words of Ray Burke, went to Tyrone for its President. You fought a great fight. As you know, had you been earlier in the fray, things would have been different. Your TV appearances made a big impression. But you raised the big question which others dodge, and I hope that this aspect of your campaign will not be allowed to die down. More power to Annita and yourself. We are proud of you.

Best wishes,

Douglas Gageby. Dorothy Mary.

In the course of his letter Conn McCluskey said: 'I expect you will get many invitations to the Park because, without you, Mary R would never have smelt it.'

That struck a responsive chord. After one of our TV appearances during the campaign, Brian Lenihan had said to me, 'Austin, when this is over, whether you or I win, we will have a session with the wives in the Áras.' I had wholeheartedly agreed. I don't know about Brian, but there was no invite to me from Mary Robinson.

28: IN AND OUT OF POWER

After the high of the Presidential election it took quite a while to settle down to the humdrum existence of Dáil and constituency work. But that was what I knew I had to do. My second Dáil election was always going to be my most difficult, when the novelty of me had worn off. The exposure of the Presidential election had helped, of course, but there were those who said, 'Well, you were prepared to leave us for the Park.' I had to be seen to be assiduous in my constituency representation, particularly as Dublin West had been reduced, as a result of the *Boundary Commission Report*, from five seats to four.

The Fianna Fáil–Progressive Democrat coalition that had come to power on 12 July 1989 continued in office, with Charles Haughey as Taoiseach, until February 1992 when Charlie was forced out and Albert Reynolds took over. Watching Albert performing as Taoiseach, it was clear to me there was not only a change of style but of substance. For all his arrogance and showmanship, Charlie had real ability and was not only on top of his job but knew, possibly too intrusively, what was happening in each Department. Albert didn't have his style and it was obvious, too, at Taoiseach's Question Time, that he didn't have the same capacity for the job as Charlie had. He tended to chance his arm if he didn't know the answer to a question. Albert had other qualities, but they were more those of the businessman than the politician. He set himself an objective and went for it, not too worried about the corners he cut. It was those qualities that made him the right man in the right place when opportunity beckoned in relation to Northern Ireland, but which also caused his difficulties with his political partners in coalition.

The coalition with the PDs he saw as, 'A temporary little arrangement', and it came to an end after only nine months. The election in November 1992 resulted in a major breakthrough by the Labour party, with 33 Deputies, an increase of 18. Fianna Fáil lost 9 seats to 68, Fine Gael lost 10 to 45 and the PDs gained 4 to 10. A government was eventually formed on 12 January 1993, a coalition of Fianna Fáil and Labour and with the biggest majority in the history of the State. With this huge majority, and an agreement on major funding from Europe amounting to IR£8 billion, those of us in opposition feared we were going to be there for a long time.

In my own constituency, now a four-seater, I had finished third, behind

Joan Burton of Labour, who shared in the swing to Labour nationally and topped the poll, and behind Brian Lenihan, but ahead of Liam Lawlor. The two defeated Presidential candidates finished second and third!

On the second day of the count I was involved in a controversy that might have wrecked any chance I had of preferment under the leadership of John Bruton. During the campaign, as opinion polls predicted a substantial increase in the Labour vote, the idea of a 'rotating Taoiseach' was floated by Dick Spring and received considerable currency in the media. Following the election result, the betting was on a 'Rainbow coalition' since Fianna Fáil had lost 10 seats. However, Labour was angry at Fine Gael for what Labour figures described as a 'condescending and patronising' attitude towards them and a poor personal relationship existed between Bruton and Spring over differences they had had in the last FitzGerald government. Additionally, Fine Gael ruled out Democratic Left involvement and Labour ruled out the Progressive Democrats.

In circumstances where the electorate had clearly voted for change, I decided, on my own personal initiative, on a course of action, without consulting with anyone, except Gerry Leahy, who supported what I proposed to do. At the count in Lucan I gave an interview to RTÉ in which I described the idea of a rotating Taoiseach as 'constitutional nonsense', but went on to say that I was prepared to put to the Fine Gael Parliamentary party some way in which Dick Spring's aspiration could be realised.

I was totally unprepared for the violent reaction. The Fine Gael Director of Elections described me as 'treacherous' and John Bruton responded with interviews on TV and radio in which he dismissed the idea, and me as well. What I hadn't realised was that on foot of the party's election disaster, the leadership feared that my interview was the first shot in a campaign to oust John Bruton, in the same way Alan Dukes had been shafted after the Presidential election. The result was that my suggestion did not receive any consideration and the whole concentration was on my alleged disloyalty. There was also the accusation that I had damaged Fine Gael's bargaining position.

As events developed and Labour went into coalition with Fianna Fáil, an arrangement was agreed whereby an expanded Department of the Tánaiste gave Dick Spring an overview of the workings of the entire government. It wasn't exactly a rotating Taoiseach position, but it was the nearest thing to it compatible with the Constitution, and there was no reason why such an arrangement could not have been worked out with Fine Gael. Two years later, when Fianna Fáil and Labour split up, there was little difficulty in Fine Gael and Labour agreeing an arrangement that gave Labour what they wanted and included Democratic Left. Lessons had been learned.

However, I deserved the criticism I received. It was not my job to have made such a controversial proposal, publicly. I made a personal statement at the next party meeting for what I described as an inexcusable breach of collective responsibility, and I resigned my frontbench position. It had been a traumatic experience, the worst part being my anger at myself for a failure of judgement of timing and place. I was comforted to find that there was little criticism in my constituency organisation, and indeed my commitment to two-way loyalty stood me in good stead. My loss of the frontbench spokesmanship role did not worry me unduly.

On 10 April 1993 the news broke, by accident, that John Hume and Gerry Adams were meeting and two weeks later they issued a joint declaration in which they said that the Irish people as a whole had a right to national self-determination, that it was a matter for agreement among the people of Ireland, and that they would be continuing to meet to pursue that agreement and the means of achieving it. The very same day as this statement was issued an IRA bomb exploded in the centre of London, killing one person, injuring thirty and causing stg£1 million worth of damage.

The Hume–Adams talks, as they became known, were a source of some concern and scepticism and indeed, in some quarters, outright hostility. I had an advantage over other members of the Dáil because of my previous involvement with Sinn Féin as a member of the SDLP team in the talks in 1988, and I was able to interpret what was likely to be happening in the light of that experience. I expected criticism of Hume, as there had been of me and him and Seamus Mallon and Sean Farren in 1988, but I was surprised and dismayed by the intensity of it on this occasion.

As the SDLP spokesperson for North–South relations in the 1980s, spending a lot of time around the Dáil, I had warned John that there were members of the Oireachtas who were not friendly disposed towards him. Some resented that he had become the effective leader of nationalist Ireland instead of the Taoiseach and the Minister of Foreign Affairs of the day. For some, it was a personal dislike; for others, just old Irish begrudgery. There were also elements in the media who were similarly inclined. I told him that as long as he was a gazelle they would not move against him, but if he stumbled, they would be at his throat. Now it was happening. Some were sincerely concerned that anyone would talk to Sinn Féin, effectively the IRA, while their murderous campaign continued, while others saw their chance to get at

Hume. In the corridors and the bars of the Dáil even some who had not displayed any overwhelming interest in Northern Ireland went out of their way to express their reservations about Hume involving himself in the talks.

The worst criticism came from the *Sunday Independent*, week after week. Two events in particular fuelled the criticism. On 25 September, Hume and Adams announced they had agreed to forward a report on their discussions to the Irish government. The 'Hume–Adams Agreement' became a source of great confusion. What was it? Was there an actual document? Why were mixed signals coming out of government in relation to the so-called agreement? We were to learn later that part of the reason for the apparent confusion was deliberate obfuscation to cover the fact that, parallel to the Hume–Adams discussions, there were secret contacts between Dublin and Sinn Féin/IRA and, more dramatically, between the British government and the organisation involved in continuing terrorist bombings and shootings.

The second development that intensified anxiety, and indeed anger, was an explosion in a fish shop on the Shankill Road in which ten people were killed and fifty-seven injured. The IRA bomber, Thomas Begley, blew himself up along with his victims. This atrocity was followed by the spectacle of Gerry Adams carrying the bomber's coffin. How could John Hume associate himself with a man so clearly committed to the organisation responsible for such atrocious acts, which, while awful in themselves, also fomented sectarianism?

The criticism came not only from predictable sources but from within the SDLP itself. I received phone calls from former colleagues concerned about Hume and the direction he was taking the party. A big part of their concern was that they had not been informed, or consulted, about the talks with Adams. Seamus Mallon MP and Joe Hendron MP were making coded statements to the media indicating their concern.

As if all of this was not sufficiently confusing and worrying, immediately after the announcement of the report being made available to the Irish government, John cleared off to America without further clarification. The rumour mill in Leinster House had a field day. Hume was having a mental breakdown was the main one. He had given an interview a week or so previously, outside No. 10 Downing Street after a meeting with John Major, during which, in response to criticism of his meetings with Adams, he had uncharacteristically said, 'I don't give two balls of roasted snow what anyone advises me, I will continue the meetings.' He was clearly under pressure. I had met him shortly before these developments and saw that he was very upset about the media criticism. He did not have the hard neck in relation to criticism that his Downing Street comments suggested. Indeed, he was much more vulnerable to it than many politicians. However, I doubted if he was having a mental breakdown, irrespective of the stress, the travelling and the lifestyle. I could understand, however, why the rumour was so current. John had a thing about his health. I had often advised people meeting him not to enquire about his health, not even to give an opening by enquiring, 'How's the form?', or 'What's the *craic*?' I later regretted such advice as it became apparent that John did indeed have a serious health problem deserving of our sympathy.

What was happening, and the criticism of John so prevalent among TDs and members of the media around Leinster House, forced me to re-evaluate my own position and my continued 100% support for him. What he was involved in was central to what was, to me, a fundamental question at the heart of Northern Ireland policy. Was a solution to be sought by attempting to bring in the extremes, or by seeking to build up the centre? It was the old 'the basis of policy should be the isolation of the two Ps of Paisleyism and Provisionalism' mantra, which had been central to my thinking back in the 1970s and 1980s and which had caused me so much soul-searching when I had first been asked by Hume to join the team in discussions with Sinn Féin in 1988. The answer to the question was even more important now, for it was not only John who was involved in what critics were describing as 'appeasement of the Provos' but the British and Irish governments as well.

I came to the same conclusion as I had five years earlier. Anything that would save lives had to be supported. It might cause political difficulties further down the road, but those problems would be more capable of solution than restoring the dead to life. My conviction in this regard was strengthened by an event that occurred in the aftermath of a horrific loyalist Hallowe'en shooting at the Rising Sun bar in Greysteel, County Derry, when seven were killed and thirteen wounded. John Hume attended the funerals and the TV images showed a daughter of one of the victims embracing him and the two of them crying in each other's arms. She said to him, 'Mr Hume, we have just buried my father. My family wants you to know that when we said the Rosary around my Daddy's coffin we prayed for you, for what you're trying to do to bring peace.' It was powerfully symbolic, but the strain was telling. Shortly afterwards, John collapsed and spent some weeks in Altnagelvin Hospital in Derry.

Around this time I was having conversations with Gordon Wilson, appointed to the Senate by Albert Reynolds and the father of Marie Wilson, the young woman who had died under the rubble of the Enniskillen Remembrance Day bombing while holding her father's hand. I, and I'm sure many, many others, had cried at his moving account of her death: 'When I asked her for the fifth time, "Are you all right, Marie?" she said, "Daddy, I love you very much." Those were the last words she spoke to me. She still held my hand quite firmly and I kept shouting at her, "Marie, are you all right?" There wasn't a reply.' Gordon was the most Christian person I ever had the honour to meet. He summed up his philosophy in a speech in the Forum for Peace and Reconciliation at Dublin Castle: 'Love is enough. If that sounds naively simple, let's try it out, because we have travelled other roads and we can see where they have brought us. Love it must be, but love in action, spelt out and worked out in strategies for peace and reconciliation.' As a new member of the Oireachtas and new to public life, Gordon came to me for advice, but I learned more from him than he did from me. Despite what they had done to him, he had been prepared to enter into discussions with the IRA in the pursuit of peace. He supported the Hume–Adams initiative. How could any person of goodwill do otherwise?

So I supported Hume, and in doing so I gave my support to the policy of attempting to bring Sinn Féin/IRA into the mainstream of political life; I attempted to repress my gut reaction, which was to lock them all up, for I was not as Christian as Gordon Wilson. In endorsing the policy of building peace by offering Sinn Féin/IRA an alternative based on political action as part of a wider alliance involving the Irish government, the SDLP and Irish America, and despite my reservations, I did my best to further these developments inside and outside the Dáil.

I had been a member of the British-Irish Interparliamentary Body since its inception in 1990, and I hope I helped in making it a vehicle for immensely improving relationships between members of the Irish and British Parliaments. I was used to meeting British Parliamentarians, but most of my Irish colleagues were not and it was a very useful learning experience for them. Meeting with British politicians on a regular basis, socialising with them, starting initially with discussion of subjects which were not contentious and moving on to subjects which were, debating with former ministers in Northern Ireland who had been identified with unpopular decisions – all of these helped to reinforce the increasingly close relationship between the British and Irish governments, which was essential to any solution of the final British–Irish problem.

I have been accused of excessive support and loyalty to John Hume. It was a criticism that surfaced occasionally within Fine Gael. Certainly I was a staunch and committed supporter of the SDLP – hardly surprising in one who was a founder member and who had been so deeply involved with it, in good times and bad, over a period of twenty years. But I had never been among those who put forward John's entitlement for sainthood. I had had my differences with him on policy matters over the years, as in relation to Duisburg, and while we had a good personal relationship, I had never been as close to him as to Gerry Fitt. John was selfish, a trait not uncommon in politicians or other ambitious people and perhaps a necessary ingredient for their success. This aspect of John's personality was first brought to my attention by Tony O'Reilly. In his capacity as founder of the Ireland Fund, O'Reilly had organised its Annual General Meeting in Ashford Castle, County Mayo, and had invited John to be the Guest Speaker. John had had to withdraw, and I was invited to replace him. My speech impressed O'Reilly, and afterwards he told me he was critical of John for keeping able colleagues in the shade and for retaining for himself contacts that would be more useful to the cause if exposed to a variety of people, such as myself.

This criticism was confirmed for me on a number of occasions, particularly in 1983 when, as a member of an all-party trade delegation to America seeking to attract investment to Northern Ireland, John adamantly refused to introduce any members of the delegation to his contacts on Capitol Hill. I was present on another occasion when, at the home of Denis Corboy, the EEC's Ambassador to the USA, there was a very heated argument between Seamus Mallon and John over Seamus' complaint that John was impeding access to some people he was anxious to meet. John was also secretive, rarely confiding fully in even his closest political colleagues and, on occasion, in my experience, not communicating information that would have enabled his colleagues to have come to better decisions. His poor relationships with Gerry Fitt and Paddy Devlin and the difficulties with Seamus Mallon were not all one-sided, nor did they all arise from political differences.

However, and I say this without reservation, from the vantage point of history, John Hume will be recognised as a towering figure, in the same league in Irish history as O'Connell and Parnell. He was courageous, had strategic vision and never for one moment departed from a complete insistence on the non-violent approach, despite all the pressures on him, his family and his electorate.

He had the wider vision to look beyond the narrow confines of Northern Ireland and Ireland to Europe and America in his quest for a solution to the Northern Ireland problem. He was lucky in some respects: he had a secure political base in Derry; the first direct election to Europe and the increase in the number of Northern Ireland seats at Westminster (which he and the SDLP resisted) came at the right time for him; Irish civil servants of the calibre of Sean Donlon, Michael Lillis, Dermot Gallagher, Seán Ó hUiginn and others were there to assist and guide him; and he has an extraordinarily supportive wife and family. But he made the most of his luck, and his commitment, courage and self-belief overcame obstacles that would have discouraged lesser men. Above all, from an early stage he had a vision of the type of Ireland he wanted and he worked consistently towards that goal. Very recently I spoke to Gerry again about John. Unfortunately, there was a history of personal coolness between the two former leaders of the SDLP. Gerry's pithy description of John, expressed in terms of praise and begrudgery and epitomising their relationship, was, 'He was a far-seeing c***.' Unlikely to be on his tombstone, but a considerable tribute indeed considering the source from whence it came.

Whatever else may be said about John Hume, one thing is incontrovertible: he was the prime mover in bringing about the process that brought peace to Ireland, and in so doing he displayed considerable moral, physical and political courage. There are people alive today who would be in their graves save for John Hume.

Throughout this time in the Dáil, Fine Gael was in the doldrums and the possibility of gaining power seemed out of the question for the foreseeable future. In February 1994, four frontbenchers went to John Bruton and, when he refused to stand down as Leader, resigned from their positions, precipitating a leadership battle. There was an assumption among many in the party, on both sides, that I would be in the anti-Bruton camp. In addition to the recent events which had led to my resignation from the frontbench, it was known that I had reservations about his Northern Ireland policy. He was not as supportive of the SDLP, or the nationalist position generally, as I would have liked. Indeed, on one occasion while we were both in the Shadow Cabinet, Peter Barry and I had seriously considered resignation.

But there was one factor about Bruton I considered to be of paramount importance: his acknowledged integrity, which was not only of importance in itself in a political leader but was crucial in circumstances where cynicism among the electorate was being confirmed by evidence of low standards in high places. So when I was invited to meet him to discuss my position, I surprised him by immediately saying I would vote for him in the motion of confidence, without even waiting for him to lay out his stall. Unlike some other members of the Parliamentary party, I had no pre-conditions and made no effort to extract promises of future preferment. He won the confidence vote – political commentators presumed by a narrow margin, since such votes in Fine Gael were not then publicly disclosed.

In April 1994 I was given the opportunity to be part of an EU team that monitored the first free election in South Africa. Noel Davern, FF TD for South Tipperary, was on the same team. Often it was only on foreign trips that one got to know other members of the Dáil well, including members of one's own party. We were honoured by the opportunity to see at first-hand and to contribute to the birth of a new democracy. We witnessed the queues to vote – the very old, the invalids, even, on one occasion, two people dead in a queue – and people walking for up to twenty miles, transported on wheelbarrows and prams, determined to exercise their franchise. We saw the fear on the faces of the local women as they ran from the two white men in a jeep: myself and Noel. We marvelled at the gleaming white blouses on schoolgirls who lived in huts without running water. And there were some humorous episodes, too. At one polling station I had the experience of a mother offering her daughter as my wife, and the daughter's response, on being told I already had one, 'I will kill your wife'!

I remember the hotel in Umtata, where we were advised not to go out after dark, and the barbed wire and the high security walls that reminded me of Coalisland RUC station. And, for obvious reasons, I will never forget the Nissan hut at the bottom of the Drakensberg Mountains where I monitored an 'election education' meeting. About 300 people were packed into the hut, which had only one small window and one door. The stench was so awful, in the middle of a hot African afternoon, that I could only enter at the second attempt. Once inside, my attention was immediately drawn to a group of men standing along the wall, tall, athletic-looking and dressed in sheepskin, they had clearly come down from the mountain. The first few rows were occupied by women, many with babies. I started to explain who I was, where I came from and why I was there. All had to be explained through the interpreter, except the phrase, 'Free and fair elections', which elicited immediate applause. Shortly into my speech a child started to cry and its mother pulled out a breast and started to feed it. This led to a number of children wanting to be fed and soon a number of them were at the breast. Then I became conscious of another sound. The gentlemen from the mountain clearly did not consider audible farting as being anti-social. I have addressed many meetings in my time, at some of which I have been heckled, shouted down, had stones and bottles thrown at me, even on one occasion shot at, but none has compared with that meeting in the shadow of the Drakensberg, to the sound of sucking and farting and the applause for 'fair and free'.

What I like, and at the same time hate, about politics is its unpredictability. In an unprecedented development the Fianna Fàil–Labour coalition split, the Labour party changed its allegiance and on 15 December 1994 a 'Rainbow' coalition of Fine Gael, Labour and Democratic Left took power without an election. John Bruton became Taoiseach, and Dick Spring, Tánaiste.

On 20 December I found myself in government as a Minister of State. What I had anticipated as a boring and frustrating five years as a member of the opposition, continually crushed by an all-powerful government, became instead a period of excitement, creativity and personal satisfaction.

I was appointed Minister for Children with responsibilities as Minister of State in three departments and I thereby became the first person to serve as a Minister in both jurisdictions in Ireland.

As Minister for Children, the first in Europe, I had specific responsibilities in the Departments of Health, Justice and Education. I came into office at a time of heightened public awareness of child abuse and matters relating to that sensitive issue would dominate my two-and-a-half years in office. Revelations, particularly in relation to Catholic clergy and religious, had shocked the public. There was a widespread feeling that there had been cover-ups and collusion and that much more remained to be disclosed. Not only did I have to deal with the past, I had to ensure, as far as I could, that similar events would not occur in the future, particularly on my watch. The previous government had been brought down on a matter related to child abuse; any negligence or misjudgement on my part would be severely punished.

On the positive side, I relished the opportunity to improve the lot of children, particularly the disadvantaged. By doing so I could make a major contribution to society and prevent serious social problems down the road. I was being given the opportunity to do some of the things that had motivated me to enter politics in the first place.

My most important function was to coordinate child-care functions across the three Departments in which I was Minister of State. I calculated that there were fifteen Departments with responsibility for children, but my three Departments were the crucial ones. Health was my primary Department and it was there that my main office was located, but I insisted that I have a Private Secretary and an office in the other two Departments. This raised eyebrows in certain quarters, but I was adamant that I required my own person, working directly to me, in each Department to ensure I could do my job effectively. So I had three Private Secretaries; other Ministers had only one! To maximise coordination I chaired a weekly meeting attended by officials from the three Departments. At an early stage I discovered that the real spur to progress was not the pressure I applied so much as the rivalry between the Departments to avoid being blamed for delays.

Some Ministers of State have a lousy job. Some Departmental Ministers keep the sexy, media-attractive responsibilities to themselves and assign the mundane tasks to their subordinates. I was lucky on two counts. First, I had Ministers in the three Departments with whom I got on well on a personal level – Michael Noonan in Health, Nora Owen in Justice and Niamh Bhreathnach in Education. Secondly, and more importantly, I had been given specific responsibilities, delegated to me and for which I had full responsibility.

I was impressed by the professionalism of the civil service. Some of those who served me, I predicted, would go far and the intervening years have proved me right. I couldn't help but make comparisons with the Stormont civil service and I was not surprised to find many more similarities than differences. After all, they both grew from the same British root. In one respect I did note a significant difference, however. The Dublin official was more acutely attuned to the political needs of his Ministerial master. Hardly surprising given that the Stormont officials with whom I had dealt in 1974 had only ten years' experience of dealing with anyone other than a unionist, and no experience at all of dealing with a nationalist. They learned quickly during the five months of the first Power-Sharing Executive and I am sure they are now, more than thirty years later, quite as dextrous as their Dublin counterparts. I was lucky also to be able to bring with me into government people whom I trusted implicitly to look after my interests: Tom Hannigan as my Special Advisor and Marie Meegan, Brenda Coyne and Jane Murphy to look after my constituency.

With the help of the people I have mentioned I was able to deliver on the tasks allocated to me, and even to advance the parameters of my job. When I took over at the end of 1994 only seventeen of the seventy-nine sections of the Child Care Act 1991 were in operation; by the end of 1996 they had all been implemented, substantially increasing the protection for children and providing additional services for them. A Children Bill (to replace a juvenile justice system in operation since 1908), which had been promised for twenty years, was published in December 1996. The Bill had been delayed by differences between the Departments, so one of the first things I did was to call together the three Departmental heads and task them with sorting out those differences. This they did in an admirably short time. The Bill was one of the biggest legislative measures ever in the Dáil. Unfortunately, the lack of a government majority in the Senate – a disadvantage of a government formed without an election – meant the Bill only got a Second Reading and the next Fianna Fáil government took a further five years to implement what was, effectively, my Bill.

School attendance legislation had not been updated since 1926. I remedied that. The law relating to child pornography was strengthened. I introduced new adoption legislation to give rights to unmarried fathers and to address difficulties which had arisen in the recognition of foreign adoptions. I brought in new regulations and guidelines for the proper inspection of pre-schools, play groups, crèches, etc. I recognised the essential part played by foster parents in the childcare system by substantially increasing foster-care allowances and committed the government to regular increases. These and other measures for which I was responsible over the short period of two-and-a-half years represented a significant contribution to the improvement of the position of children in our society. I was proud to be able to claim, when I left office, that the interest of the child had been paramount in everything I had done, and that Ireland was a safer place for children because of me.

There was one initiative I took as Minister that I was not able to implement before I left office, but I hoped I had bequeathed to my successor a situation that would leave him with no alternative but to follow on. At the end of 1996 I announced that I supported the establishment of an Ombudsman for Children, and in a follow-up document, *Putting Children First*, it was stated that 'the Minister of State is fully committed to the principle of the establishment of an Ombudsman for Children'. I knew that there were the usual civil service reservations regarding an Ombudsman, in terms of restrictions on their powers. There was no way that an Ombudsman could be established before the election given that the views of fifteen government Departments, the voluntary sector and all the organisations dealing with children had to be taken into consideration. Even if we won the election, there was no guarantee that I would be appointed Minister of Children again, and if we lost, the civil service opposition to the measure, along with the usual reluctance of incoming governments to continue with proposals of their predecessors, might mean the Ombudsman proposal would not be implemented. There were two factors in my favour. First, the proposal was popular with the public and was much wanted by the strong childcare lobby. Secondly, the government would find it convenient to be able to say to an upcoming conference on the United Nations Convention on the Rights of the Child that such a radical move was being contemplated. I therefore pushed forward the consultation process and encouraged the agencies involved with children to show their full support for my proposal, in the hope that by the time the election came around the Ombudsman idea would be so firmly rooted as not to be reversed.

The election went against us, but in opposition I was able, rather deviously, to facilitate the Taoiseach in misleading the House and in so doing greatly assisted the Ombudsman process. The following exchange between the Taoiseach, Bertie Ahern, and me was reported in the *Official Report on The Order of Business in the Dáil* on 17 December 1997:

Mr. Currie   'In view of today's news, the obvious continuing necessity for greater protection of children at risk and the fact that the government reneged on its commitment to introduce mandatory reporting, when will an announcement be made on an Ombudsman for children?'
Taoiseach   'The commitment to the programme will be met.'
Mr. Currie   'When?'
Taoiseach   'In due course.'
Mr. Currie   'The proposal should have been implemented before now.'
Taoiseach   'The proposal, which is well thought out, will be implemented in due course.'
Mr. Currie   'Will the Taoiseach confirm it is a commitment of government?'
Taoiseach   'Yes.'
Mr. Currie   'The Taoiseach should inform the Minister for Health and Children of that because he was not aware of it.'

I did not tell the Taoiseach that a commitment to establish an Ombudsman was not in the Programme for Government, or that his Minister for Children was heeding official advice not to proceed with it. I was told afterwards there was consternation in the Department when the Taoiseach's commitment was heard. Clearly the Ombudsman for Children would now have to be implemented. It was, but it took five years.

My involvement in government enabled me to better represent my constituency and to deliver on some long-delayed projects and the rapidly expanding Blanchardstown area benefited in particular. The James Connolly Memorial Hospital was able to embark on a much-needed and oft-postponed major Development Plan because of my efforts, supported by the Minister for Health, Michael Noonan. A new Garda District Headquarters was delivered after years and years of effort by the local Gardaí and the community. A site was purchased for a Regional Technical College in Blanchardstown.

These were significant successes, delivered by political clout. They also provided a good illustration of the competition created in a multi-member constituency. Joan Burton, the Labour Minister of State at Foreign Affairs and Justice, was also a TD for Dublin West. She was extremely competitive, and rightly so as it turned out as she lost her seat in the next election. The Minister for Justice, Nora Owen, also represented a part of the greater Blanchardstown area as a Deputy for Dublin North and she also had a strong personal interest in pushing the Garda station in Blanchardstown. Unfortunately, on the day arranged for the sod-cutting ceremony, Nora had to be away in Brussels. She decided I should do the job in her stead and communicated her decision to the Department and the Gardaí. To my embarrassment, and that of the Garda top brass, but to the amusement of everyone else, Joan turned up at the ceremony demanding that she also cut a sod. The ceremony was delayed while another spade was procured. The imposing Garda station we have in Blanchardstown today obviously gained from the doubling of resources at its inception!

As the first Minister for Children in Europe I represented the government at childcare conferences at home and abroad. Occasionally, Annita came with me, but it was a trip to Australia and New Zealand representing the government at St Patrick's Day celebrations in 1997 that she still talks about. When we arrived in Sydney after the long journey, she had to go outside the airport building to have a cigarette, and even outside there were designated areas for smoking. 'I'm never going to go through that again. This is the last time I'll come to Australia,' she said. An hour later, travelling across Sydney Harbour with the sun shining and the Opera House in the background, she turned to me and said, 'I'd love to stay here forever.'

It was hard work – five cities in five days and then on to New Zealand. In addition to speeches and receptions and reviews of parades, I concluded an agreement with the Australian Health Minister that provided health insurance for young Irish people working temporarily in Australia and in New Zealand. I also had discussions with government Ministers about juvenile justice legislation and an Ombudsman for children. We appreciated greatly the hospitality and friendship of Dick O'Brien, the Irish Ambassador, and his wife, Bernadette, and of the Honorary Consul General in New Zealand, Rodney Walshe. On all trips I was conscious of the workload placed on the civil servants who travelled with us and on the members of the Diplomatic Service who looked after us. Not always an easy job and sometimes taken for granted.

Although I was in government I did not have any direct responsibility for the Peace Process, but as Minister of State at Justice I was able to observe and to have occasional discussions with Tim Dalton, the Secretary-General, who was deeply involved in the Process and was a man whose judgement I respected. My main involvement in Northern Ireland was as a member of the Forum for Peace and Reconciliation, to which I was appointed by John Bruton in October 1994.

The Forum emanated from a Joint Declaration of the Irish and British governments, which indicated that, as part of the development of a process of political dialogue, arrangements would be made by the Irish government 'to enable democratic parties to consult together and share in dialogue about the political future'. The real purpose of the Forum was to provide an opportunity for Sinn Féin to come in from the political cold, to bind them tightly into the political process and to provide a transition into normal political life. Every political party, North and South, was represented – except Unionists, who refused to participate – and all of the main political personalities attended. The Fine Gael delegation was led by John Bruton, while I was second-in-command and Delegation Coordinator. When John became Taoiseach, shortly after the Forum first met, he continued to attend as often as he could, but in his absence I deputised for him, effectively representing the government. The Chairperson was Mrs Justice Catherine McGuinness and the Forum Secretariat was headed up by Wally Kirwan, who had played such a valuable role in the previous Forum and who, as an Assistant Secretary in the Department of the Taoiseach, had an overview of Northern policy that helped guide the Forum to constructive conclusions.

Meeting in the splendid surroundings of Dublin Castle, the Forum discussed every aspect of the Northern Ireland problem and attempted to make up for the absence of the Unionist parties by hearing from anyone who was prepared to state the Unionist position. Members of the public were invited to make submissions. Distinguished visitors who addressed us included the President of the EU, Jacques Santer, Senator George Mitchell and the Deputy President of South Africa, Mr FW de Klerk.

However, as far as the main Dáil parties and the SDLP were concerned, these addresses were secondary to the task of bringing the Sinn Féin delegation, led by Gerry Adams and Martin McGuinness, to a common position with the rest of us, a position that would have a realistic chance of being acceptable to unionists. In particular, we strove to win them over to agreement that the consent of unionists was necessary to bring about any change in the constitutional status of Northern Ireland. And this, despite all our blandishments and several false dawns, they refused to do.

In other respects I saw significant changes from 1988, the previous occasion when I had been in close contact with representatives of the republican movement. They had clearly learned from John Hume. 'Hume-speak' – words and phrases identified with John – poured out of them as if they were their own. Another change, this one most definitely not learned from John, was their mode of dress. Gone were the sweaters, the open-necked shirts and the sports jackets to be replaced by designer suits and shirts. The age of '*Tiocfaidh Armani*' Sinn Féin had arrived. In another respect, they were a damn nuisance. The message was clearly 'Engage': they were always there, smiling, with the hand out. It was dangerous to go to the men's room, where it was almost impossible to avoid them. I had great sympathy with members of the Unionist party when, at a later stage, in Stormont, they complained of being harassed in an attempt to make them shake hands.

John Bruton has been blamed by Fianna Fáil and Sinn Féin for the lack of progress on Northern Ireland during his term of office, and some responsibility has been imputed to him for the deterioration which resulted after the ending of the ceasefire. The criticism was and is unfair. The core on which the Peace Process was built was the relationship between the Irish and British governments. The SDLP, the republican movement, the US government, all had their role to play, but they were tangential and their efforts would have run into a brick wall had they not been based on the solid foundation of a good relationship between the two governments. In particular, if the British government had not been amenable, no progress would have been made. Unfortunately, while John Bruton was Taoiseach, John Major was in a weak political position in his own Parliament. Indeed in June 1995, in order to assert and to confirm his leadership, he had to resort to the stratagem of resigning as Leader of the Conservative party and then offering himself for re-election, forcing his opponents to 'put up, or shut up'. A sizeable section of the Tory party considered his dealings with Dublin and the Republican movement as 'appeasement', and Major showed considerable courage in standing up to them. For example, a leak of part of the text of the *Framework Document*, which led *The Times* to say that the document brought 'the prospect of a United Ireland closer than it had been at any time since partition in 1920', led to Major having to hold a late-night meeting to reassure prominent backbenchers. Major couldn't afford any hostages to fortune. How unlucky for Bruton, and how fortunate for Bertie Ahern, that just over a month after the defeat of the Rainbow government a government was elected in London with an unassailable majority and a Leader determined to make his mark on history. If John Bruton had been elected to a second term in these circumstances, his contribution to a Northern solution might be more positively judged.

Apart from my participation in the Forum, I was not involved in any developments in relation to Northern Ireland. I took the opportunity, any time I got the chance, to advise the Taoiseach of my views, but I was not consulted nor were my opinions sought. I was sufficiently egotistical to think that my experience of thirty years and my involvement in every development over that time in Northern Ireland may have made my opinion of some use. I had made a point of keeping in touch with the North, indeed with ten brothers and sisters living there it would have been difficult not to. I clearly had good contacts with the SDLP and, particularly since Duisburg, Unionist devolutionists were keen to talk to me. If my advice had been sought and acted upon, some things might have been done differently. But I had to content myself with expressing my views to the Special Advisor to the Taoiseach, Sean Donlon, the former Secretary of the Department of Foreign Affairs and Ambassador to Washington and the man who, more than anyone else, including John Hume, had built a special relationship with leading Irish-American politicians. I could only hope his advice was being heeded.

29: ENDINGS

June 1997 and its general election brought to an end one of my most satisfying times in politics. Dublin West was still a four-seater, but with substantial boundary changes, so I knew it would be a hard campaign. I was third on the first count and was elected on the ninth. Nobody was elected until the sixth count, when Joe Higgins (Socialist party) made it. Dublin West, with all the new housing and boundary changes, had become very volatile. In 1989 Brian Lenihan had topped the poll (from his hospital bed in America). In 1992 it was Joan Burton. Now, five years later, she lost her seat and Brian Lenihan (Junior) topped the poll on the first count, but Joe Higgins was first elected. I considered I had done well, but it was, of course, a great disappointment that my party and I were out of government.

I had fully expected that the Rainbow government would be re-elected. Within hours of the dissolution of the Dáil, the Leaders of Fine Gael, Labour and Democratic Left were at the Shelbourne Hotel presenting a united front and emphasising how well they had worked together in government. This, along with unprecedented prosperity, seemed to me to provide the necessary ingredients for a return to power. I knew from knocking on doors prior to and during the election that a big number of voters were determined to make Labour pay for its alliance in government with Fianna Fáil, but I was surprised by the extent of the Labour losses, from 33 to 17. Fine Gael increased from 45 to 54, and Democratic Left stayed at 4, but the combined numbers did not add up and a minority Fianna Fáil–Progressive Democrat government took over, with Bertie Ahern as Taoiseach.

In the aftermath of the 1997 election I took stock of my position. Had we won, I would have expected to be back in government in some capacity. It was generally accepted in the Dáil and in the media that I had performed well as Minister for Children, and I might have been reappointed to that post. I would have liked to have had some involvement with Northern Ireland, but realistically, in view of my experience in the last administration, that wasn't likely. Anyway, we were now in opposition and I had to come to terms with that reality. I was almost fifty-eight years of age and would be sixty-two/sixty-three if the Dáil ran its full term. It was highly unlikely that I would serve in government again. I had been fortunate to have a long political career, but now I was getting tired, and a bit bored. I decided I should aim at announcing my retirement on the fortieth anniversary of my first election, on 1 July 2004, when I would also be approaching the normal retirement age of sixty-five. This meant I would have to win the next election. That was, of course, highly presumptuous of me and to that extent I got what I deserved.

Life in the Dáil was often boring, sometimes exciting and, on occasions, funny. If I could have made one change to make the Dáil more interesting, it would have been to seek to enforce a rule that major government announcements had to be made in the Dáil. A practice had grown up, and here successive governments of different complexions were all to blame, of making major announcements at press conferences and other media events outside the Dáil. It might have ensured greater publicity and deprived the opposition of the opportunity of immediate response, but it also took away from the credibility and relevance of the Dáil. If such major announcements had to be made in the Dáil, as is normally the case in Westminster, there would be fewer empty seats in the House – and in the Press Gallery.

The best example of what I mean was the occasion when a major announcement had to be made in the Dáil, for it was there the action was. It happened in December 1994, when Dick Spring spoke in the vote of confidence that would determine the future of his coalition with Albert Reynolds. To a packed House, and with most of the country watching on television, or listening to the radio, he kept his intentions until the end, keeping us all waiting with bated breath. Then he concluded, 'For the reasons I have outlined, it will be obvious to the House that neither I nor any of my colleagues can vote confidence in the government at the conclusion of this debate.' History in the making! A really great Parliamentary occasion, of which there are too few.

Certain words and expressions cannot be used in the House. In addition to four-letter words and such insults as 'hypocrite' and 'liar', unparliamentary expressions include 'guttersnipe', 'rat', 'communist' and 'yahoo'. However, an expression I used following a well-publicised row between Minister Máire Geoghegan-Quinn and the board of Aer Lingus was ruled out of order by the Ceann Comhairle. I alleged she had 'handbagged the Board'. The Ceann Comhairle ruled that 'the reference to "handbagging", particularly with reference to a Lady member of the House, is deemed to be unparliamentary.' I have often wondered how it would have been described if alleged of a male member of the House!

Other moments stand out: Albert Reynolds giving a press conference outside No. 10 Downing Street on his first visit there and referring to 'the mainland'. At a time when he was describing John Bruton as 'John Unionist', it made me wonder who had the unionist mentality.

The same Albert nominated to the Senate a Northern Ireland businessman, Edward Haughey, who was alleged to have been a financial supporter of the Conservative party. Mr Haughey took the Fianna Fáil Whip and was the party's Northern Ireland Spokesman in the Senate. He was a member of the Fianna Fáil delegation at the Forum for Peace and Reconciliation. The Leader of 'Fianna Fáil – the Republican party', Taoiseach Bertie Ahern, renominated him to the Senate. Mr Edward Haughey is now, in 2004, known as Lord Ballyedmond, is a member of the House of Lords and takes the Unionist party Whip. Was there a conversion, or something?

In 2000, on his visit to Ireland, I met one of my great heroes, Nelson Mandela. My delight and pleasure at meeting him was complete when he asked me about my experiences as a civil rights leader; someone had obviously briefed him well.

There was another event that gave me considerable personal pleasure and satisfaction. Donal Barrington, a great constitutional lawyer, had acted as an advisor to the SDLP during the Constitutional Convention at Stormont in 1975 and subsequently he and I had become friends. He and his wife, Eileen, had been very kind to us as a family, inviting us to stay in their home on a number of occasions. Donal subsequently became a member of the European Court, but because of an oversight this office was not considered as service that would have qualified him for membership of the Supreme Court, for which he was ideally suited. As luck would have it, I was the one given the duty and honour to steer the Bill removing this anomaly through the Senate.

Finally, a Dáil story to illustrate the difficulties that can be created by a difference in accents, in this case between Tyrone and Kerry. While Spokesperson on Law Reform in the early 1990s, I had to make a speech attacking the government's delay in bringing forward a divorce referendum and its dependence on the Catholic Church's ability to end a marriage by declaring it null and void, a process I described as 'nullity'. In the course of my remarks I intended to say: 'Nullity, in many cases, is a lie. To build family law on a concept that a couple who believe themselves over many years to be married, a union which has produced children, were never in fact married, is farcical. Yet, on the evidence of the Family Law Bill, currently in Committee in the Dáil, nullity is being enshrined at the centre of our family law. Instead of being a little-used alternative to divorce, it is becoming a substitute for it.' My usual secretary, Marie, was on holiday that week and her temporary replacement was from Kerry. She was a very good secretary, but had some difficulty with my Northern accent. I dictated my speech and it was typed up and sent to the Press Office. Shortly afterwards I got a phone call. Why was nudity a lie, and how was it being enshrined at the centre of our Family Law as a substitute for divorce?

My main interest was still in Northern Ireland and now that I was a backbencher again I was able to contribute to the debates and ask questions on the matter. The Ceann Comhairle and his Deputy recognised my special interest and would usually call me, although often towards the end of the discussion after the frontbenchers had had their say. I found Bertie Ahern very approachable. On Wednesday mornings, after the Order of Business, he could generally be found in the Members' bar having coffee, and we would often have a chat about the North. In the Dáil I continued my previous practice of lobbing up a ball for him to hit, giving him a chance to agree with me and put the agreement on the record. In particular, I would give him an opportunity to express his views on the Disappeared, agreeing with me that it was barbaric, that details of their whereabouts were not being supplied by the republican movement and demanding that they do so. Eventually, there was limited success when some of the bodies were recovered, but unfortunately, to date, not that of Columba McVeigh. The murder of these people, their secret burials and the failure to reveal their whereabouts to their relatives remains one of the most barbaric violations of human rights of the entire Troubles, and the republican movement, Sinn Féin and the IRA must never be allowed to forget it.

Since the beginning of the Peace Process, I, and others, had been reluctant to attack the IRA with the ferocity they deserved. For fear of destabilising the Process, I had pulled my punches. The murder of Garda Gerry McCabe on 7 June 1996 forced me to rethink. Now, in 1997, it seemed to me the IRA had been long enough on ceasefire for this no longer to be a risk. Additionally, the IRA assessment of its own capacity to return to war after a previous ceasefire suggested strongly that it would not happen. Also, would the leadership risk the probability of losing out on their new lifestyles, or the possibility of being killed, or going to jail? I thought not and started to put the boot in. I found that when I did so, their one TD invariably got offside. When he expected critical references he would absent himself from the Chamber. I was surprised that when I went on the attack I received little support from other members. They would congratulate me afterwards, of course. Too many TDs were conditioned to think in terms of vote transfers in multi-member constituencies. It was to take some time for the threat from Sinn Féin to their own positions to sink in, especially in Fianna Fáil.

The highlight of my third Dáil (1997–2002) was, of course, the report of the Good Friday Agreement in 1998. My delighted statement of welcome said, 'This is the first day of the rest of our lives, the first day of the rest of our history. I wish to congratulate all those in all of the parties who have made this day possible. I have always believed that reconciliation will be brought about by representatives of our two traditions working together in government to overcome the political, social, economic and cultural problems which affect us. The constitutional and institutional contexts in which this can happen are now available. I look forward, with confidence, to endorsement by the Irish people'.

I appended to my statement the following:

Extract from Official Report of the proceedings of the Northern Ireland Assembly for 28th May 1974, the day the Power-Sharing Executive ended.

Mr. Currie (Department of Housing, Local Government and Planning) – 'Irrespective of what happens and how this community may go in the future, somebody at the end of the day is going to have to come in and pick up the pieces, no matter how shattered those pieces are...'

(Hon. Members: 'Hear, Hear')

'When he does that, someone will remember – and I should like to think a lot of people will remember – and say, there was an idea about once; the idea was partnership in the North between Catholic and Protestant (Hon. Members: 'Hear, Hear') – and partnership on this island between Irishmen.'

(Hon. Members: 'Hear, Hear')

It had taken twenty-five years and terrible death and destruction, but the pieces appeared to have been picked up.

I couldn't help thinking, when the second Power-Sharing Executive came into office, that had I stayed in the North I would probably have been a member of it. After all, most of the SDLP members of the Executive were older than I was. Nor could I help making comparisons between the new Agreement and that reached at Sunningdale, twenty-five years earlier. I did not, of course, publicly initiate or contribute to such a debate at the time because of the destabilising possibility mentioned earlier, and also because I did not wish to increase support for dissident republicans. But I had, and have, strong views on the matter. In many respects, Sunningdale was a better deal for Irish nationalists and republicans. Taking that into consideration, there are few better examples in history of the futility of violence in achieving political change than the thirty-year 'war' in Northern Ireland.

The Belfast Agreement is more detailed than Sunningdale and indicates lessons have been learned from the failure of the previous Agreement. On the central issue of the constitutional position of Northern Ireland and the circumstances in which a united Ireland could be brought about, there is no difference at all. The principle of consent of the majority in the North is absolutely fundamental to both. The section of the 1998 Agreement dealing with self-determination is new and clearly designed to reflect the Sinn Féin position. The promise of such a commitment had encouraged Sinn Féin to join the process and had been central to Hume–Adams. It was, therefore, extremely important and without it Sinn Féin's agreement would not have been possible. But what advance did it really represent in republican terms? The Irish people can exercise their right to self-determination, but 'this right must be achieved and exercised with and subject to the agreement and consent of a majority of the people of Northern Ireland'.

The Government of Ireland Act 1920 was repealed. Ironically, it was this Act that gave those of us involved in the civil rights campaign the leverage to force Britain to intervene and to eventually suspend the Stormont government and Parliament. When Peter Mandelson suspended the Power-Sharing Executive in 2000 and created a precedent followed a number of times since then, to the present day, the repeal of the Government of Ireland Act 1920 (Section 75), trumpeted by Sinn Féin as a historic victory, did not make any difference. Sovereignty still resides in the mother of Parliaments.

The Good Friday Agreement also achieved something that unionists had been demanding for many years and which had not been achieved at Sunningdale: the deletion from the Irish Constitution of 'the illegal claim to Northern Ireland' represented by Articles 2 and 3.

The British-Irish Council was, of course, a new development. The use of the phrase 'totality of relationships' brings us back to the Haughey era. But from the viewpoint of Irish republicanism, the creation of a body so clearly designed to balance North–South relationships in the eyes of unionists and its emphasis on placing the Northern Ireland Assembly in the context of devolution within the United Kingdom was hardly an unmitigated blessing!

Power-sharing is central to both agreements, but the Good Friday Agreement is more inclusive in that all parties are entitled to membership of the Executive if they have sufficient votes, whereas in 1974 only those parties which supported the Executive and accepted its institutions were able to participate in the government. The new position allowed the DUP to have Ministers who did not attend meetings of the Executive: hardly the best way to ensure the coordination and collective responsibility which good government requires.

In relation to North–South institutions, the Council of Ireland of 1974 has been superseded by cross-border bodies. The loss of the Council of Ireland is a strongly negative factor for Irish nationalists, particularly the loss of its Parliamentary tier, which was to bring together sixty Parliamentarians, North and South. It would have enabled backbenchers to meet to discuss matters of mutual interest and to get to know each other and appreciate each other's points of view. The symbolism of an All-Ireland Parliamentary Assembly was probably its undoing, but its deletion hardly represented a step forward for those in the republican tradition.

One of the major differences was the provision in the Good Friday Agreement for referenda, North and South. The substantial majority for the Agreement and the institutions created by it gave it an authority never before given to any institutions, North or South. That authority and legitimacy has been partially eroded by events since then, but who can doubt the situation would have been worse had the original mandate not been given?

The question obviously arises, following comparison between the two Agreements: what were the Troubles about? And especially, do the differences justify the loss of one life, never mind the loss of over 2,000, as occurred between the fall of Sunningdale and the Good Friday Agreement? Specifically, from a Provisional republican point of view, how can they justify their opposition to Sunningdale, their support of the Good Friday Agreement and the role they played in the twenty-five years in between in terms of the loss of life, the maiming and the destruction, the blight on so many lives, including their own members', for which they were responsible?

I have noted a judgement by Gerry Adams in *The Irish Times* (15 July 2004): 'The British state in the North is a unionist state. Its symbols and emblems are unionist. So are its agencies. And its management.' Was it for this that nearly 4,000 died and countless lives were ruined?

I have seen and have welcomed many changes in the republican movement in my political lifetime. The movement has travelled a long way since Sunningdale. In 1974, its members did not recognise either State in Ireland, or their institutions. They refused to take seats in the Dáil, or Stormont, or Europe, or in the local authorities. They refused to recognise the courts. They did not recognise the authority of the Gardaí, never mind the RUC. Those of us who entered the Dáil or the Northern Assemblies were traitors. Under no circumstances could they accept that one part of the nation could break away from the rest, and that which had – the unionists – should be coerced into rejoining. On this basis, war could be waged by the IRA on behalf of the Irish people without any mandate from them and this would continue until an Irish Socialist Republic had been established.

I do, of course, strongly welcome the enormous changes in republican thinking and indeed predicted most of them. In 1986, after the Árd Fheis decision to take seats in the Dáil, I said, 'The decision to abandon abstention in Leinster House will lead to full participation in it and to full acceptance of its institutions and will lead also to participation in a new Northern Assembly and eventually, though this will take a bit longer, attendance at Westminster.' While they have taken up their offices and other facilities at Westminster, they have not, as yet, taken their seats. They haven't so far found the right formula!

I wish to put on record my appreciation of the leadership qualities and indeed the political courage displayed by the leadership of the republican movement, and of Gerry Adams and Martin McGuinness in particular, since they adopted the Peace Process. What a tragedy it took so long and so many lives were needlessly lost.

I regret that certain developments since the Belfast Agreement was signed have obscured the very real gains the Agreement represented for unionists. The major achievement for them in the Agreement, and particularly in its endorsement by the great majority on the island, is that the unionist tradition on this island is copper-fastened and protected. The Sunningdale Agreement and the many Declarations by successive Irish governments and by the SDLP over the years had established the consent principle, but the Good Friday Agreement was the first time the republican movement had ratified it. For unionism, it was an achievement of fundamental importance.

So where do we go from here? I am confident that the clock cannot be turned back. The principles embodied in both Sunningdale and the Good Friday Agreement, based on equality and partnership in the North and between North and South, will remain. This does not necessarily mean they will remain within the precise structures created in the Belfast Agreement. Changing political circumstances must be accommodated and the structures may change as a result, but if that happens new structures will evolve which will have the same principles at their core. To put it bluntly, it is only on the basis of partnership between the two traditions in the North, and partnership between North and South on this island, that Northern Ireland can be governed.

I hear talk about the imminence of a united Ireland, even suggestions that it will occur for the centenary of the 1916 Rising. Granted, this talk emanates mostly from Provo leaders anxious to reassure their support base, but it is nonsense, indeed dangerous nonsense. It flies in the face of reality: the reality of unionist opposition, still as strong as it ever was, and the reality of partitionism in the Southern part of Ireland. Nor will a united Ireland come about as a result of Catholics–nationalists outbreeding Protestants–unionists – what I call the rabbit theory of politics. Recent statistics show this is not going to happen, certainly not in the near future, and anyway, what sort of country would it be and what would be the conditions of life – and death – in a Northern Ireland wracked by such insecurity?

During the first Power-Sharing Executive in 1974, the late Cardinal Conway was asked on a radio programme whether Sunningdale and its involvement of Catholics and nationalists in the government would make them content to remain within Northern Ireland, or would their success encourage them to press harder for a united Ireland. The wise Falls Road man replied, 'I am prepared to leave the answer to that question to history.' That is my answer, too. There is no inevitability about the future of Northern Ireland. That will be for future generations to decide. This generation has played a very significant role in redressing the mistakes of those who last attempted a settlement, in 1920. Many have made huge sacrifices in doing so. In the context of the Good Friday Agreement and any updating of it, with the development of the institutions as time progresses, with equality for all in Northern Ireland, with partnership between North and South, our children and grandchildren will have the freedom to make their own political choices.

Within Fine Gael, the opponents of John Bruton finally got their man in January 2001. I voted for him in the motion of confidence, which he lost by 39 votes to 33. I spoke in the debate and made the point that Fine Gael was developing a tradition of getting rid of leaders just when the particular virtue of the leader was beginning to be recognised by the voting public. In the case of Alan Dukes, when it was becoming apparent how he had put the country first in his Tallaght Strategy, and John Bruton, who stood out as a beacon of integrity in a sea of corruption. I thought it also created a very bad precedent that the final move against Bruton was based on an opinion poll.

To succeed him, the 'Dream Team' of Michael Noonan and Jim Mitchell was proposed. I voted for Enda Kenny, whom I believed to have hidden strengths, with a steely commitment and leadership qualities obscured by youthful looks and a personality that belied his basic seriousness. The 'Dream Team' won by

44 to 28. In the ensuing election, I contemplated just how close were dreams and nightmares.

As a result of the increased population my constituency was again revised, only this time it was serious surgery. Under our Constitution the maximum number of seats allowed in a constituency is five. The population of Dublin West would have required six seats, so the Electoral Commission, in their wisdom, divided the constituency in two and created Dublin West and Dublin Mid-West with three seats each. It was a disaster for me, separating Lucan, where I lived, from Castleknock, my other best area of support. When I spoke on the changes in the Dáil, I complained that in my time in the Dáil my constituency had been reduced from five seats, to four, and now to three. 'If I were still in the North and Unionists were still in power, I would know what was happening to me,' I said facetiously.

I took some time to make up my mind, for both constituencies were equally difficult and I had good personal as well as political friends in both. Eventually, I decided on the new constituency of Mid-West, despite the fact that more than half of it would be virgin territory for me. Two factors decided me: I wanted to represent the area where I lived, where I and my family were making new friends and contacts on a daily basis; and in Dublin West there was an excellent candidate, Sheila Terry, who would have a good chance of succeeding me.

I knew I had a serious challenge on my hands and I prepared for it. I moved my constituency office from the Dáil, where most Dublin TDs had their offices, into my constituency so as to maximise the local service, and I initiated a programme of walkabouts, leaflet drops, local meetings and anything I could think of to raise my constituency profile. I was pretty confident that the election would not come until the very end of the Dáil term, and I programmed myself to peak then. I never worked harder in any of my constituencies than I did in the two years preceding that election. Though a member of the Foreign Affairs Committee, I declined all offers of foreign trips and took minimum holidays. I was a nuisance to Annita and the family, involving them in canvassing and distributing leaflets, enlisting their friends to help; they had never worked so hard either.

On account of the Tribunal disclosures of low standards in high places, many of them specifically relating to the Lucan area, and in the belief that the voters would give preference to candidates at whom the finger could not be pointed, I sent to every household in the constituency a copy of my tax-clearance certificate, stating I was fully tax compliant. I was the only candidate in the constituency to do so, and possibly the only candidate in the entire election to do so. In so doing, I ignored the advice of one of my more cynical canvassers, who said to me, 'Austin, a lot of the people out there are of the opinion that if you can't help yourself, you are unlikely to help them.'

I didn't see the double-decker bus coming down the road until the very last minute. It was Brenda Coyne, the constituency Secretary, who saw it first, a few days before polling. We had just concluded the canvass of a housing estate in Lucan, where I thought we had received the usual good reception. But Brenda said, 'There is something wrong.' Operating separately from me, a few doors ahead or behind, she had detected a change in people's attitudes. I started to watch out for it, and she was right. We lost the election in the last few days.

The primary reason for our loss, I think, was because Fine Gael was not seen as an alternative government, nor as the leader of one. Indeed, in those same days when we were losing, the Progressive Democrats were gaining precisely because the electorate perceived that Fianna Fáil would be returning and the PDs were needed to act as a restraint on them. I hope I went out with dignity. I was well beaten and had no complaints on that score. I had, as I have already said, intended to retire in two years' time anyway. It would have been nice to have chosen my own time, but that's politics. My sense of rejection was eased by the knowledge that over twenty of my Fine Gael colleagues, some of them long-serving with distinguished records of public service, such as Alan Dukes, Jim Mitchell, Nora Owen, Jim Higgins, Charlie Flanagan and Alan Shatter, had also hit the dust.

At the count centre I quoted Enoch Powell, who had observed that all political careers eventually end in failure. I announced my retirement from active politics, thanked my party workers and my family and all those who had voted for me, and departed the political scene. That was May 2002. The following morning, sleeping late after a very late night, the telephone at my bedside awakened me. It was our daughter, Estelle. She had given birth to a daughter – to be called Josephine, after me – just an hour earlier. What better illustration of life after politics?

EPILOGUE:
LIFE AFTER POLITICS

A few months after my retirement from politics, our neighbour in Ballyowen Lane, in Lucan, where we had lived since 1991, decided to sell and the purchaser, with the intention of building apartments, made us an offer we couldn't refuse. We now live outside the village of Allenwood, in County Kildare, back in the rural setting from which I originated and which, in my mind, I never really left.

We have wonderful neighbours, the best one could possibly hope for. One of them tells me I have already caused a revolution locally. I come from an area in County Tyrone that has a reputation for early potatoes. I brought my father's expertise with me to Lucan, and from there to Kildare. This year, our first in our new home, I planted a small quantity of my Home Guard spuds, as usual, just before St Patrick's Day. My neighbours planted British Queens at the same time. To their surprise, I was harvesting three weeks before them. The 'revolution', my neighbours tell me, is that for the first time in history they will plant my rather appropriately named Home Guard next year. But they don't know that I have a secret weapon. Bullet-proof glass from my former home in Donaghmore is very suitable for keeping the frost off early potatoes! When my time comes, an appropriate tribute on the headstone might be: He grew great spuds.

Our five children, of whom I am extremely proud, are all university graduates and have good jobs. They all have an interest in politics, but so far only one, Caitríona, has stood for election. She is a councillor on Tewkesbury Borough Council in England. I am pleased the commitment to public service has continued to the next generation. So too, I think, would have been my grandfather, Neal O'Donnell (and his Presbyterian mother!).

We have, at last count, seven wonderful grandchildren.

Tyrone has won the Sam Maguire cup – though not, unfortunately, twice in a row.

I will be sixty-five next birthday – not bad for someone who did not expect to survive his thirties.

We are content and in good health.

Annita and I hope to live happily ever after.

INDEX

439